DOWNTIME

The Lost Years of Doctor Who

Dylan Rees

Second edition published
April 2017 by Obverse Books
Cover Design © Cody Schell
Cover Artwork © Blair Bidmead

Printed by TJ International

CONTENTS

Introduction

With some cities made of song, some cheetah people made of faux fur and the temperature of a cup of tea rapidly decreasing, the Seventh Doctor and Ace walked off our screens for the foreseeable future in late 1989, ending classic *Doctor Who*'s twenty-six year run on British TV.

While *Doctor Who* was rarely out of the headlines during its sixteen year hiatus — there were rumours of Spielberg movies, D-list Doctors and a near miss with 'The Dark Dimension' — *Doctor Who* fandom, on the other hand, went underground. Through Virgin Publishing and BBC Books, fans produced numerous novels for past and present Doctors, Jon Pertwee popped up on radio for a brace of last hurrahs, the official magazine continued to thrive, video and DVD releases filled our shelves, and eventually Big Finish began producing all new audio adventures for the Doctor and his companions. All of this has been covered before, of course. However there is one area of fan innovation and creativity that frequently — and unfairly — finds itself over-looked. A medium that provided a creative outlet for numerous writers, actors and production staff (some of whom later went onto work on the show in a more official capacity and some who already had) — the straight-to-video, and later audio, spin-off.

Before we go any further, it is important to establish what we mean by 'a spin-off'. Dictionary.com defines it as "any product that is an adaption, outgrowth, or development of another similar product." For the purposes of this book, therefore, we will define it as any product that was commercially released and featured characters from, or inspired by, *Doctor Who*. So, as well as productions like *Downtime* and 'The Devil of Winterborne' — which featured several of the Doctor's companions and enemies, all licensed from their copyright owners — we will also be looking at series like *The Stranger* and *The Wanderer* (aka *Fred*), whose *Doctor Who* influence is clear, if less formal. We won't, however, be covering not-for-profit fan films that attempt to be nothing but ersatz–*Doctor Who* nor audio series like *The Scaryfiers* or *Soldiers of Love* which, while they feature many actors who have appeared in *Doctor Who* and are certainly aimed at the same audience, take little in the way of direct inspiration from the series itself. Also not on the agenda is the film *Soul's Ark* (wrongly listed as a BBV production on Wikipedia) or the audio series *Layton's Mission.* While these titles feature *Doctor Who* actors and are science fiction, they are little more than passion projects for the makers and sit more in line with fan films than professional productions.

We also won't be covering the documentary and interview output of companies like BBV and Reeltime in any great detail, as, let's face it, a

Making Of the Making Of might be pushing the boundaries of audience interest!

Over the last decade, *Doctor Who* fans have been spoiled with the number of spin-off series the programme has generated. The BBC unleashed both *Torchwood* and *The Sarah Jane Adventures,* while Big Finish has now released over thirty *Doctor Who*–related ranges!

In this time of plenty, it is easy to forget that, in its initial run, the programme spawned only one official spin-off: a single episode of *K9 & Company*, starring Elisabeth Sladen, reprising her role as Sarah Jane Smith, and John Leeson as the popular metal mutt. A number of other ideas were floated around that never made it to screen, including "The Destroyers" (a star vehicle for the Daleks, pitched to US networks by creator Terry Nation[1]), another series focusing on the military side of the *Doctor Who* world staring U.N.I.T.[2] and, lastly a Victorian-set endeavour for the much loved characters of Jago and Litefoot from 1977's 'The Talons of Weng-Chiang'[3]. For this author, without *Doctor Who* on air I was looking for my new *Who* fix wherever I could get it. I was too young for the *New Adventures* novel range, not a fan of comic strips and was quickly catching up on the television stories I'd missed on satellite TV channel, UK Gold. So where would I get my regular dose of new *Doctor Who* from? I'd seen adverts for something called *The Stranger*, staring Colin Baker and Nicola Bryant and I'd heard mention of Sergeant Benton featuring in his own story, *Wartime* — I'd even heard rumours that the Yeti were on their way back somehow.

Then at some point in the early 90s I joined a local fan group — the Birmingham (later Wolverhampton)-based 'Wolves of Fenric'. There, a collection of fans would sit huddled around a video player and watch *Doctor Who* rarities, orphaned episodes, fifth generation tapes, 72 edits and other cult TV gems. At the back of the room was a merchandise table containing VHS releases, fanzines and other assorted bits and pieces. It was there I first took the plunge and brought a copy of *The Stranger* video 'The Terror Game'. Although it wasn't *Doctor Who,* it grabbed me right from the get go and I could have almost imagined a post 'Mindwarp' sixth Doctor ending up at that club, bereft of mind and memory.

After that, I quickly devoured the past releases and awaited the next ones with bated breath. To me — and to many others — these videos were our only source of new '*Doctor Who*'.

These straight to video releases not only satisfied the fans' need for further adventures; they also introduced a number of important names to the *Doctor Who* creative world, including Mark Gatiss, Nicholas Briggs and Rob Shearman — all of whom would cut their teeth on fan films and audio adventures that would influence their career direction.

This book will explore the history and production of these video and audio spin-offs and follow the careers of some of the people who would go onto become stars in their own right, as well as others who — for one reason or another — never quite achieved the same level of fame or acclaim. Through low budgets, last minute rewrites, stars dropping out and films made under impossible conditions for no money at all — this is a story of passion, dedication and fan ingenuity.

A brief note about the research

While every attempt has been made to cover each release as completely as possible, the nature of such semi-official productions means that not everything was recorded in the same detail as a BBC show like *Doctor Who*. While BBC Productions have an abundance of paper work, archive materials and interviews, many of these fan films and audios relied on the good will and the hard work of the people involved, and — obviously — didn't have a large organization watching over them, making sure records were kept of all operations.

This book, therefore, relies on interviews and articles published at the time, along with the wealth of video material that accompanied many of these films as well as brand new interviews conducted by the author with over fifty people involved in the fan productions of the time.

Chapter 1 — Bring on the Dancing Horses

Throughout the 1960s, *Doctor Who* fans enjoyed exciting adventures across time and space, as their heroes encountered a cornucopia of hideous creatures with whom to do battle, from the rubber clad Voord to the lumbering Quarks and the Nazi-inspired Daleks. Each of these was presented in a 'monster of the week' format, igniting children's imaginations across the country and encouraging them to seek out further exploits of both the Doctor and his enemies. Their continuing adventures could be seen off-screen on cigarette cards and in comic strips, while on the high street, fans could purchase any number of goodies to relive the excitement. The Doctor's encounter with the Zarbi, for instance, could be viewed again through the 'Give a Show' projector (albeit with a reduced run time). Similarly, the battle between the Mechanoids and the Daleks from 'The Chase' could be re-enacted thanks to Cherila Ltd's Swappit range of action figures. And up to four eager young fans could play the excitingly titled 'Dodge the Daleks' board game (essentially Snakes and Ladders with Daleks) — remembering to "avoid the Sylther take extra turn!" These products inspired a sense of make-believe in youngsters, encouraging them to imagine further adventures for the mysterious Doctor (yet to be named a Time Lord or steeped in layers of continuity). The merchandise also reflected the age of the audience — the cigarette cards (so named because they originated in cigarette packets, before being sold with more child friendly products) came enclosed in ice lolly wrappers, and games were for ages five and up.

By the mid to late 1970s, the programme — and indeed the landscape of television — had changed. The Doctor was no longer a doddery old man lost in time, space and monochrome — the black and white era had given way to the blazing colour of the Pertwee era. This in turn gave way to the lurid aura of the early Tom Baker era, where the stories were darker and the imagery on screen reflected that.

The changes made to the series mirrored the changing nature of its fans. While young children still loved to be frightened by what was on screen, those who had started watching the show in 1963 were now young adults with their own ideas about what *Doctor Who* 'should' be like. Whereas the show had once been twenty or so minutes of thrills and scares on Saturday evening, now it was to be poured over, dissected and analysed — *Doctor Who* fandom had begun to organise itself.

Perhaps the most important step in the organisation of fandom was the formation of the 'Doctor Who Appreciation Society' (D.W.A.S.), whose founding members included Jan Vincent-Rudzki, Jeremy Bentham, Stephen Payne and Keith Barnfather.

Barnfather in particular, was instrumental in bringing the society to a wider fan base. "I've always been one of those people who likes to do something new. I was the first editor of *Celestial Toyroom* [the society's newsletter]. I edited, I'm guessing about 6 to 10 issues of that and was getting a bit bored doing that. I think it would be fair to say I came up with the idea of doing the convention but we were all involved in the concept of what we would try and do. So we all took responsibility for certain aspects. Although it's true I was ultimately responsible."[1] As the society grew, a number of local groups sprung up around the country. The most famous meeting became the monthly gathering of D.W.A.S. members at the Fitzroy Tavern in central London. This was attended by the great and the good of *Doctor Who* fandom of the time, including Barnfather, David J. Howe, Andy Lane, Kevin Davies, Gary Russell and various others whose names will become familiar as our history progresses.

Not only was fandom inspired to organize, but they were also inspired to create. Fanzines and fan fiction flowed out of every corner of the country, from A5 photocopied pamphlets to glossy A4 magazines. However, the fiction didn't stay on the page for long, as fans also produced their own amateur films. *Doctor Who* writer and historian David J. Howe took part in a number of these productions.

"Back in the late 1970's I was very involved with friends down in South London: Gavin French, Paul Tams, Owen Tudor and Paul Simpson. These guys were in my immediate vicinity but we were also involved with Kevin Davies, Sue Moore and people up in North London and we were all making 8mm movies. We were all doing our own *Doctor Who* productions in whatever way we could manage to do. We were all teenagers doing this great stuff. We built our own Daleks, we built our own K9s that looked nothing like the real things and we were having fun making films and knocking about with them. It was great fun and as technology improved so did the ability to make things improve."[2]

Kevin Davies had come to the attention of fandom as a film-maker very early on. "I'd made a little animated film called *Dr Hoo* which I showed at the very first convention and Keith Barnfather gave me my first budget, five quid, to get the film processed quickly."[3]

The showing of this short led to Davies becoming involved in a number of other productions.

"Mark Sinclair saw this film and said 'would you like to do the titles for my *Doctor Who* feature film?' It was an hour and fifteen minutes and at the 1979 convention it got screened, there were three big reels of 8mm and the audience were kind of waning and I remember him going on the microphone and saying to the packed lecture theatre 'you'll be glad to know there's just one more reel left.' It was terrible."[4] Sinclair was the head of the drama department at the D.W.A.S. (yes, they had a drama department) and the film in question was 'Ocean in the Sky'.

"His idea was it would be the third cinema *Doctor Who* film," chuckles Mark Ayres, who was brought in to do the music. "We had a leading lady who went through puberty in the two years that we shot it and an aged retired actor playing the Doctor who, bless him, couldn't remember his lines." The film was shot on Super 8 film, which at the time was the only format available and was incredibly expensive. The limited money meant every shot had to be done in one take and so the outcome was of varying quality, but Ayres remembers it with fondness. "Looking back on it, it was terribly, terribly amateur, but also enormous fun."[5] 'Ocean in the Sky' was self-funded by Sinclair, with the TARDIS alone coming in at around £300. The script was written by Owen Tudor, with later revisions done by Tom Marshall. The role of the Doctor was played by 70 year old, retired actor Leo Adams, an alumni of Manchester Rep.

Over the next few years numerous fan productions circulated on the convention scene including Gavin French's 'The Destructors'; 'The Thosian Strategy', starring Paul Mark Tams as the fourth Doctor; and Tams' own endeavour, 'The Image Makers', which Ayres considers one of the more professional productions.

"'The Image Makers' was actually, for its time, quite a polished little movie. They very cleverly worked within what was possible, so they just made a half hour thing."

While some fans were inspired to produce their own home video adventures for the Doctor, others produced brand new stories on audio. Audio Visuals (AV) was the brainchild of D.W.A.S. members Gary Russell and William 'Bill' Baggs. The productions were recorded and sold on tape through mail order and at conventions by the AV team, which included a number of names now familiar to fandom, including Nicholas Briggs, John Ainsworth and Nigel Fairs. Their work also attracted a number of guest stars from the world of televised *Doctor Who*, including Michael Wisher who had played Davros, and Peter Miles, perhaps best known as Nyder in 'Genesis of the Daleks'.

Through these audio plays and amateur films many enthusiasts made their first step in converting a hobby into a career. It is these people who pushed their creativity beyond novice productions, and in doing so, made some truly memorable films and audio adventures, each inspired by a programme they loved. Their next steps saw them brush shoulders with Doctors and companions (albeit often in different guises), and bona-fide *Doctor Who* monsters.

Most excitingly for one group, their next endeavour would see them producing a brand new adventure for one of the Doctor's most trusted allies.

Chapter 2 — Life During Wartime

'Benton Is Back!' was the headline sprawled across a double page feature in the October 1987 issue of *Doctor Who Magazine* (*DWM*).

"If you want to know more about this popular U.N.I.T. member, now's your chance to find out..."[1] touted the article. Adorned with colour pictures of a slightly older, slightly more rugged looking, but still recognisable John Levene, the article detailed the return of one of the Pertwee era's most prominent characters, promoted from Sergeant to Warrant Officer Benton.

The story of *Wartime* goes much further back than this, however. It began with Keith Barnfather, who had managed to obtain an entry level role at the BBC VT Library.

"I worked in VT for about a year. Channel 4 was being set up in 1982 and I was poached, which was rather nice. I worked there for about two years, setting up their video tape and broadcast library on the technical side and then I moved upstairs to business development, which was like the BBC Worldwide of Channel 4. That's when I started getting involved in bits of editing and bits of production work. I just realised that's what I wanted to do with my life. In 1984 I had a few opportunities to earn money doing other things, so as well as getting up and going out on my own I set Reeltime [Pictures] up. I went to work part time at that and part time at a couple of other jobs and eventually started working full time at Reeltime."

Reeltime Pictures Ltd's main focus was corporate films — however they also launched a successful range of *Doctor Who* interview tapes, titled *Myth Makers*, hosted by Audio Visuals' own Doctor and convention panel host, Nick Briggs. Early contributors to the range included Kevin Davies, broadcast specialist Andy Grant, musician Mark Ayres and fanzine writer David J. Howe.

"We were all frustrated producers and directors," explains Barnfather when asked if these productions were a way of venting that frustration. "I always had in the back of my mind that as well as doing the stuff for the bread and butter I would then be able to do all the things that had something to do with stuff related to my interests. But I always tried to approach everything as a business and it's not easy because a lot of the *Doctor Who* stuff was done for love, not for money." [2]

The initial titles were done on modest budgets of six to seven hundred pounds per tape but found a loyal fan base within the *Doctor Who* community. As the number of titles grew, so did the ambitions of the production team. As Andy Grant remembers, "Keith was looking to adding value to them because the original format was Nick Briggs and the interviewee sat opposite each other, you intercut the pictures, it was tried and tested but it wasn't very adventurous. So I had access to the facilities, obviously there is no great budget on these things but it was a bit of fun to do it as a narrative piece."[3]

Mark Ayres, who was by now working at TV-am, provided the music for a number of these early releases and also directed a couple. "We just got more and more ambitious. They went from being simple interviews sat at a kitchen table to doing them on location and then getting quite absurd with Mary Tamm playing Alice in Wonderland, it was just utterly bizarre! So we got more and more ambitious because we were all frustrated and all wanted to make real television."[4]

By the late 1980s a vocal section within *Doctor Who* fandom felt that the programme had lost its way. It is well documented that producer John Nathan-Turner had faced a backlash, via fanzine *DWB*, from fans over the direction the programme had taken during Colin Baker's tenure as the Doctor.

Keith Barnfather was one of these fans. "Colin as a person I like immensely, but I felt his period was a total disaster. I actually stopped watching *Doctor Who*, I didn't watch 'The Trial of [a] Time Lord'. When I did watch it, I loathed the music, I loathed the direction, I mean I like Bonnie Langford professionally but... you know."[5]

It was, perhaps, then with a sense of disillusionment towards the show he had once followed avidly and to the frustrated drama director within him, that Barnfather set about planning his first foray into the world of fiction. "I wanted to prove the point that it could be done. At the time a lot of what *Doctor Who* was about wasn't what I wanted to see. And I felt we could make a point about that. As much as making a point about being able to do it."[6]

Barnfather's first idea was to attempt to produce a licensed *Doctor Who* product with the BBC's blessing. "I made an approach to the BBC in the 1980s to do an independent drama officially by licensing it, and the producer at the time, John Nathan-Turner, felt that it was impossible to make that kind of production on the money that we were envisaging and he turned us down and I respect his decision in doing that."[7]

While Nathan-Turner never went on record discussing Barnfather's approach, the reason for his decision seems clear — having two concurrently running *Doctor Who* productions might confuse viewers. With money tight on *Doctor Who,* it's not difficult to imagine the potential damage which could have been caused by an even lower budget production.Undeterred, Barnfather got together with his old friend from the D.W.A.S., Jan Vincent-Rudzki, to develop a very different kind of story, to star former Doctor and assistant, Jon Pertwee and Elisabeth Sladen.

Vincent-Rudzki recalls, "The idea must have come from Keith, certainly not from me. It was called 'Bell, Book and Candle', so it was about magic, or perhaps the appearance of magic; not sure. I know I named Jon Pertwee's character Famulus (an old word, which can mean magician) and that he had a large country house. I recall Elisabeth Sladen had seen the script and pointed out that I had her driving, which she was not able to do! I recall Keith was considering directors, but it didn't get beyond that." [8]

Barnfather sheds a little more light on the situation. "We did go quite a long way. We went down to [stately home and tourist attraction] Longleat, and met Ralph Montague [the owner] who I knew, and looked around the place. We were going to use some of the old cars from the [on site] museum and things like that, and film in the house but I just think we were too ambitious at the time. That's why *Wartime* came out because making that was less ambitious." [9]

Interestingly, this approach of using a former Doctor in a Doctor-like role would be the template used to launch *The Stranger* series a few years later.

Lifelong D.W.A.S. member Andy Lane had left university with a physics degree, but had always had aspirations as a writer. He cut his teeth on fan fiction for various fanzines and had been writing reviews for *Starburst Magazine* under the editorial guidance of Stephan Payne.

"I met Keith Barnfather at the regular monthly pub meetings at the Fitzroy Tavern or whatever the precursor to that was and we'd got talking and he knew I was a writer or a writer wannabe. It wasn't so much *Wartime* at the time; he was talking about bringing me in to do some scripts for corporate training videos. I went round to Keith's house at the time and had a couple of drinks and dinner and on this occasion he broached the subject of a *Doctor Who* spin-off using the character of Sergeant Benton and said 'Would you be interested?' and I said 'yeah I'll give it a go'." [10]

For Lane, it was an idea that very much appealed. A chance to flex his writing muscles and hone his skills as an author. "The idea that it was fan fiction but doing it as a script as opposed to a fanzine. You know with a fanzine you'll get a couple of hundred readers but some kind of semi authentic *Doctor Who* spin-off with a real *Doctor Who* actor that was like gold dust at the time. Nobody had ever thought of that!" [11]

Lane wouldn't be the only writer credited for *Wartime* — Helen Stirling worked on the script with him. The couple were living together at the time and had met at one of Barnfather's parties. Lane recalls that Stirling was able to add a much needed dramatist's point of view to a script that was otherwise being written by a prose writer:

"She had a history of drama studies [and] she did a degree at Crewe & Alsager College. She's much more a performer than a writer. I guess I brought her in for two reasons. Number one because she forced me to, and number two she could give me a sort of actor's perspective. She actually helped with the pacing of lines and the ability of the actors to deliver." [12]

A number of restrictions were placed on the writers: the drama had to be thirty minutes, have Benton as the star (as copyright had been granted by his creator Derrick Sherwin), they couldn't have prosthetics, the cast had to be minimal and it had to be set around an Edwardian folly.

The locations were brought to the table by associate producer John Ainsworth. He had grown up in Bolton and visited the area of Rivington in the borough of Chorley numerous times, where, in the 1920s, an industrialist named Lord Leverhulme had set up home. As Ainsworth explains "He had made a fortune and decided to build his home and these quite exotic gardens. They're on this bizarre hillside with lots of little stone houses and a tower, it was all very overgrown and sort of semi wilderness."[13]

Having taken photos of the area, he showed them to Barnfather, who was so impressed by them he agreed to shoot the film there. Lane and Stirling were provided with photos of the locations when planning the story. They numbered the location photos, worked out where the action took place, and wrote scenes around them.The first idea pitched by the two writers, about a group of religious aliens, was rejected by Barnfather. "I sent [Andy Lane] away saying I don't think this works. From the point of view of the narrative suddenly we get these aliens showing up as [Benton]'s driving through Britain and it was a bit shoehorned and it just didn't work. I felt the science fiction element was written in as a necessity. If it wasn't necessary for it to be science fiction it worked better on that occasion for it to be a ghost story."[14]

With this in mind, Lane and Stirling set about developing a ghost story concerning Benton's past. Andy Lane remembers "I pitched [that] it should be more of a psychological drama. Trying to get into Benton's head and exploring something in his own mind about an aspect of his childhood that was unresolved."[15]

The script was developed under the title *Brothers in Arms*, which Barnfather rejected on the grounds of there being an album by Dire Straits of the same name about to be released. Therefore it was renamed *Wartime*. The script for *Wartime* went through minimal drafts — the only major change being the addition of a framing sequence of Benton and his driver in the jeep which the writers only reluctantly included.

"He [Keith Barnfather] wanted there to be more external threat which I put in against my will because it never got explained as to why there's a plot that we don't know anything about." [16]

As scripted, *Wartime* finds Benton haunted by ghosts from his past. Andy Lane discussed the turning of a two-dimensional character into something a little more interesting:

"I wanted to actually do something about Benton's character who I thought had been underused and had been pretty much a sort of humorous thug in a sense, since he's big and burly and he rushes around and shoots things. Mainly just me being pretentious, as you are when you are in your twenties. I just wanted to get under the skin of who Benton was." [17]

Levene had long since given up acting and had never formally trained as an actor — and the script required him to play a lot of emotional scenes. When asked if Levene was entirely successful at portraying the emotions, Lane doesn't think so. "Bless him, no. Did I know that? I could have guessed that just by watching him on *Doctor Who* but I think being arrogant as a twenty-whatever I was, I thought 'why should I write down, I'll write up and let him stretch for it'. Which I think, actually thinking about it, is a reasonable thing to do. If you just write for the character you know you just end up with the same thing repeating over and over again. You've got to try and give people something more to do." [18]

John Levene had started out in television as a supporting artist before graduating to small speaking roles. He had played both a Cyberman and a Yeti during the Patrick Troughton era before securing the role of Corporal Benton in the 1968 adventure, 'The Invasion'. Benton returned, this time as a Sergeant, during the Pertwee years and would become a regular up until the early part of Tom Baker's mammoth seven year run. After giving up acting in the late 1970s he set up his own audio visual company Genesis Communications. Barnfather had met Levene at a *Doctor Who* convention in the early 1980s and they then went on to film a *Myth Makers* tape together. Barnfather also employed him to do some corporate work through Reeltime.

Upon asking him to take the starring role in the company's first drama production, Levene was unsure. "When I was approached I first refused," Levene told Steve Eramo in 1994, "given that I had not thought I wished to act again. Once I was shown the script, which was very reasonable and well written by two people who were beginning a career in TV. I found it a joy to come back and reprise the role."[19]

With Levene on board, Barnfather had then to find an actor who would take on the strict militaristic role of Benton's father. His first, and only, choice was character actor Michael Wisher. Wisher had had a long and varied career on British television appearing in shows such as *Z Cars*, *Dixon of Dock Green*, *Colditz* and of course *Doctor Who*. A fan favourite for his portrayal as the original Davros in the 1975 serial 'Genesis of the Daleks', Wisher had met Barnfather when the former was a guest at the very first *Doctor Who* convention in 1977 and they immediately hit it off. As a result, when Barnfather launched the *Myth Makers* range he asked Wisher to be the first interviewee.

"Michael was a good friend, my father died when I was 18 and Michael had become a bit of surrogate father. We used to meet quite often and have a pint down the pub and talk about life and the universe and everything. It was almost unnecessary to think of who to cast in the part. I've always had a great deal of respect for him. He lent a believability to it. He really is the pivot; he really holds that whole thing together."[20]

The rest of the cast was sourced locally. A relative of Ainsworth's was a member of the Bolton amateur dramatics group, and so when someone was needed to play Benton's mother in addition to two children to play the junior Benton and his brother Johnny, Mary Greenhalgh and her son Paul were cast as mother and son, while Steven Stanley was cast as Johnny. The final two pieces of casting were Paul Flanagan as the unnamed man pursuing Benton, and Peter Noad, playing Private Willis alongside Levene. Noad was a local army officer who had a keen interest in acting, and who was helpfully able to borrow an army Land Rover from his regiment in exchange for a charity donation. All were cast without Barnfather meeting them, but he did visit them the day before the shoot to talk them through the script.

Cast in place, Barnfather recruited a team of fans and industry professionals he knew he could count on to make the shoot go as smoothly as possible. As well as associate producer John Ainsworth, Mark Ayres was brought in as sound recordist, camera operator Robin Lee also joined the team and the Unit Manager was Richard Landen. Nick Briggs acted as Assistant Director (Briggs also played a small part in the film, albeit behind a gas mask). A close friend and colleague of Barnfather's, Briggs was the natural choice as a trustworthy right hand man. However, he had mixed feelings on the project. "To be blunt, I was gutted that he hadn't asked me to write it, but I was happy to be involved. I wasn't sure whether John Levene would be a credible leading man, but I thought it was a fun idea."[21]

Barnfather now feels Briggs deserves a bigger credit than he was originally given. "In many ways I was directing it with him. I was consulting with him on everything, we always did. The group of us that did all of this were a pretty tight knit group." [22]

Briggs disputes this, feeling Barnfather is being overly modest regarding his own achievements. "That's extraordinarily generous of Keith. What a nice man he is. My memory was that he was very much directing it, but that he would consult me. We didn't really know what an assistant director's job was, so Keith and I sort of improvised. Keith would do a lot of explaining of his shots to me, on location, telling me how the scene would cut together. He's very much an editor at heart, and can immediately see how he wants a scene to cut together. I can't remember us ever disagreeing, because it was very clear in my mind that he was in charge. My main function in this regard was for me to back him up and make sure he felt confident he was doing the right thing. I did direct a couple of bits here and there, but not much."[23]

The script, story boards and shooting schedule were all prepared and the cast and crew embarked on a two day shoot in Bolton, despite Barnfather never having visited the location. As the only local on the team, Ainsworth navigated the cast and crew to the locations and the hotel they were staying in. When they arrived at the location they found that the nearest roads and available parking were some forty minutes' walk from the area in which they were shooting. This immediately set the production back — and they would soon fall even further behind schedule. Barnfather blames this delay on a lack of experience.

"I think we were unprepared because we were working on such a low budget. We weren't flexible enough if things went wrong and we simply couldn't get enough done in each day. Sometimes you have to go through it. You can't read it in a book; it's impossible. You need to live it to know it. It wasn't so much the planning as doing it." [24]

"It was extremely hard work and quite chaotic." recalls Briggs of the shoot. "He had a very firm idea of what he wanted, but was always battling to get it. So my first main memory was of Keith, rather valiantly, having to fight for what he wanted. And he got it. Keith has some great leadership qualities. He persists in situations like this, and, frankly, he had to. But it was quite unrealistically scheduled, so we did run out of time"[25]

Day one of the shoot was Thursday 30th of April 1987, which saw the scenes of the Benton family having a picnic shot in the morning. After lunch, shots of Wisher and Greenhalgh dancing were recorded, before they moved onto more picnic scenes. Greenhalgh was then wrapped for the day, while the scene of kids playing were filmed.

The following day began with Wisher's death scene and the battle flashbacks, with Briggs donning army get up and gas mask (to disguise the fact that the *Myth Makers* host was appearing in the video). In the afternoon the kids were back, to record more of the footage of them running through the folly. Filming then moved on to the fight scenes between Levene and Flanagan (the stunts were coordinated by Flanagan and had to be rehearsed on the spot). These took a considerable amount of time to shoot, due to the complicated nature of the action, with the final scenes of the day comprising the confrontations between Wisher and Levene.

While the shoot may have been running behind schedule, Barnfather doesn't feel it made tensions or tempers high. "I got the right people there. We had a wonderful atmosphere. Everybody knew what they were doing. The problem was they didn't have the experience to do it efficiently and jobs were handicapped by lack of experience and lack of knowledge."[26]

Indeed, Briggs' main memory of the shoot is "…it being loads of fun. My dear friend John Ainsworth was working on it, as kind of local liaison and location manager, and he and I had lots of silly laughs together."[27]

Ainsworth recalls a number of scenes where time was against them. "The guy who played the soldier had to be somewhere, to join his unit and they just needed one last shot and basically he said 'I'm going to drive where you want to me to drive but I'm going to carry on driving off to where I need to be,' so they had to get it on this take otherwise he just wasn't coming back." [28]

The crucial confrontation between Benton and his father was left until the end of the final day. "It was quite a dialogue heavy scene and we more or less filmed that as it was going dark and I think they knew it just wasn't going to be usable." [29]

Although he didn't attend the shoot, Andy Lane also feels that a lack of experience was a running theme throughout the production process. "I think with the exception of Michael Wisher we were all in over our heads because we were doing something none of us had done before. I'd never written a fiction script for acting before, Keith had never directed drama before and so we were all kind of making it up as we went along." [30]

As well as talking through the technical aspects of shots with Barnfather, Briggs was also able to offer a much needed actor's insight into the scenes, to help the first time director. "He felt he had a lack of expertise in that area. So I think I was able to give him some pointers about characters and motivation and that sort of thing now and again."[31]

His role also involved logging shots and making notes of time codes, something Briggs had already done on a number of corporate projects for Reeltime.

It became apparent almost immediately that the team weren't going to get everything they needed shot in the two days allotted. Deflated, Barnfather returned home with a half-finished film. "We wrapped it and I went back, and then I was left with this huge decision and I looked at the rushes afterwards and there was some good stuff in there and I just thought I've got to go back and finish this if everyone will do it. I mean you probably could have cheated and done a load of stuff in a studio somewhere and cobbled it together. But I phoned everybody up and said 'look guys is there any way we can go back?' and everybody said yes."[32]

Two weeks later, on 15th May 1987, the cast and crew returned to the locations to complete the film. Once there, they soon found themselves in trouble after stopping at Watford Gap Service Station. Designated driver Ayres recalls, "In the back of the van we had all the props which included a number of rifles, and Keith decided that to avoid any trouble we'd secure them and make sure they were covered up. So we all went in to have breakfast and we came out half an hour later and we drove off and as we got to the exit slip road going back on to the motorway, there was this screech of tyres. Two police cars came in at a V either side and blocked the front, and another two at the back. There was a tap on my window and there was a guy with a gun and he said, 'Leave your hands where they are, we are armed police officers.' Keith in the back said, 'oh no, we are just a film crew and...' and I just said 'shut up, just be quiet!' The guy then reached in and took the keys out of the ignition and we very gently got out the van."[33]

Unbeknown to the crew, they had been seen adjusting the guns by a member of the public who had called the police. With on-going trouble in Northern Ireland, there were armed police response units patrolling the M1 permanently, as it was suspected the IRA were running guns along the route. Fortunately the crew could prove the guns were fake and they were sent on their way without further action being taken.

The day began with the previously abandoned confrontation between Benton and his father. This was re-filmed in full before moving on to a shot of Levene running through the Folly. The team then went back to the road side to record some cut-aways for the fight scenes, with Briggs standing in for Flanagan, as he was unavailable. They then filmed the action set around the jeep for the rest of the film, including the opening radio conversation, before finishing the day with shots of the children by the Folly's water feature.

Levene was pleased to be back in uniform. "I found it a joy to come back and reprise the role. With so many years having passed I thought it would be interesting to see how Benton had survived."[34]

Levene also kept the cast and crew amused throughout the shoot with a series of his (now legendary) bad jokes. Ayres has affectionate memories of the lead. "I'm very fond of John but he is a unique character. You have to remember as well I'd grown up watching John on the telly and Benton was a favourite character. He maybe wasn't as important as maybe John would like to think he was [laughs] but he was a favourite character."[35]

Briggs, found himself in admiration of the would-be star. "John Levene and I got on really well. He may not be the best actor in the world, but he really threw himself into this. He gave what felt like 150%. He'd committed to it and by gum he was going to do his level best to make it work. I think he had a lot of self-doubts, and I remember at least one occasion when he turned to me and said, 'I bet you're thinking, Christ I could do a better job of acting than him!' And I think John was right, I was thinking that. But I was wrong to think it, because, actually, John brought a huge amount of 'leading man charisma' to the role. He really led the cast and took on the responsibility of entertaining us every second of the day. Granted, some of that entertainment was not always entirely welcome, but bless him, he was determined to do it, and I love him for that. I think he's a genuine, British eccentric, and he made me laugh like a drain."[36]

Levene had never been a leading man before *Wartime* and according to Ainsworth was very excited by the prospect, but also had to deal with the pressures that come with leading a company. "He was quite nervous, he had real trouble remembering his lines for some of the dialogue heavy scenes. In fact one of my jobs on the re-shoot, for the big scene where he confronts his father on the bridge, was to stand out of shot holding this huge placard with all his dialogue written on it, so it was there if he needed to refer to it. He took the occasional glance at it and in the editing we would always cut away at any point that his eyes glance at me holding the board." [37]

Wisher also stayed in good humour throughout the shoot. Pitching in to help carry kit from location to location, he sang songs about Lancashire and teased Ainsworth with a few white lies about the area. "Michael was full of stories, strange stories about Bolton, which I had never heard of and was a little doubtful about their authenticity. He said phone calls were cheaper from Bolton, that's why all solicitors were based in Bolton — it was very strange. He'd quite happily tell us these little stories." [38]

Ayres too was amused by Wisher's presence on the shoot. "Michael was unique; an incredible man, just very, very enthusiastic. He was one of those actors who just wanted to act and he was constantly acting, constantly performing in the nicest possible way."[39] Briggs described Wisher as "lovely", adding that he was "so warm and supportive and trusting and in spite of his dodgy politics and lengthy 'anecdotage', largely wonderful company. I feel privileged to have known him." [40]

Initially due for release in October 1987, the video was finally released in August of 1988. Barnfather recalls this was due to post production issues.

"The only medium that was available to us at that time was U-matic and the only machine I could afford to own at that time was a type two U-matic. The type ones did fast forward or backwards but the type two was single speed forwards and backward. You pre-rolled it. You hit the button you wanted. Imagine what that was like, and it took a long time simply because of the fact it was a very slow process."[41]

Also present for the edit was Briggs, who recalls the challenges they faced with the primitive equipment. "Again, Keith was in charge, doing the bulk of the work, but we sat at those edit machines and discussed it as we went through. It was before the days of non-linear, computer software editing, and video editing at that level in those days was still quite primitive. I remember we couldn't even be frame-accurate!"[42]

The incidental score was provided by Ayres, who was given pretty much free range. "As ever with this sort of thing, it was do what you want. Now I was more interested in the electronic stuff but everybody else seemed to want to push it orchestral. But it was all very cheap synthesizers back then. I had an eight track machine, a sampler, a couple of synths and drum machine and that was it. So it was something vaguely orchestral with a half decent strings sound and the rest was electronic."[43]

Despite his experience in the sound department of a live TV show and doing *Myth Makers*, this was Ayres' first experience of doing a full scale drama. "I really learnt on my feet. It was the first time I'd got heavily into synching to picture, working out tempo maps and all that kind of stuff. It was a real learning curve." [44]

The graphics for the opening sequence were created by Kevin Davies. A radio conversation between Benton and his erstwhile UNIT commanding officer, Brigadier Lethbridge-Stewart (played, as on television, by Nick Courtney) was also recorded to play over the opening.

With the edit done, Barnfather organised a premiere at the Horse and Groom pub in central London on 5 June 1988. In attendance were the majority of the cast and crew including Michael Wisher and John Levene. Also on hand were Nicholas Courtney, *Who* director and writer Peter Grimwade and *Doctor Who* historian Jeremy Bentham.

Barnfather remembers the event fondly. "We all wanted to get together and drink the health of the baby. It was also because I wanted to see what people thought. Nick and I were happy, we thought it was good enough to release but you want to know what other people think and the general reaction was pretty good, it was enjoyable." [45]

The rest of the team also enjoyed the final product according to Ainsworth. "We all thought it was quite amazing, considering the restrictions under which we had done it and they did actually get everything they wanted. In the editing process, they did a really good job and Mark Ayres' music pulls it together."[46]

One person who wasn't entirely pleased, however, was Andy Lane — but not because of the quality of the film. "I was embarrassed. Which is the way I tend to feel whenever I do something that's then acted by somebody else. You realise the limitations of your own writing in somebody else's mouth, because in your head it sounds fine and somebody else does it and actually it's a bit clunky, isn't it? I don't know if it's a common thing for a writer but I always imagine there is only one way to say the lines but actually an actor can find a different way of saying it." [47] To this day Lane has only ever seen the film once.

Wartime was made on a modest budget of £5,000, with many of the crew volunteering their services for expenses only (a commonplace practice in low budget film making). While the sales figures for these productions are unavailable, it performed well and made its money back, as Andy Lane, who wrote the project for free, reveals. "About five years down-stream Keith said 'I've made enough money from *Wartime* now that I can pay you for it.' So he gave me 500 quid which was nice." [48]

The film achieves admirable things for its small budget and the limited technology available. While Lane was right, the framing story is never really explained, it doesn't need to be as that isn't the main focus. What's important is the background we get for Benton: his family life, the loss of his younger brother at an early age and the relationship he had — or didn't have — with his father. Benton wanted to impress his Dad and joined the army to emulate him.

It perhaps gives credence to Levene's performance in *Doctor Who* itself. Despite being one of the heavies, he never looked comfortable wielding a firearm and there was lightness to his touch and a humour that makes the viewer feel he'd look more at home preaching flower power than fighting Ogrons. Benton isn't an obvious soldier, he's a lost little boy still trying to prove to his father that he has what it takes to be a man.

Wartime was generally well received by fandom, with *Doctor Who Magazine* saying of it, "Displaying considerable skill for editing and story-telling, the Reeltime production of this U.N.I.T. inspired tale makes the most of the factors that marked the Jon Pertwee years on *Doctor Who*, and made the programme so popular. Mystery and action, with a suspenseful build-up to the haunting proper, make this project well worth seeing."[49]

Despite his reservations at the premiere, Andy Lane is proud of the project. "It's telling and very important that it actually works not as a *Doctor Who*, I think it actually works as a drama in its own right. I'm actually happy with it but I was not happy with it as a *Doctor Who* spin-off. Talking about it, it occurs to me consciously or unconsciously that what I was doing was *The Stone Tape*. The idea that a location can absorb a history of something that's happened then replay that scene later on." He goes on to add, "I had a great time doing it and I felt privileged to be involved in something that had a blessing from people involved in *Doctor Who*. It started me on what is now a career as a writer so I learned a lot."[50]

Barnfather can also look back on the film objectively. "Over the years it's become a bit of an institution. I mean nowadays people buy it because it was the very first drama spin-off and I think people tend to look at it in that context. It certainly isn't something I would want to put up there as being my best work, but at the same time I'm very proud of *Wartime* and what we achieved at that time." [51]

Levene was also proud of his contribution. "For me *Wartime* was a personal triumph, in that I hadn't acted in front of a camera for over thirteen years."[52]

While the makers of *Wartime* are modest about their achievements, it's a testament to all those involved that over the next three decades many people would take inspiration from what Keith they did — creating a new sub-genre of *Doctor Who* and a micro industry in itself. While *Wartime* runs at a mere thirty-five minutes, its legacy would last for decades.

Chapter 3 — Strangeways, Here we Come

Before Nick Briggs had aligned himself with Reeltime Pictures he was predominantly known in *Doctor Who* fandom for playing the Doctor (in an unofficial capacity) on audio. As a member of the Southampton branch of D.W.A.S. Briggs met the group founder and convention organiser, the seventeen year old Bill Baggs.

Baggs had recently set up 'Audio Visuals', an amateur group of actors and writers who had produced their first *Doctor Who* audio play, 'The Space Wail', written by Gary Russell and starring the somewhat reluctant Stephen Payne as the Doctor. Having not enjoyed the experience and having no aspirations to act, Payne stepped aside after one outing and Briggs took over the role for four seasons.

By all accounts a charming and charismatic individual, Bill Baggs had a drive behind him that fuelled his many ventures within the world of *Doctor Who* and beyond. His passion for television production — spurred on by his love for *Doctor Who* — had led him to join the BBC in a clerical position in 1986. From there he transferred to Bush House as an Assistant Picture Editor and then spent three months at Pebble Mill in Birmingham as a video editor, before ending up in News and Documentaries at BBC Nottingham.

He later told Marcus Hearn that this wasn't where he wanted to be, however.

"What spurred me into action was a mixture of things. Firstly, the desire to make a film because I'd tried several routes to get into drama within the BBC and failed. Secondly an interest in science fiction and *Doctor Who*. There was however also the knowledge that because of Keith Barnfather's *Myth Makers* and things like that, there was a potential for selling tapes and getting your money back."[1]

Baggs' ambition to produce a film had already manifested itself towards the end of the 'Audio Visuals' range. "As part of the 'Audio Visuals' set we made this film, *Scarecrow City*, which was a pile of dog shite but fun and it was a steep learning curve and it was a fascinating way of working and so this was kind of the culmination of all the 'Audio Visuals', *Scarecrow City* and my desire to produce something visual."[2]

While *Scarecrow City* proved a disappointment for Baggs, he was undeterred and ultimately had bigger ambitions. "I mean, it all stemmed from a burning ambition of mine to take over the world," he explains light-heartedly. "Ever since doing Audio Visuals I'd always harboured a desire to make films, and I guess at that time, I was probably very keen to direct *Doctor Who* or even produce the show."

While at the BBC, Baggs joined their amateur dramatics society, the BBC Aerial Theatre Company, where he met nineteen year old Christian Darkin, who was somewhat perplexed at the lethargy of the theatre group.

"I went along and met a few other people who were likewise annoyed at having got nothing for our membership fees (including Bill). At the meeting the entire committee stepped down, so the company was going to close. We decided that since we'd bothered to turn up to the meeting, that must mean we were interested, so everyone present decided to turn the company around. Bill took the chairman's job. I did publicity and ran a magazine, and we got a treasurer and a couple of other roles filled and we started putting on plays. We did a performance every six weeks for two years and ended up taking one of my plays to the Edinburgh Fringe."[3]

As well as being a member of the BBC's theatre group, Baggs was also a member of the BBC Film Club — it was through this group that he was able to fund his first film, produced as part of a training project for the group members. Baggs commissioned Darkin to write the script.

Was it always to be *Doctor Who* in all but name?

"Pretty much — Bill and I discussed it, but it was the availability and willingness of the actors that gave me most of the restrictions in what I was writing."[4]

The script, entitled 'Summoned by Shadows', was written and developed over the winter of 1990, at a point when the future of *Doctor Who* was still uncertain. It's a testament to Baggs and his skills as a producer that he convinced the BBC to fund what was essentially a rip off of one of their own programmes. It is perhaps equally telling regarding the level of care the BBC felt for *Doctor Who* at the time.

In casting the film, Baggs decided to approach both Tom Baker and Colin Baker to play the lead, feeling that if the former didn't want to take the part, the latter would.

"Colin, I think was always interested — it was just a case of whether he was available. I also contacted Tom Baker because, although Colin was the first choice, quite often when you're doing these projects you don't always get who you want, so you have to cover yourself. At one point I was going to use Deborah Watling because I hadn't confirmed Nicola Bryant. I think I also approached Sophie Aldred as well."[5]

He also enquired about non *Doctor Who*-linked actress Charlotte Coleman, later to star in Richard Curtis' smash-hit movie, *Four Weddings and a Funeral*.

In the end, Bryant couldn't commit as she was currently in the middle of a nine month run as Daisy Buchanan in a production of *The Great Gatsby* and was unsure that she could get the time off. Although Baggs went through official channels to get his leads, he had also approached them in a number of other ways, she remembers. "I just met Bill in the

BBC bar; I didn't know anything about him, he was just a fan as far as I'm concerned, but he had approached both Colin and myself. I thought 'this could ruin your career'. I was worried that it could turn out really disastrous. You can't tell where something might end up — on some TV screen, or some director might be round for dinner, and it could be terrible, and ruin you."[6]

Bryant was eventually persuaded with a little help from a former *Doctor Who* producer. "John Nathan-Turner asked us to help out because I think Bill had written to JNT and said 'oh please would you be interested in helping me get started'."[7]

With his two leads in place, Baggs told the genre press that he saw this film as way of bringing more life to the short-lived sixth Doctor. "I wanted Colin Baker because I felt that people thought he had been hard done by in *Doctor Who* and knew there was a very strong line about becoming a hermit (in 'The Twin Dilemma') that would have been very easy to pick up on."[8]

In 2006, Baggs admitted to Mike Haberfelner that perhaps he hadn't been entirely truthful about his first and second choices. "Well, actually [Colin] wasn't my first choice... bless him." His first choice was the aforementioned Tom Baker. "Also I was arrogant enough to think, given Colin didn't have a good tenure as the Doctor, being such a cool director I could do something with his character and give him a chance to show his acting talent."[9]

It's odd to imagine an alternative universe where the Stranger was portrayed by a grey haired Tom Baker, accompanied by a middle-aged Deborah Watling. Given Tom's notorious bad temper, penchant for the absurd and habit of changing scripts, it is perhaps a blessing that Baggs ended up working with the more restrained Colin. For the rest of the cast, Baggs asked people who he had previously worked with on the 'Audio Visuals' range, including Heather Tracy, Helen Hewlitt (soon to become Mrs Baggs) and John Wadmore, who had been recruited to the AV range by Nick Briggs — the two having met at a drama evening class in Southampton. Not a big science fiction fan, Briggs persuaded Wadmore and other members of the class to take roles in the AVs under a series of aliases. For 'Summoned By Shadows', Baggs cast him as a deaf mute — a challenging role for any actor.

"I did a bit of research, I went to the library and I found a few books on sign language and I learnt a few...funnily enough since then I've got level one BSL (British Sign Language)." [10]

There was no money in the production for the supporting cast, but, despite being a jobbing actor, Wadmore had no complaints. "It was done on the cheap. I presume Colin and Nicola were paid a fair wedge. The rest of us it was all expenses, we weren't really doing it for the money. If you're an out of work actor and someone offers you a profit share in a money losing role you do it because you are better off doing that than doing nothing. "[11]

For the villain of the film, Baggs turned to fan favourite, Michael Wisher. Wisher had lent his vocal talents to a number of 'Audio Visuals' plays, meaning Baggs was able to call on him. *Wartime* writer Andy Lane offered his opinion on why he thinks Wisher lent his talents to so many fan productions.

"I think a number of *Doctor Who* actors, the bit part actors or side actors, like the acclaim they get for having done that stuff. They kind of feed off that. So if a group of fans go 'can I give you some money to do something for me?' a lot of them are likely to say 'yes'. I don't think he [Wisher] ever got the recognition that he deserved — look at the range of acting that he does just in *Doctor Who*; actually he's playing a whole range of different parts."[12]

In order to get his directorial vision on to screen, Baggs needed a competent Lighting Cameraman/Director of Photography. He approached a freelancer who was working at BBC Nottingham, Dick Kursa. "Dick was somebody who stood out as being good at lighting and caring about what the image looked like so he was the obvious candidate and very enthusiastic and very creative."[13]

Before filming commenced, the cast and crew had a read through at the BBC rehearsal rooms in Acton. Everyone apart from Bryant was in attendance. With a budget of £3,000 in place, filming took place over three weekends in the spring of 1991.

The first scenes to be recorded were those of the titular Stranger in his self-imposed isolation on a vast alien landscape — AKA a Sand Pit in Surrey — exactly the sort of location that Bryant and Baker had been all too used to during their time on *Doctor Who*. In fact they had filmed 'Attack of the Cybermen' in the same location a few years previously.

As can be seen onscreen, the weather for the shoot was poor, resulting in a number of transportation issues. The make-up bus Baggs had booked had to be parked half a mile from the location, as it was feared it would not be able to get out of the mud and wet sand at the end of the day. This caused endless delays to the shooting as cast and crew had to be ferried to and from the bus.

Cameraman Dick Kursa also had trouble with the sand. He was the last to leave the location on the first day and when he came to start his car he couldn't reverse out of the mud. Being miles away from any sign of civilisation, and this being before the days of mobile phones, he was forced to spend the evening sleeping in his car until the rest of the team returned the next day to help him get it out.

The following Saturday saw scenes of Bryant at a lavish party hosted by Wisher's character. These were shot at a house in the middle of a Wimbledon park. The next day the team moved to BBC Lime Grove studios, where the prop stores were raided in order to create the set where the final showdown between Wisher and Baker would take place. Baggs has since described this as the least successful part of the play, only saved by some inventive lighting.

The final weekend of the shoot started in Shepherd's Bush Market, where they filmed the opening scenes, with Wisher seducing the natives into searching for parts to his broken teleport device (the Sunday of that weekend was, in fact, given over to scenes of scavengers on a desolate waste land searching for the aforementioned parts). The wasteland in question was an abandoned building on Wood Lane near BBC Television Centre that would later become a BBC car park.

Once filming was complete, Baggs utilised his place of work — BBC Nottingham — to edit the film, using their facilities, in his spare time. When he reached the segments set on the waste land, he realised he didn't have enough footage of the scavengers, so quickly scheduled pick up shots to be filmed at a local skip, using many of his colleagues at BBC Nottingham to play supporting roles.

As well as these pick-ups, Baggs also had to shoot the model sequences of the controller's spaceship. The model was constructed by BBC Special Effects artist Mike Tucker and shot in Kursa's garage against a black back drop with which Baggs was very happy. "He was very clever, those sequences were very simple but very effective and his imagination and creativity really shine through, so I was dead impressed with that."[14]

The model in question would later be adapted and reused in the BBC *Children in Need* special, 'Dimensions in Time'.

The plot of 'Summoned By Shadows' is a simple one, with the Controller splitting into several different versions of himself — clearly inspired by the 1979 Douglas Adams-pseudonymously penned 'City of Death'. Wisher gives a stand out performance as always, making each character different, but with subtle similarities. A smarmy smile and the same condescending attitude to the planet's natives can be seen in each aspect of the Controller. Colin Baker's performance is equally pitch perfect; gone is the blustering arrogance of the sixth Doctor. Instead, here is man who is haunted by his past — when he says, "I misunderstood the nature of the universe" it is not difficult to believe that this character has been part a life changing catastrophe.

Darkin created a back story for the character of the Stranger that lies closer to its copyrighted BBC roots than might be expected. "I felt [as though *Doctor Who* struggled for its identity and] that there was a big change between the reckless/antagonistic Doctor of his first season where he appeared uncomfortable with the universe and his place in it, and the more chummy version in his second where he appeared to have come to terms (kind of) with the universe, even if he didn't fit too well into it."[15]

Eighties' *Doctor Who* in general proved rich in themes that Darkin wanted to mine for his *Stranger* story. "In some ways I felt the change in [political] atmosphere in society and TV had driven a trend in drama that was dark, serious and cynical over the previous few years. The drama of the 80s focused less on heroes and villains, on right and wrong, and more on shades of grey, where every character was a little soiled and every positive idea was a little flawed. And *Doctor Who* followed this trend. Characters like Lytton and even his own companions — Turlough for example — weren't clearly on one side or the other. Frequently things resolved badly or darkly ('Black Orchid', 'Mawdryn Undead') or were resolved by people doing bad or suicidal things (who are the good guys in 'Resurrection of the Daleks' for example?). This culminated in the fifth Doctor's last story where everybody was pretty much out for themselves, nobody survived. The Doctor's heroism counted for nothing in that story because the story (like the rest of television) had no place in it for a hero."[16]

So how did this manifest itself in *The Stranger*?

"I see the Doctor in 'Summoned by Shadows' (let's call him the Doctor for now, shall we?) as having had a few more adventures after 'Revelation of the Daleks', finding that his new way of behaving didn't lead to any better outcomes than his attempt to be a hero and finally ending up making some catastrophic mistakes in worlds where he tried to meddle. He then followed through on the instinct he had when he first woke from his regeneration in 'The Twin Dilemma' — he became a hermit."[17] On the dubious nature of the copyright, Bill told *Doctor Who Magazine,* "The story isn't *Doctor Who*. 'Summoned by Shadows' is a complete story in its own right."[18]

Colin Baker also shed a little light on this. "I suppose I was asked to play the Stranger, because I once played a character on television called the Doctor, and there are parallels to be drawn between the two characters — who is this strange person? Where does he come from? He seems to be able to involve himself in worlds and places other than our own. It's a bit like 'Who is that masked man?' Who is the Stranger? He's called the Stranger because wherever this man is, he's a stranger, there's no place where he is 'right'. He has with him Miss Brown who we learn about as each story progresses, but who is someone who has been caught up with this man's restless peregrinations through... time? Space? I don't know."[19]

As mentioned, Darkin never had any doubts when writing the film that Baker's character was anything but the Doctor. While Baggs may have made it clear to the press that this wasn't *Doctor Who*, he knew he was playing a dangerous game, so asked Bryant to drop the American accent she used playing Peri Brown in *Doctor Who* and play Miss Brown with her own accent. "Basically Bill made it clear that he was just scurrying the lines of legal usage, it was obviously very close to *Doctor Who* the science fiction time traveling situation but obviously they didn't want any connotations of me playing Peri so I think that was the simplest way of making that clear."[20]

'Summoned by Shadows' received a premiere at BBC Bush House to an audience of friends and colleagues. It proved a modest success, with *Doctor Who* Magazine calling it "[a] very well made video production, beautifully directed and acted" going on to say "some great visual effects and the acting of the three guest stars, as well of the ever good Bryant/Baker team make this well worth the £11.45 asking price."[21]

The film was available to purchase from specialist outlets and direct from Bill Baggs himself, with copies of the tape being duplicated in the family sitting room. The film was released under Baggs' newly established company Bill and Ben Video or BBV, Ben being short for Helen, Bill's partner.

While not the most accomplished piece, it proved that *Wartime* was not a one off, and showed what could be achieved on the smallest of budgets. Future BBV collaborator Mark Gatiss offers his memories on the film: "I remember reading about the first couple — 'Summoned By Shadows', I think — and someone had said, 'See how Colin Baker and Nicola Bryant could have been, and weep.' I remember watching them and thinking that although they didn't look very flashy, in terms of trying to portray real characters they were a massive improvement on *Doctor Who*!"[22]

And how did Bill Baggs look back on the film years later?

"I felt 'Summoned by Shadows' was quite a jolly little story. But I was most interested in how it looked, shot to shot. I had a very clear idea of what I wanted Colin to do, and I think his performance is smashing — it was very low key and moody and it was right for that thing. I am, in retrospect, quite pleased with it as a first effort, it shows imagination. I could do a bit better now."[23]

Baggs would indeed go on to do much better. BBV's back catalogue would expand greatly over the coming years, far beyond its roots as a simple *Doctor Who* clone.

Chapter 4 — Strange Love

Keen to capitalise on the success of 'Summoned By Shadows', Baggs quickly commissioned a second film. This time he turned to actor and writer Nigel Fairs for the script. Fairs had played the Doctor's companion Truman in the AVs and also provided a number of scripts for the range. One of these would be the basis for this new outing for *The Stranger*.

Entitled 'More than a Messiah', the original script saw the Doctor and friends land on a planet where the natural infrastructure has been corrupted by civilization and modern technology. The planet produces an anti-body in the form of a young woman, who falls in love with the Doctor. Fairs explains why Baggs wanted to bring the audio play to life. "Bill thought it was one of the most visual of the Audio Visuals, and I think he was right in it because it was all about ecology, plus he liked the idea it was character based as well." Rushed into production, the film would arrive just six months after the release of 'Summoned by Shadows'. It is likely that Baggs thought that by using this pre-existing script the development time would be minimal.

So did Fairs have many changes to make to the script?

"No, funnily enough the biggest change was one I had in the original script (before the AV was recorded). I went back to the original, original script because when I first wrote it for Audio Visuals my companion character was new and I didn't know anything about him because I hadn't played him yet, so I sort of cut him out of the story quite early on and let Trish's (Patricia Merrick) character — who was called Ria — carry on the thrust of the story and when it came to record it Bill asked me to swap it round so my character, Truman, took the main bulk of the story. Well, in the video it's the other way round — again my character gets sidelined."

Both Baker and Bryant returned for the second outing of *The Stranger* along with former Hammer actress Barbara Shelley as Charlotte, and Peter Miles as Bernard, named after Fair's grandparents. Much like Wisher before him, Miles had appeared in the AV range, was a convention regular, and an underrated character actor of stage and screen. Often called upon to play evil types, he was drawn to the character of Bernard because it offered him something new. "He's having a breakdown through over working. Being neurotic is wonderful as an actor and he's not bad or evil"[1].

Seventh Doctor-era assistant Sophie Aldred was called upon to play the female anti-body created by the planet. Baggs and Aldred had met at a convention and Sophie immediately took to him. "Well, Bill had originally asked me to do 'Summoned by Shadows' as well, but whatever I was working on meant that I couldn't do it. Eventually I bumped into Colin

Baker and he said I had to do the next one as it was such a laugh. It turned out I had a few spare dates when Bill asked me to do 'More than a Messiah'."[2]

While Baker and Bryant were playing very much to type — at least in *Doctor Who* terms — Aldred relished the chance to play someone different from her *Doctor Who* character, but for the same audience. "I've always been very much of the mind that life is an adventure and you do what comes up and so I toddled off with that lot down to Cheddar Gorge to do something completely different."[3]

Again the production was afforded a rehearsal day with the cast and crew assembled to immerse themselves into the story world. The plan was to shoot the film itself in Lanzarote. Previously used in the *Doctor Who* story 'Planet of Fire' (which Shelley also stared in), the island's volcanic landscape offered a stunning and alien looking location. Nigel Fairs also took on the role of Nic in the film — a part which required him to be submerged in water for the opening sequences where Nic and his lover Mark race a speed boat and encounter Aldred's character, who kills the latter. "I volunteered knowing we were in Lanzarote. I wrote these wonderful scenes where I was thrown off a motor boat and washed up on the shore. I ended up being frozen to death on Telscombe beach on 12th January and in a lake in Nottingham. As we were approaching it, this was the middle of winter, there was a motor boat going round the lake that we were going to film in cutting up the ice."[4]

The film's location was changed at the last minute to England due to Colin Baker's wife being in the later stages of pregnancy at the time. Baker had previously lost a child to cot death, and did not want to stray too far from home should there be any complications. The majority of Bryant, Fairs, Miles and Shelley's scenes were filmed in the New Forest with the cast and crew staying in the same chalet they filmed in. While a great looking location, Bryant was less than enthusiastic about sleeping there: "They had corrugated metal roofs so none of us got any sleep because the weather was really dire through the whole shoot, but we all had a lot of fun, really it was pretty relaxed."[5]

Sophie Aldred (who was there for one night only) agrees. "We were in a hut somewhere, having a really good laugh with Nigel Fairs, and [I] met him really properly for the first time and just thought what a lovely bunch of people and thought how professional they are. It wasn't that different from a *Doctor Who* shoot."[6]

While at the New Forest, several scenes were shot with the ape-like natives, with Mark Trotman donning a mask designed by Sue Moore (whose prosthetics are perhaps the least convincing part of the film). Fairs, however, finds them amusing for other reasons. "Do you know I can't watch it, I can't see it objectively because the guy playing the ape was just so sweet and in such pain, with all that latex and glue. I can't see it and think it's a bad mask or a funny wig or whatever the criticisms of it is. I just see him."[7]

Fairs also helped out with the dressing of a particular scene. "There was a body coming out of the ground that had offal all over it with a fake hand, and I had to dress it with the offal, it was disgusting."[8] Also shot in the New Forest was a scene where the forest itself attacks and pins down Miss Brown where Bryant suggested to Baggs how to achieve the best results. "Nicola Bryant was lying on the ground and I had the wide shot established so you could see all the undergrowth attacking her and she quite rightly pointed out that maybe an equally good position would be to stick the camera in front of her face so that the camera could see all the acting she was doing!"[9]

With the New Forest filming complete, the cast and crew headed down to Cheddar Gorge to shoot the cave scenes between Baker and Aldred, and the film's finale, over a long weekend. The caves were still open to the public with the crew having to stop every time visitors came through. This was the first time Bryant and Aldred had worked together, although they had met briefly at conventions. "Nicola and I hadn't really talked much before and I gave her a lift down to Wookey Hole Caves where we were filming. We were talking so much that we got lost and turned up two hours late because we were chattering so much!"[10]

The hotel at which the cast and crew were staying also temporarily became a location when a number of pick-ups between Shelley and Bryant were filmed in one of the hotel rooms.

It was in the caves that Aldred filmed the bulk of her scenes with Colin Baker.

"We got on like a house on fire and he was always so lovely to me, and really very complimentary about my acting and we enjoyed our scenes together which were slightly saucy. I quite enjoyed the fact that we were stripped to the waist, wherever we were in Wookey Hole. I mean, we were absolutely freezing cold — it was cold down there — it was also very damp but again I was used to that, I was young; I just really got on with it — and it was fantastic make up. I loved having all that green stuff all over me. At that time I was just really eager and keen to do what I loved — which was acting."[11]

Aldred found Baggs a very competent director. "Bill always ran a very professional operation; he actually gave us more direction than we'd ever got on the actual set of *Doctor Who*. He was a very good leader in that he knew what he wanted but also knew how to get people together who were going to get on with each other and have a good time."[12]

While it was all good natured and fun at the New Forest, things were a bit more stressful at the caves. Peter Miles recalls "[i]t was such a tight schedule that poor Bill Baggs had to direct and direct until he got so far into the script every day because he could not afford to go into too much detail, you just had to shoot when ready because it was such a long story."[13]

Baggs is in agreement. "I think I bit off more than I could chew... I think I was completely unrealistic as to how much we could film in a day... normally you have about four scenes to shoot in a day, I had something like twenty... and I still hadn't really got the hang of how much footage you can realistically shoot in a day without exhausting your cast, pissing off your crew and just doing your head in yourself."[14]

With pressure mounting, Baggs tried to change the complex final scenes over Fairs' reservations. "Things did get very tight and we were always running out of time. The only time I really put my foot down was when Bill suggested, whilst we were filming, that Bernard shoot himself because he didn't think he was going to get the planet blowing up and that was so not his character, so I really put my foot down and said 'no' but that would have been to save time. I completely get it where he was coming from — it would have been easier if he'd shot himself and we didn't have the planet blowing up but no I was adamant about that."[15]

Fairs blames some of the tension on the caves themselves. "It has quite an oppressive atmosphere especially if you're working, well its underground I suppose it's going to. It was quite weird and tempers were really getting frayed"[16]

Fortunately, Barbara Shelley was on hand to help ease the atmosphere. "I watched her go around every single person one by one and just say a little word and I just noticed it was like a ripple effect with the whole crew and cast just relaxing and it was down entirely to her doing that thing."[17]

Despite being in over his head, Baggs was grateful to his cast for dealing with his lack of experience. "People were very accommodating. I think they loved my enthusiasm and they were willing to put up with my naivety for that reason."[18]

He later blamed his issues on lack of personnel. "I definitely remember being overwhelmed and at the same time [I had] tunnel vision, which I think you've got to be if you are going to get something done. I'd just been unrealistic about it because as well as directing it, I was producing it and production managing it and script editing it."[19]

Providing the music for 'More than a Messiah' was another name familiar to Audio Visuals listeners, Alistair Lock. Needless to say, a lack of resources and budget meant the process was more complicated that it is today.

"My set up was very simple; my computers could just about run an old keyboard, an old Roland sound module and two little other boxes. I was sent a VHS with a time code burnt in, I'd have that as reference and I'd record a tempo track where I would actually have a mix of the soundtrack and mix of myself counting saying 'we are coming into one minute and 25, 26, 27' and then I would start counting the tempo and so I would have a recording of me saying where the hit points were, as well as being able to watch the video tape." [20]

After all this was done, Lock could then start composing the actual soundtrack, but he was still dealing with limited technology. "Because my sequencer was so primitive I would have to change the tempo in real time, I couldn't just program tempo changes, so it was a bit loose but I'd record it to a VHS which was the best audio recording medium I had." Once the master was recorded Lock delivered it to Baggs in Southampton "where he would run it onto a beta tape so he could synchronise it to the master recording using a very simple mixer."[21]

Baggs' former colleague Gary Russell was one again in full praise of the film, giving it a stellar review in *DWM*. "'More than a Messiah' has some quite stunning visuals, a marked improvement over 'Summoned by Shadows' (and those were very good), some wonderful acting (Miles and Shelley steal the show from the three leads — an unintentional theft, I'm sure but one from which the video benefits) and above all an incredibly complex, but thoroughly clever script. Writer, Nigel Fairs (who also plays Nic, the tourist Bernard shoots) excels at humour and juxtaposition of drama and irony, and has created a really good ecological thriller, with a conscience."[22]

For all its bravado, 'More than a Messiah' is a very different story from anything the official show had done. Peter Miles' character, on the surface, is a slightly mad, pompous, upper-class toff. But he is actually a man having a nervous breakdown, abandoned by the very system that broke him in the first place. It's almost heart-breaking how Shelley's character tries to justify his faults when it's obvious to everyone else that he is losing the plot. She is willing to accept him and can't live without him so choses to die with him. The Stranger's story is even less like the TV show it tries to emulate. The film doesn't quite manage to pack in all it needs to in its short run time in order to convince us that the Stranger has fallen for Aldred's character — though he is certainly at peace with her in a way he clearly isn't with Miss Brown — but it is clear to the viewer that he is almost tempted. Indeed the love angle is very much what Fairs was aiming for when writing the film — "the message was about love and what a disaster that would be if the Doctor fell in love. I thought the Doctor wouldn't fall in love with a secretary or a dolly bird like Captain Kirk he'd probably go whole hog, if he was going to fall in love he'd fall in love with a planet or a concept or something a bit off piste."[23]

It is easy to picture the same *Doctor Who* fans who had objected to John Nathan-Turner's more controversial decisions reacting to the Doctor falling in love. But because this isn't actually *Doctor Who*, it could push those boundaries and still be acceptable. Fairs sums this up perfectly "one of my favourite reviews I've ever had for my *Doctor Who* things was in [the *Doctor Who* Appreciation Society fanzine] *Celestial Toyroom* and it said 'this is *Doctor Who* with teeth.'"[24]

'More than a Messiah' may not have the emotional molars (to stick with the teeth analogy for a moment) of post-2005 *Doctor Who*, but this is an early attempt to create a more personal and emotional story for the Doctor/Stranger.

And it does it very well indeed.

Chapter 5 — Jumping Someone Else's Train

With the first two *Stranger* films firmly laying the foundation for BBV's *Doctor Who*-in-all-but-name range, Bill Baggs commissioned Nick Briggs to write the third film in the series. And whereas 'More than a Messiah' had been rushed in front of the cameras, this next script would be given a longer pre-production period, as Baggs told *DWM* in August 1994. "On 'In Memory Alone' however, I had about six months to tackle that because in-between commissioning that and getting a first draft, I got a job in America and had three months over there to go over the idea."[1]

In spite of being one of the main writers for the Audio Visuals range and being involved in numerous fan productions, this was Briggs' first semi-professional writing credit. He was not a fan of Baggs' idea of doing *Doctor Who* in all but name. "I thought he was bonkers to do it and risk being sued by the BBC, but I was hungry for the experience and keen to be involved." [2]

Briggs' thoughts on the previous two films varied widely. "I thought 'Summoned by Shadows' was really, really dull, but there were moments of inspiration in it. I really like Colin and Nicola's performances. But it was a real oddity. Sort of like a student short film mixed up with a very low budget episode of 1980s *Doctor Who*." [3]

'More Than a Messiah', on the other hand, was a production for which he had more of a soft spot. "I thought the script of the second one was much better. It was based on one of the Audio Visuals *Doctor Who* scripts I'd been in, playing the Doctor! I seem to remember it had some very spurious partial nudity in it. Bill was very into putting that sort of thing in. Must have been his hormones." [4]

Despite his reservations about the film's "flawed" predecessors, Briggs could nevertheless recognise the potential for the series. "I could see something exciting that I could be involved in. I felt I could tailor-make something more appropriate for the budget. I wanted to err on the side of weirdness and mystery. Shapes in the dark, shadows in the smoke. Always a good way to cover up a lack of money!"[5]

Briggs had previously discussed what Baggs wanted from him, when he commissioned him. "I think he had the idea that he wanted something a bit more action based which for some reason he thought I was good at doing.[6]"

The gestation period gave the concept a chance to grow, Briggs confirms. "The original thing I came up with was very un-*Doctor Who* — not that this is anything like *Doctor Who* at all! (he said deeply ironically) — and it had that very *Blade Runner*-esque setting, and was really the script for a feature film. He was terribly keen on doing it, as was Dick

[Kursa], the cameraman; and then he suddenly thought 'no, we haven't got the money to do this, and maybe this is something we can do later', and he said, 'In the meantime, I'd like to do one like the other two — so how would you feel about adapting one of your Audio Visuals plays: what about "Conglomerate"?' 'Conglomerate' is an Audio Visuals play, which I actually wrote — which people don't know about because I did it under a funny name! But I said 'I can't go back to something I wrote four years ago'. One moves on — not wishing to sound pretentious — but, you know what I mean, you can't rehash something old. So I said 'I tell you what I'll do: I'll take the starting point of that' — and the starting point of it was, it was set on a railway station — 'and then I'll just create whatever comes up', and that's how I did it."[7]

While Briggs wasn't very keen at the time to rehash his old 'Conglomerate' audio play, he would later use it as the basis for his second series of *Fourth Doctor Adventures* for Big Finish.

With the idea locked in place, Baggs asked Briggs to write specifically around two locations he had in mind — the aforementioned train station, and a large underground vault. And so Briggs began work on fine tuning the script while Baggs was away in the States.

"'In Memory Alone', started out as a story about a weird alien railway station visited by the Stranger and Miss Brown — but, under Bill's direction, it became the story of the Stranger and Miss Brown's struggle to find their identities through their experiences in a weird alien railway station. The difference is subtle but enormous in terms of story-telling.[8]"

While the finished script is very much Briggs', Baggs made sure he was involved in the plotting. "I've always had quite a heavy hand in the text because that's something I enjoy and whether it's to the detriment or the betterment I guess it's for other people to decide. But Nick had particular ideas of what worked and what didn't work and it was very difficult and I seem to remember he wanted to know who the fuck was the Stranger? And who the fuck was Miss Brown? Which I didn't have a problem with. I like the mystique of it but I was happy to accommodate his thinking, that was his way of trying to make them be something, he wanted it all to make sense so not only was he rewriting 'Conglomerate', he was making sense of who they were as characters. It wasn't my thing really but I was happy to go along with it because it was an interesting progression." [9]

Upon writing his first film script, Briggs was understandably enthusiastic. "I was really excited to be doing it." But he found a new set of challenges in dealing with Baggs. "Writing for Bill Baggs was a very valuable experience for me. It taught me that you can never predict what a director/producer might say about your script. It was that moment of growing up when you, emerging from child-like naively, realize that other people are not 'inside your head', as it were. They will not instantly see what it is you're getting at. I know this sounds a bit crazy. But it was the beginning of my trying to learn how to be more precise in my work. So it was immensely valuable to me. It was painful, not least because, by any standards, Bill had the most bizarre way of thinking. I still don't really understand what makes him tick. The difference now is that I'm blissfully unconcerned about why Bill Baggs makes really bonkers decisions. At the time, of course, I was fully ensconced in his 'world'. He was my boss and he was the central creative force."[10]

The two leads were most impressed with the script, with Bryant citing the new direction as a positive change. "From my point of view, it's great to be able to start from scratch — I think that's one of the most enjoyable things about it — we're able to develop the relationship very slowly and we don't have to go the route that perhaps we would have gone before. So the relationship is much more interesting, and develops on a much more even keel." Baker too, was full of praise. "I think it's a very clever script, it has little echoes, to me, of a series which I used to enjoy, called *Sapphire & Steel*. There is something about the 'world' all this has been filmed in, which is strange — not here, not anywhere else... where the hell is it?"[11]

'In Memory Alone' is unique in *The Stranger* series in that it is the only film not to feature any other *Doctor Who* actors. In fact, the only other human(ish) part is played by Briggs as the somewhat aloof Minor. While Baggs may have saved money on the cast, the shoot itself would be far more costly, with fifty percent of the action taking place on a train station platform at night and using a real locomotive. Night shoots considerably hike up the budget due to the extra lighting required and the above average fees that have to be paid to cast and crew for the inconvenience.

The first block of filming on 'In Memory Alone' took place between Saturday 17th and Monday 19th October 1992. The majority of the Saturday was spent constructing the room in which Minor's survival suit was concealed. The location for this was the basement of BBC Nottingham (Baggs' place of work).

Julian Bote of *Celestial Toyroom* visited the set and described the location in detail. "Most of it's a brewery that was emptied then built on. It has another level below it (we could tell this by the holes knocked through the floor for the newer building's support pillars), attached to which are caves leading on and under other buildings surrounding ours above. Bill 2 (the caretaker, popping in to make sure we were okay) explained the people of Nottingham once lived in the caves, and the Luddites more recently."[12]

Due to its location, the crew were able to take advantage of the BBC facilities (such as make-up and car parking) along with the local amenities that the centre of Nottingham offered. Principal photography began on the

Sunday, with Briggs being the only member of the cast required. Also absent from the Sunday shoot was camera operator Dick Kursa, who refused to take his kit down into the damp basement, and so he was replaced by Darren Cox. The majority of the day was taken up by CSO shots of Briggs in his various guises, followed by a heavily made up Minor revealing his charred corpse. The scenes called for a lot of smoke which was produced by a smoke machine as well as Baggs using more conventional means. "I dropped some matches, I tried to create this smoke effect, they were smouldering, so I kind of kicked them through a hole in the floor to the level below thinking they would go out... and the next morning I had a phone call from one of my colleagues at work saying 'I don't wanna alarm you Bill, but we've all been evacuated and they're saying it's you...' The fire brigade was called and it was me, but luckily the building wasn't burned down, it was just full of smoke."[13]

Despite this case of accidental arson, the weekend shoot was completed with little incident. Monday saw the arrival of Bryant and Baker, who recorded their scenes in the tunnels beneath BBC Nottingham. The crew then took Tuesday off and returned to work the following day to record scenes of Baker and the Drudger (the ticket inspecting robot) on a specially hired, classic locomotive driven on the Grand Central line that runs through Leicestershire from Rothley Station.

Unusually, production took a break for several months after this due to other commitments of its cast and crew. Production would not resume until the 17th of January 1993. The first of a two day block would see the team return to BBC Nottingham's basement to shoot the climax of the film with all three cast members present. The final day would see a long and arduous night shoot back at Rothley Station, where all the scenes on the station platform would be recorded. The crew began setting up in the mid-afternoon, with the cast following to rehearse the action with Baggs. The locomotive was again on hand to run through the station as Baggs recalls. "Shooting at night at that railway station was extremely romantic and these enthusiasts who ran this steam train would just do anything for us, even though it was a major effort just getting that train in and out — and they were happy to do that a couple of times, so that was really exciting."[14]

With the 90 hour shoot complete, Baggs began post-production in full, although a rough edit of the first block's footage had been assembled in the downtime between shooting. The music for 'In Memory Alone' was provided by 17 year old Harvey Summers, who had just finished school and was looking for work.

"A friend of mine at the time was a huge *Doctor Who* fan (I loved it too but my friend was a real collector) and he had discovered Bill Baggs' first spin-off film which had his address on the end credits. Being interested in music for pictures, I decided to send him a demo, so I wrote new music for a couple of scenes from that first video and I think I also did an arrangement of the *Doctor Who* theme. Well, Bill liked what he heard and commissioned me to score 'In Memory Alone'. It was pretty basic in those days, I had an old VHS VCR, a simple rig comprising of a couple of synths and an Atari ST computer for sequencing! I'd line up my cues by hitting play on the VCR and computer at the same time as I didn't have the luxury of time-code! Amazingly, it all worked. We hired a friend's studio for a day so I could do the final mix and add the live clarinet which was an integral part of Nicola's theme."[15]

'In Memory Alone' is something of a reboot for *The Stranger* series and would mark a sharp change in direction, as Baggs recounted to *DWM* several years later. "With 'In Memory Alone' we didn't know where to go next. Nick Briggs, who wrote it, came up with the plot device where they lost their memories — effectively this meant we could start again. It's about the journey of having to work out who they are, what they are doing in this place and how they're going to get away from it. It was a very complicated one to do because I was on the way to sorting out who I was as a director, and my style, so there was a lot of it that I didn't enjoy at all. I think the end result is very good though."[16]

Briggs developed the idea, drawing on his own experiences. "It's all to do with people finding a role in life — the actual drama from moment to moment is nothing to do with that! That's just the underlying idea. I suddenly realised that the whole thing is full of my own neurosis about, you know: who I am, where am I going? What does anything mean? Because the main characters arrive here; they don't know who they are, they don't know what they're supposed to be doing, and the whole play is them trying to find out who they are, what it is they're supposed to be doing, and how the hell they get out of this awful place."[17]

The third *Stranger* film is the most accomplished of the spin-offs at this point. It is well directed, packed with atmosphere and has a script filled with great ideas that surprise the viewer at every turn. Baker is at his most Doctor-like in this film, having forgotten some of the angst that weighed down his character in the first two productions. It is an ambitious production that is occasionally let down by its small budget (the survival suit's gun being one available in High Street toy shops, for instance) but the direction is solid and the performances are pitched perfectly.

DWM 199 contained a competition to win one of five copies of 'In Memory Alone' and also a glowing review, citing it as the stand out video of the range — "it outshines both its excellent predecessors." The review also reiterates a previous point. "'In Memory Alone' once again demonstrates how good Colin Baker and Nicola Bryant could have been, and indeed sometimes were, despite their critics, in *Doctor Who*, given better scripts and direction."[18]

The review was written by *DWM* editor (and colleague of Baggs from his *AV* days) Gary Russell, who had to be careful when covering projects of this nature. "I gave them coverage because yes, they were doing something with the *Doctor Who* brand, and they were industry professionals I knew and respected. We had to tread a thin-line at *DWM* because strictly speaking they were *illegal* (certainly it is not over the line, they balanced a fine tightrope walk towards "passing off" or IP conflict) but I always wanted to be supportive. The second reason, less altruistic, of course, is that I edited *DWM* when the programme was a dead duck and I needed things to fill pages. And these productions always had people to talk to and, more importantly, colour photos to print!!" [19]

The final cut of the film relies on a certain amount of mystery and never quite explains several details, a fact that perplexed star Colin Baker. "I would have liked to have seen a clearer narrative in this case but that is not my decision. We've seen the director's cut now; I'd like to see all that stuff put back in to see if it works."[20]

Indeed, Baggs cut some of the explanatory dialogue, leaving more mystery behind the cause of events. "During the filming I realised I wanted some changes to the story. I actually began to understand more about what I like about a story and what makes it work for me."[21]

This process took place on location, with Baggs in full consultation with Nick Briggs. "Bill has been keen to cut gobbledygook explanations all the time. The trouble is, you have to strike a balance with these things. I know for example, *Star Trek: The Next Generation* — which I love — in recent years has started to be full of more and more of what people lovingly call 'Geordibollocks' where Geordi La Forge goes off on these incredible explanations of things which actually don't mean anything, but they've got a sort of internal logic to them. And I had a lot of that in this story, which Bill has asked me to cut — so it's become more and more like *Sapphire & Steel* as we've gone along, because all the explanations have been cut!"[22]

Baggs also made several alterations in the edit with which Briggs was less enamoured. "Bill's favourite phrase is 'I must challenge these [scripts]'. He really tends to change things during filming and editing. For instance he cut a lot of speeches during 'In Memory Alone' and when I saw the first edit of it I was really frustrated because it wasn't telling the story in the way I wanted it to. I had a long, fairly heated, discussion on the phone and he told me 'You've got to learn that not everything you write works!' And when you think about it, Bill had been struggling away editing this thing and then a bastard comes on the phone lecturing him on how it should be done."[23]

In 2013 Colin Baker shared his thoughts on 'In Memory Alone', citing it as a favourite. "That was for me was one of these stand out scripts of that very kind of strange interregnum time when we did those *Stranger* stories and those that watch them still say I love the one on the train."[24]

At the time, both Baggs and Briggs seemed ready to discuss the creative and collaborative process, and Briggs is now able to speak about his experiences more frankly.

"I was very grateful to him for the work and the experience, but to be blunt, I think I thought, perhaps unfairly, that he was a bit of an idiot at times. He was, I thought at the time, a lot younger than I was (although, as you get older, these age differences seem less important), and he hadn't had the same education I'd had at drama school. I'd been taught all about scripts and writing and acting and all that stuff for my degree, and Bill had more or less gone straight from school to being a tape librarian in the BBC World Service. I had to keep telling myself that, just because he knew nothing about drama or acting, it didn't mean that he didn't know what he was talking about. He was very dogmatic and determined. He had virtually no tact and was extremely rough with people. He would argue like crazy about almost everything, and most of the time it would just be a jumble of words that meant nothing to me — but I would strive and strive to find out what he was getting at. I think he possibly knew what he was talking about, but he hadn't had the appropriate educational experience to clearly structure or express his thoughts. But all that said, he could be loads of fun and really good company. We used to laugh like crazy with each other, so we were friends. He would come and stay at my place and we'd talk endlessly into the night. The whole process of working with Bill was relentless, though. It was a constant battle and he would make the oddest decisions. Colin Baker called him, 'Bilbo the Bastard Baggins' and that's more or less how we all felt about him. And he sort of loved that, I think. He was harsh, he underpaid us all and worked us like dogs, but hey... it was his money he was using (or perhaps the money of others who'd fallen under his spell) and he was determined to 'do stuff'. That's quite a charismatic, powerful thing for him to have been doing. It drew people to him. People were hungry for experience on 'making movies'. I was one of those people. Looking back, it all feels like utter madness, but I think it was essential experience for me."[25]

'In Memory Alone' would be the last *Stranger* film marketed as a *Doctor Who* knock off, and as a final hurrah for the series in this guise it is certainly the most successful. This would also be the last we see of the Stranger's companion, Miss Brown, and we will learn more about Bryant's departure from BBV in the next chapter. The Stranger's story would take a very different route in its coming releases but it certainly made its mark in these first three films and they act as a loose, unintentional trilogy. From the weary traveller, burdened with the mistakes of his past, in 'Summoned

By Shadows', via the healing process channelled by the girl in 'More than A Messiah' and the Stranger taking responsibility and putting everything back in its proper place, all the way to the completion of the Stranger's journey of cleansing and renewal 'In Memory Alone', the Stranger attempts to put his past behind him and start anew.

Unfortunately his past isn't quite finished with him.

Chapter 6 — November Spawned a Monster

1993 marked *Doctor Who's* thirtieth anniversary and to celebrate this landmark the BBC planned a number of special releases and events. The home video range saw the release of two special box sets — a Dalek themed tin containing 'Remembrance of the Daleks' and 'The Chase' and a TARDIS shaped tin containing the fourteen part epic 'The Trial of a Timelord'.

Meanwhile Virgin Books would continue to release its range of *New Adventures* with fresh instalments from the pens of Andy Lane, David A McIntee and Paul Cornell. They would also release the coffee table book *Time Frame*, written by David J. Howe, which covered all thirty years of the series. Domnitempeoral Services and the D.W.A.S. in association with BBC Worldwide would host 'Panopticon 93' in London with guests from every era of the show and all five surviving Doctors in attendance; while Kevin Davies would put together the superlative documentary '30 Years in the TARDIS' for broadcast on BBC One.

All this was well and good, but what *Doctor Who* fans really wanted was brand new *Doctor Who,* and their call was about to be answered by a number of parties. The first production to be announced in celebrating the anniversary came from Reeltime Pictures, entitled *Downtime* and featuring Nick Courtney reprising his role as the Brigadier, as well as the return of second Doctor foe, The Great Intelligence.

Shortly after this production was announced the BBC announced its own special, 'The Dark Dimension'. Centring on the fourth Doctor and featuring cameos from all the other living Doctors, this production would be produced by BBC Home Video in conjunction with BBC One. In light of this, *Downtime* was postponed until 1994 (the story of which can be found later in this book). Ultimately, 'The Dark Dimension' would never get past pre-production, with the plug being pulled by Amblin Entertainment's Philip Segal, who was attempting to get a brand new TV series of *Doctor Who* made in America.

With both of these productions on the back burner, Bill Baggs stepped up to the plate with a production he had been planning for some time. Keen to produce another film for the *Doctor Who* audience, but away from *The Stranger* series, Baggs approached his BBC Nottingham colleague, and former *Doctor Who* script writer, Philip Martin.

"I can't remember the sequence of events, but Philip wrote a script which I didn't like at all. I'd given him a brief and thought I'd been extremely clear. I said 'this is something like *Doctor Who* but isn't *Doctor Who*'. I was very clear I wanted a political thriller but he basically wrote a

Doctor Who script. It was called 'Doctor Who and The Formentors'. I think he misinterpreted who I was and what I was. I think he thought I might have been a barking fan or someone who didn't really know what he was doing. It was a tongue in cheek effort and I wanted something a bit more serious. I can't do comedy."[1]

Unsure if he could do anything with the script, Baggs asked Briggs to cast an eye over it. "It wasn't a bad piece of work as such, but more a testament to a complete misunderstanding between Bill and Philip. Part of me felt that Philip looked at the fee, and wrote what he thought the money was worth. It felt like a very rough, first draft. But the main, hilarious thing was that it was a *Doctor Who* story. It had 'the Doctors' in it. I'm pretty sure Bill had asked Philip not to do that, but he'd done it anyway. I told Bill it was unusable, and I think he agreed." [2]

Much to Baggs' disappointment, he was forced to abandon Martin's effort. "I was very excited to work with Phillip because I liked 'Vengeance on Varos' and all the things that he'd done, but it was a very interesting experience and it was bloody hard going back to someone who's finished a script and saying 'I'm not going to do because it isn't what I want.'"[3]

With Martin's script abandoned, Baggs asked Nick Briggs if he could come up with something more suitable in a couple of months — the result was a script entitled *The AirZone Solution*.

Baggs had very clear ideas about the direction this film should take, as Briggs later recollected. "With *AirZone*, Bill had gone through my original draft and virtually re-written it into something which vaguely resembled my submission, then I rewrote what he had written, which had given me an idea of the direction he wanted the script to go."[4]

The finished script was an environmental thriller that owed much to one of Baggs' favourite BBC dramas, as future BBV collaborator Tim Saward explains. "*Edge of Darkness* for him was the epitome of what was a successful TV drama, it was credible, it was serious, it was earnest, no jokes at all and if you look at the *The AirZone Solution* that was Bill's attempt to do *Edge of Darkness*. It was like a government conspiracy and had environmental issues and I think, in a way, that was what he wanted to make his films." [5]

Briggs felt he was able to incorporate Baggs' desire to recreate *Edge of Darkness* into a workable script "I found a way of writing the impossible brief of having three 'Doctor-like' characters but sort of in an *Edge of Darkness*-ish plot. I was preoccupied with environmental issues too and had also liked *Edge of Darkness*, so I was very much up for it."[6]

Although not initially intended to be a celebration of *Doctor Who's* 30th Anniversary, Baggs aimed high when casting *The AirZone Solution* and called in some favours, as he now had the only *Doctor Who* related drama being produced at this time.

The first members of the cast to be brought on board were Colin Baker as Arnie Davies the weatherman, Nicola Bryant as his long suffering partner and Sophie Aldred as Rachel Lonsdale. Baggs then asked Baker if he could persuade Peter Davison to join the cast. "Colin first mentioned it to me several months ago," explained Davison at the time. "He said he'd done a couple of these things and 'would I be interested?' and he gave me one of the tapes of one of these things, so I could sit through Colin acting (laughs) and I thought it was rather good too and so I said 'why not?' and so eventually a few months later a script arrived and I read the part and ended up playing another."[7]

Davison was originally meant to play Anthony Stanwick, but had to take the reduced role of Al Dunbar as he was appearing in the West End production of Arthur Miller's *The Last Yankee* at the same time. Baggs still recalls the excitement of getting the star to sign on. "I remember being in my flat in Nottingham, on the phone to Peter Davison, using my Bill-Baggs-charm to convince him that he actually wanted to be in this movie. It was like hedging around the subject, but eventually, he just agreed to do it. When I put down the phone, I really flipped out with excitement (that shows you how sad I am)."[8]

With the role of Stanwick still up for grabs, Baggs asked Sophie Aldred if she could persuade Sylvester McCoy to join the production. "Sophie Aldred had told me that she had enjoyed very much working with the group who made these and that they were quite keen for me to become involved, and I should look upon it favourably,"[9] and so McCoy signed up to play Anthony Stanwick. Aldred then had to pull out of the production due to a schedule clash. Joining the three Doctors and Bryant was up and coming Scottish actor Alan Cumming, who Baggs had worked and become friendly with on the Screen Two production *The Last Romantics*.

Cumming later spoke of his involvement on his website. "*The Airzone Solution* is a sort of *Doctor Who* homage, and indeed features four actors who played the Doctor in the cast. It was made in those wilderness years between *Doctor Who* series on the BBC, and I became involved with it via my friend Bill Baggs who directed it and who was an AD on *The Last Romantics*. We shot it in Nottingham, and I liked being a baddy."[10] Also joining the cast were Heather Barker, who had previously starred in 'More Than A Messiah', writer Nick Briggs, *DWM* editor and *AV* producer Gary Russell, and spin off regular Michael Wisher.

A late addition to the cast was third Doctor, Jon Pertwee, as Baggs recalled. "While we were already shooting, Jon Pertwee got to hear about it from Sylvester, and he phoned me up about the film, saying 'So, you are doing this film. Why am I not in it?' and I didn't have an answer, so he basically forced me to put him in it... which of course I was really pleased to do."[11]

With the cancelation of 'The Dark Dimension', McCoy thought it would be fun to get Pertwee involved. "I then phoned up Jon Pertwee and told him I was doing this. Jon said 'Why am I not in it?' and I said that my impression was that everyone was apprehensive about asking him. You know, the Great Jon Pertwee! All that stuff. So he said. 'They shouldn't be frightened of me!' and he phoned up and volunteered and they were delighted. So he got into it — and so that was four of us. I kept suggesting that we ought to have in the background a big hat and a scarf on a peg somewhere, just to make it the kind of complete package, because — as coincidence would have it — it was done around the Thirtieth Anniversary. Quite a coincidence!"[12]

With Pertwee keen to be involved, but production well underway, it was Pertwee himself who suggested how he could be incorporated into the script, at least according to him. "I told him, 'Write me in as an establisher', and he said, 'I'd love to do that'; and I just mentioned it to the boys and they love the idea, and that's how it came about. I'm only doing a pit and a cough in this one."[13]

Bill Baggs recollects that Briggs was aware of Pertwee's eagerness to be involved. "Nick apparently had expected this phone call, so he already had an idea how he would introduce Jon and give him a couple of scenes, and that worked out really well."[14]

Briggs however remembers the conversation slightly differently. "Bill phoned me one evening and said 'You know that scene where Peter Davison's character is watching the edit of his *AirZone* documentary? I reckon there should be an old bloke there, a sort of mentor.' By that stage they had started shooting so I asked who he'd got in mind for it. 'Jon Pertwee' came the reply. Jon had been on the phone to him and just wouldn't take no for an answer. Bill kept saying, 'Yes, I'd like to work with you in the future,' and Jon just went on and on, 'I want to work on this one please'"[15]

As this was the first time the four actors had been on set together, Briggs describes the event as "[r]ather special." With the actors frustrated over the aborted 30th Anniversary special, "[t]hey were all very angry about what they felt was the bogus 'The Dark Dimension' production. They'd been sent scripts and had been flabbergasted to see that, rather tactlessly, it had been written with Tom Baker's Doctor playing a huge part, with each of them appearing for just one cameo scene each. Colin Baker arrived for the rehearsals with the two scripts, 'The Dark Dimension' and *The AirZone Solution*. He slammed them both down on a desk and said, 'Do you know what the difference between these two scripts is?' I quaked in my boots. 'No...' I ventured. He pointed to my script and said, 'I'm going to be doing this one!' [16]

After four days rehearsal *The AirZone Solution* commenced shooting over four weeks in late summer 1993. The film featured the four Doctors sharing scenes together, some for the first time (Davison and Pertwee had occupied the same screen in 1983's 'The Five Doctors', and in the same year Davison and Baker had acted together in 'Arc of Infinity'). For McCoy, however, it was the first time he had worked with his fellow Doctors in this capacity. "It was great to work with Colin, we'd met at conventions and got on well, but I'd never worked with him. It was wonderful to find out that when we worked together, it looked very good on screen. And Peter as well! It was lovely working with him although we didn't have as much to do together."[17]

Davison too was in agreement, opining that it is a common myth that there are egos and rivalries between the Doctors. "It was fun, there's not the sort of egos flying around between Doctors, I don't find, at least not most Doctors (he says casting a knowing glint at the camera), that people believe and I've always been open to working with other Doctors and it was fun. We dragged Jon Pertwee in and I had the great honour of holding Jon Pertwee's cue cards because he was brought in the day before he filmed and hadn't had time to learn his big long speech"[18]

Scenes featuring the four Doctors at Dunbar's home and surrounding streets were filmed in Epsom at Baggs' parents-in-law's house. The film called for a number of action scenes and a car chase which McCoy particularly enjoyed. "*AirZone* was great. I got to drive — stunt driving in fact. Considering, I'm blind — I did it without my glasses — and I actually can't drive, whoever was operating the camera was a very brave man! I could hardly see him!"[19]

Filming then moved to elsewhere in Surrey. *DWM* editor, and former child star, Gary Russell was there to play a small part. "Bill [Baggs] just phoned me up one day and said, 'Colin and Nicola are down here asking why they're not seeing you.' And I said, 'Eugh, I want nothing to do with your bloody film!' And he said, 'Why don't you come down for a day, I need someone to play an assassin? You can wear a suit, and I'll give you a gun to play with.' And I said, 'You're on.' I'd never held a gun in my life before. And that was great fun. So yes, that's why I did that. But that was just helping Bill out, helping a mate out. I did a couple of his small films, just for the sheer hell of it."[20]

AirZone also featured a scene which raised a few eyebrows amongst fans, in which Colin Baker and Nicola Bryant's characters made love. As can be seen on the DVD's out-takes, both the actors took it in their stride, finding the situation amusing. Baggs never expected the scene to court controversy. "I was surprised by that, it was a deliberate thing on my part. If I remember rightly, Nick was a wee bit resistant, but it was again part of this thing of adding something extra at the time." [21]

In fact Briggs takes no responsibility for the scenes in question. "Let me be clear, there was no sex in it when I wrote it. Bill put all that in. I was writing the script knowing that Nicola and Colin would be in the production. But I expressly argued against the sex scene, not out of prudishness, but because I just thought the notion of Colin and Nicola having sex would be a bit... yuk. I was flabbergasted when I saw the scenes. The last conversation I'd had with Bill about it, I thought we'd come to an agreement that there would be no sex and that the two characters would just have a sort of innocent but close friendship. It was Bill who had them living and sleeping together. But this sort of characterised one of the less pleasant of Bill's characteristics. If he couldn't win an argument with you, he'd just let you think he'd agreed with you, then go and do what he liked without telling you. He was quite dishonest in that respect. But, you know, it was his gig, he was paying the bills. There's no law against fibbing to writers, especially vastly inexperienced ones! But anyway, I thought the sex stuff was just... so wrong... and inappropriate... and added nothing useful to the plot. And it was hilarious, I thought, that we saw more of Colin's flesh than Nicola's!"[22]

The final day of the shoot was one of the most challenging, not least because McCoy only had a limited amount of time to get his scenes in the can. "We filmed *The AirZone Solution* in Nottingham, but I was supposed to be rehearsing a play in Belfast! I flew over from Belfast and drove straight to Nottingham, filmed all day long, stayed the night in Nottingham, got up really early the next morning, and then left just in time to get a plane from Birmingham back to Belfast for the opening night! I was driven straight to the theatre from the airport — and I was running half-an-hour late, so they held up the play until I got there! It was an extraordinary thing to do. The play went down a storm."[23]

The day also featured one of the largest groups of supporting artists gathered for a production of this nature. The extras were sourced from the great and good of *Doctor Who* fandom, making the atmosphere more akin to a *Doctor Who* convention than that of a film set, as Colin Baker recalls. "The extras all worked extremely well and there was a very taut atmosphere. Certainly given the fact that the audience was made of people who were *Doctor Who* fans, the less one had to do in front of them the better in a way, because you weren't distracted by trying to entertain them or how good an actor you were; you could actually get on with what you wanted to do, it's not like doing it in front of normal extras who couldn't give a stuff what you are doing. These ones were extremely keen but they were there for other reasons."[24]

The editing of T*he AirZone Solution* took a month, and was completed the night before the thirtieth anniversary convention, Panopticon 1993. While the film had no official premiere, it was available to buy for the first time on the Saturday of the event. With none of the cast having seen the final film, they were given preview copies as they were all in attendance.

AirZone also saw a wider release than BBV's previous output, with Colin Baker (who was director of his own production company Visible Ink) helping broker a deal between Bill and Pickwick Video, who also re-released the first three Stranger videos onto the high street.

The *Edge of Darkness* parallels are obvious, even if the production is more daytime soap than high end drama. The storytelling is about as far away from classic *Doctor Who* as you can get, within the sci-fi genre, weaving a political thriller, a ghost story and a dystopian future together to produce a competent film. The near future setting plays to the budgetary limitations, making for the most assured of the BBV films to date. Briggs' script is simple but effective, and delivers just enough tension to keep the viewer hooked for the film's duration. The direction is solid but uninspired, with Baggs seemingly having developed a confidence in his own abilities. The supporting cast are uniformly excellent, even if the odd extra seems more like someone's mate dressed up, than a genuine supporting artist. Seeing the four leads acting together is a fan pleasing moment, with each of them bringing some of the star quality that no doubt got them the role of the Doctor in the first place. And if you try hard enough, I'm sure you could retcon this into the *Doctor Who* canon somehow, just for the sheer delight of having them share the screen one last time.

Reviews were generally favourable, with *Celestial Toyroom* describing *AirZone* as "by far the best video production that I have ever seen and is considerably better than many that make it onto broadcast television."[25]

DWM's Craig Hinton also felt it was of broadcast standard: "Well worth a watch, and easily deserving of television exposure."[26] One criticism levelled at the film by fandom was that it had nothing to do with *Doctor Who,* and while this is true, it is a solid drama in its own right with each of the leads giving compelling performances that are far removed from their *Doctor Who* counterparts. However it must have been a shock to fans used to *The Stranger* series to see something so different from both the BBV output and *Doctor Who* itself — but it's worth remembering that this was only an anniversary celebration by default. Similarly, while the controversial love scene isn't jarring to the narrative and isn't explicit in any way, the reaction from fans seems to be due to their being unable to separate the actors from previous roles they've played.

While not the thirtieth anniversary special fans were expecting, it was a welcome surprise for its *Who* hungry audience, enthused McCoy. "It was a nice celebration. If the BBC couldn't get it together, thank goodness someone else did. Bill made it possible for something to be done to make a kind of celebration with all of us together."[27]

Gary Russell also feels it was a good addition to the anniversary celebrations. "That was probably the only time you've got all those actors together, actually, because even in 'Dimensions in Time' they weren't all together. It was Bill's attempt to do a thirtieth anniversary *Doctor Who* story, without doing anything to do with *Doctor Who*."[28]

For Davison, it was more about testing the waters, working on this kind of production "It was fun for what it was. It didn't prove to me that Bill had quite got it. In a way, it was in the best traditions of early *Doctor Who*: the sets wobbled, and people who were supposed to be dead kept blinking, but Bill was finding his way. I thought the script was quite good, but it concerned me that I might turn on the telly and see it! It was just a lot of fun rather than a professional job."[29]

Baggs, on the other hand, remains proud of the film. "It was tremendous fun to work with these people who I have been a fan of for as long as I can remember. Again it was tough because it was such a complicated story to tell in such a short space of screen time. I feel it is a tremendous achievement but think the story would have been better in two hours."[30] Briggs felt it was his most successful script to date. "I was very pleased with the finished product. It is more accessible to a viewing audience"[31]

The ambition of *The AirZone Solution* is admirable. The fact that Baggs managed to get together four Doctors for the 30th Anniversary was cause for celebration enough. But why did these well known actors agree to appear in these low budget and low profile films? After all, Baker himself expressed his doubts about working on these types of productions while on set on 'In Memory Alone'. "I enjoy making these a lot, but in some ways I shouldn't because I feel I should be insisting on working in a totally professional environment, which this isn't — in the sense that these people don't make films as part of their full time jobs. However, while they're here, they go about in a very professional way."[32]

It seems much was down to Baggs himself. Tim Saward describes him as "very charismatic and he was very persuasive." [33] It was these qualities that many of the cast and crew of these productions were drawn to, including Sophie Aldred. "His gift of the gab, his energy, his enthusiasm, his leadership qualities. He was a great one for a scam and a good old scammer and I thoroughly enjoyed working with him." Peter Davison, perhaps the most successful actor post *Who* (at this time at least) also agreed. "It's a very commendable project. Sometimes you get used to the BBC people coming in, either the writer or director who really don't have any interest in doing the things; it's just a job. Here, we have Bill, who's very intent on doing this project, although on a very shoestring budget. The sincerity is there, and it's the right way to go about things. That makes it nice to do."[34]

While the money apparently wasn't great on these productions, it seems some of the actors (particularly those with low television profiles at the time) thought Baggs was a rising star in the world of television drama, including Colin Baker. "I think it's going to be the start of a lot of stuff that Bill's going to do and I hope I'll be involved in it, because I enjoy working with him. I think Bill's a very talented man." [35]

Bryant concurred. "I think ultimately it would be wonderful if we were making feature films. Aim high and see how far we can go. I hope we'll stay as a team and keep going. We'll probably go back and do some more with the Stranger and Miss Brown, because they're very popular."[36]

When asked why the stars did these films, Nick Briggs certainly feels it was a combination of all the factors that others have mentioned. "I can't give you a definitive answer. I think Bill put enough money on the table to make it not entirely a waste of their time. They certainly wouldn't have done it without that. But I think the key thing was the charisma of Bill. He had a steely certainty in his eye that people sort of found attractive, I think. It made them think, 'Hey, this young guy is really going places'. He had a real drive, and people are drawn to that. And there he was, setting up a production. He actually made these things happen, often by what seemed like sheer will power alone. He was able to say, 'Here's a script, come and do it for this money'. He was offering them a credible job. And I think they liked his ambition. I think actors are always looking out for the next rising star. Who knows, there might be an alternative reality where Bill got really successful? Not in our reality, though."[37]

Baggs had his own thoughts on why well-known actors appeared in his films. "Being blunt: money, doing something creative, working with someone you like; I think those are three quite strong reason to do anything. I think although I've had my run ins with people at times, I run a professional set up and if you are an actor you kind of invest in somebody like that who you think is going somewhere" [38]

Nevertheless, Baggs was grateful for their support. "People were very accommodating, I think they loved my enthusiasm and they were willing to put up with my naivety for that reason."

This goodwill had, however, run out for one actress on *The AirZone Solution*. This would be the last appearance of Nicola Bryant in any BBV production. "Colin and I gave our services for free, we didn't get any money and he finally said with *AirZone Solution* he would pay. So I flew back from Los Angeles to do the film, I paid for my flight and we never got paid! I know that from the make-up artist who never got paid, she provided all her own stuff and her other half who worked on it as well and he was promised a lot of money for all the stuff that he brought he didn't get paid. Sometimes it's nice to help people out but on the other hand we were kind of abused." [39]

Baggs, however, recalls things slightly differently. "Certainly money comes into it, she wasn't demanding huge sums of money, but as a producer you're juggling what is selling your film and how best to spend the budget. I mean Nicola is inevitably going to be not as expensive as Colin, but she's going to be more expensive than a new actor and I could maybe get two actors. There wasn't any falling out, I probably didn't think about it and now I feel sad about that. Nicola can be challenging to work with on some levels but from an acting point of view she was always there." [40]

Whose version of events is to be believed is up for debate, but by most accounts at the time Baggs appeared to be paying his stars, although the fee was negligible. There may be a certain element of memory cheating on from both parties. If Baggs was taking advantage of Nicola Bryant and Baker why did the latter go on to work with Baggs for a number of years after *AirZone*? And with his loyalty to, and friendship with, Bryant, why did he not side with her rather than Baggs? On the other hand, due to the amateur nature of these productions, without proper contracts in place and with very little paper trail, Baggs may have promised money and conditions in negotiations that he couldn't deliver or forgot about. We've already heard about his persuasive nature and enthusiasm, which may have played a hand in securing Bryant's services, even if Baggs was unable to deliver on his promises.

What is undeniable, is that Nicola Bryant helped launch the BBV range to the *Doctor Who* audience and her contribution is part of what makes the first few films so successful. Her departure also marked a change in direction for *The Stranger*, from *Doctor Who* knock off to serious sci-fi drama. With *AirZone*, Baggs attempted to present himself as a serious film maker and it would be this ambition and mentality he would take with him onto his next ventures.

Chapter 7 — Earth is the Loneliest Planet

Having decided to change the direction of *The Stranger* series following the climax of 'In Memory Alone' and the success of the *The AirZone Solution*, Baggs was unsure of which direction to take next. Initially, he considered the continuing story of Colin Baker's *AirZone* character, Arnie Davis. "There were scripts, it was debatable whether it was popular enough to star on its own, but I did have a couple of scripts and Nick had some other ideas. For me, I wanted to do something on a basic level that produces an income but what that really means is what the people want and in the end I went back to *The Stranger* and that was more creatively interesting." [1]

On returning to *The Stranger*, Baggs initially discussed his plans with writer Iain McLaughlin. "Before *The Airzone Solution* came out I pitched a script to BBV for *The Stranger*. It was set in an old country house with paintings of historical figures who came to life. Time in the house seemed to be all over the place. A mysterious old tramp sent the Stranger and Miss Brown to the house. I spoke to Bill Baggs on the phone about it. He mentioned that Nicola Bryant was out of the picture and there would be a new companion and he'd be in touch about that, but I never heard from him about it. Every character was written with a *Doctor Who* alumni in mind. The Tramp was written with Jon Pertwee in mind, the grand lady was written for Mary Tamm and Frazer Hines was definitely the lost Jacobite. BBV were using *Doctor Who* actors, so it made sense to write roles for as many as possible. The core of *The Stranger* film became the *Time Hunter* novella, 'Echoes'. Everything else changed." [2]

Why this script never came to fruition is unknown but shortly after this Baggs invited another writer to develop the story and fill in the blanks of the Stranger's past. "A script came in from John Guilor, an actor-writer from Yorkshire, which I thought had potential. Unfortunately, it didn't work out and I was so frustrated that I gave Gulior the chance to write one further down the line and gave it to somebody else. The nub of it was my idea — the history of the Stranger which is what is revealed in 'The Terror Game'."[3]

Gulior's script was a vastly different take on what was eventually seen on screen. "I wrote a script called 'A Secret with Purpose', in which it was revealed that the Stranger had a dark past. The only thing I can tell you about it is Bill wasn't happy with the lack of character development, in that he felt none of the characters were changed by the events of my story. I argued that only the Stranger should change since it was him and revelations concerning him that drove the whole thing. But to be honest, it was my first ever TV script and I didn't really know what I was doing. I'm not sure I actually knew how to re-write something in those days and I sent him a new draft which basically had about two pages which had been changed to sort out a couple of more minor niggles he had with it. I then became disinterested in the project and he became disinterested with what I had to offer."[4]

With Gulior out of the picture, Baggs turned, once again, to Nick Briggs, to whom he showed one of the previous efforts. "Bill actually had a different script from somebody else," Briggs remembers, "which he gave to me and said, 'I think I'll film this. What do you think?' I remember saying, 'Well, it's awful.' And so he just said something like, 'Oh yeah, it is, isn't it? You write something, then.'"[5]

Despite Baggs discussing a backstory with Guilor, Briggs seems to think the change in direction was down to him. "That was me. I couldn't bear the dishonesty of writing something that was meant to be *Doctor Who*, but the TARDIS was just out of shot and no one could say 'Doctor'. I'd got round it in 'In Memory Alone', because I'd had Colin and Nicola's characters losing their memory. But with 'The Terror Game', I set out to establish a 'new continuity'."[6]

The new tale revealed a dark past for the Stranger. But Baggs insists that none of it was planned in the early stories. "We were making it up! It wasn't relevant at the time — but now I'm keen to make things clear and I've changed styles. Anyway, I gave the idea to Nick and said 'right I want the first draft in a week — this is what I want to happen.' I went down to London and picked it up, read it on the train on the way back and 'phoned him as soon as I got to Nottingham. I said 'this is wrong and this is wrong, that's right, like that, gotta develop that.' So that's how the relationship works."[7]

The other caveat that Briggs was given, was to lose Bryant's character, Miss Brown. "Bill told me she wasn't going to be in it. That was part of the brief. I know they'd had lots of disagreements about expenses and things, but this might have been at the root of that. I don't know for sure."[8]

At the time, Briggs seemed only too happy to guide *The Stranger* on his new path. "The seemingly bizarre veering away from the core audience's main reason for buying the tapes was driven by two factors — Bill and me. Bill wanted to use these productions as audition tapes for *Eastenders* and *The Bill,* and I wanted to create a solid, workable story basis for *The Stranger,* rather than leaving the audience to make assumptions based on *Doctor Who.* I did however, still want to deliver stories with a *Doctor Who* 'feel' to them — for my sake as well as the audience."[9]

While Briggs wanted to keep them with relevance to a *Doctor Who* audience, there was a definite shift in tone. "In *Doctor Who,* the plot invariably wins. *Doctor Who* stories are, largely, not about a person's emotional journey or some kind of psychological awaking, they are about mysteries which need to be solved. These mysteries and battles are, of course, all the more engaging for the audience if the characters caught up in them are realistic — but it is the actual unfolding of events, not the characters' reactions to them, which drives a *Doctor Who* story. These were the kind of stories I attempted to write for *The Stranger* series. However, Bill's agenda was to focus the stories on character. He wanted *The Stranger* series to be about the Stranger's inner turmoil first and the events in the stories second"[10]

Consequently, the Stranger's past was dug up, and Briggs made a brave and somewhat shocking choice for the character. "The impetus for the story was for the Stranger to discover that he wasn't such a nice person and that he'd done something appalling in the past, so it's really about your past catching up with you and also the fact that just because you have done something wrong in the past it doesn't mean you can't put it right or change your mind."[11]

Briggs idea was to make the Stranger a terrorist, feeling there was a strong story to tell within this world. "Terrorism is all to do with perspectives. What the French Resistance did in the Second World War was terrorism, if you were a Nazi. From our point of view it was fighting a bad thing... It's a question of how incensed and personally involved you can get in on issues and I think it's possible for people to get so involved in an issue that they don't see the broader question. And they think the most important thing is that they get this view across — nobody's listening so they're going to make a loud bang which hurts people, that makes them listen. It doesn't work, of course, because they make louder bangs your way and it just becomes... worse"[12]

Later Briggs revealed that the new more adult nature of the film was down to the producer/director. "This was what Bill wanted and I was very happy to go that way. We enter a period here where, to all intents and purposes, we were supplying Bill with a show reel. Nothing wrong with that. And this was his attempt to show the world that he could do a gritty, terrorist story. He seemed constantly frustrated by my including science fiction in the storyline, but I did point out that this is what his audience expected."[13]

With the Stranger's past agreed upon, Briggs had only one week to deliver his first draft and only another week after that to deliver his final script. In the meantime, Baggs set about casting the film.

With Bryant out of the picture, Baggs needed a new female lead to play the Protectorate agent and night club manager, Tamora Hennessay. For this role he approached former fourth Doctor companion Louise Jameson, who agreed to play the part. The script also called for a new double act, Egan and Saul — two terrorists known as Preceptors who knew the Stranger (now known as Soloman) from his past.

For the part of Saul, Nick Briggs convinced John Wadmore to come back to the series (having previously appeared as the mute in 'Summoned by Shadows'). "I'd given up acting and I was working in social services which meant I could take time off, so Nick would say 'we are doing this over this weekend,' and I'd just put in for leave." [14]

The turnaround was so quick that all the events are blurred into one for Wadmore. "Nick wrote it and said that 'there's a part in this are you interested?' and I said 'yeah ok'. We ended up filming in a disused night club somewhere in Nottingham, he borrowed the equipment, the costumes were all our own and we stayed on somebodies floor. I have no idea what it was about — something happens, somebody gets beaten up, somebody disappears, no idea!" [15]

For the part of Egan — the terrorist leader — Baggs approached a face familiar not only to *Doctor Who* fans but particularly familiar to Colin Baker — David Troughton, the son of a former Doctor, Patrick Troughton.

A successful actor in his own right, Troughton had appeared in numerous TV series including *Doctor Who*. He had also shared a flat with Colin Baker in their younger years, and Colin had been best man at his wedding. Despite his *Doctor Who* credentials, Baggs was adamant this had nothing to do with his casting. "That wasn't the reason I chose him, it's coincidence, I think David Troughton is an excellent actor and that's the sole reason why I chose him. He's the type of character actor who can turn his hand to anything. I'm not going to sit back and say 'your father was Patrick Troughton or your brother's Michael or you've been in *Doctor Who'*[16]"

Troughton understandably had reservations about doing the production at first: "I think he was unsure about why he has been cast. I made it very clear why I chose him very early on and we were both complimentary to each other. He leapt in with both feet once he'd decided to do it. I think he is very reluctant to highlight the family link. When he came to do publicity he said 'no *Doctor Who*' and that's fair enough. He's made a name for himself in his own right and that's the real reason why I chose him. Also, within the industry, David has a lot of clout and it does me good to be seen working with him in videos."[17]

Briggs too, remembers the star being hesitant about the reasons he was chosen. "It concerned David. And he took the job on condition that it was nothing to do with his father having been the Doctor. But Bill reassured him. Bill greatly admired David in his own right, although he was mindful that the *Doctor Who* connection would do no harm."[18]

Troughton later told Robert Cope about the approach. "My agent phoned up and said 'There's this funny bloke called Bill Baggins who is interested in doing a video which is sort of *Doctor Who*-ish'. So I phoned him and he seemed a personable sort of chap, on the ball, so I thought 'What is all this?' I phoned Colin Baker who I knew was going to be involved as well, because he was my Best Man years ago — we've been great mates, although I hadn't seen too much of him recently. He explained it was all on the level and where the videos were sold, and as I was doing nothing else I thought 'OK, let's have a couple of weeks working with Colin', because I'd never actually worked with him before."[19]

For the final two roles, Norman and Raven, Baggs cast closer to home, with AV contributor Nicholas Pegg and writer Nicholas Briggs taking on the respective roles.

Wadmore and Troughton's performances are one of the highlights of the film, one that Briggs is happy to admit was mainly down to their chemistry. "They are great performances. I was keen to get John Wadmore in again. And I was very excited about David Troughton doing it. Those two really struck up a friendship and great working relationship. I like to think they took their cues from the script, but they really brought it alive."[20]

During the pre-production period, Briggs once again encountered the more difficult side of Baggs. "Bill said to me 'this bit where he goes up the stairs and you have him put his hand on the wall' and I said 'yeah' and he said 'that's not going to work, I think he has to put his hand on the banister' and said 'I don't care, whatever' and he said 'no no no, not whatever, Nick, it has to be the banister,' and I said, 'I don't mind either way' and he said 'No you've got to understand that it's the banister and not the wall,' and I said 'as long as he makes contact with the building'. But it wasn't enough for Bill for me to say I don't mind either way, I had to disavow myself from my point of view and completely agree with him otherwise he wasn't happy, and that was the bizarre thing of working with Bill. Then I found out eventually that the only reason for it, was that the staircase he had in mind to shoot it next to didn't have a wall next to it, it just had a banister. But it's all mysterious with Bill. He can't tell you the full account, he just has to get you to agree with him and then he's happy; a very strange mentality." [21]

A ten day production schedule began with rehearsals on March 19th and 20th 1994 at the BBC rehearsal rooms in Acton. Shooting then commenced on the Monday at a night club in Nottingham (again near BBC Nottingham) where the bulk of the action took place. The day kicked off with only Nicolas Pegg in attendance, with both Baker and Jameson arriving later in the day. The next few days saw Wadmore and Troughton join them to film scenes set within the night club, the flat above which acted as Egan and Saul's base of operations.

Wadmore was particularly in awe of Troughton. "He was lovely. You have to remember David is a Royal Shakespeare actor, he is in the business, he lives in Stratford-upon-Avon, worked in the RSC most of his life and at a various times the National Theatre. Plenty of television stuff, and stuff like that. He's a really good established actor and he's a really nice bloke as well." [22]

Troughton himself was very complimentary about the script, and was happy to be involved. "Bill Baggs is a marvellous director. First of all, he can get a company together for no money so I think he'll go far. Because if you want to know we get diddely squat for this, absolutely nothing — we are here for the love."[23] Again, Baggs managed to persuade an established and respected actor to take on a role for free, again perhaps with the promise of bigger roles and bigger films enticing him into doing this low key production. Briggs once again remembers the shoot with fondness, despite the heavy workload, describing it as "[l]oads of fun and frustration. Bill driving us all very hard. David Troughton being an absolute hoot. John Wadmore getting off with the make-up girl. Far too much drinking and smoking. Curries. David said, 'I'm only here for the "big night out"!' Yes, getting to the pub after shooting was a priority... although not always possible, because of the punishing hours we worked. But the whole 'being away from home' and in a team together aspect was fun."[24]

The Thursday of that week saw the team embark on their first bit of filming beyond the confines of the night club. The film visited Easter Marina in Nottingham for the confrontation scenes between Egan and Soloman. The crew then filmed the opening of the story in which Soloman arrives and passes out in an alleyway. The next few days were spent in and outside the club, with Briggs donning bandages and filming his scenes as Raven, and Louise Jameson returning for more scenes — with this being the only day that all members of the cast were on set together. Baker was happy that his character was being developed into something other than a *Doctor Who* clone. "*Who is that masked man?* can't go on forever, the fugitive cannot run forever, eventually there has to come a point where you find something out. He was a terrorist, an idealistic assassin, and what I like about the development of that idea was that it invites obvious comparisons to the world we live in today." [25]

'The Terror Game' also saw Briggs providing a score for the production, which he puts down to budgetary restrictions rather than a desire to score a film. "He certainly didn't pay me much, so I think there was an element of cost-saving. I can't remember how much I wanted to do it. It was quite daunting, because of the low level of technology available to me then. And the production wasn't mixed or dubbed properly, because Bill was just using a BBC East Midlands news edit suite — sometimes during live broadcasts of news programmes! — and they didn't have proper sound facilities. So the music does sound terrible. And, naturally, Bill fiddled around with it and used the music in places it hadn't been composed for. He always found it difficult to leave things alone and accept other people's decisions. He was the leader and it was his vision."[26]

'The Terror Game' was first advertised in the June edition of *DWM* and released the following month. In his review Craig Hinton found it a somewhat mixed bag: "The Terror Game yet again demonstrates everything that sums up *The Stranger* series: excellent acting, top notch directing... and a plot that fails to ignite" going on to say "My major criticism with 'The Terror Game' is the plot. There's simply too much of it! In trying to reveal the Stranger's origins, too many things are thrown at the viewer which get in the way of the action."[27] Robert Hope of *DWB* had much the same criticisms of the plot but still found it a satisfying watch. "Bill Baggs' high production values and guiding light at the directorial helm has turned in another video of quality which should add to BBV's growing reputation for excellence."[28]

Briggs wasn't aware of the review, but feels the criticism were not entirely just. "I never really took much notice of anything the late Craig Hinton said, bless him. Lovely chap, though. I only ever saw him when he was hopelessly drunk. I don't think I read that review. I don't think there was too much plot at all. Things only appear to have too much plot when they're not explained properly. And Bill kept taking out all the explanations, so things appeared very unclear... which then confuses the audience, making them think there's too much going on. I'm not sure why Bill was preoccupied with removing explanations. He was very keen on everything being very uncertain. I remember thinking at the time that this was about a fundamental uncertainty within him, that he was projecting on to everything he made. But that's enough amateur psychology for now!"[29] This was the first time *DWM* had anything largely negative to say about any of *The Stranger* productions, and it may be no coincidence that this is also the first review that wasn't written by Baggs' friend and former colleague, Gary Russell. Russell later said that "ultimately the quality wasn't always as high as the preceding release and as time passed, one had to be careful not to be seen as just a mouthpiece promoting my "mates" at the expense of critical distance."[30]

In hindsight, the criticisms that were levelled at 'The Terror Game' don't really stick. While there is a lot of exposition in the story, it all flows naturally within the dialogue, or as naturally as sci-fi can be integrated within day to day character drama (it's certainly not as clunky as anything George Lucas has written, for instance).

The character of Norman helps to ground the drama, providing much needed comic relief to the otherwise heavy nature of the unfolding plot. The criticism that the character development gets in the way of the action is an odd one; this isn't an action story, it's a character piece and any action is contained in a small sub plot about Soloman's last mission to kill

Raven. In hindsight, maybe it's a sign of the changing nature of fandom — where it once looked for action adventure, it now looks for character and back story.

And while modern *Doctor Who* (re-launched in 2005) often delivers both in 45 minutes, 'The Terror Game' is a smaller tale that gives real weight to the character of Soloman and introduces a duo worthy of Robert Holmes in Egan and Saul. By modern standards it moves at a relatively slow pace, but for fans in the 90s who were used to four and six part *Doctor Who* stories, the pacing must have seemed positively Olympian in speed. If we compare the BBC release of that month (the six part 'The Seeds of Doom') to 'The Terror Game', the two couldn't be more at odds in their story telling and pacing. 'The Terror Game' successfully re-launched *The Stranger* series and the back story could easily be applied to a modern day drama — with very little tweaking — and produce a relevant and insightful drama.

'The Terror Game' set BBV on a new course for the next few years, as Bill Baggs later told Mike Haberfelner. "'Terror Game' was like the beginning of something new, we were trying to do something different from *Doctor Who* and changed the character completely so instead of a hero he's kind of an anti-hero. It was like grown up filmmaking and gritty and I kind of got into my stroke with it..."[31]

Chapter 8 — The Ordinary Boys

With Baggs and Briggs both determined to bring *The Stranger* very much down to earth (and use these productions to garner other work within the broadcast industry) they set about developing the fifth title in the series.

A script began being developed almost as soon as 'The Terror Game' was complete. Entitled 'Breach of the Peace', this video would be the least sci-fi oriented of them all. Briggs suggested this was partly in reaction to the response to the previous film. "The Terror Game' we think suffers from having too much science fiction in it, so this one has got hardly any in. Colin Baker thinks this doesn't matter because the characters will be known from 'Terror Game', so I hope he's right."[1]

With Egan and Saul thrust to the front of the action and a plot more suited to a police procedural drama, Briggs was pleased to be moving out of his comfort zone "I suppose it's true to say that if Bill let me, I'd write in [*Doctor Who*]... but it's nice to be pushed in this direction. It was great fun to do 'Breach of the Peace' and hardly have any science fiction in it. That was a really good experience for me."[2]

The police procedural aspect of 'Breach of the Peace' was specifically designed as an audition piece for weekly police drama *The Bill*, as Baggs was only too happy to admit. "Of course, 'Breach of the Peace' is a complete and utter rip off; that's exactly what it was meant to be... I really enjoyed doing 'Breach of the Peace' it was a dream, because it all fell into place really. Because there is none of this strange language that you have... That they were aliens was actually immaterial in a way."[3]

Colin Baker, David Troughton and John Wadmore all returned for this foray into a grown-up game of cops and robbers. Joining them were newcomer Holly King and Nick Briggs — this time in the role of Evans, and sporting a very fetching moustache. The main guest star of this production was Caroline John, who had played third Doctor companion Liz Shaw in Season Seven — here she was to star as Detective Chief Inspector Diana Sellars.

John had had very little to do with *Doctor Who* since leaving the role, so when she appeared on the convention scene in the early 90s she was taken aback by the prospect that this could lead to other acting work. "I was asked to be in this by Bill Baggs at Blue Box [a convention]. He gave me the script to read which I thought was great so I said OK, I'll do it."[4]

As with David Troughton, Baggs was keen that his stars, including John, knew that although the film was sold to *Doctor Who* fans, his primary concern was to get the right people for the part. "I think she's aware of her connection with *Doctor Who* and the effect that will have on the video because she knows Colin Baker is in it. I wouldn't say she's very conscious of it but I'm sure she's realised that's part of the reason she was chosen. After all, I gave her the script at a *Doctor Who* convention. But, again, I've admired her work and thought it would be good fun to work with her."[5]

However, Briggs reveals, that John wasn't the first person approached for the role. "Caroline was about third choice for the role. Bill had tried Imelda Staunton, but she'd made it fairly clear, I'm told, that she didn't like the script, when Bill offered more money and the message came back from the agent, 'The money isn't the issue.' That makes me laugh. I have the distinction of Imelda Staunton rejecting my script. And quite right too." He feels that this rejection was down to a fundamental problem with the format. "You see, because Bill was trying to fund these things by making them for *Doctor Who* fans, but also making them look like they weren't science fiction, there was something fundamentally dishonest and confused about these productions. And the scripts reflected that. I'm sure that reading them when you had no connection to the *Doctor Who* world must have left someone like Imelda Staunton thinking, 'What the hell is this? It's neither one thing nor the other.' But I was keen to carry on, despite this fundamental compromise, because the experience was largely fun and really useful for me... and I was being paid. And I was very poor."[6]

Production once again returned to Baggs' current place of residence, Nottingham, and was recorded in May of 1994. While the outside of Nottingham police station appeared in the film, the interior of the police station was in reality the AST Training Centre in Beeston, where the unit could use the office space for shooting, and the extra room for hair, make up and technical storage. BBC Nottingham also loaned their newsroom to the BBV team to utilise as part of the busy police department, as it was not in use on weekends. According to Briggs, Baggs was once again weaving in and out of legal loopholes in order to get the production done on the cheap. "That was mostly based around Bill's house on the outskirts, in Beeston, but they illegally filmed outside the police station. And all the interiors were done in BBC East Midlands, in their old building on the Mansfield Road. I'm not sure Bill had permission to shoot there either, but we just did it on Sundays, I think."[7]

Both Colin Baker and David Troughton were busy working on other productions at the time of shooting, the latter touring with the Royal Shakespeare Company. In order to accommodate both of them, Egan and Saul were kept apart from Baker's Soloman for the majority of the story. With the two terrorists disguised as detectives, Briggs was keen to bring them to the forefront of the drama. "What I like about Egan and Saul is they have no conscience, the people on this planet are an irrelevance to them. David and John developed that in such a humorous way, not a send up way but a humorous way that we couldn't wait to get them into CID and have them going around the place pushing people about, being annoying and irritating and not giving a damn about it"[8]

While Wadmore was game for returning, did he want to see the character develop beyond its villainous roots? "No, not really. I think he was very two-dimensional in that respect. He's supposed to be quite flirtatious, he'd been dallying with one of the bobbies (one of the local girls) but I think he was fairly basic really." And what did Wadmore think of the more grounded police setting of the drama? "It made sense at the time, these two were after the Colin Baker character, and it made sense that they'd track him by any means."[9]

Troughton too enjoyed returning to the role, but was under no illusions as to why he or indeed Baggs were there. "Bill is basically doing CV videos. He wants to be a proper director and he's getting all these good actors and he's got us for absolute shite [because] we all have a bloody good laugh, and he sends them off to prominent people in the industry. The reason we're doing this as a police one is that he keeps being told 'Do one like *The Bill!*', which he has done. I just hope Bill remembers all this when he's as famous as Spielberg and doing his 900th film. But I've really enjoyed it, it is one of the happiest jobs that I've ever done because there is no pressure. I hope he will, he'll go far."[10]

Caroline John agreed that it was the atmosphere that made the production. "It was quite low budget, totally low. The good thing about doing those is it's very small and everyone's totally relaxed and having fun." [11]

Overall, *DWM*'s Craig Hinton — having disliked the previous story — had no major qualms with 'Breach of the Peace'. His only reservations were the "excessive bad language" and Nick Briggs' and Caroline John's "atrocious" accents, before going on to say that "Nick Briggs' story is straight forward and dynamic — the hunt for the Stranger — and the only disappointment is that it finishes too soon." As before, he praised Baker's performance - "[t]he Stranger is the part Colin Baker is born to play", and expressed a wish to see it given wider exposure. "I just wish someone "up there" would recognise the potential and bring it to television. It deserves it."[12]

Robert Cope of *DWB* was also impressed with 'Breach of the Peace', citing it as his favourite of the five. While Hinton may have disliked John's accent, Cope couldn't have been more complimentary. "Perhaps the performance that most stands out this time is Caroline John's no nonsense "Yorkshire lass", Diana Sellers. From the outset she struggles to retain order within her station against the impending threat of the two mercenaries that have been thrust upon her, and like many a good officer she relies on her instincts to search out the truth behind the cloud of mystery that has started to prevail. John reaffirms that she is a first rate talent and this role seems to suit her perfectly — enough to make her return to the series a worthwhile thought." [13]

'Breach of the Peace' is an interesting if not entirely successful delve into the world of police drama. All the performers are on point as usual, with Egan and Saul once again stealing the show. The plot is simple and the guest characters well fleshed out in a relatively short run time, although there is some clunky exposition at the beginning. As an audition piece for other work, it is as competent as any contemporary soap, but Baggs lacks any particular directorial flair that would have made him stand out from any other number of aspiring directors at the time. It would be interesting to know what Baggs' potential employers thought of 'Breach of the Peace'. His get up and go attitude was admirable, even if his technique lacked originality. Any such employers must have also been slightly bemused by the sci-fi elements of the story — before the film has started the video greets viewers with information regarding the alien nature of its protagonists; not exactly the back story a soap opera executive would be expecting on a police drama.

Although only 26, Baggs' drive and ambition was clear at this point and it was a brave decision to ground the series. On the sci-fi content (or lack of) in *The Stranger* series, he stated, "I have no driving ambition in that particular genre, it just happens that I do science fiction because I like it, because it's convenient, because I know it's going to sell, being brutally honest. What I can never get away from — and it doesn't worry me at all — is that there's a market there. And what I do is use that market to make something that I hope will be of interest to them but at the same time may well be of interest to other people in the sense of a programme idea, and also as a way of showing off what I can do."[14]

In 1998, Briggs was more reflective on the success and failures of 'Breach of the Peace'. "Each successive *Stranger* story was stripped of incident and story complexity in favour of emotional angst. Unfortunately, the net result was often that story details, the reason for the emotional angst, became fuzzy. Leaving the finished products lacking clarity and perhaps more importantly science fiction. We were trying to make serious, emotional drama, and in the process we were confounding the expectation of our core audience. It was an interesting exercise, but the end result was, arguably, not completely satisfying for anyone."[15]

Both Briggs' and Baggs' confidence was clearly building at this point, even if they would later see the flaws in this production. Baggs certainly had big plans following the release of 'Breach of the Peace'. "I'm waiting to see if 'The Terror Game' and 'Breach of the Peace' do well in terms of sales. If Pickwick are interested then I will consider resigning from the BBC and do six productions a year. So the goal would be to release *Stranger* tapes,

AirZone tapes and anything else I can think of but I think the *Stranger* tapes would be the backbone."[16]

Briggs too was keen on the idea. "I have a vague memory of his mentioning this. I would have been up for it. I would love to have created some narrative cohesion. But I don't think the market would have supported it."[17]

Baggs hoped to keep his audience on side. "I want to keep the *Doctor Who* audience with me because they are one element of the market, but at the same time I'm trying to expand the market so that I can access other areas and do other things as well. I think that Keith Barnfather is quite happy to do things that are like *Doctor Who* and that's fine, because he's trying to make money out of it. I'm trying to do more than make money. I'm trying to sell me, and the skill I have."

Paradoxically, he went on in the same interview to say, "I'm trying to wind down the *Doctor Who* now, so I'm manipulating the market if the audience doesn't come with me that's fine — I'll have learnt from that. I want to impress potential employers, and if they just think *they are ripping off Doctor Who* then where's the imagination as far as they're concerned? Interestingly, I've been down to see the people at *EastEnders* because of *The Air Zone Solution* and I'm very hopeful of getting a block of episodes to direct." [18]

One look at Baggs' IMDB page reveals he never got much further in his bid for other work, listing as it does only his BBV output and a short film *The Last 28*. He later revealed how near he got to the next step up, however.

"I got very close, I had interviews with *EastEnders*, I had interviews with *Emmerdale*, I had interviews with *Brookside*. I don't think I ever had interviews with *The Bill* but I certainly had feedback from them so it was that close. It's a huge disappointment to me that I never really broke into that arena but I did get very close. I don't know if my face didn't fit or I wasn't good enough or whatever." [19]

Briggs however would have slightly better luck. "I once got pretty close to writing an episode of *The Bill* but it was like staring into the pit of Hell."[20]

When interviewed for this publication, Briggs elaborated further on this. "I did have a 'near miss' for writing a script for *The Bill*, but it was years later and nothing to do with this. When it came to it, I realized the problem was that I just didn't want to write *The Bill*. I'm not aware that Bill got anywhere near directing any television drama."[21] Briggs would however, go on to write several episodes of *Family Affairs* for Pearson TV and Channel Five and a drama for BBC's *Children in Need* — 'Bowlin' All Over' — but if his experience with *The Bill* is anything to go by, this was unlikely to be the result of his BBV work. Nevertheless, this experience must have helped, even if it wasn't a direct influence.

Chapter 9 — Shake, Dog, Shake

Kevin Davies and Mark Ayres had been involved in *Doctor Who* fandom since the late 70s. Between them they had worked on fan films, ran local groups, contributed to fanzines and Ayres had even worked on *Doctor Who* itself in the late 80s. They had also worked for Keith Barnfather on *Wartime* and various *Myth Makers* releases.

Inspired in part by the success of *Wartime* and a general impetus to create, they had long talked about making a *Doctor Who* related drama, although as Davies explains he would have done things differently to Barnfather. "Keith was more practical than me, he decided he was going to do something manageable. So he thought, as a first attempt let's just do something simple: a straight forward ghost story exploring the background of Sergeant Benton, and he was probably right to do that. My way would have been to immediately dive in head long and be really ambitious and have everything thrown in and probably it would have been a bit of a botched mix." [1]

Both Davies and Barnfather were keen to make a bigger film than *Wartime* and with Reeltime's *Downtime* already pushed back from 1993 to 1994, there was a healthy competition between them, according to Davies. "We'd tease him saying 'why don't you something properly,' there was a bit of a rivalry when it came to doing the videos of what we wanted to do like *Downtime* vs *Shakedown*. There was definitely a bit of vying with each other to see who could get there first."[2]

If anything, it looked like Barnfather would be the first over the finish line — he was a business man and producer who had carefully planned his next foray into film, while by Davies's own admission, he and Ayres simply didn't have the finance. "We wanted some producer to come along and give us the money to do something." [3]

Downtime was due to premiere at the *Dreamwatch 94* convention in October of that year. However, just three months before the event Barnfather was forced to postpone the production for another year, leaving *Dreamwatch* — who were using the film as the selling point of the convention — without its main attraction.

Kevin Davies and Mark Ayres were approaching the end of post-production on the VHS release of Davies's 30th Anniversary documentary, now retitled 'More Than Thirty Years in the TARDIS'. Seeing an opportunity, Davies approached *DreamWatch* editor Gary Leigh about creating a replacement film. Leigh was only too happy to have something to fill the void, but couldn't afford to fund the whole thing, having promised only a portion of the funding for *Downtime*. As a result, Leigh approached super fan, record producer and missing episode hunter, Ian Levine.

Both Leigh and Levine had waged a somewhat vocal war against *Who* producer John Nathan-Turner in the late 1980s and this would give them a chance to make a *Doctor Who* drama the way they wanted. However Ian Levine's involvement came with a certain stipulation, as Ayres later explained. "Ian Levine was not my biggest fan. Ian Levine was not a fan of anyone who had continued to work with John Nathan-Turner after he had fallen out with him and so therefore, I had worked on *Doctor Who* after Ian Levine had deemed that *Doctor Who* wasn't worth watching. I was the enemy! I said to Kevin, 'I'll do this as a favour to you. But does this mean that I am going to have to mix an hour long film with Ian Levine music on it? Does this mean I'm going to have work with a man who absolutely hates my guts?' but as a favour to Kevin I agreed to do it but it would be really tough and I wasn't looking forward to it." [4]

It wasn't just Ayres who had a difficult relationship with Levine, according to Davies. "It quickly became obvious that I was stuck in the middle between how Ian wanted to do things and how everyone else wanted to do things, and it was a bit difficult. Then Gary said 'if this is going to work we have to get rid of Ian,' and of course it came down to me being the middle man to tell Ian 'I'm sorry we are going it alone'." [5]

So how did Ian react to this?

"He ranted and raved as he did, a bit. In the end he knew it was Gary who wanted control of things and they were never going to agree on how it should go and how much money should be spent. Ian can be very dictatorial, it's just his manner, he's got a heart of gold underneath it all but not many people get to see that and I've always managed to stay friendly with Ian while he's fallen out with just about everyone else I know."[6] With Ian Levine out of the picture, a new financier was needed. This arrived in the form of entrepreneur Jason Haigh-Ellery, and in early June Gary, Kevin, Mark and Jason met for the first official pre-production meeting for the film at Centrepoint London.

With just ten weeks from conception to the premiere of the film, Davies needed a reliable writer to deliver the script. "I was at Mark Ayres' house and we were talking about it and I said 'we need to get a proper writer; it can't be a fan'. We wanted to do a classic *Doctor Who* story as we remembered it, the glory days of the Pertwee and Baker era. I think Mark had worked with Terrance Dicks on *Myth Makers* and he had his number and said 'why don't we ask Terrance to do it?', I said 'you can't ask Terrance to do an amateur film' and he said 'why not? we've got a little bit of money' so he rang him up at 10 o'clock at night and he said 'how much' and I think we gave him 1500 quid and he said 'yes'." [7]

Dicks of course, was a prolific *Who* writer with countless titles to his name, but the idea of writing a fan film amused him. "They wanted to do an original script, not with *Doctor Who* because of course that was BBC copyright, but a science fiction thing with the Sontarans. They were people I'd met at conventions and things like that and they approached and said 'would I be interested?' and they paid a fraction of a proper fee for a script writer. They were very short on both time and money but they were a nice bunch of lads and tremendously enthusiastic so I wrote it for them in a great rush."[8]

The basic premise of *Shakedown* was worked out between Dicks and the production team. "Mark and I took Terrance Dicks out for lunch," recalls Davies, "and we told him what we wanted, which was something along the lines of 'Horror of Fang Rock' (the Dicks' penned Season 15 adventure). As you can see the blueprint is there; a little bottle show, simple story — beginning, middle and end, proper story. We just gave him the idea of a strong female character as the captain, a kind of a Ripley character [and] a bunch of characters that get bumped off one after the other." [9]

With the script set to feature the popular 70s menace the Sontarans, the film would see them sharing the screen for the first time with their rivals the Rutans, at Dicks' insistence. "That was my idea. In 'The Time Warrior' (which is the first Sontaran story) Bob Holmes put a line about 'you're still in this endless war with the Rutans', and later on I did a *Doctor Who* script called 'The Horror of Fang Rock' (sic) and that was set on a lighthouse. The monster that came out of the sea was a sort of giant jellyfish and was also a shapeshifter that could imitate humans. And that struck me just as a sort of joke in continuity to amuse myself and since the Sontarans were very sort of defined and military, it would be nice if they had a sort of blobby formless enemy and nice sort of contrast you see. They're definitely not going to get on so I then used the Rutans from time to time, including in *Shakedown* as the natural enemy of the Sontarans." [10]

In the same meeting Dicks also decided upon the details of the solar yacht crew, much to the amusement of Davies. "It was Terrance that said about this Solar Yacht crew, that they should be all be pretty well to do people, because they take part in yachting races, there's got to be a bit of money involved and I remember his quote — he said 'there's nothing people like more than seeing rich bastards get it in the neck' so that was his idea to have them all quite wealthy and make them bitch at each other."[11]

The script for *Shakedown* was completed in two weeks. "We shot pretty much the first draft," remembers Ayres, "but we got from Terrance exactly what we love about Terrance's work — a really good solid story with a beginning a middle and an end, and a good monster and bit of moral point and that's what Terrance always provides for *Doctor Who*."[12]

With the concept in place, Davies went about securing the rights to the potato headed warriors. "The Sontarans we knew we could do things with. We went to Robert Holmes' widow to get her permission and we gave her something like 350 quid and she just wrote a letter saying 'thank you very much and good luck' and that was as much as they had any involvement in it." [13]

But while the concept belonged to the Holmes' estate, the design of the Sontarans was owned by the BBC. Which prompted Davies to re-think the design. "We couldn't get anyone at the BBC to tell us if we were allowed to use the BBC design of the Sontarans. We got the rights to use the name and the characters, but not the look, so we started redesigning them." [14]

The task of re-designing these iconic monsters was given to the duo of Derek Handley and David Miller, although Davies was originally a little disappointed with the design. "I don't think they are the best sculptors but I think what happened was they made the early version, but then it was given over to Sue (Moore) and Steven (Mansfield) to lend a more professional finishing touch, they did a bit of work on it and gave it back to Derek who produced all the different moulds of the finished thing and the helmet which I thought was lovely. I really liked the mottled skin tones. They were very much Susan. She was inspired by what was current then, which was *Babylon 5,* those textured skins."[15]

With the masks in production, Davies was still keen to chase the BBC for permission, just in case the design edged too close to the BBC model. "They worked out very well, we had a very good team on that but at that point we were still trying to get someone at the BBC to give us an answer. I'd made stuff for BBC Video and we had contacts at Enterprises and we heard from them that our letter was being passed from desk to desk because nobody knew what to do with it." The redesign turned out to be a good decision, as when news came it was not good. "On the very first day of shooting, I finally got a fax through from a legal bod at [BBC] Enterprises saying no they couldn't give them permission to use them, by which point we had already built our Sontarans because we knew that was going to happen, but we kept the vague overall silhouette." [16]

The next task was to cast the crew of the *Tiger Moth*. Davies had already had some input on developing the lead character. "I'd been reading Tracy Edwards' book and I thought about transplanting that character. She was quite inspirational; the idea of her as a space going character. I thought, why not have a solar yacht and have people manning the rigging of the solar yacht as a sport."[17]

The lead character in question was Lisa Derrane, the *Tiger Moth*'s captain. Davies's first choice for this role was Elisabeth Sladen. "She thought about it, she was in for the ride, she had the script and everything and she reluctantly had to pull out because she said she had to give all her time to Sadie. She was a full time mum at that point, she hadn't done any acting for a while. I absolutely adored Lis Sladen, she's still my favourite companion ever, but she could be a bit neurotic to say the least. She used the excuse that Sadie (her daughter) was about to start at a new school and on those first two weeks of the new school we were shooting and she couldn't commit to us. So we were disappointed and a bit fed up that we'd got that far and all of a sudden we lost our leading lady and I said 'well if it can't be my favourite *Doctor Who* girl it has to be my favourite *Blake's 7* girl', which was Cally"[18] and so Jan Chappell was approached and agreed to play the part."

Also on board at an early stage was Sophie Aldred, who Ayres had worked with on *Doctor Who* and with whom Davies had also collaborated on a number of projects. Aldred fell in love with the character Mari, who was very much a spoiled brat. "What a gift of a part. I just love anything that is different and stretches me and also I was aware I was going to be showing the fans something different I could do as well."[19]

Although Sophie Aldred was very keen on the part, Davies did briefly consider switching her to a different role. "We did toy with the idea — because we already knew Sophie quite well — when Lis dropped out, we asked Sophie if we can't find anyone else to take the role of Lisa and she said if it helps you, yes I'll do it, but I don't really want that, I want to be the silly girly."[20]

One actor who had been attached to the project for some time was 60s *Who* companion Carole Ann Ford. She had been brought to the table by Ian Levine, much to the reluctance of Davies. "They were great friends. Now as much as I love Carole she might not have been my first choice to be truthful."[21] But cast she was, in the role of Zorelle.

One minor part ended up causing a major issue for Davies. "Brian Miller, Lis's husband was going to play Robar, who was going to be the father figure, but we realised if we got an older person to play Lisa, Brian wasn't old enough to be the father figure to them. So there was a bit of an awkward moment when Lis found out that we'd been talking to Michael Wisher about playing opposite Jan Chappell. She thought that we'd dropped Brian because she pulled out, which was slightly awkward because we hadn't asked Brian to be in it. We hadn't actually cast anyone else at all until Lis pulled out, she got completely the wrong end of the stick and balled me out over the phone saying 'how dare we drop Brian just because she dropped out.' I said 'it's not that at all, it's about casting the right mix of people.' So that was a bit unfortunate and I didn't actually speak to Lis for a couple of years, but it was all friends again next time we met up, but it was a bit awkward at the time."[22]

Other people approached for the part included two people who were more known for their work behind the scenes on *Doctor Who* but had started their careers as actors — Christopher Barry and Barry Letts. Also approached was William Russell, with the part eventually going to Wisher in one of his last roles before his untimely death the following year. The final star of the piece was Brian Croucher (who Davies had met when directing *The Making of Blake's 7* for BBC Enterprises) as Kurt.

Completing the human cast was the role of Nikos, the posh, good looking partner of Aldred's Mari. While the other cast members had been plucked from the worlds of *Doctor Who* and *Blake's 7*, Davies held an open casting session for this role. "I went through various different people. JNT suggested Dominic East [sic] who had been the Rani's assistant in 'Dimensions in Time' and it's to my shame that I wouldn't take him because JNT suggested him." [23]

In the end a recommendation came from someone closer to home. "It was Brian's agent who said 'I know a young chap who would love to play it, he's a big *Blake's 7* fan he would love this, will you see him?'[24] and we went to see him and we hit it off immediately and I thought 'yes. this is the guy'." The actor in question was Rory O'Donnell. Finally, for the two lead Sontarans, Davies cast Tom Finnis as Commander Steg and Toby Aspin as Lt. Vorn, having worked with both actors on previous projects.

The next step was to find a location, although initially Davies recalls there were talks of building a set. "We had two grand for building a set and studio, which isn't enough. You can build a small set with two grand or you can hire an empty studio for a week or two if you are lucky and I said 'do you remember Douglas Trumbull used the inside of an air craft carrier for the inside of the valley forge in *Silent Running*? What about the HMS *Belfast*?'." [25]

HMS *Belfast* was a former warship turned floating museum moored on the River Thames that Davies and Ayres had spotted while recording for 'Thirty Years in the TARDIS'. "We paid our money as tourists, went on board and that was it," Davies recollects. "We talked to someone on board and they said 'there are other areas below decks that the public can't go,' and we went 'ahh ok'." [26]

Ayres too remembers their visit. "It was very cramped, it was very hot but there was all these engine rooms that weren't being used for anything else and were too dangerous to let the public in."[27] Enthused by their discovery Davies arranged a meeting with the ship's owner. "He thought we were just mucking about as kids, because we were late twenties/early thirties and were not even BBC! We gave him the two grand and we got the run of HMS *Belfast* for two weeks." [28]

The *Belfast* offered a solid, ready built spaceship set with the crew having to make very few adjustments in order to make it more futuristic. All that was required was to hire in a couple of computer banks from a prop store and build an air lock set within the ship.

The location now secured, the cast and crew gathered on board for a read through. It was at this point that it became apparent that there had been a mistake in the casting of the two lead Sontarans, as Davies explains. "Tom had a very rough and ready kind of voice but we realised that the comedy wasn't there and it didn't sound right, Tom was struggling to read it." [29]

Worried and under pressure Davies made an inspired decision. "Everyone was looking at me knowing that it wasn't working, I suddenly remembered something that had happened years ago on the Rainbow stage show of *Hitchhiker's Guide To The Galaxy*. The two lead actors a week before the performance had swapped roles and I thought to myself, 'let's do it' and we swapped them and it suddenly came alive, it was so bizarre."[30]

And so the read through continued with Aspin now playing Steg and Finnis as Vorn.

Filming commenced the following week for an intense two weeks of night shoots. Due to the sound of reverberating footsteps coming down from the upper decks, the crew were forced to shoot from 6pm onwards when the museum was shut, although the crew would sometimes arrive early to set up. As the first drama Davies had ever directed, he was lucky to have a very patient cast. "They were all lovely, they put up with an awful lot of crap, partly because it was the partially sighted leading the blind. It was a semi pro crew and a lot of people weren't being paid." [31]

Due to other work commitments, Ayres wasn't always present but was on the end of the phone to help out when needed. "There were a few crises. There was one point where the crew were mutinying because there was no food, because we couldn't afford food and I just said to Jason, 'You've got to order sandwiches, even if it means losing some props but you've got to feed the crew' because they were stuck in in this hot ship and a crew marches on its stomach, if the crew is hungry you'll have very bad morale."[32]

The crew for *Shakedown* was made up predominately of fans, some professional, others just keen to assist, although there was one member of the crew, the sound op, that was not a fan by any stretch of the imagination, as Davies recounted. "[She] came in... was not a fan and didn't understand why were all so excited about it all. She put up with it for a bit but she wouldn't do anything beyond the agreed set of hours, she played it pretty much by the book and it was difficult to get to know her. So we went through several different sound people. I think we had to pay a small amount of money to a professional sound person in the end." [33]

DreamWatch Magazine's Robert Cope visited the set four days into the shoot, when the crew were running behind schedule "The atmosphere was notably tense as shooting had fallen behind schedule due to technical problems, and everyone was immersed in catching up on lost time."[34]

In order to get things back on track, an Assistant Director was recruited half way through the shoot in the form of David Rowston, much to the relief of Davies. "I needed someone to do the kick bollox screaming. He was employed to be very unpopular. I didn't really know him." [35]

Another crew member was brought in by Sophie Aldred herself. "I had a friend of mine, Paige Bell, who was doing the make-up. She was training to be a make-up artist at the time and she did me the most fantastic hair do with all these funky little knots and that was great fun."[36]

Aldred herself was all too used to low budget productions and seemingly enjoyed working with some of her sci-fi peers. "It was a lovely bunch of people. I'd just met my, what was then to be my, husband, so I was on a bit of cloud 9 anyway. It was a little disorganised, a bit of sitting around but there's always a lot of sitting around in filming and I always love meeting the people, the people are what make the difference on any film set, I got on very well with everybody. I'd not met any of the *Blake's 7* lot before and we shared some bond. I know I'm quite a positive person but I just love the process of filming anyway and they proved that you don't have to be a massive experienced professional to do work, you get a good team together and you are all doing something that you want to. So I just don't think there is any point sitting around moaning because it's taking a long time because that's what you are there to do." [37]

Aldred was also a big fan of her costume. "I had this extraordinary costume which I loved wearing, which was made by a designer that makes lamp shades. Basically it was a lamp shade and it was a knitted thing, which was incredibly glamorous."[38]

Despite having a lesser financial stake in the production, executive producer Jason Haigh-Ellery got very hands-on during the shoot, according to Davies. "Jason was very keen to be involved; in fact he was our stunt Sontaran. Jason had a background in judo, he was on a major judo team I believe, so he did a couple of stunts for us dressed as a Sontaran."[39]

For these stunts, a special Sontaran costume was built with a rubber neck piece to prevent the wearer breaking their own. Conversely, Davies found Gary Leigh to be slightly out of his depth. "Gary was very bewildered by the whole thing and just had to trust in us. In fact, he came up at some point where we were effusing over some minute detail, looking at the watch and thinking 'what it was costing?' and came up to us and said 'Kevin, our audience is not that discerning' and he was right, we were fussing over the tiny details and he couldn't see it, but we've always laughed about it." [40]

After the initial shoot wrapped, there was still the matter of recording all the model shots for the film, including the Sontaran War Wheel and shuttle. Model maker Dave Brian was in charge of building these and they were recorded at Westbury Design at Pinewood studios some weeks later. With a tight budget and limited time Davies struck a deal with the owner. "The guy who owned the place said we could have their studio, which included a little dolly for a set price, but there was only so much left, we'd spent it all on the big shoot. We could come in for one day and we said 'what about if we came in and used it for 24 hours?' and they said 'well we won't be here but you're welcome' so that's what we did. We did a 24 hour shoot. We were exhausted by the end and I drove home with Tony Clark, who I was dropping off in Crouch End and he remembers grabbing the steering wheel because I'd nodded off and I was heading towards the traffic island." [41]

Davies did a rough VHS edit of the film at home but the majority of was edited at BBC Birmingham by Paul Vanezis over three long weekends. Davies thought Vanezis was an "amazingly talented editor" but the edit offered its own problems. "We were working in 'Kevovision' as they called it, because it was widescreen which was new and everything had to be widescreen. But it wasn't any known format, because we didn't have the right technology to do it, we were just shooting Beta SP, so I just got the monitor and used a bit of gaffer tape and said 'right that's wide screen'. And we just cropped off the top and bottom with tape. So on the original rushes you can see everything that's above and below what was meant to be in the frame."[42]

Once the edit was complete, Ayres was on hand to provide a score, sound effects and do the final mix. "Things had moved on massively by that time. I was using computer sequencing, I had a 16 track tape machine, I had much better synthesizers, samplers, again much the same gear that at that time they had at the Radiophonic Workshop. I'd turned my attic at home into a studio. We did it in stereo, whereas *Wartime* had been mono, lots of sound design effects, a much more polished score and mix than I had been able to achieve previously."[43] The final sound mix was done overnight, the night before the films debut screening.

Shakedown was premiered on October 29 and 30th 1994 at Dreamwatch 94 in Earls Court London. The entire cast and crew were present, with the film being shown in three parts like a traditional *Doctor Who* story, with part One on the Saturday night and parts Two and Three on the Sunday. The Dreamwatch convention was not only a launch for *Shakedown* but *DreamWatch Magazine* too, which used *Shakedown* as a promotional tool over its first few issues. Davies was very appreciative of the responses at the event. "It was a really good reaction. I was very pleased especially as in the audience we had people like [*Doctor Who* director] David Maloney, who were taking part in the convention and they all said very nice things. I remember Jan Chappell got blotto, she had way too much to drink before her panel and it got a bit embarrassing."[44]

Dicks was also pleasantly surprised by the outcome. "I thought it was very good considering the incredibly limited resources they had. And it's been surprisingly popular ever since and at the time it came out it actually made money, which was almost unheard of from that sort of thing."[45]

Shakedown was released on VHS in October 1994, with two hundred limited edition gold-embossed, signed copies were available to attendees of the Dreamwatch convention. A *Making Of* feature was also released on a separate tape. While Davies' work was pretty much done, Jason Haigh-Ellery and Gary Leigh would spend the next year promoting the film at conventions, through stalls in dealers' rooms and on stage panels. The film was re-released into High Street shops in June 1996 along with the *Making Of* by Reeltime Pictures.

Shakedown received a wider spread of publicity than any other spin off, largely down to the two executive producers, although this may also be due to the accessibility of the plot, which relied very little on continuity or foreknowledge. Craig Hinton of *DWM* noted of the cast, "[a]ll are outstanding, but Sophie must be mentioned in dispatches for the moment she hits the deck with enough force to shake the camera"[46]

He had more mixed feelings towards the Sontarans, however. "They've got new uniforms. And new heads. And they bear more than a passing similarity to the Vogons from *Hitchhikers Guide to the Galaxy*. But overall, the Sontarans are amazing. I say overall, because you have to swallow the bitter pill of Tom Finnis' dreadful Lieutenant Vorn — who makes Stor from 'The Invasion of Time' sound like Laurence Olivier with a rubber head on — before you can delight in Toby Aspin's Steg. Steg is certainly the best Sontaran to ever grace the screen, surpassing even Kevin Lindsay's Linx and Styre. He possesses both a commanding authority and fascinating personality: these combine to electrify every scene in which he appears, and his put-downs of his educationally subnormal lieutenant are a joy to behold."[47]

In retrospect it seems odd now that people would be bothered by a comedy Sontaran, considering the popularity of Strax in the new *Doctor Who*, but at the time it must have been quite jarring to see a Sontaran with a comic edge.

The print advert for *Shakedown* featured various other quotes from more mainstream publications, with *Wired* citing it as "brilliant", the *Evening Standard* calling it "[a]n action packed sci-fi thriller" and *SFX* quoted as saying it was "[a] claustrophobic slice of science fiction action…."

The video was also available in the United States and launched by Sophie Aldred and some Sontaran troopers, at the Visions convention in Chicago. Other promotional appearances included an appearance from Terrance Dicks and Kevin Davies on Radio 4's *Anderson Country*. Aldred also showed up on *SKY News* to discuss the film, and a squad of Sontarans popped up on Channel 4's breakfast show *The Big Breakfast.*

Shakedown may be the most successful of all the spin offs. It is accessible, simple, fun and frightening in equal measure, and best captures the spirit of the show from which it took its inspiration. The actors are largely on form, although Carole Ann Ford's performance can grate a little, while the Sontaran duo are brilliantly conceived and add more depth to the race than most of their classic series appearances. The effects are of a high standard for the period and the budget, with the Rutan's natural form still look beautiful today. Kevin Davies stands out as one of the most accomplished of the spin off directors and it's a crime that he never got to direct more television drama beyond two episodes of *Space Island One* for Sky.

The following year Virgin Books asked Terrance Dicks to do a novelisation of the script for their *Doctor Who* range. "Virgin said we've seen *Shakedown* and we want you to write it as a *Doctor Who* book and I said 'there's one major problem with this, the Doctor isn't in it' and they said 'well put him in it' and I thought about it, I didn't want to rewrite *Shakedown* because I thought the *Shakedown* script worked very well in its own terms, so I came up with what I think was rather a cunning solution, which is a sort of *Shakedown* sandwich. For the first third of the book the Doctor is chasing a Rutan spy and he get's there just too late, the spy smuggles himself away on the Shakedown ship but he (the Doctor) knows where it's going, so he can go to the destination and wait for it there, which is what he does. So you get the first bit of the story with the Doctor and his accomplices, the middle third of the book is a novelization of *Shakedown* completely as it stood and the last bit of the book is the Doctor meeting the ship and the story goes on from there, so that worked out quite well I think." [48]

Shakedown was made on budget of £25,000 and recouped its costs over the next few years. Dicks was surprised by the success of the film "much to my astonishment it did very well and I actually got royalties on it, so I was really very pleased with the unsuspected success of *Shakedown*, it made a lot of money out of not very much." [49]

How does Davies view the film now though?

"I look back on *Shakedown* and laugh at the madness of it," he reflects. "It was hugely ambitious. I always refer to it as my rather belated student film, I still thought like a teenager, I was still very naive. I must tell you also, I did *Shakedown* when I was unemployed, I was freelance I hadn't got any work on, I think I may have even signed on at the time, but I turned down work to do *Shakedown*. I turned down the National Lottery launch commercial."[50]

Ayres too looks back on it with fondness. "For what it was, I think it was pretty good. It certainly isn't perfect, it does drag in the middle, but considering it was made on little money and in no time, I think it works pretty well." Perhaps most importantly, he concludes "I think it's a testament to a lot of people's enthusiasm and some really hard work." [51]

Despite the success of *Shakedown*, this was the only venture into on-screen *Doctor Who*-related dramas for *DreamWatch*, Davies and Haigh-Ellery. But there was briefly a conversation about a follow up series, as Davies recollects, "[A]t one point we tried to get Channel 4 interested in doing a series of Lisa Derrane, using *Shakedown* as a pilot. We sent it to whoever was Head of Drama at that time, and I got a rather sniffy message back saying 'we don't feel like investing in any science fiction at the moment, because we've already got one science fiction on the go'. That was Dennis Potter's *Cold Lazarus*. I felt a bit miffed at the time, because of this one off thing they were doing, which from their point of view was more highbrow and high profile, but it didn't really make the great splash that they thought it would."[52]

With a series not viable, did they ever consider mounting a sequel? "There may have been talk of it, but not a direct sequel, certainly I only ever thought of it as a one off. I think that lightning doesn't strike twice. I think we were lucky to pull it off then with an awful lot of good will. Gary put the money in, we just blitzed it, we all went crackers, because we all thought this is going to be fun and you couldn't expect people to do that on a regular basis without being paid." [53]

If not a *Shakedown* sequel, there was certainly talk of a number of other projects that involved both Davies and Haigh-Ellery. At a convention in Coventry in the late 90s, Davies mentioned in a panel the possibility of doing a Davros origins series, but when asked about it now he remembers nothing of it. Although one production touted goes right back to the genesis of *Shakedown*.

"The whole idea of doing a Sontaran spin off came from back in the eighties where I wanted to do an 'Arena' [a 1967 episode of *Star Trek* which sees Captain Kirk and a Gorn in a fight to the death on an alien planet] type story. I wanted to do one human and one Sontaran, kind of like 'The Sontaran Experiment', out on a moorland somewhere and have them fighting each other and I briefly revived the idea after being on the Isle of Man shooting *Space Island One* (for Sky)[54] with a Sea Devil. We were going to come up with a brand new type of Silurian — a River Devil — which was going to be like a Sea Devil, only more enhanced with more prosthetics on the face and when it opened its gills, it was going to be like Rainbow effects so it was going to be like a Rainbow Trout. There was a dam with an outward bound centre on the Isle of Man and I thought if we could hire that we would have all the scenery we need with the lake." [55]

Another project mooted between Davies, Haigh-Ellery and *New Adventures* author Paul Cornell was *Phoenix,* which would have starred Sophie Aldred, of which Davies can only remember some minute details. "She was some kind of secret agent in a futuristic world. I think it was a spin off of a *New Adventures* type thing and I briefly got involved and we had a series of meetings" [56]

Cornell describes the project as a "spies-in-space script I wrote. I don't know if we ever got as far as casting. I wrote a few things for Jason, back in those days, including an episode of a soap about stock car racing! He was trying all sorts of new things. The script would, I now think, have required a Hollywood-size budget rather than a video one, but Jason and I would mention having another go at it every time we met. Phoenix was a secret agent for the Irish in a solar system split between nations, a concept I later used in my Jonathan Hamilton stories."[57]

Davies was somewhat amused by Cornell's ideas. "I could never see it happening, Paul Cornell being quite heavily committed politically, had written Ireland as a superpower in the future and I just laughed and said 'no one is going to buy that' and he got very cross with me." [58]

Davies also felt the project would have needed a larger budget to realise its ambitious script. "[Sophie] was going to go in one of those carts, that weld the inside of pipe lines, she was going to be riding a bomb through a pipe line in the centre of a city and she'd got to dismantle the bomb before it's delivered to the city and blows up." [59]

Although this idea never came to fruition, Cornell and Davies did briefly collaborate on another pitch. "I also wrote a 'Three K-9s' pitch for Kevin, which I called 'Three Dog Night!'. It involved the Hellfire Club, an attempt to return Britain to the 18th Century, a re-hash of a plot I'd used for Jason's female Doctor audio play, starring Jo Ware." [60]

Ultimately none of these ideas would ever come to fruition and Davies would not direct much drama after *Shakedown*, while Haigh-Ellery would play a big part in the future of *Doctor Who* spin offs in another medium entirely. However, *Shakedown* stands as testament to the sheer will power and ingenuity of fans who managed to pull off a seemingly impossible task in a short space of time with limited resources and funds.

Chapter 10 — Ghost of Modern Times

Hot on the heels of *The AirZone Solution*, Baggs was keen to reunite his star studded cast in a sequel. In August of 1994 adverts began appearing in the fan press for 'AirZone 2'. Initially, a sequel from the pen of original writer Nick Briggs was briefly discussed. "I think there were plans to do a follow-up to *Airzone*, but I think I got busy doing some theatre. So Bill decided to find another 'inexperienced' writer, the lovely Mark Gatiss."[1]

Baggs welcomed Gatiss to the fold, on the recommendation of Gary Russell. A lover of the macabre and a talented writer, actor and comedian to boot, Gatiss had earned a reputation as one of the shining stars of Virgin's *New Adventures* range, with his 'Nightshade' novel being a fan favourite. While it was Bill that wanted to do a direct sequel to *AirZone* Gatiss was keen to take the actors in a new direction, and any consideration of a follow-up was quickly dropped in favour of an area Gatiss was more comfortable in. "I was very much drawing on my youth — living opposite that mental hospital!"[2]

Baggs told *DWM* at the time. "It's designed to frighten, scare and horrify, but I wanted to bring in some elements of *Doctor Who* in a way, because that's the audience we're selling to." [3]

It was Baggs who gave the film its mysterious title — one with which Gatiss was less than enthused. "I didn't want to call it that. I don't know what on earth it means!" [4] Interestingly, when the film was first advertised, it was billed as "BBV Presents... The Stars of *The AirZone Solution*. 'The Zero Imperative', a horror story for the new millennium." Drawing on the success of *AirZone*, rather than the *Doctor Who* connection, it perhaps represents Baggs' desire to move away from *Doctor Who* and build a catalogue of original content.

Also joining the production was a new co-producer, in the form of Andy Grant and his company World Leisure Corporation Ltd. (WLC). Grant was a former operations engineer for cable channel Greenwich TV. He had previously worked with Reeltime's Keith Barnfather on the early *Myth Maker* videos, directing the Colin Baker volume and providing equipment for the low budget productions. He had also released a number of *Doctor Who* related records and provided the audio and visual rigs for some of the larger *Doctor Who* conventions of the late 80s, including a live link up around the building for Panopticon 7. His company WLC was a much larger venture than either Reeltime or BBV, as Grant himself explains. "World Leisure Corporation was a company I actually bought, it was the World Leisure Corporations of America. WLC Broadcast was the main division, WLC Pictures was the production side, Event One was the music side. We had a massive office at 22 Soho Square at that time with 16 staff."[5]

Grant had met Baggs at a Panopticon event several years earlier, where they were both working with Barnfather. Their paths would cross again at Panopticon 1993, as Grant recalls. "He was peddling some of his earlier dramas at the time and he wanted to go up a notch, so he approached me about co-producing. I had a look at what he had produced, it was not bad for a low budget. With the technology available, it was very difficult to do an hour plus of drama anywhere near BBC's broadcast standard. You haven't got that sort of money available and with the best will in the world, you've got enthusiastic amateurs and volunteers. There is a difference in the quality of lighting, sound recording, camera operation, continuity, but then again, it works!"[6]

With several, clearly more profitable, irons in the fire, why did Grant decide to align himself with a smaller company? "I agreed to do them because I looked at it, with the portfolio of work I was doing and thought that it may open further doors. We had connections with mainstream broadcasting, that might have seen the films as pilots and we might have been able to develop something further."[7]

With money tight on these productions, Baggs was relieved to have somebody to help him ease the financial burden. So what sort of stake did Grant and WLC actually have in these films? "Basically I had little to do with the day to day shooting of it. I was on some of the locations, but I was busy with a lot of things at the time, but I put a fair amount of money into it. The main issue with cost, was the fees of these people; to actually get the talent costs money."[8]

Baggs remembers WLC's involvement slightly differently. "He provided the equipment, which at the time was very helpful, so it was on that level the deal that was done. There was no direct involvement."[9]

Due to the conflicting nature of these accounts we may never know exact details of their agreement, but we will learn more of the financial nature of their relationship later.

With Baggs intent on re-creating the success of *AirZone*, he didn't have to go far in casting his leads. "'Zero Imperative' was kind of a multi-Doctor story (that was kind of the idea of that one), a sort of follow-up to *The AirZone Solution,* but not using the same characters. Mark Gatiss always looked at it as our own version of *Carry On*, with the same actors in a different concept, and that worked pretty well."[10] At the time, Gatiss hoped the change of characters wouldn't be too difficult for an audience to accept — after all they had already accepted that these were not *Doctor Who* productions. "*AirZone* sort of started a precedent, which could be continued, either as a direct sequel or as something entirely different. As it stands, I think what you've established is a sort of *Carry On* ethic, that could be continued indefinitely really. A group of familiar actors — or familiar to some people — who are just shifted into a totally different story." [11]

The main protagonist was always going to be Baggs' leading man, Colin Baker, as Peter Russell. It was hoped his main co-star would be Peter Davison as Dr Colin Dove, but as Gatiss later told *DWM*, Davison wasn't keen. "Peter Davison did not want to do it, he didn't like the script, but he was included as a patient at the end"[12], a cameo that would later cause friction between Baggs and his lead. With Davison unwilling to participate, Baggs offered the role to Sylvester McCoy, who was only too pleased to be playing against type. "I tend to get asked to do a lot of comedy, but the parts I've been asked to do in these videos are more serious. I'm not slumming in any way."[13]

Having muscled in on the action late last time, Jon Pertwee was eager to take a more active role in 'The Zero Imperative'. Gatiss (who was also appearing in the film) was a child of the 70s and considered Pertwee his Doctor, and was over the moon to be working with his hero. He purposely wrote scenes for his character with Pertwee's Dr. Jeremiah O'Kane. "I remember being totally excited because it was my first attempt to write any kind of teleplay — to use that word that nobody uses anymore — and it was something vaguely *Doctor Who*-ish. And of course, Jon Pertwee was going to do it!"[14]

Other *Who* alumni included a brief cameo from Sophie Aldred, and Louise Jameson as Patricia Haggard. Other notable cast members included Baggs himself as Daniel, and an old flame of his, Patricia Merrick, who played Dr. Julie Gilchrist and acted as Second Assistant Director. "I first met Bill at a *Doctor Who* convention in the mid-80s but lost touch with him after a few years. Then as luck would have it I bumped into him at another convention in 1993 — he mentioned he was doing a *Doctor Who* spin off and I registered my interest." [15]

'The Zero Imperative' is notable in the BBV canon, as it is the first to feature a licensed character from *Doctor Who*, in the form of third Doctor companion Liz Shaw, played once again by Caroline John. Although as Baggs told *DWM*, it was touch and go whether they could use the character at all. "I telephoned BBC Enterprises with the idea of trying to get permission to use the Liz Shaw character. I wasn't sure who actually owned the rights, but we went ahead using Caroline anyway, playing a similar character called Abbott. The Friday before we started filming I got a fax through saying we could use the character as long as the BBC got an acknowledgement at the end. They didn't even charge me for it!"[16]

How did Gatiss cope with the ever-changing legal status of the character?

"When it was pending permission I just wrote the first draft for Liz Shaw, then just changed the name and took out all the UNIT references.

Then at the last minute, when we got permission, I put them all back in again!"[17]

Caroline John was intrigued by the prospect of returning to a character she had played some three decades previously. "I'm the same character but I'm not blonde, and I'm a lot older, so there are just one or two references to what I was. I've gone back to Cambridge University from leaving U.N.I.T., and they've called me up because they've set up an organisation called the Preternatural Research Bureau that looks into anything out of the ordinary, things the everyday police can't deal with. There are a few references — for example, I'm looking at a picture of Nick Courtney and I have the line 'this reminds me of something else'. I also put in the line 'in my salad days' because I hope people won't think they're going to see Liz Shaw of years ago. I'm older, I've got family. I am the same person but I've moved on." [18]

It is Liz Shaw's inclusion that makes some of the previous statements of intent about this film a little confusing. If BBV were attempting to sell their films based on the actors rather than their connection to *Doctor Who,* why include an actual bona-fide *Doctor Who* companion? Surely it would be harder to sell them in different roles if this film is set in the *Doctor Who* universe. Putting Liz Shaw in a film with Sylvester McCoy is one thing but putting her opposite the man who played her Doctor is another; would Liz not notice the resemblance? Baggs may have said he wanted to move away from *Doctor Who* but this film actually takes him closer than he had ever been before.

The final piece of casting came a little out of left field: playing Liz Shaw's side kick was former glamour model, Linda Lusadi. Although she had notched up a number of early acting credits, she was predominately known for her career as a page three model. As Baker told *DWM,* he had been appearing in 'Not Now Darling' in Bournemouth alongside Lusadi and recommended her for the part. "I spoke to her about it, and she was very keen to become involved. She is a very good actress and is keen to break the image that she obviously has. I suppose tentatively at first Bill thought 'well that might work,' and I said 'Look — she will deliver the goods, and more so.' and she has." [19]

Caroline John was taken aback by the choice. "I thought my side kick was going to be a man, and my boss, and when he told me it was going to be Linda Lusadi, I thought 'flipping heck!' But it's a very good idea and it's a very good relationship, an older woman and a young one"[20]

Commencing filming in late summer 1994, 'The Zero Imperative' was shot entirely on location in a disused psychiatric ward of Horton Hospital in Epsom. Mark Ayres, who was on sound recordist duties (and whose uncle had previously been Chaplain there), was somewhat surprised to find some of the patients still in close proximity. "The rest of the hospital was still active, so there was still a secure wing on an upper floor with a sort of balcony, where they housed the secure patients. There was a sequence we were shooting with Carrie and Louise wandering through the grounds of the hospital, having a discussion and there were patients above us shouting at them. It was just a thoroughly odd shoot.'[21]

With the crew having the complete run of the building, it was possible for them to dress each room as the script required and use any spare rooms for production purposes. These purposes included accommodation for the crew, as Ayres recounts. "It just about had electricity, but not overnight. It had no running hot water and we stayed in cells. It was just weird, just thoroughly odd, it was like the beginning of a horror movie. There was one night where everyone else decided to go home and there was just me and one of the assistant directors in cells, at opposite ends of this corridor and it was very, very spooky." [22]

The atmosphere on set was charged but fun, with the entire cast chipping in to make things run as smoothly as possible, as Baggs relayed to *DWM*. "Nobody's on the going rate which is a bit of a dilemma because people are working harder than they normally would because it's a smaller unit. People are flexible — one minute they're acting in a scene, the next minute they're making tea for the other actors, which is brilliant. Everybody knows the level on which it's been done and yet they really seem to have enjoyed themselves. It's a fun team and people believe in what we're doing."[23]

For a press conference scene, Mark Ayres (with heavy beard) is part of the on-screen press corps, but what you cannot see is the audio mixer on his lap as he mixes a scene in which he appears. Patricia Merrick found herself multitasking in several roles. "It was a steep learning curve and there was a variety of jobs I ended up doing on the production side: on 'Zero' I even ended up being the sound department for a day... which basically involved being the boom operator and mixing the sound (I think that's the technical phrase). [Ayres recalls that he had to take the day off to complete the final mix of the video version of *More Than Thirty Years in the TARDIS*]. One scene was somewhat challenging — Liz Shaw had to come rushing through a door to find Dr. Dove dead on the floor. There I was standing precariously on a chair balancing the boom and frantically adjusting the sound levels on the mixer to offset the bang of the door and then increasing the levels to catch Carry's whispered line." [24]

Both Gatiss and Baggs enjoyed the team atmosphere and collaborating on the project as a whole. "Mark and I worked really well together. He had some quite big ideas and has an obsession with horror, which comes out in the *P.R.O.B.E.* series and other bits and pieces he has done. The collaboration was very good, he's very different from me, that's all I can say."[25]

Gatiss too was fond of his cohort. "Bill was very... dogmatic. I really liked that. We had a great time, and it was very interesting, the whole process. Lots of fun, but he had some very strange ideas as a producer." [26]

When asked about these ideas, Baggs is somewhat coy, but does elaborate on one aspect. "Mark was very keen to camp it up. There is one particular character in that, the morgue attendant, it was played for laughs I mean he had a big fricking cold sore and that's not me, I'm much more interested in straight drama. That's Mark's area and there's nothing wrong with it, it's just not what I wanted to do and I wish I'd resisted." [27]

While overall things seemed harmonious between Baggs and Gatiss, the latter did little to enamour himself to Colin Baker. "Bill Baggs was trying to save money — as he always did, bless his heart — and there was a bit where Colin was supposed to rescue Caroline John from a cell. And in order to save paying Colin, Bill got me to put Colin's jacket on and use my arm. Of course, when Colin found out he went crazy. Quite rightly probably, especially when it was actually his own coat rather than a costume. But he chose to haul us over the coals in front of an actor called David Terence, who was a man I had great respect for and brought him in especially. It was so cripplingly embarrassing, and from then on things had been a little difficult between us"[28]

Indeed, there was no wardrobe department on the film, and the actors were asked to provide their own clothing for their characters, with Caroline John borrowing suitable clothing from her sister as she had nothing appropriate for Liz Shaw to wear. If there was any conflict between Baker and Gatiss, the same could not be said of his relationship with Pertwee. "He was an absolute dream, I have to say. We'd prepared his cue cards thinking he was too old but he learnt it all. In the middle of a take he barked, 'Where's Mark, where's Mark?' I was pushed forward and he said, 'You're a bloody good writer, my friend. This is the most stable dialogue I've read in a very long time'. I just turned to mush! He was great. He was really great."[29]

Partly due to his health, but also his reputation, Baggs had some reservations about giving a larger role to the 'great' Jon Pertwee, reservations that proved unfounded. "It's funny, I had so many fears about working with JP and he was tricky on the set but never with me. He was charming and very professional and in a lot of pain on 'The Zero Imperative', because he'd just had an operation. I had a conversation with his wife Ingrid [sic] about whether he should do it at all. But the bizarre thing was, for him, he was healing through the process of doing it, because he loved being on set, he loved acting, that's what he wanted to do, so to not do it for him would have been more destructive than putting up with pain of moving around." [30]

When Pertwee had one of his more cantankerous moments, Baggs had a pacifier in the form of Ayres. "He could be bad tempered at times, quite irascible. But I got on very well with him and there were a couple of times when Bill said 'Mark, can you handle Jon for me?' So I basically just used to agree with Jon that everybody else was an idiot and that it was he and me against the world and he quite liked that."[31]

Pertwee was present for three days towards the end of the shoot and enjoyed himself immensely by all accounts, despite the pain he was in, once again relishing the chance to share the screen with his *Doctor Who* peers. "We are tremendously close, most of us, there's one we don't get on too well with but all the rest of us work together and we've got a great brotherhood."[32]

Colin Baker was pleased at the calibre of people these productions were starting to attract. "Jon is a very imposing figure, and you think he's going to be difficult to work with, and he's not going to like working on the low budget productions because there aren't any facilities and we haven't got the money. Like with Linda, it's wrong. He's been great to work with."[33]

Pertwee also enjoyed working with Lusardi. "She put us all to shame this morning at the press call, she was very professional and knew exactly what to do for the photographers, arranging us all." [34]

The press call in question took place on the last day of filming, at the same time as Peter Davison was arriving to film his secret cameo in the film, as Gatiss recalled. "Bill was frantically trying to wave him around the back, so nobody knew."[35] Despite this slight distraction, the secret was safe, although the only picture that made it into the national press was of Pertwee with Lusardi much to the annoyance of the other Doctors.

The final day also saw the crew de-rigging the location they had taken over during the past few weeks. Patricia Merrick was there to lend a hand. "Mark Gatiss, Ed Salt and I tried out 'mattress' sledging; which basically involved throwing yourself on a mattress and hurtling down a flight of stairs. Fortunately we all survived the experience." Merrick also had fun chauffeuring Pertwee around. "Driving Jon Pertwee I heard lots of his amazing stories, and how he taught me to double-declutch; which came in very handy when, a few years later, I took my HGV class 2. To this day I always think of Jon when I double-declutch!"[36]

Baker was once again keen to stress his commitment to these sort of projects, especially as they veered away from *Doctor Who* knock-offs. "Instead of other people using us for purposes that don't help us, we are all jointly using that association in order to produce a product that is totally different. Jon Pertwee is playing someone totally unlike his Doctor, so is Sylvester and indeed, I hope so am I."[37]

Gatiss (who had been vocal about his dislike of eighties' *Doctor Who*) was quick to offer a back handed compliment about one of his co-stars. "I think Sylvester is actually more like the Doctor in this than he ever was on television. He's very good in it, and it's a combination of darkness and humour that I think is coming across well."[38]

While the chemistry between the leads was clearly working and everyone seemed happy with the results, despite the low budget, Pertwee seemed particularly excited to be back in front of the camera. "This is the sort of role I'd like to do more often. I've enjoyed working on it, and it's been very good for me because there are very few roles around for older men. I'm not really doing any favours by being here because I get as much out of it as anyone else. It's great fun to work with other Doctors because we see each other a lot at conventions.[39]

It's interesting to note that while Pertwee was revered amongst his co-stars and the crew, any ego he was reputed to have, did not play into this and he saw this as a great opportunity in his twilight years. If we delve further into Pertwee's career at the time we find a very vulnerable actor, desperate for one last hit. Chris Leach worked with Pertwee on a long gestating pilot for a potential series called *Starwatch* in the late 80s and early 90s. In this extract from a 2012 issue of *DWM* we learn a little more about Pertwee's eagerness to stay active.

"So why had Pertwee kept the faith in *Starwatch*? Chris had his own theory. He says the actor despite being 'energetic and full of life' knew he was at the end of his career, but didn't want to be put out to pasture just yet. Chris represented the opportunity of perhaps one more show. Even after *Starwatch* was no longer a going concern, Pertwee asked Chris to sell an idea he had for a radio series starring himself and Geoffrey Bayldon. Chris recalls that, despite his protestations, he knew nothing about the medium, Jon said, 'Well, you must know some people!' Says Chris: "I thought, 'He's putting all his energies on to me to try and sell something because I'm his connection to the industry.' But I knew absolutely nothing and no-one.'"[40]

Indeed Pertwee's last regular recurring role on TV was as the voice of Spotty, in children's cartoon *SuperTed* in the late 80s. By the 1990s his career consisted of a handful of minor acting roles and celebrity appearances as either *Doctor Who* or *Worzel Gummidge,* as well as numerous appearances at *Doctor Who* conventions. 'The Zero Imperative' would be the last acting role Pertwee filmed. In May of 1996 he died of a heart attack while on holiday in America. His BBV co-star Colin Baker paid tribute to him "He was a man of such presence and stature. I can't believe he has gone — it is a great shock. Of all of the interpretations of the Doctors his was the most straight in terms of avoiding comedy."[41]

While it's doubtful his work with BBV would lead to the renaissance he hoped for, it's worth noting that while physically frail, Pertwee puts in a great performance in his two outings with BBV and with his death the *Doctor Who* world lost one of its greatest ambassadors and showmen.

'The Zero Imperative' received a cast and crew screening at *Doctor Who* convention Manopticon 94 in Manchester, where it caused further friction between Baker and Gatiss, due to Peter Davison's surprise cameo. "When it got to the end, everyone looked around at Colin, expecting to see his smirking face. And he was just furious! Furious! I think it was because he thought he'd made something which wasn't *Doctor Who* — which was something 'of its own' — and therefore this cameo would just pull it right back... or maybe he was just annoyed that his thunder was stolen by sodding Peter Davison."[42]

Baggs later admitted he made a mistake not telling his star about this cameo. "It was because it was kept entirely secret and I totally understand Colin's point, because it was — in retrospect — a bad idea, although I think it's quite fun. If I'd thought about it, I wouldn't have done it. That's not a slight on Peter, who I thought was very generous to do that, but Colin was investing in it, thinking it was one thing and then suddenly some guy shows up at the end, who is also one of the other Doctors, that he didn't know anything about, that tops it. It's a bit insensitive, I suppose and I get that, it wasn't what he signed up for, it wasn't in the script, it was like an add on and was all kept very secret. And actually I do understand Colin's reservations about it."[43]

Ayres also remembers Baker's response "It massively upset Colin, he was absolutely furious, he said it cheapened it and again he was probably right."[44] Whether this was the first crack in Baker and Baggs' relationship is impossible to say but this was certainly the beginning of the end of their working relationship, as they would go on to do only one more film together.

While Baker's reaction to the film was less than ecstatic, audience response was generally favourable. *DWM*'s Craig Hinton had recently been very disparaging about Gatiss' *New Adventure* 'St. Anthony's Fire', but he was far more complimentary about this release. "I am pleased to say that he has completely redeemed himself with the latest offering from the ever-fruitful Bill Baggs production company, 'The Zero Imperative'... Not only has he written a tantalising psycho-drama, but his acting abilities are also put to the test — and he comes out with flying colours."[45]

He went on to say very positive things about the cast and crew, particularly Pertwee. "Jon Pertwee maintains his dignity even though he is playing a man on the edges of senility."[46] Hinton did however question the use of *Doctor Who* actors versus *Doctor Who* characters. "Having set it in the *Doctor Who* universe (I refuse to use the term Whoniverse, even if tortured!) with Liz Shaw, the presence of so many Doctors often caused a reality check, as I had to remind myself that Pertwee wasn't in his familiar role, for example. This was made more difficult by the odd 'in-joke', especially in the closing few minutes when the survivors are nibbling their Swiss roll and sipping their Earl Grey. It is almost as if Bill Baggs had shrunk back from the Stranger's domain to return to the more familiar ground of *Doctor Who.*"[47]

Both Hinton and *CT*'s A. N. Bradbury were confused by the film's resolution. "The story moves along well, until the end when, once again in typical BBV fashion, it suddenly gets very confusing. The story is resolved, but I am not sure how."[48] Bradbury goes on to remark, "I wish that a little more care had been taken in the scripting to make what is a fairly good story a very good one." [49]

Even BBV stalwart Nick Briggs was somewhat vocal about the addling climax of the film. "I became slightly confused by the plot of 'The Zero Imperative' the first time I saw it. I thought 'God this is exactly what I do.' I thought all the lines were good, I kept thinking this is really good dialogue and I like what these people are saying, but I wish they wouldn't say so much."[50]

In the same film, Gatiss goes on to clarify the plot. "The idea of the 8 or 9 murders around the hospital, was that Zero was simply reaching out from his cell to these people, but because this force was behind him, over time he touched mentally another sensitive, it blew them apart essentially or killed them horribly, very horribly. And that I think, I just didn't make sufficiently clear."[51]

The reason for the lack of clarity in the film may not, however, have been down to the script, at least according to Mark Ayres. "I think it's fatally flawed in a number of areas, not least because Bill cut the one scene that explained the plot, which I thought was bizarre. People say 'there's no explanation.' There is and we shot it, but Bill decided he wanted it a bit like 'Ghost Light', you had to make your own mind up about it."[52]

Years later, Gatiss reminisced about his first jaunt into the spin off media. "I honestly haven't seen it for years, though I would like to see it again. I wouldn't like to come across as the sort of person who's ashamed of his juvenilia. I mean, at one stage it could have been the only thing I ever did! I wouldn't swap it for the world."[53]

'The Zero Imperative' is a chilling ghost story, that is genuinely unnerving in places, although the direction isn't as sympathetic to the horror as it could be, lingering on shots for too long and lacking any real eye for gore. Said direction, is once again competent but nothing special, while the score by Mark Ayres contributes a certain pathos to the action. The script is uneven and a little clunky in places but does offer a genuine mystery. It gives each of the leads some hearty dialogue and has them playing very much against type. Caroline John's performance as Liz Shaw is equally as able, but there is very little in the character to denote that this is the same person we saw in the early 1970s and she could easily be a generic cop. The production is however let down by lack of clarity in the story and some truly atrocious sound, although the sound issues were later fixed for the DVD release.

Perhaps most importantly, 'The Zero Imperative' is notable for introducing Mark Gatiss to the spin-off world. While he had published two books by this point, it's worth remembering not all fans read these publications, so for some this would be their first exposure to someone who would become heavily involved in *Doctor Who*'s future.

It also marks the passing of Jon Pertwee and it's sad to see him playing a role that so reflects the cruelty and frailty of age, so close to his death, even if mentally (but not physically) Pertwee still had his wits and charm about him. It is worth taking a moment to consider a future that never was. Had Pertwee survived into his eighties, he would have no doubt been a part of the early Big Finish releases (he would have been the same age as Tom Baker when he signed up to do Big Finish in 2012). It would have been great to hear Pertwee in action one last time.

Unfortunately, time was against him, and this would be one his his last appearances in a *Doctor Who* related drama.

Chapter 11 – Back to the Old House

In November 1994 *The Stranger* series took an unexpected detour back to an arena that Baggs and Briggs were more than familiar with from their Audio Visual days, producing two audio productions staring Soloman and his associates Egan and Saul. With 'The Zero Imperative' costing BBV a comparative fortune, Baggs needed time to recoup the costs as Briggs elaborated. "Bill knew that he wasn't going to be able to do another video project after 'The Zero Imperative' until early this year, but he's very conscious of the people who buy the tapes and he wants to do things to say we are still here. So I suggested, and I suggested it a long time ago, that we do *Stranger* audio plays."[1]

With audio being a format Briggs thrived in, Baggs (who was busy working on the BBC's *Children in Need* show) pretty much gave him free rein to direct and write the two plays. "Although Bill Baggs certainly had some input into the script in this case, it didn't undergo the massive rewrites which always occurred on the video productions. Bill hated explanatory speeches and would frequently cut them in order to keep the pace of the story going, unfortunately with the unpleasant side-effect that certain story elements were left unexplained. It wasn't unreasonable for him to want to do this, because the Stranger's back-story had become a huge, almost unfathomable thing. Yes, I take the blame for that. Every time I attempted to clarify it, several more questions would pop up."[2]

The advantage of the audio medium meant budget was not an issue. On audio Briggs was determined to unleash his more outrageous concepts, with the first story 'The Last Mission' being the most outlandish of the two. "This adventure was a definite attempt to do all the things that our video budgets simply wouldn't allow for at the time. Computer graphics were nowhere near affordable in those days, so a vast city-scape, a spaceport, flying cars (straight out of *Blade Runner*) and weird semi-invisible monsters would never have featured in my plans for a Stranger video. However, with an audio format, such possibilities came within our reach."[3]

Briggs also saw this as a chance to bring a cohesive narrative to *The Stranger* story. "It also became possible to tie together all the loose ends of the saga so far. There were two reasons why I was able to do this. Firstly, speech is audio drama's primary means of communication (so explanatory narrative would not be stylistically intrusive). Secondly, I was given a significant amount of autonomy, as I was directing. Anyway, in the story, Soloman recalls, in flashbacks, the events before 'Summoned by Shadows' which led to the end of his terrorist career. The 'last mission' retold here relates to flashbacks seen in 'The Terror Game', depicting Soloman in formal evening dress murdering a woman."[4]

As well as Colin Baker, David Troughton and John Wadmore, 'The Last Mission' also features a cameo from Holly King, reprising her role as Rose, and the vocal talents of fan favourite Elisabeth Sladen, of whom Baggs was particularly in awe. "It was great to work with Lis Sladen, who I'd met at conventions, and there was this mutual respect. She was very delicate at the time, very sensitive but I loved working with her, her performance was very good very strong."[5]

The star's involvement came with one condition, much to the surprise of Briggs. "Lis Sladen insisted that Bill directed it. So I directed the play, but let Bill do the talking to Lis. This is hilarious, in retrospect, considering how well I ended up getting on with Lis. But she was nervous of fan projects and was, at that stage, convinced by Bill's confidence and track record — and she had no idea who I was. Mind you, it was Bill who told me that she didn't want to be directed by me..."[6]

'The Last Mission' was recorded in mid-November 1994, alongside a second play, 'Eye of the Storm'. Briggs later told the BBV website that this second play had a troublesome genesis. "The script travelled a somewhat rocky road to completion. Another author was originally commissioned to write the second audio play, mainly for reasons of time and convenience — Bill and I thought I didn't have the time to write two scripts. I acted as script editor for this one, but, to cut a long story short, it started off fairly ill, caught a nasty case of re-writes, then just died on the page. Bill asked me to bury it and write something myself, quickly."[7]

The script in question was from the pen of Simon Messingham, who had just had some success with his *New Adventures* novel 'Strange England' (released in August of that year). Briggs found himself at loggerheads with the author when trying to make the script work. "He's a nice guy, Simon, but I found his approach to writing totally at odds with mine and I don't really think his heart was in the story he was writing. When I asked him questions about why something was happening in the story, he'd just shrug and say things like, 'I dunno, seemed like a good idea'. I remember thinking that he didn't seem to be able to take the job seriously. I threw his script out because it didn't make any sense to me." [8]

With the new script hammered out quickly, Baggs and Briggs agreed on the latter using an alias so it appeared BBV had a larger roster of writers than they actually did. "For the sake of modesty (at the time!), I used a pseudonym (Arthur Wallis) and bashed out 'Eye of the Storm' in about a week. Consequently, it's a flawed script and gets a bit ragged at the end." [9]

Despite, his displeasure with the script, he was pleased with the performances. "It was acted beautifully, especially by Karen Henson (as Meta) who, to my intense disappointment, was not available to feature in the video version which followed."[10]

Briggs was also impressed with David Troughton, who had several emotionally charged scenes with Karen Henson. "He had a lot of emotional stuff to do in the second one, and he immediately latched onto it with hardly a word from me. The moment I started talking about the thing with him and Meta, he was nodding furiously and just got on with it."[11]

Briggs also found a new respect for Colin Baker, as this was the first time he had engaged with him on a directorial level. "Colin's acting comes far more from his intellect. He distils problems down to the choices involved. Most of the time, he will have an instinct for a scene or a line and will offer it up, giving it in his first reading. Mostly it's spot-on, so there's no discussion. But sometimes he will be keenly aware of the alternative ways of playing a scene, or the possible alternatives in interpreting the plot. In that case, a discussion is needed. Does my character already know about this, or am I discovering it as I say it? Am I aware of the implications of what I do? Those are the kinds of choices to be made when playing any part. Having an actor who asks those sort of questions really makes the writer/director think. Sometimes, Colin will highlight an area of doubt that you haven't thought of. He's a very clever, sharp man and he doesn't mince his words if he's on the trail of something. He's always careful to be polite, but he can be very forceful in his pursuit of the 'truth'. Once you and he have arrived at a decision, that is the point when Colin engages the emotional side of his performance and lets his instincts take over. He's also very analytical about his performance. He will often stop and say, 'I was crap in that, let's do it again!' I like that. I like actors who take responsibility for what they do. He's very self-aware and keen to give his best."[12]

'The Last Mission' is a prequel that ties into the many strands of narrative that exist in *The Stranger* videos. The script allows Baker to play a nastier version of Soloman, who is in full terrorist mode and he can be found assaulting the newly recruited Saul. In contrast to this performance, the entire thing is tied together by a narration performed by Baker, who delivers the introspective dialogue with a vulnerability that is rarely called for on screen as we get a chance to get inside Soloman's head. Briggs paints a vivid world that could only be achieved on audio full of alien swamps, invisible monsters and bustling spaceports. Both Troughton and Wadmore are once again on form and only Lis Sladen lets the side down. Despite playing a character completely different from her *Who* counterpart, she somehow manages to pitch the performances remarkably similarly to that of Sarah Jane.

The second play, 'Eye of The Storm', has much in common with the previous two videos, developing the earthbound exploits of our three leads further. Briggs' eye for characters really shines through in the guest stars as, in the 55 minutes run time, we learn just enough about their past to make them interesting as they each go on their own journeys. When it is revealed Meta has special abilities, it becomes clear she was the face they saw. Her penetration of the web has left a crack that it is trying to fix by engulfing the cottage and all who reside in it in a fog. At centre stage is the relationship between Meta and Egan, who develop feelings for each other but it's Troughton who steals the show, managing to portray not just a man who is going through an emotional crisis but a man who has never had emotions to be in crisis before.

Originally scheduled for December of 1994, the two plays were released on audio cassette in early 1995. Baggs was ultimately happy with both. "I think they're great and it made sense and added value to the BBV portfolio." Briggs too enjoyed them and relished the change to be back in the audio medium. "Mainly because I did most of the sound editing on the audio plays, and for me editing audio plays and doing the music, sound effects, and all that is hard work but it's almost the most fun I can have." [13]

Critical response was also favourable. *DWM*'s Craig Hinton said "The audio production values are consistently high, with some quite spectacular use of special sound — I even jumped at one point! From the savagery of the storm to the eerie Dimensional Web, every aspect of the setting is effectively conveyed. Nick Briggs' music, while very reminiscent of the *Doctor Who* theme at times, complements the action all the way."[14]

The cassettes however failed to ignite the interest BBV hoped for, as Briggs later recalled, while on the set of the final *Stranger* film. "I don't think that they've broken all records at the moment. I think there is this problem that we were on video then we went to audio, and everyone thinks what a step backwards!"[15]

The failure of the cassette tapes to be a huge hit didn't deter Baggs from attempting another venture into audio, however, this time in collaboration with Virgin Books. Virgin had been releasing Doctor Who *New Adventures* since 1991 and Baggs thought these were ripe for adaptation into the audio format. "I met Peter Darvill-Evans, [editor of the range] I can't remember why but I went to the Virgin offices because they had the licence to produce the novels, and I couldn't understand why nobody would be making the fucking audios of these novels, so we put a joint pitch in. I convinced them that this would be worth doing and they were obviously thinking of my Audio Visuals experience, but the BBC weren't interested."[16]

The landscape of *Doctor Who* could have been very different had BBV and Virgin been successful with their pitches, and both companies would make further ventures into the world of *Doctor Who* audio, as we will see later. However, it is understandable that the BBC would not want to give out the *Doctor Who* audio licence at this point. BBC Radio had recorded two audio productions staring Jon Pertwee as the third Doctor: 'The Paradise of Death' and 'The Ghosts of N Space', and were potentially planning further stories. They were also in the process of developing the ever evolving *Doctor Who* film/TV show/pilot/TV movie (delete as applicable) as a co-production with various US broadcasters, and as such were keen to retain all licenses related to the property. Indeed, unbeknown to them, Virgin Books were only a year or so away from having their own licence revoked by the BBC.

Chapter 12 — Break up the Family

Now aligned with WLC Ltd., Baggs was looking for ways to further boost the profile of BBV. In doing so he returned to the world of *The Stranger* but this time intent on shooting a feature length production in order to test the waters for future projects. "It's my intention to direct a major production later this year, featuring the Cybermen, that will be a long, intensive and technically complex production. I wanted some practice at a ninety-minute play first. I'm comfortable with the *Stranger* material — we've done this story as an audio and I trust the writer and know the cast. It seemed a sensible safe-area in which to practice and learn the special demands of a production of that length."[1]

Returning to the previous year's audio adventure, 'Eye of the Storm', he asked Briggs to adapt the script for video. But was Baggs ever worried about asking fans to shell out money for something they had already purchased?

"No, it didn't even enter my head [laughs] If a story's worth telling... I don't know what the audience think about [buying the same story twice] maybe because, again, it was suitably different [from the original]." [2]

Briggs found this idea typical of Baggs' approach to film making "He was always pushing for something to be done quickly, and he said something like, 'Well, you've already written that.' And it was certainly a more affordable idea than the other audio play, which had alien settings, I seem to remember."[3]

With Briggs already familiar with the text, he seemed a lot more confident with this film than he had been with the others. "'Beholder' is ninety minutes long. It is adapted from an audio version we made last year, so we knew there was enough plot to fill sixty minutes, which allows us to do some nice character work. We can, for instance, develop the character of Hunter, the scientist in charge of the research project, and give him more motivation and background."[4]

One major change was made to the script for budgetary reasons by Briggs. "Naturally, the first thing that had to go was 'the storm', then the mysterious creeping fog. In the video, we replaced the fog with zombie soldiers. I played one of those zombies... and I think that's a good enough reason to prefer the audio play — don't you?"[5]

Newcomers to the production included David Troughton's wife Alice as Sheila, who found hidden depths in the character. "Sheila on sort of face value, she was just a sort of very butch lady with a gun, who without asking questions in the first few minutes shoots someone in the leg and she could be a very bland butch sort of lady, but what was also in there was her relationship with Meta, her relationship with Saul, although they were touched on fairly, sort of fleetingly, they had to be because of the pace of the film."[6]

Also joining the cast was Geoffrey Beevers, who had had a number of roles in *Doctor Who*; most notably the Master in 'The Keeper of Traken'. "I attended a *Doctor Who* convention early [in 1994] with my wife Caroline John, who once played a companion, Liz Shaw, in the series, and it was there that we met Bill Baggs. Carrie has done two of these plays already. I was asked if I wanted to appear in 'Eye of the Beholder'."[7]

The film also featured an obligatory cameo from Briggs and second AD Patricia Merrick. One bit of casting that Briggs was less than pleased with was Bernadette Gephears, playing Meta. "Karen Henson, who played Meta [in the audio], is one of my favourite actresses. I must work with her again. She's terrific. Such a shame she wasn't in the video ['Eye of the Beholder']. The girl we got kind of loused it up." [8]

Production took place in late February 1995 at Orchard Cottage in the village of Cote in Oxfordshire, which was hired out for three weeks for the cast and crew to shoot and stay in. Colin Baker once again appreciative of the chance to play Soloman. "It's quite a good script, though this one. This could actually be the best script we've had so far, in terms of development of characters, and the relationship between Soloman and Egan. [Egan] is forced very quickly to re-evaluate his standards and priorities which is very good, it's fascinating." [9]

Once again Baker enjoyed being reunited with his co-stars, David Troughton and John Wadmore. "It's a bit dangerous because we enjoy ourselves too much. We tend to muck about a bit. David in particular is a very powerful actor, but he's wonderful because he doesn't take acting seriously except when he's doing it."[10]

Beevers too found himself in good company and enjoyed the atmosphere that BBV created on set. "Oh it's lovely, much more relaxed than working on a television production. I'm playing this marvellous character, a Ministry of Defence scientist who is investigating the mind powers of a young girl, trying to find out if her psychic abilities can be used as a weapon. He also has something of a crush on her which makes things interesting dramatically. It's good fun, and Bill Baggs knows exactly what he wants; he's a very thorough director."[11]

Troughton meanwhile found delight in the range of scenes he got to play as Egan, even if the schedule was a gruelling one. "All my part has been done in five days," he told Baggs in an interview, "which is not normal shooting, you'd have gaps, you'd go home but I've been here five days. One morning I was in bed for four hours, then I was outside fighting aliens. I mean it's extraordinary, the contrast, but that in a way helped because I've had a through line all the way through. I mean you do it in a different order but the thoughts from one scene are fresher in your mind than if you waited a week and did it again, so that's been helpful. What hasn't been helpful is that it's been hard work."[12]

While the previous BBV films had relied on post-production effects to simulate the firing of weapons 'The Eye of the Beholder' featured the use of live weapons that fired blanks, under the instruction of an armourer, as Baggs later recounted. "What I remember is these loud guns going off and everybody had to wear these ear defenders, which governed the whole filming process, everything had to be safety first. And Alison Troughton was in it, and in one scene a gun goes off pretty near her face, and some kind of shrapnel came out of the gun and struck her face. Which was really scary, but she's alright."[13]

With *The Stranger* now in completely different territory to its origins, *DWM* asked Baggs if it was still relevant to its audience. "Oh yes, absolutely. Don't forget that Soloman, Egan and Saul are three aliens from another dimension. That is the science-fiction core of the series. They come from the Dimensional Web, a fantastical place. There is no point in mimicking *Doctor Who* because that, ultimately, has nowhere to go. We do have letters from people who are upset because we have moved away from *Doctor Who* but we get a lot more congratulating us on the direction we have taken. Of course, when I am making a *Stranger* story, I am conscious of what will appeal to the *Doctor Who* fan market but I think that if Nick and I continue to do what we believe in, we will produce a better and more popular product." [14]

Having developed Soloman's story over the last two films, Briggs was keen on developing the Stranger's former friends. "In a way it's Egan's story, but it's also Soloman coming to terms with his friend changing and working out how to help him." Briggs continued, "This whole video is about Egan realising that there are no moral certainties any more. Because you have to have great moral certitude to be able to stick a bomb under an innocent person's car. Because you think my cause is so important, this person I've never met, I'm not even going to bother thinking about what their family think... I am certain this is more important. The argument in this video basically says you can't be so certain. There are other questions, open your perspective and you can see the crying wife of the person you've killed and so on: there are other perspectives."[15]

Indeed it was the nature of Egan's dilemma that attracted Troughton to the new script. "The thing that interests me is, I'm not human yet here we are on earth in a human body. I think we could explore that much more, like that little Lucozade number I did in the first one, [Egan is disgusted at the taste of it and questions why humans drink it] things like that, that suddenly you come up against somewhat 'what are they doing, these humans? Do they really do that?' So that's why it's interesting, the gradual humanization of them their being absorbed." [16]

Colin Baker seemed satisfied with the character development the script offered him and his co-stars. "This play turns the tables on some of the characters. It is informed by the earlier ones, but stands up on its own. So if readers are wondering, 'What happens if I buy *Stranger* number six and I haven't seen numbers one to five?' then they needn't worry — it's a story in its own right. It also has a lot more science-fiction than 'Breach of the Peace', and it's more interesting for that." [17]

Baker also seemed gratified that the series had found its own identity. "It started off as a sort of *Dr Who* clone. I mean we don't admit that too much but it was kind of son of Who. But it's developed, mainly due to Nick Briggs' scripts, into something beyond that, and something totally different, and it's actually quite rewarding because I've got far more history behind the Stranger than you actually can have with *Doctor Who*. Because each regeneration you are starting with a clean sheet really, even though you've got the baggage of other regenerations. But *The Stranger* now, you've got the history of Soloman being a preceptor and coming from the Web and all that."[18]

The video is perhaps the strongest release of *The Stranger* series, at least in terms of script and acting. The three leads are on fine form, as is Geoffrey Beevers, even if the other two guest stars are a little theatrical. It is a great character piece for both Soloman and Egan, the latter being humanised by his encounter with Meta, while Saul's reluctance to be anything but a complete swine is a great contrast to their emotional journeys. On the downside, the music is occasionally inappropriately used, the sound recording is dreadful and the lighting is a little uneven. The direction remains a little too static in places but the action scenes are well shot. While it does little to prove Baggs could handle a 90 minute sci-fi war film, in the vein of his proposed Cyberman film, it does show he had a handle on the Stranger's domain at least.

'Eye of the Beholder' was released as two 45 minute instalments over two video tapes in July 1995. Reviews for the film were full of the same praise as the previous tapes, citing the broadcast quality of the film. *DWM*'s Barry Ethridge commented that "Bill Baggs is a formidable director whose talents deserve a wider audience," before going on to state, "I can recommend the tapes unreservedly."[19]

He did however have qualms about the decision to spread the production over two tapes — although he did also note that "the same criticism applied to many BBC Video releases." Baggs later justified this decision. "I did this two tape thing that was probably a mistake. But at the time it was done for financial reasons because in my head I could justify charging twice as much, because it was costing me twice as much, as the story was twice as long, but it was a logistical pain in the arse!" [20]

With positive reviews and a happy shoot for all involved, the future appeared bright for the Stranger. Baggs shared some of his ideas for the future of the series while filming 'Eye of the Beholder'. "We were talking on set when David [Troughton] was here... One idea which was quite interesting, I thought, was that in the next story Egan's character ends up in Soloman's body, and then... so they all move around one. Which I thought was quite interesting... so everyone's thinking about it and are keen to do more, which is good, and I think they're very strong characters so I'd like to do more. I mean what I would really like is for a television company to think, God I like that, that's a good idea for a series. That's what I would like to happen." [21]

Baggs was still adamant that he wanted to move on to bigger things, but was taken with the idea of moving the series onto TV. "That would be nice, that would be an ambition of mine... I mean, ultimately, I want to do television drama and feature films..." Baker, too, was keen. "I think there's an edge of a possibility — I don't think it's a very strong possibility but there is an edge of possibility — that somebody might pick it up as an idea. Especially now it's got David and John in it because I like that combination of characters... You'd have to go back and make the whole lot again, I mean you'd probably start from scratch but I think Soloman, Saul, and Egan, not myself and the Stranger, is a great idea for something."[22]

With all this positivity, it is odd, then, that this was the last in *The Stranger* series, and ultimately the last time Baker and Baggs would work together. In later years Baker would try and distance himself from these productions and would have stern words for Baggs, but at the time he seemed more than game to continue. "Yeah, I'd very much like to carry on. It's an extraordinary role. I've become so interested in the characters. I want to do more so I can find out for myself what's going to happen to Soloman."[23]

So while it seems it was hoped that BBV would return to Soloman and co, Baggs later recounted that it was a natural parting of the ways. "It wasn't a deliberate thing, it just turned out that way. I go for the path of least resistance; there's an element for me of just getting stuff done and I didn't want to be wedded to one person all the time. I admire Nick. I think he's very talented, but it would have been a mistake to stay with just him and finding Mark Gatiss opened up a whole new world."[24]

When questioned more recently about further instalments, Briggs too was unaware it would be the final film. "I didn't know that at the time. But there was a sort of pattern with Bill's productions, where he'd exploit people just that little bit too far and then they'd finally crack and say, 'No more!' I think that's possibly what happened with Colin Baker and David Troughton. I was certainly extremely unimpressed with the end result of 'Eye of the Beholder'. I thought it was an enormous step backwards in terms of production standards. The music was terrible and the whole thing just looked a bit rough and amateur to me."[25]

One person who was in no doubt over why the series ended was Andy Grant, who was also soon to part ways with BBV. "Soon after that, there was no money coming in and I co-owned rights on it, so therefore he couldn't do anything with that series without my permission."[26] The split between BBV and WLC is documented in the next chapter, but it seems that in striking a deal with Grant, Baggs may have relinquished some of the rights to *The Stranger* series and this would have an effect on his future output when this relationship went sour.

Ultimately, the Stranger was left holding a smoking gun and being menaced by zombie soldiers. The series had come a long way in its six film series, from a simple *Doctor Who* rip off, to a story with its own mythos and legacy. And while it didn't have the impact of Big Finish's later output, the series nevertheless helped in the rehabilitation and reappraisal of Colin Baker's performance in the eyes of fandom. It also went some way to showing what Nick Briggs had to offer as a writer, in terms of stable dialogue and well-rounded characters. While the series couldn't run forever, it would have been nice to see where Soloman and co went next.

The Stranger remains an interesting footnote in the history of *Doctor Who* and another example of the passion, dedication and creativity that existed within fandom.

Chapter 13 — The Headmaster Ritual

As early as August 1994 BBV let it be known that a Cyberman production was in the pipe line. In a two page advert masquerading as an article entitled 'The BBV Story So Far' in *DWM* 215 they announced "Alongside the *Stranger* series, BBV has already commenced pre-production on a sequel to *The AirZone Solution* and a chilling CYBERMAN adventure. 'Sword of Orion.'"[1]

While no further details were given, the title would appear as a footnote on a number of BBV adverts over the coming year. 'Sword of Orion' was of course the title of a Briggs penned *Audio Visual*. While Baggs was determined to see the project through ("I was intent on doing a Cyberman thing."[2]) Briggs disputes that it was ever really a remake of the AV play. "I think Bill put the title 'Sword of Orion' out there first, to encourage people to pay, because he knew that round about 500 people had brought 'Sword of Orion' — the original — and it was loved. People really thought it was the bees' knees, at least those 500 people did, and I think he was trying to provoke investment, in a sort of pre Kickstarter way and I think that happened a bit." [3]

Baggs it seems, was intent on pre-selling his next film to the audience he had built up over the previous BBV releases. "All these projects had got very loyal core supporters," confirms Briggs. And while he considers this to be a "small number" it would, nevertheless, have supported BBV's output. "I think Bill was keenly aware of that, so he thought if I say we're going to do 'Sword of Orion', we might not end up doing 'Sword of Orion' but I want to do some kind Cyberman-ish thing. So he put that out there at the bottom of adverts." [4]

According to Briggs, this project soon evolved into a film called *Sentinel*, which he describes as "Cybermen taking over an island."[5] Both the idea and title would eventually be recycled for a future BBV project. Briggs cited the setting as "one of my comfort areas for a storyline... set[ting] things on islands or near the coast, because I love all that." It's a setting not dissimilar to many classic *Who* stories. "It's the isolation thing isn't it? I think it's *Doctor Who*ish to do that because if they isolated something, it meant that they didn't have to pay hordes of extras." [6]

Over the next year, Baggs looked for people to fund the project, as its budget was way outside the level BBV could afford solo. The early adverts were seemingly a means of generating interest from financial backers, and Baggs could also be found handing out flyers at conventions, looking for sponsors. By April 1995 the script had changed titles to *Cyber-War* and was officially announced in *DWM* alongside the much delayed *Downtime*. Briggs describe this new effort as "much more like a trench warfare thing, on an alien planet that I later kind of revisited when I did that Fred adventure."[7] He also recalls some preliminary pre-production. "I seem to remember Bill and I went and looked at locations."[8] Despite this Briggs still wasn't sure if the project was achievable. "I think at the bottom of my mind, was the nagging problem of 'how would we get the rights to use the Cybermen?' But Bill sort of waved his hands and said 'no, no, no, leave that to me' of course eventually he solved it by not getting the rights!" [9]

Intriguingly, the *DWM* article informed fandom that the film was being made in association with WLC again, and that the script was being developed by Briggs and Baggs, with a redesigned version of everyone's second favourite *Who* monster to appear, apparently with the full blessing of the BBC and the estates of Cybermen creators, Kit Pedler and Gerry Davis. Baggs later admitted these negotiations may not have been as complete as he suggested at the time. "I was struggling to get the rights. When I approached the BBC about Liz Shaw I also approached them about the Cybermen and I've got a piece of paper that gives me both, but there was also the agents aspect of it and I never got a fucking reply."[10]

Briggs was of the opinion that it may not have been easy to get the BBC on side. "I think his interpretation is a little optimistic, I think the BBC probably said that, knowing that the estates wouldn't give permission. Also in those days, there wasn't really the whole apparatus in place at the BBC so they'd say 'well, as long as the owners of the Cybermen think it's ok, yeah sure'. Probably thinking, (A) we're not interested, (B) this is never going to happen and (C) if he does ask them they'll say no." [11]

Returning to the plot of the prospective movie, Baggs shared some details on the project. "We are certainly using a *Doctor Who* monster, but in a different context. The script I am developing — which at this point is called *Cyber War* — is more like a war film, it's very action-orientated. I think the Cybermen are well-suited to that, and I think fans would like to see them again. There are all sorts of new things that can be done with the Cybermen." [12] The project was further discussed on BBV's own documentary, 'The Doctors: 30 years of Time Travel', released in May 1995. At that point, it was mooted as seeing the Cybermen face off against The Ice Warriors, although Baggs says this was never seriously considered. "I think that was more talk than anything because there were these maquettes."[13] The maquettes in question were used to illustrate the project on the documentary but these were actually created from Chris Fitzgerald's creature designs for the aborted 'The Dark Dimension' and used without his permission.

Briggs on the other hand, thinks by this point the film had dropped the *Cyber War* title all together and the Ice Warriors were very much part of the project. "The basic plotline was that some piece of technology had come to Earth," he explains. "It was a machine that built itself in some way, when the scientists started playing with it and it built itself into a transmitter that attracted the attention of the Cybermen, so it was like a cyber-seed of some kind." It was only after this story line was completed that that Baggs asked for the inclusion of the Ice Warriors. "This original story was just about the Cybermen being attracted to Earth by this bit of technology and then an almighty battle to stop them. The new version of it had this other character, who was an alien spy on Earth, who was going to — for whatever reason I can't remember now — help the Earth stop the Cybermen taking over."[14]

This character would be a new take on the fan favourite, which he describes as "...driving about on a motorcycle, with a helmet over her head, was a woman but she was an Ice Warrior. So she had a helmet on and then she took it off and there was like another helmet underneath."[15]

This new script came with more stipulations from Baggs. "I think he was talking to Adrian Rigelsford at the time,"[16] recalls Briggs.

Rigelsford was the author of the abandoned 30th anniversary special 'The Dark Dimension' and the *Doctor Who* book 'The Doctors: 30 Year of Time Travel' on which BBV had recently based a video documentary of the same name. Rigelsford courted some controversy, however, when he apparently obtained lost interviews with William Hartnell, Roger Delgado and the last interview with Stanley Kubrick, the validity of which have been highly disputed. He was later convicted of stealing and selling 56,000 photos from Associated Newspapers' archive, for which he received eighteen months in jail.[17]

Briggs describes him as "someone who had a very interesting relationship with the truth and who, some might say, was prone to rewriting reality as he's speaking." [18]

It seems Rigelsford was offering a possible funding solution for the project. "I think Adrian was saying to Bill that he could get some sort of computer game company involved. And so Bill got it in his head that he could get a load of money out of this computer game company. I mean all of this, I'm sure was Bill being strung along. Adrian just has these ideas you know, three times a minute. And so Bill said to me, 'you know what you've got to do is write a script that has the structure of a computer game?' and I think the only computer game I played at that point was *Doom*." [19]

Briggs duly incorporated the new element into the script. "I got this idea that it was about going around and going up different levels," though he found this new prerequisite somewhat limiting. "I definitely worked long and hard on that and remember thinking this is going to be terribly comprised as a story if we keep having to make it like a computer game."[20] Nevertheless, the project got to a reasonably advanced stage. "I definitely wrote the full story line and I'm fairly certain that I wrote some script for it," Briggs recollects. Baggs too supports this view. "There was a script, maybe not a completed script, but certainly 20 pages that Nick had written." [21]

In the debut issues of *SFX* magazine, Baggs once again laid down his intentions to make the film. "Cybermen to me are the most frightening enemy in *Doctor Who*. They're tall, they can do anything a human can do, only they're far stronger. What I would like to do is explore every opportunity to make a very powerful war film, with the Cybermen as very strong enemies. I'm hoping it'll get picked up for broadcast." [22] However, while WLC was announced as a partner on the production, it seems the announcement was somewhat premature. "I remember talking about it and pulling it, because of having had difficult experiences with BBC Worldwide," recalls Grant. "The licensing on things like Daleks and the Cybermen was very dodgy ground, you needed to find the right person in BBC Enterprises to sign it off or they wouldn't take the project seriously, but the moment it became professional and it became above the radar they'd jump on it left right and centre."[23] Thus, while publicly everything seemed to be going well for this production, behind closed doors things were in a far less advanced stage than BBV led fans to believe. With WLC not keen on the project, Baggs put it on the back burner and turned his attention to a more affordable production.

In looking for this next project, Baggs decided to build on the success of 'The Zero Imperative', mainly "because Liz Shaw was fine, she was entirely BBC and I had the rights."[24] Baggs also puts this down to his excitable nature as a young film maker. "You've got to imagine there is this young man who just loves filming and being creative and getting people together. And so I was like 'I've got *The Stranger*, I've got Liz Shaw, I've got the Cybermen. What's the easiest thing to do? What's the quickest thing to do?' And so 'The Devil of Winterborne' comes along." [25]

In developing the new idea, Baggs decided to play on the *P.R.O.B.E.* team that was established in his previous film, and having struck up a good relationship with Peter Davison, use him as the major guest star. Peter was arguably the most successful of the former Doctors at the time and to this day is still a regular face on screen and stage.

Returning to *P.R.O.B.E.*, Baggs once again asked Gatiss to come up with a suitable script. "After 'The Zero Imperative', Bill Baggs asked if I'd like to do something else, and I said I'd love to. There was no sense this time of it being any sort of multi-Doctor thing, and I think Bill was keen to produce something that he could maybe send into Carlton or one of the TV companies to say 'I've made this drama that happens to star Peter Davison'. That way it looks more like a star vehicle rather than a *Doctor Who* knock-off. Also I was keen to write something that was less sci-fi and more like TV drama.[26]

If Baggs was intent on creating a TV series from *P.R.O.B.E.,* then the casting of 'The Devil of Winterborne' is as bold statement as any. With the bankable name of Peter Davison already on board, Baggs also recruited Charmian May, another familiar face on British TV, with significant roles in the sitcoms *You're Only Young Twice* and *The Good Life*. Returning alongside Caroline John from the *Doctor Who* stable was Louise Jameson, one of the more recognisable faces to potential mainstream viewers. Geoffrey Beevers and Gatiss also joined the cast, the latter in a different role from his previous outing with *P.R.O.B.E.* "It was the best part in it!" he stated later. "What I regret about that was that later on he starts to speak and become very expositionary, where he really should have stayed mute. He was proto-Mickey from the *League* [*of Gentlemen*] TV series."[27]

The production also saw Davros actor and *Archers* regular, Terry Molloy join the BBV team alongside newcomers Stephen Dolomore, Daniel Matthews and Gatiss' comedy collaborator Reece Shearsmith. Of this casting Gatiss later told *DWM*, "I said 'd'you want a job?'", before going on to explain Shearsmith wasn't exactly a fan. "Well Reece has a *Doctor Who* connection. But Reece has a strange, episode three connection, it's always strange! Where he was living in Hull and just about to leave school, he and his friend Phil became mono-obsessive about Season Twenty-Two. To this day, if you get him in the right mood and prick him with a pin, he can do impressions of the Borad and Maylin Tekker. It's so unexpected! I mean, of all the things to know... So he knew of it, but like any of us, he was just trying to advance his career." [28]

For Peter Davison, conversely, the part of Gavin Purcell was a welcome divergence from what he was normally offered. "One of the main reasons this was good to do, was because it was a very different sort of character to parts I've got lumbered with over the years." This was the case, even if the character turned out to be something of a red herring at the end of the story. "You think he might turn out to be nastier than he actually is, he is a bit of a manipulated being. It was a great chance for a while to act like the villain of the piece which I don't normally do."[29]

When pushed for memories of the filming, most of the cast can supply only glimpses, like Patricia Merrick, now promoted to 1st Assistant Director, who recalls "[t]he freezing cold when we were filming on a bridge over the M25" Mark Gatiss' main memory is of "[t]his beautiful school where we filmed. We had such a good time — it was like being at Hogwarts! It was out of term time obviously and we had gorgeous weather. We were lucky to have Chairmian May, who was a superb actress, and Peter was lovely. It was a gang show."[30]

Later, at Manopticon 5, Caroline John went into more detail on her experiences on this second *P.R.O.B.E.* "I really loved it! It was really small and we have a wonderful team, the crew is brilliant and Lou and I really enjoy it. I thought I cannot go back to remembering what Liz Shaw did. I watched all my tapes of that time and thought 'now go ahead'. She's 25 years older, just use that; practical, slightly scathing occasionally, but get on and try and probe out what needs to be done. We had terrific fun I must say, there isn't the pressure you have in large concern like the Beeb. You don't feel like Big Brother is looking over your shoulder. Big Brother is directing it and that's Bill Baggs and we have a very jolly time, but we work oh so hard. I mean sometimes in television it's at least 4-5 pages, we do at least 10 or 12 if not more."[31]

For Jameson the shoot offered a number of challenges, most notably the part itself. "The reason I like *The Devil of Winterbourne* so much was the fact that I was given a part that was originally written for a man, I believe, and I didn't think it would be as much of challenge as it actually was, because my personal power lies in the fact that I'm a woman more than I realised. It wasn't until I played that part that I thought 'this is actually a man's dialogue' It doesn't have any of those wily ways that we women have."[32]

BBV chose to advertise *P.R.O.B.E.* rather cheekily as "Britain's answer to *The X-Files*", a series that was currently re-igniting interest in genre shows around the world. Gatiss jovially opined, "It was also part two of what I suppose you'd call a 'video series', the *P.R.O.B.E.* dramas with Liz Shaw. 'Britain's answer to *The X-Files*' I believe it was called by Bill Baggs! And that was true actually, in so many ways. The only difference was that they did 26 episodes a year and we did one! But that was the only difference..."[33]

When asked if she thought it was worthy of the title at Manopticon, Caroline John replied jokingly. "I don't think my kids would. I mean, I enjoy doing it. I'd love to do more. I wish one of the bigger companies would buy it but it's doing quite well I believe. It's being sent abroad and things like that."[34]

Indeed, Baggs was selling this first film to small broadcasters in North America, and even managed to get the show on the British Sci-Fi Channel, much to the annoyance of his co-producer Andy Grant. "I'd originally said I could open the doors to broadcasters, then I hear it's being broadcast and I'm saying 'well, when did I sign this off?'" — although he admits he would have taken them to much the same places, "Again the Sci-Fi Channel would have been a target, but around this sort of time we did have the multi-channel mainstream telly. I was looking more at the US because I have connections with some of the cable channels there. The Sci-Fi channel in the US would basically take anything, although it would have to be cut into four parts for commercial breaks."[35]

At this point in time, it's difficult to say whether the *P.R.O.B.E.* series would have been more successful had Baggs not gone behind Grant's back in finding distributors. But Grant's larger organization certainly would have held more weight than the excitable young film maker.

Despite WLC being credited as co-producer on the next two *P.R.O.B.E.* films, Grant is adamant that this was the last he had officially to do with Baggs. "I'm probably credited or the money has been used or the name has been used to open doors without my permission on stuff."[36]

Grant's parting with BBV was not a happy one "They [the films] did fairly well, but Bill Baggs didn't pay any of the money. I believe I'm one of many that are owed a great deal of money. If I remember, he did make a fair amount of money out of it. What happened is I think it was his then wife who had this heavyweight lawyer, who basically said 'well sue me' and I looked at it but the contract between us was so ambiguous that it would have cost a lot of money to achieve anything and it wasn't worth the time or effort. With projects like that, the money was fairly substantial but in real terms not so much, so it would have cost more to recover it."[37]

If these allegations are true, it's hard to defend Baggs' actions. But, equally, without knowing the full details of their agreement it's difficult to comment. Grant still runs a successful broadcasting business — if he had been bankrupted by these films it would be understandable that his bitterness might skew his memory and opinion, but Grant seemed neither bitter nor broken by these events when interviewed, he merely relayed these events as he remembered them. Much like Bryant before him, Grant was sufficiently taken with Baggs to invest a large amount of money where Bryant invested time, and both of them felt cheated by him. Unfortunately they wouldn't be the last people to feel this way.

'The Devil of Winterborne' is possibly the most accomplished of BBV's productions. Baggs' directorial style has really stepped up a notch and he makes great use of tracking shots, while Dick Kursa's lighting is suitably atmospheric in places and Mark Ayres' score adds weight to an already tense script. All the cast are on top form, with the newcomers easily holding their own against the regulars. Gatiss' script really gets a chance to breathe over the film's 90 minute run time; the dialogue is punchy if not a little functionary in places and the script offers a genuine mystery that keeps viewers guessing. Gatiss has clearly learned from his mistakes on 'The Zero Imperative'. His plot is concise and features a soon-to-be Gatiss trope of borrowing from programmes of the past in its *Inspector Morse/Dial M For Murder/Ruth Rendall Mysteries*-like setting, and its 'what we got up to in the school holidays' plot, even if what they got up to was far more adult with a good deal of boy on boy action. While it is progressive in that sense, its biggest failure is that instead of trying to create a new format, it borrows too much from the TV of yesteryear while comparing itself to the biggest TV show of the time. In that respect it fails to craft its own identity but it's easy to see how, with a bit more money and time to develop the story, *P.R.O.B.E.* could have gone to a series.

Released in September of 1995 over two tapes, the film was then re-released in 1996 on a single tape to bring it in line with its sequels. Upon its re-release, *Celestial Toyroom*'s Cate Caruth was not impressed, however. "Somehow it is a little pedestrian, and the shocks are too far apart to bring the viewer to the edge of the seat. It didn't quite scream as a mystery either, as there are some obvious pointers to the culprit quite early on."[38]

Her review was also damming of the supporting characters. "I found some of the characters were unconvincing too, a common problem when a story is set in a school."[39] Caruth also didn't care for Davison's performance. "Davison's portrayal of Purcell, the current head teacher of Winterborne School, failed to impress at all, either as a teacher or as someone who has raised a teenage boy."[40] *DWM*, on the other hand, called Davison's understated performance "artistically justified by the subtle ambiguity he brings to the part" and generally enjoyed the production. "In many ways, 'The Devil of Winterborne' is the most successful of the direct-to-video productions made in recent years featuring ex-*Doctor Who* personnel, by not being particularly reminiscent of the series."

The reviewer concluded with a clear interest in the next installment. "The series has great potential, but 'The Devil of Winterborne' treats its audience with a great deal more respect that its successors."[41]

This was still early in Gatiss' career, and these films saw him placed in a fortuitous situation that few up and coming writers could expect to find themselves in, as he discussed at the time. "It's the opportunity to write rapidly and efficiently and get something actually produced and see what it turns out like in a very short space of time and act with people I admire and want to work with and because it's a lot of fun"[42] While *The Devil of Winterbourne* is not without its flaws, it nevertheless is a well-structured and competently written script that shows the potential of Gatiss.

Chapter 14 — The Same Deep Water as You

Of all the spin-off productions produced in the interim between the classic series finishing and the show's triumphant return in 2005 *Downtime* was the most high profile, most ambitious and ultimately the most expensive production. Its story stretches right back to the release of *Wartime* in 1988.

With his first film being a modest success, it was always Keith Barnfather's plan to shoot a follow-up. Indeed, the article covering *Wartime* in *DWM* 140 promised more drama in the future. "If *Wartime* is a success, there are hopes that a further story, featuring other members of U.N.I.T. will be made, with the working title *Return to Devils End*'..."[1]

Return to Devils End eventually materialised as a documentary featuring the cast and crew of the classic Pertwee story 'The Daemons', revisiting the episodes' location to discuss its making. Barnfather is doubtful that *Return to Devils End* was ever meant to be anything more than a documentary. "I don't remember *Return to Devils End* being mooted as a drama, it was always a documentary. We did a little trailer for [it] that looked a little bit like a drama trailer. Loads of little shots of Aldbourne and it said '*Return to Devils End*... Coming Soon' and it may well be people misconstrued it as a drama."[2]

Despite this, there were brief discussions about adding some fictional elements to the video. *Wartime* scribe Andy Lane was asked to contribute. "I did have some talks with Keith about *Return to Devils End*. It was going to be some kind of framework for the actors to be wandering around. So you'd get these intermittent sequences all the way through, of them being observed by somebody and somehow their actions are being influenced. They start acting in strange ways and almost reliving the story as well and it turns out to be Terrance Dicks at the end playing with the video recorder." [3]

Notwithstanding the confusion in fandom over the format of the follow up to *Wartime*, Lane was nevertheless asked to submit ideas for a second film. "The proposal I wrote was the return of the Great Intelligence and again it was going back to trying to explore the inner life of characters. I had the Brigadier going to a medical clinic for a heart operation, and his daughter was there and they had been estranged. So, there's a bit of awkwardness between him and his daughter. What neither of them realise is the Great Intelligence has taken over the director in charge of the clinic and he's implanting the Yeti spheres into the chest of heart operation patients. So you'd get this lovely scene where a patient's dressing gown falls open and you could see in the chest the metal curve of the ball coming out of the flesh and breaking out. I also had scenes of the spheres rolling through the air conditioning system, which I thought was great."[4]

Neither Barnfather nor Lane can remember why this idea was rejected but it's easy to see how differences between them may have caused a parting of the ways. The rights for the Great Intelligence and the Yeti had been secured by Barnfather, who was also keen for John Levene to return. Lane, on the other hand, had different ideas. "It was just the Brigadier and I remember thinking those Yetis are not going to work, probably as a result of *Wartime*. I thought nobody is going to be able to build the Yeti realistically. It's also the problem that the Yeti work fine in Tibet and to get them underground you kind of have to shoehorn them in quite a bit, but they don't work anywhere else." [5]

Despite this original idea being rejected, Barnfather was still keen to do another film. "*Downtime* took a long time to make, mainly for financial reasons because it rather snowballed. I got terribly involved in a lot of corporate business work, so I didn't really have the time to work on it, but I secured the rights a long time before the script was written, so I knew that we were alright and so there was no deviating from the basic elements'"[6]

The, at that point untitled, drama was officially announced in June 1992. The aim was to shoot it in early 1993 and have it ready for the 30th anniversary of *Doctor Who* later that year. In June, Barnfather shared his intentions with *DWM*. "As the BBC seem unlikely to produce any *Doctor Who* for the foreseeable future we wanted to ensure that fans had some new drama to help celebrate the anniversary"[7] The same article stated that while no writer was attached, the drama would be 50 minutes in length and Nick Courtney had signed up to reprise his role as the Brigadier, while Mark Ayres would act as composer. The soundtrack (along with the *Wartime* score), the piece concluded, would be released by Silva Screen and a signing session with cast and crew would take place in November of 1993 to celebrate the release (this did not, in fact, occur).

By July 1993 more firm details had been announced — John Levene had signed up to reprise his role as Benton, *Doctor Who* writer Marc Platt would be taking on scripting duties and legendary *Who* director Christopher Barry was also on board. "I was still prepared to take on anything then, and it seemed a challenge that Keith Barnfather thought I'd be up for. Although he couldn't offer me 'real money', he made it seem attractive enough to tempt me — and I fell."[8]

Barnfather agrees, feeling Barry wanted one last challenge. "He needed to do it, he hadn't directed for seven or eight years and he really wanted it, he just had that last moment left in him to do it and we caught that."[9]

Just a few weeks after Reeltime had issued these solid details about *Downtime*, the BBC announced their own *Doctor Who* anniversary special *The Dark Dimension*, a multi-Doctor tale from BBC Worldwide. In the same issue of *DWM* announcing *The Dark Dimension,* Barnfather had less positive news about *Downtime*. "I'm delighted that the BBC will be doing a drama to celebrate the Doctor's anniversary. Obviously, anything Reeltime wished to do would be overshadowed by their film and so we have decided to put *Downtime* back until 1994."[10]

While publicly the postponement of *Downtime* was due to the return of *Doctor Who*, Keith later admitted there were very different reasons behind delaying the production. "It was literally financial, I could not afford the budget and I had to put it off. And what happened then was, Kevin Davies came to me and said '"I've got an idea for a drama, it's a lot cheaper than *Downtime*, would you be interested?'" which was very kind of him but if I couldn't do *Downtime* I didn't want to do put the money I did have into something else."[11]

The Dark Dimension would ultimately never make it to screen, with the BBC celebrating the 30th Anniversary with the heavily criticised *Children In Need* Special 'Dimensions in Time' instead.

With production delayed until 1994, writer Marc Platt had a chance to develop the script further. "I grew up loving the Yeti, but what was I supposed to do with them as a writer? All they do is lumber about and hit people! I then had to think of a reason for the Intelligence to return. There are moments in 'The Abominable Snowmen' when characters talk of it being cast out in its own dimension, so I started digging about in Tibetan Buddhism — and discovered the concept of the 'bardo' (a term used to designate the period from physical death to physical rebirth). I decided that the Intelligence was stuck in a dreamlike limbo, desperate to escape into a material world." [12]

Even with the basic concept in place, Platt had to jumble an ever increasing cast list, in part because Barnfather wanted to add to the Brigadier's personal history but also because he wanted to strengthen the *Doctor Who* connection to the new story.

Consequently, Barnfather recruited Debbie Watling to play the head of New World University, the organisation that the Great Intelligence was controlling on Earth. In the meantime, the production had lost the services of John Levene (according to Barnfather, the character of Sergeant Benton never made it into a draft of the script, despite Levene signing up in pre-production. Levene moved to America in late 1993 which would have prevented him from taking part in the film in any case) and so Barnfather approached the BBC to use the character of Victoria Waterfield — who Watling had portrayed in *Doctor Who* in the 1960s.

Platt was thrilled to be writing for the character. "She had been left alone in the wrong place at the wrong time. A celestial orphan! Victoria's beliefs and values were not fitting for the period — that made her lovely to write for. The poor girl is very screwed-up. Debbie was sure that

Victoria was still a virgin — and I absolutely agreed! We had a long talk about what to do with the character."[13]

Watling was pleased with the direction in which the character was taken. "She was written in *Downtime* as a powerful woman — power suits and all that — and she was a total control-freak, the head of the facility, but you could see little bits of the old Victoria coming through."[14] Watling also informed Barnfather that her father, the actor Jack Watling, was keen on appearing in the production. So Platt was given the task of incorporating the character of Professor Travers, who had been in both the Yeti serials from the 1960s. "They [Travers and Victoria] worked together beautifully, but the story kept changing as we managed to get more and more people on board. It was a bit like writing 'The Five Doctors' — and it probably ruined Keith financially!"[15]

With production scheduled to take place in summer of 1994, some of the funding for the production would come from Gary Leigh's DreamWatch Publishing. The premiere of the film was scheduled to take place at the *DreamWatch 94* convention on the weekend of the 29th and 30th of October. An advert for the convention read, 'The official premiere of the final story in the yeti trilogy, written by Marc Platt and directed by Christopher Barry. Starring Nicholas Courtney as the Brigadier, Deborah Watling as Victoria and Jack Watling as Professor Travers, plus special cameo appearance to be announced. The cast and crew will be present to sign copies of this exciting fifty-minute, made for video drama which will go on sale for the first time at DreamWatch 94."[16] Interestingly, a sidebar in the convention magazine noted that John Levene would be in attendance and featuring in the production, despite his character apparently never making the script. It is possible that the team hoped to secure him for a cameo if he was in the country when shooting commenced. The assumption that things were still in flux at this stage due to the erratic nature of low budget film making is unavoidable.

That assumption appeared to take on an aura of fact when, at the last minute, both Watling and Courtney became unavailable — both having secured parts in West End productions ('Don't Dress Down For Dinner" and 'The Mousetrap', respectively). With both actors being pivotal to the film, Barnfather had no choice but to postpone the production for another year.

In the absence of a film to premiere at their event, DreamWatch Publishing withdrew funding from the film, opting instead to produce Kevin Davies' *Shakedown* film. This left Barnfather searching for a new partner to take on the financial burden of the production with him. He approached Andrew Beech of Domnitemporal Services Ltd (DSL) who ran England's biggest *Doctor Who* Convention, Panopticon "They were doing really well with their conventions at that time, but they felt they needed something new to try and up their profile, and bless them, for whatever reason they couldn't afford to fund half of it, but they felt they could afford a third." [17]

With DSL on board, Barnfather approached another name prominent in the fan community, Ian Levine. Levine had recently left the *Shakedown* production and was happy put up the final third of the money. According to Beech, the final budget was £56,000. On the DWO podcast, Levine claimed he put up £15,000 of the production's budget, while on the Outpost Gallifrey forum he claimed "I put up most of the money. Far more than either of the other two producers."[18]

The exact split is unconfirmed but one would assume Beech and Levine would have fronted £15,000 each, with Reeltime coming up with the rest. As Levine was a well known record producer, one further change would be made to the team — Mark Ayres would leave the project, with Levine insisting on producing the score himself.

With production delayed, Barry took time to get to grips with the story. "Marc Platt's script was ingenious in weaving together the two *Doctor Who* stories on which *Downtime* is based. At first, not knowing those stories, I couldn't understand the script at all. Eventually, with many rewrites — mostly at my suggestion — things became clear — and Doctor or not, I think the script was successful in the end."[19]

The script featured a supporting character in the shape of a female journalist, but Barry had other ideas about this character. "I'd been to a *Doctor Who* convention in Chicago in the meantime, and there I talked to Lis Sladen about the possibility of playing the journalist character, who I'd always seen as Sarah. She said, 'If you're directing, I'll do it. I trust you'." [20]

Sladen, however, revealed to *DWM* during filming that the process took a little longer than just a simple meeting at a convention. "He said he could really see me in it. He didn't say then that it was Sarah Jane. So I said yes. Then I bumped into him a few times and he said that it was on the back burner. Some time passed, and then I got the first full script a few months ago. Keith Barnfather contacted me and asked me what I thought. I said that I quite liked it and asked him how he saw the part. He told me that he actually saw it as Sarah Jane, and would I go for that if he could get the right to use the name. I asked if it would then be written more in the style of Sarah Jane, because she deals with situations in a very particular way, and that has to be taken into account. Keith said if they could get the character and I was willing to play her, then they would do just that."[21] Barnfather therefore negotiated with the BBC to use the Sarah Jane Smith character and Platt made adjustments to the script. "She was far too good to waste, so I beefed up her part! Lis didn't want to play Sarah as the young girl from the television series."[22]

Production was now firmly locked in for March 1995, and the premiere of the film was scheduled for Panopticon 95 on 2nd and 3rd September in Coventry. Reeltime set about casting the rest of the film. Former K9 actor John Leeson was recruited to play the DJ Anthony, Geoffrey Beevers — best known to *Doctor Who* fans as The Master — played Harold Haroldson and James Bree (previously the Keeper of the Matrix in 'The Trial of a Time Lord') played the Lama in the opening scenes. As well as these names well known to *Doctor Who* fans, Barnfather recruited Peter Silverleaf as Christopher Rice, Mark Trotman (brought on board by Alistair Lock) as Daniel Hinton, Miles Richardson as Captain Douglas Cavendish and Richardson's real life wife Beverley Cressman as the Brigadier's daughter, Kate.

Richardson and Cressman had met Barnfather at an event in early 1994. "It was in the Coal Hole pub on the Strand," remembers Richardson. "My then wife Beverley had attended a course called ISA, which was some type of self improvement ethos. I didn't go, so I never got to the bottom of it and there was a get together of people who had attended the course. They were a mixed bunch. As well as Keith there were a range of diverse people including Les Dennis, who was going out with Sophie Aldred at the time, so that's also when I first met her. I don't remember much about Keith at the time, but then, I did meet a lot of new people that night. I obviously left an impression on him, as he offered me employment a few months later."[23]

With the three shareholders in the film all having their own agendas and a number of fans being part of the crew, Barnfather was relieved to have Barry in the director's chair, as he was someone who everybody respected. "Having Christopher Barry as director meant people didn't play silly buggers on location. It suffered from an abundance of people who had their own views, being too closely financially involved. But at the same time the script was agreed so we didn't have to worry about it from that point of view, it was more a question of lots of big fish in a little pool and I include myself in that."[24]

So was Barnfather ever tempted to direct the production himself?

"If I could have employed somebody I could trust as a production manager, I would have tried to have directed it myself. But bear in mind, I think both Ian and Andrew would have said they could have directed it themselves. So if I had come in producing and directing that would have caused a lot of problems so I didn't even consider it." [25]

Barry's presence also went down well with the cast. Richardson found his stamina and method impressive. "He had cut his teeth on the early days of television. He was also a very hands-on director. In the days of monitors and now bluetooth letterbox, sometimes you don't even see the director as he is in another room from the action. Chris was old school and though we had an able camera operator in Keith, Chris would always look down the lens just in case."[26]

Before shooting commenced, a read through took place at Reeltime's studio at London Bridge. "I have very strong memories of that," reminisces Barnfather. "We got the entire crew together and the entire cast together, with Christopher, and we read through it and that's when the script came alive and I loved that moment." [27]

A gruelling ten day shoot began in spring 1995. Courtney — now well into his sixties — found it exhausting. "The saga of *Downtime*. A punishing schedule, which Chris Barry handled extremely well. We worked damn hard every day. I was very tired at the end of those ten days. I only had one day off!"[28]

While it's easy to sympathise with Courtney, who had come from a background of a heavily unionised television industry, it's important to note that the landscape of film and television making had changed in the UK. *Downtime* — like most television — was now recorded single camera, with twelve hour plus days and very little time off being the norm. Things may have been tough for some of the older members of the cast and crew but no tougher than it would have been on any other production at the time. Barnfather was more than happy with how the production ran. "We nailed it, we got that in the time scale every day we did what we said we were going to do, Reeltime had been going for 12 years by then, I knew exactly what I was doing." [29]

Shooting began on the morning of Friday March 24th 1995 in South West London, with the all the interiors of the Brigadier's house being done first. The afternoon was given over to recording a scene where Harroldson and Hinton walk past a TV shop. This was filmed on a high street in Clapham Junction. The next day saw the crew head to Kensal Rise Narrowboat Pool, where the bulk of Kate Stewart's boat scenes were filmed.

Sunday 26th March saw the team head to the aptly named Watling Street in EC4 for scenes set on the busy streets of central London. Initially, almost everyone involved believed these would have to be faked elsewhere. Surprisingly then, they were allowed to film there with very few restrictions. No-one was more surprised than Barry. "Well in fairness, I never thought we'd get such a free hand in the City of London as we did that Sunday morning." [30]

Friends and family were brought in along with their cars to make the streets seem busier than they were, and writer Marc Platt can also be seen playing a businessman. The university scenes were originally written to be recorded at Canary Wharf, but the location proved too expensive. As a result, the scenes were moved to the University of East Anglia, with cast and crew being given free run of the campus as the students were on holiday. "My memories of East Anglia are bleak to be honest," recalls Barry, "in that we were held up by a snowstorm at the university and were almost blown away in a sandstorm on the beach! The university people were very good and let us go anywhere we wanted. We even lived in student accommodation whilst filming there."[31]

The first shots to be recorded were those set in the University's computer room and then in and around the lift area. At the same time, Nick Briggs popped in to film footage for an updated version of Watling's Myth Makers tape. The Tuesday of that week was scheduled to be given over to exterior shots of the university but due to the bad weather conditions these had to be postponed. More interior shots were therefore brought forward, including those of Kate inside New World University from the film's finale, and all the scenes in Victoria's office (though the shooting was interrupted by a fire alarm going off!).

On the 29th, the company were able to go ahead with the exteriors. This included the film's grand finale, where the heroes are captured by the Intelligence and surround by the University's brainwashed students, known as Chillis. Over 30 extras were present, mainly real life students at the university. They were recruited via an advert in the student paper Concrete and paid a small fee. Filming went on well into the evening as the crew returned to the University's basement where the generator room was used to film more scenes from the climax.

The next day saw the sun come out in full and scenes involving the Brigadier and Sarah Jane walking along a canal were filmed outside of the university before all of the scenes in the DJ's studio were recorded in the afternoon. Some more external shots were also filmed, including Daniel's death at the beginning of the film. Finally, the crew went back to the generator room to complete the scenes there.

Originally the 31st was to be given over to a shoot at Norwich Castle to film the opening scenes of a young Victoria in Detsen Monastery. But as they were running slightly behind schedule this was cancelled and more exterior shots from beginning of the film were recorded.

For the scenes set on the Astral Plane the crew spent the 1st of April on Holkham Beach in Wells-next-to-the-Sea, where windy conditions caused issues for the crew. The 2nd of April saw the crew returning to Kensal Rise and the narrow boat before they headed over to the Forte Crest Hotel in Regent's Park where the Brigadier's meeting with Cavendish took place. This point was effectively the wrap on the main bulk of the shoot.

Like Courtney, Elisabeth Sladen found the shooting schedule difficult. She was another actress who had been used to the old methods of television production and had long since given up acting. She shared her memories of the shoot at the Manopticon convention in Manchester in 1996. "There again you're working until twelve at night. If that was a 'real production' everyone would be saying 'overtime'; no such thing. You go back, you iron your clothes, you get ready for the next day. I think with the limitations, to pull something off like that, it's incredible. I remember all my speaking scenes were on the day I shouldn't have been there. I stayed an extra half day and all I could think about was 'bloody hell I hope I don't miss the train home' because it was snowing and you had all that whack to do. You just do it and you just hope it works." [32]

Barry, on the other hand, found it exhilarating not to be tied down by the production methods of yesteryear. "There seemed to be a terrific well of enthusiasm also, that might have been lacking at the BBC. I seemed to have complete freedom. And we weren't tied down by Union Hours."[33]

Nick Courtney was impressed with Barry's stamina and resilience in the face of adversity. "Christopher Barry directed this story with his usual flair and energy — though, in an uncanny rerun of 'The Daemons', the poor man's production was plagued with frequent snowfalls when exterior work was required to be done. He still managed to complete the filming on schedule, however, and the finished product — considering the whole thing was shot in ten days — was a credit to all concerned."[34]

Newcomer Cressman was also impressed by the enthusiasm of the cast and crew. "I really enjoyed it and I felt very lucky to be involved. I got to work with some fab actors and I had not really had that much film experience. Christopher Barry our director was a delight to work with as [were] Deborah Watling and Lis Sladen, to name but a few. I was the new youngish actress in the cast and Deborah and Lis were very helpful and fun. Of course, I adored Nick Courtney; he was like a father figure but of course with this great twinkle in his eye. It was a real team effort from all of the crew and cast. As with any movie, especially on a low budget, you have to be really flexible and easy going."[35]

Courtney too enjoyed his scenes with Cressman, stating that she performed the role "admirably" and appreciated the chance to explore the Brigadier's personal life. "Marc Platt wrote some very good scenes for myself and Beverley. I should very much like to work with Beverley again, not least in order to develop further the relationship between the Brig, his daughter and his grandson." [36] Meanwhile Cressman's partner also welcomed the chance to work with Courtney. "It was the first time I met Nick Courtney, who was a delight to work with. I will be honest and say that his acting was a bit two-dimensional, but if you can make two dimensions work — why bother digging for the third. He and I got on very well together, mainly because we had a lot of acquaintances in common."[37]

Also present for the university shoot was David J. Howe, who simply wanted to help out and be part of it. Howe had previously interviewed numerous *Doctor Who* actors and production staff, and had heard all sorts of anecdotes about being stuck inside monster suits. Here he was about to find out firsthand the issues an actor in a monster suit goes through. "I'm one of the Yetis in the attack sequence, when they all come through the woods and kill all the soldiers. I was one of those Yetis lumbering though the woods, not being able to see very much. Discovering very quickly why *Doctor Who* monsters lurch, because it's the only way you can move. Not being able to see, not being able to hear and just hoping to hell there was nothing on the floor that was going to trip me up."[38]

Barry found the Yetis easy to direct. "The Yetis were very obedient! And not any different from directing the Daleks."[39] Writer Mark Platt was less than impressed with the final look of the Yeti creature, however. "The costumes weren't very good either. I used to have an old handmade rug that was much the same colour and rather more frightening. We managed so much on such a tiny budget. But the Yetis were a bloody let down. And why do monsters all walk with their arms outstretched? I should have said something when the wretched creatures started doing it in *Downtime*. It looks terrible!"[40]

Beverley Cressman also found the Yeti costumes a little unrealistic. "The yeti was hilarious. With the scenes on the narrow boat, the yeti came in and we had to be petrified. Well it had bicycle lights for eyes, one kept going out and of course it was really hard not to giggle."[41]

While the bulk of the film was now in the can, there was still the matter of shooting the previously postponed opening of the film. This scene would see a young Victoria revisiting Detsen and was shot in tourist attraction London Dungeons, in July 1995, with camera operator Robin Lee doubling for Jack Watling. The scenes run time was extended at the request of executive producer Ian Levine who thought Victoria need a stronger motivation. Watling was worried she wouldn't be able to recapture the character or the look of her youth "I read the script and said to the director, 'Hang on! It says here that I'm 19 years old. And well I'm not. If we're going to film this sequence make sure it's very dark,"[42] but in the event the character came back to her relatively quickly. "I became Victoria instantly! Older, yes, but Victoria was still there."[43] While shot in sympathetic lighting, it was perhaps a mistake to include these scenes which did little to convince the viewer this was a younger Victoria.

With all the footage now recorded, Barnfather did an offline edit before handing it over to Paul Vanezis at BBC Birmingham for the online edit. Special optical effects were added at Framestore in London, while the soundtrack was mixed at Nonelinear Ltd in central London by Roger Stevens. The score had been put together by Levine who felt this was his chance to prove a point. "I personally felt very strongly about the incidental music used in *Doctor Who* during the 80s. I felt it was too electronic, I felt it jarred with the action, it grated on the nerves and I wanted to make a stand and prove that you could use proper orchestral incidental music and make it much more frightening and atmospheric." [44]

The film finally premiered to 600 fans at the Panopticon 95 as advertised, with all the cast and crew present, as Barry later recollected. "When it was first shown at Panopticon, it received terrific applause from a packed hall."[45]

Not everybody was as pleased — producer Ian Levine stormed out of the convention hall. "Half the music that we wrote had been removed. Without my knowledge. Which they would have had every right to do, if I hadn't been one of the producers."[46]

The music had been a bone of contention for the other producers, and for Barry. "I didn't like the music, which was far too overpowering and unsubtle, but it was insisted upon by the main financial backer who'd composed it!"[47]

Music aside, Barry was happy with the final film "On the whole I'm pleased with the result. I was trying to be true to *Doctor Who*'s traditions, and as it was aimed at *Doctor Who* fans, it needed to be true to their perceptions. At the same time I wanted it to stand alone so people who might pick it up in a shop wouldn't be confused. Considering what we were trying to do and the fact that we did it all for nothing and for fun, I think we achieved a lot."[48]

Barnfather was also pleased with the result. "It had gravitas and the general feedback from it was it was extremely good. I've never made anything I've been entirely happy with and I suspect if I ever do I'll probably retire."[49]

Response to *Downtime* was actually somewhat mixed, with Courtney's performance being highlighted as the stand-out part of the production. *DWM*'s Dave Owen concluded, "The undeniable star of the show is Nicholas Courtney, giving quite possibly his best performance ever as the Brigadier. There's a soft side to him, as demonstrated by the genuinely moving scene where he discovers, aboard his daughters houseboat, that he is a grandfather." [50]

One criticism of *Downtime* was that it tried to cram too many things into its short runtime (some fans would level a similar criticism at post 2005 *Doctor Who*, so at least in that respect it was ahead of its time!). In fact, *Downtime* is a curious mix of the old and the new, and it's actually quite jarring to see Sarah Jane and the Brigadier in the modern world with an alien menace that can infiltrate computer systems that would seem as alien to their 1970s counterparts as the Intelligence itself.

Where it succeeds most, though, is in humanising the Brigadier. It also serves as a cold reminder of what life is like for those left behind by the Doctor — Victoria has become jaded and removed from a society she never wanted or expected. It's no wonder she forms a bond with the Intelligence, perhaps the only identifiable element she has in this time period.

While the least effective element is the Yeti costumes, which really should have been shot in the dark, the production values generally are incredibly high for a film of this nature and it's not too far from what an early 90s series of *Doctor Who* shot on video tape might have looked like. Christopher Barry's direction also lends a credibility and style to the production that is absent from a number of other spin-off videos.

As well as its Panopticon premiere to the fans, a press launch was arranged a week later at Riverside Studios. With such high production costs, Reeltime had to ensure the film reached the widest audience possible to maximize sales and fortunately Barnfather negotiated a distribution deal that got the video into major high street retailers. With distribution secured, it was decided not to waste the opportunity and so Barnfather offered to re-package and re-release BBV's back catalogue and *Shakedown* onto the High Street. Barnfather is quick to deny any rivalry between him and Baggs, however. "I've had a number of people say to me 'was there a rivalry?' but Bill and I never had a problem, why would I? He is the only other person who ever got off their arses and done something."[51] Rivals or not, all spin-offs now carried the Reeltime logo, and Barnfather was essentially making money off his competitors.

Shortly after its High Street release, Virgin Publishing — who had a monthly range of past Doctor and present Doctor book length adventures — asked Marc Platt to novelise *Downtime* as part of their *Missing Adventures* range. While Platt made minimal changes to the story, he did include a brief cameo from both the second and third Doctors. Released in January of 1996, the book also featured a foreword written by Barnfather and an eight page insert of behind the scenes photos. The success of the novelisation of *Downtime* inspired Virgin to ask Andy Lane if he wanted to novelise *Wartime*, a request which he politely declined. "I honestly couldn't see it. I mean it's a short story, you'd have to put in a whole different plot, probably involving aliens but I really couldn't see it, it wasn't going to work."[52]

The story of *Downtime* doesn't entirely finish there. In 2012, producer Ian Levine shot new material for an extended version of the story. The material in question acts as a framing device for the story and stars Sylvester McCoy as the seventh Doctor. Although Levine asked permission of Reeltime and DSL before he constructed his new edit, it was done under the proviso that they had approval before anything was done with it commercially, as the new project was and is in breach of BBC copyright. Barnfather opined, "I think that's Ian getting a little bit carried away. I've seen it, he asked my permission before he did it, I think it's crap! I don't think it's right to produce a concept and then try to shoehorn it in to something else. We didn't make *Doctor Who*, we made *Downtime*. I certainly wouldn't agree to that being released and I don't think the BBC would either."[53] Levine would pitch the release to the BBC DVD range, who rejected it. McCoy would later distance himself from the project, claiming he was unaware of what the production would entail until he arrived on the day. Levine also asked Barnfather if he could do a similar thing to *Wartime*, which Barnfather declined.[54]

Some years later, another *Doctor Who* spin-off would attempt to incorporate a sequence from *Downtime* into one of their episodes. As script editor Gary Russell told Starburst Magazine. "We tried to get a clip of *Downtime* for *The Sarah Jane Adventures* at one point, but they wouldn't play ball. We wanted to use it in one of the sort of flashback sequences, and it would literally have been a clip — of Sarah with the Brigadier, I think. And the people behind *Downtime* said no."[55]

This is more than likely down to the complicated rights situation between the three producers. For many years *Downtime* was one of the few *Doctor Who*-related productions unavailable on DVD. This was simply due to the fact there were three different companies involved and negotiating such a process was a difficult one. Also unreleased was the hours of behind the scenes footage that was filmed with the intention of releasing a *Making of Downtime* video. Despite being advertised, the video was never finished, though the DVD did eventually materialise via Koch Media in November 2015, complete with a 70 minute *Making Of* feature.

The DVD release actually caused minor controversy when Mervyn Haisman's (co-creator of the Brigadier and the Yeti) granddaughter and executor of his estate issued the following statement. "It has been brought to my attention that Reeltime Pictures and One Media are releasing *Downtime*, the *Doctor Who* spin-off film made in 1995, on DVD. This is being done without my consent or permission. As Executor of the Haisman Literary Estate, and thus copyright holder of Lethbridge-Stewart, Professor Travers, the Great Intelligence and the Yeti I should have been approached over this. Attempts to negotiate have fallen on deaf ears, and my rightful claim has been refuted by the producers. I have now been forced to take legal action to protect the copyright of my grandfather, Mervyn Haisman, after their refusal to renegotiate an agreement made twenty years ago for a film made for straight-to-video release only."[56]

The claim was refuted by Reeltime Pictures, who responded via fan site, *Doctor Who News*. "Reeltime Pictures has been approached by Hannah Hatt regarding the agreement we signed with her grandfather, Mervyn, in 1995. As we explained to her, the agreement is still in force and covers any exploitation that we might choose to undertake. Certainly no other party involved in the project has raised an issue with their agreements and we have assured her that no renegotiation is necessary. There is little else we can do at this time other than to wait upon any legal representation she might make." [57]

The outcome of this issue has, at the time of publishing, yet to be determined.

Downtime certainly upped the game of spin-off productions — demonstrating what could be done on a still relatively small budget, with competent effects and action sequences, great character work and a broad range of locations. It also showed the limitations of low budget film-making in the realisation of the Yeti creatures themselves. As Barnfather admits "it's without doubt the biggest budget spin-off production ever made, but it hasn't made its money back and it properly never will."[58]

Andrew Beech also discussed the sales figures in an article in *TARDIS* magazine a couple of years later. "The DOWNTIME project was well received on the whole, but so far sales have recouped only half of the 56,000 pounds cost. So the prospects of making another film of that kind are not good."[59]

Indeed, nobody would attempt a production on this scale again, with *Downtime* proving the limited appeal of films like these. If there was a bigger audience out there it would need a bigger production and marketing budget to reach it and when you are dealing with money of that value, you might as well be making *Doctor Who* itself.

Chapter 15 — There's a Place in Hell for Me and My Friends

Early 1996 was a quiet time for *Doctor Who* spin-offs, at least in part due to the market becoming oversaturated. The last two years had seen nine major video releases, although Baggs later insisted. "It wasn't deliberate but the thing is the market is beginning to shrink."[1]

Another factor may have been the return of *Doctor Who* itself. While the show's revival had been a hot topic amongst the fan press and the tabloids ever since it disappeared from TV screens in 1989, there was very little in the way of actual news to back this up. But on the 10th of January 1996 Paul McGann was announced to the world as the eighth Doctor, in a $5million co-production between the BBC and Universal Television, overseen by executive producer Phillip Segal. The film would also feature a cameo from Sylvester McCoy, who would hand over the title to McGann.

Indeed it was McCoy who informed Baggs of the show's return. "I remember sitting in a convention and Sylvester turning to me and saying 'we're doing a film', very quietly and privately," with the actor revealing to Baggs "that he'd been cast and that there was this film going on. So my immediate reaction was, let's get a film crew together, which of course he was more than happy to agree to and that's how 'Bidding Adieu' came about."[2]

'Bidding Adieu' was a video diary of McCoy's time on the 'TV Movie', with Baggs sending Gatiss along with him to capture the mood of the event, even if they weren't actually allowed on set. "He [Segal] was very anti the whole thing, but then he saw it he said 'I wish I'd given you permission to do it'. Helen, my wife, was pregnant at the time, so I sent Mark Gatiss and a camera man. We didn't know what we were going to get so there is whole bit which is Mark Gatiss doing pieces to camera that we never used."[3]

Baggs had crossed paths with 'TV Movie' executive Phillip Segal several times at conventions before and after the film. "I made it my business that he knew who I was. He was a very intricate guy and we got on like a house on fire." So was Bill hoping that if the film went to a series, he might land a directing role on it. "It was spoken of but then I realised he was Mr all talk and no action."[4]

Ultimately, the 'TV Movie' failed to ignite the interest that was hoped for and so we will never know if any serious consideration would have been given to a Baggs-helmed American *Doctor Who* episode. In the end, the impact of the 'TV movie' was minimal. As Baggs himself puts it "[it] happened so quickly, then it was gone. It never presented any kind of threat at all."[5]

With a new series of *Doctor Who* back in development hell, Baggs returned to the *P.R.O.B.E.* series. Once again, Gatiss was asked to provide a script and he promptly began work on a story he called 'Ishmael's Star'. Gatiss had Jeffrey Holland in mind for the titular character and he later told Anthony K McCail that it was "about a war criminal who had some plan about a comet. It was going to be the last *P.R.O.B.E.* story, and it was going to be a prequel to the others. For no good reason! It was going to be about how Liz Shaw retired from Cambridge. Anyway I wrote about half of it, and then Bill Baggs didn't want to do it because it would be too expensive. So I worked on this other idea."[6]

Gatiss opted instead for a contemporary tale, entitled 'Unnatural Selection', but once this was delivered, instead of working on rewrites, Baggs had a different, additional request for Gatiss. "And then, in his cost-cutting way of wanting to shoot stuff back-to-back, Bill said 'Could we do a sequel to *Devil of Winterborne*?' which I didn't really want to do, I have to say."[7]

Despite his reservations, Gatiss turned around the sequel quickly. "I wrote the script, for 'The Ghost of Winterborne', which is about 50 minutes long, and I finished it, and I pressed the wrong button on my computer and it all went. I actually sat there and, instead of going crazy, I started again. Straight away! I had this extraordinary vivid mental picture of the whole script in my head. I worked right through the night. Bill was coming to pick it up the next morning, and I literally hadn't gone to bed. I was literally just finishing it when the doorbell rang, I said, 'You won't believe this, but I have just written this all again for the past nine hours!'"[8]

All the regular cast returned for the two stories, with 'Unnatural Selection' also featuring an appearance from Charles Kay. A regular face on both stage and screen, he was one of Baggs' favourite actors. "He I approached through his agent. I loved him in *Edge of Darkness*. There are a list of actors you want to work with and he was one of them and fate was on my side."[9]

Devil of Winterborne on the other hand, saw the surprise return of Charmain May, not least because she had been killed off in BBV's previous excursion into Winterborne. Gatiss again was reluctant to include her. "Bill said, 'It's a shame we can't have her back... Well, why don't we, anyway?' I was eventually persuaded that she could be the twin sister of the original character. I wasn't there on the day in question, and the line was inserted: 'Hello, I'm her twin sister.' When I saw it, I almost killed myself at the sheer horror of it! There are ways of introducing twins, but that's not one of them."[10]

'Unnatural Selection' and 'Ghosts of Winterborne' were shot over two weeks in the summer of 1996. To put this in some perspective, the average single camera drama with a fully experienced crew would expect to shoot five minutes of screen time a day, a day being around 12 hours. Both of these films are 50 minutes in length, so that would require a total of twenty days. Baggs later admitted his shooting schedule for this was a bit too ambitious. "What a fucking nightmare, I mean it was hilarious, but I think it was rather fanciful on my part." [11]

Needless to say the rest of the cast and crew found the schedule demanding. Patricia Merrick recalls it being "[n]ot so fun; the stress of filming back to back in the space of two weeks was hard."[12] With a limited crew, the cast once again had to take care of their own wardrobe, as Caroline John told an intimate audience at her *Wine and Dine* interview in 1999. "The last two were a bit hectic, we worked from about 8 o'clock in the morning until 12 at night on two. [and] I laid out the costume I'm wearing for day one, day two, day three day four of the first story, and again for the second, so I had about ten different changes. If you don't have a change, Bill will take a scene which you have played for day four in the story and put it in day two. So it makes no sense and makes you look crap. I'd say 'Bill, you cannot have me in a different costume, where I've only worn it for day four' so he can't do that so much." While it's standard practice for most dramas to shoot out of sequence, Baggs would also jump around in the shooting order on the day, as John went on to say. "He'd say 'right, we are going to use the minister's room' and I'd think 'wait a minute, is this story one or story two? What costume am I wearing? What are the lines?' I luckily learnt all the lines before I started and then you have no problem. But it was very short notice too, because usually on an ordinary film the costume lady would go to the first assistant and say 'what scene are we doing for the morning? What's the order?' so she could put out the costumes and know that 'Carrie's going to need costume one from story one and three in that order'. I had to do all that by myself and sometimes I'd come down and he'd 'say we've changed our minds'." [13]

Her husband, Geoffrey Beevers, had a similar experience, as he recounted at the same event. "I had the same. It was 'Unnatural Selection' where he obviously hadn't filmed enough shots of me reacting to the character, rising up out of the bed. So if you look at it carefully you'll see that he uses the same shot of me reacting in slightly different situations. And that's bad, it makes you look bad because you could have had six different reactions, and he's only got one for it, and he's used the same one again in a slightly different situation." [14]

Not only did Baggs jump around in the schedule, he also decided to sacrifice a very important area of production in order to accommodate his self-imposed demanding schedule. "One of the other things that was happening for me as a director, because of the set up time, I wasn't getting the number of shots that I needed. Part of the problem was because it was taking so long to light, which it would do, and I made a choice to compromise the lighting to get the number of shots."[15]

With a hectic production schedule and constant cost cutting, Gatiss had become increasingly infuriated with Baggs. "I was getting very frustrated with the fact that BBV was cutting corners constantly. Everything was being reduced. It really got to breaking point when we went back to the same school to film 'Ghosts of Winterborne' — which I guess was logical — but Bill wanted to film 'Unnatural Selection' there as well. And even though this school was a big place, we re-used some of the same areas. It was clearly the same place. It was just a very unhappy experience with the way the script was chopped up... I was just so tired by then."[16]

The climax of 'Unnatural Selection' featured an impressive transformation of Gatiss' Emerson into a creature supplied by the BBC Special Effects Unit, as played by Boom Operator, Ben Hicklin. The creature then had several bullets unloaded into it, a process that came as quite a shock to the unprepared Hicklin. "It physically knocked me back, because they're really powerful. Then the next one went off and I just felt myself going back, and going back, and going back and eventually I ended up in these shelves on the floor and I was in this filing cabinet."[17]

After a brief moment on the floor, Hicklin realised he had to get up again for the creature's final attack. "Because one of these charges hadn't gone off and I'd got these ear plugs in and my adrenaline was pumping, I was oblivious to everybody else. I was even oblivious to the camera... and [as] I fell on my front I thought 'thank God for that'. I felt this hand on my shoulder and Mike Tucker's assistant came over and pushed me down, and I just heard all this muffled shouting 'right don't get up, don't get up, don't do this, don't do that, don't do this' and I realised that one of these charges hadn't gone off and like everybody was going 'what do we do now, what do we do now 'and Mike was going 'ok, everybody remain calm', with his fire extinguisher and his goggles and headphones and his ear plugs and everything." [18]

Thanks to the rushed nature of the production, Mark Ayres also found the post production process a lot less enjoyable this time round. "As time went on they got increasingly cheap, and increasingly more hurried. By the time we did the last one I had two days to do it, with no money and no time."[19]

However, it wasn't all bad memories, with Peter Davison glad to be returning to the character of Purcell. "I quite enjoyed doing those. Bill got a bit more ambitious, and a bit better. I know Mark Gatiss, who wrote the scripts, and it was nice to play almost a bad part. You thought for a while he was very bad, which was nice." [20]

When watching these two films you can see how the penny pinching and tight schedule has had an adverse effect on the overall quality. Which is a shame, as both films contain some of the strongest camera work a BBV production had produced to date. There are some great uses of a crane in 'Ghosts of Winterborne', for instance, and the dream sequence/flashback at the opening of the film is also creatively shot. The climax of 'Unnatural Selection', meanwhile, sees some fantastic dolly work, while the lighting in places is also commendable, particularly in the aforementioned climax and in the prison scenes in 'Ghosts of Winterborne'. However, in both films it feels like the creative team have picked some choice scenes to concentrate on regarding camera work and lighting, while other scenes feel hastily put together, with flat lighting and poorly shot sequences that contain camera judders that would have been re-shot had there been more time.

There are also certain scenes where the cast look uncomfortable, either because they don't know where they are in the script or through sheer tiredness, and one can't help feeling it would have been better if they had had one more take. All this is a shame as, with a bit more care and attention, these stories could have been really special, with the series on the cusp of carving its own identity.

'Unnatural Selection' was released in October of 1996, preceded the month before by a re-branded *Devil of Winterborne*, with *Ghost of Winterborne* following in November.

DWM's Dave Owen was not a fan of 'Unnatural Selection' joking that it suffers from "Acute deteriorating sequelitis,"[21] although he was quick to praise Charles Kay and Mark Gatiss' performances, saying of the latter that his performance proved "as did his Edinburgh Fringe '96 revue, *The League of Gentlemen*, that he is an equally versatile performer and writer."[22] Ryan O'Neill of *Celestial Toyroom* was equally impressed by Gatiss. "Mark Gatiss puts in a chilling performance as the mysterious Emerson; unfortunately what is gained in performance is lost through sloppy writing and careless direction"[23] before continuing in similar scathing tones. "In execution, 'Unnatural Selection' just doesn't work as well as it could, the story flits from one scene to another with a frequency which makes the story difficult to follow, the actors perform their lines visibly struggling to make them sound credible."[24] Owen enjoyed 'Ghosts Of Winterborne' far more, though. "The series becomes far more watchable,"[25] he admitted, even if he does call the explanation behind the identical character "ridiculous" and still cites 'Devil' as his favourite episode. "This series has great potential, but 'The Devil of Winterborne' treats its audience with a great deal more respect that its successors, which amongst all the other blood, guts and offal, contain a large portion of tripe."[26] Katherine Rhodes on the other hand had only harsh words for the final tape. "The plot is virtually non-existent," she declared in *Celestial Toymaker*, concluding that "[a]part from the name of Liz Shaw, the story has absolutely nothing to do with *Doctor Who* and to call it a spin off smacks of cashing in on the fans."[27]

Perhaps most damaging for Baggs however was that in shooting these two films at the same time, he had been forced to make many compromises that would affect the company's reputation. This was the final film that Lighting Cameraman Dick Kursa (billed simply as lighting director on the film, with the camera operator being Andy Bell) worked on, for instance. It seems by neglecting the lighting, Baggs had alienated his long-time collaborator. "That was probably why, but also Dick was quite an expensive choice. I didn't begrudge him what he charged but I was beginning to realise the cost in making these things,"[28] says Baggs. It is also clear at this point that Gatiss and the rest of the cast's patience was wearing thin, and double banking (as Baggs admitted) was clearly a mistake. On the subject of the third film, Gatiss is frank in saying "it was a load of rubbish", before elaborating that "'Ghosts of Winterborne' was this unnecessary sequel, which spoiled the original one by being too literal." He was also disappointed with 'Unnatural Selection': "the whole thing wasn't as good as I wanted it to be. I sound like Tegan, but it wasn't much fun anymore."[29]

These are also the first two productions to receive largely negative reviews in the fan press, proving that while the fans would accept limited special effects and ideas that weren't realised to their fullest potential due to budget restraints, they would not accept lazy production and a lack of vision. Finally, the two films were also co-funded by both the Sci-Fi Channel and Who North America, who provided a small amount of money in return for the broadcast rights. Perhaps if a bit more care and planning had been taken these inexpensive (at least in broadcast terms) productions could have led to a series, but this wasn't to be. Indeed, while these films still made their money back, they were less successful than their predecessors and would make Baggs reassess his film-making strategy in the future.

Chapter 16 — Walking in my Shoes

Despite *Downtime* not being a financial success, Keith Barnfather was still keen to return to the world of *Doctor Who* related drama. His next venture began life in early 1997 and would come out of a conversation with composer Alistair Lock. "I was doing some music for a Reeltime documentary and Keith and I were talking about it. [I said] 'wouldn't it be fun to do another drama?' and he kept saying 'well it's budget you see, it all costs and we don't have much,' and I said 'It's the old thing, it could be set in a lift as long as it's interesting enough,' because as long as the characters are interesting, you can do it in a small place."[1] With this in mind, Barnfather came up with the idea of using popular third Doctor enemies, the Autons.

Nick Briggs had had an extended hiatus from the spin-off scene, his last film being 'Eye of the Beholder' in late 1995. During this time he'd done a theatre tour of *Brideshead Revisited* with Barbara Murray, Nigel Davenport and Richard Todd, followed by panto in Chelsea, then a stint in rep the following summer, and rounded 1996 off with another panto. By early 1997 he was brought in as a Marketing Assistant for the Sci-Fi Channel by friend John Ainsworth. It was then that Barnfather approached him about writing his new film and briefed him on what he required from the production. "I commissioned the script from Nick. It was 'I think we should do the Autons as we've got the rights, let's keep it tight; you know, in a warehouse' and Nick went away and wrote the story." [2]

Barnfather also came up with the title, as Briggs remembered. "Keith said 'I know what the title's got to be, it's got to be *Auton*. Because that says who's in it and also it begins with A so it will be at the top of the shelf."[3]

Briggs was also given a number of characters to include in the drama. "The original brief was to do a short, low-budget drama that involved the Brigadier, Kate and Cavendish to link to *Downtime*. And that was duly written over a period of a few months."[4] In writing the script, Briggs not only brought in David J. Howe to offer his advice on the Autons, but also used his experience of watching other spin-offs to create what he called a "*Doctor Who* feel plus something extra."[5]

"*Shakedown* was particularly satisfying because it achieved what it set out to create — a late 70s *Doctor Who*-style story with monsters and spaceships. What it set out to create, however, wasn't enough for me as a viewer. I came to the conclusion that there must be a more appealing mid-ground between the glorious but superficial crash-bang-wallop of *Shakedown* and the angst-ridden navel-gazing of some of my *Stranger* stuff." [6]

Initially, Barnfather was to direct the project but he relinquished this role so that Briggs could try his hand at directing for the first time. With Barnfather producing the project, Nick Briggs directing, and Bill Baggs acting as First Assistant Director, *Auton* would be the first time the three of them had worked on a drama together. However, Barnfather was forced to reconsider his position due to financial issues at Reeltime. This lead to he and Briggs discussing postponing the project for another year. "I didn't have the money to produce it at that moment. I felt it was unfair on Nick to postpone, who was desperate to direct it, he desperately wanted to do it."[7]

With this in mind, Barnfather approached Baggs about BBV taking on the project. "Bill didn't have anything in the pipeline, so I felt I was holding people back if I didn't let Nick do it and he asked Bill if he could do it and Bill, luckily, was really keen."[8] While Baggs may have been keen on the project, he was unsure about letting somebody else direct the film. "It came with several strings attached if you like. Normally the way I work is I commission a script and generally I am fairly involved with the script writing process, with the writer. I like to have my say basically. And here was a project that had already been commissioned by Keith and Nick Briggs was the writer, and basically they'd already worked out what they were going to do."[9] The trio discussed the proposition over dinner, as Briggs later told *DWM.* "After exchanging a few sharp words with us, [Bill Baggs] finished his food quickly and left the restaurant," and although shocked by this, "Keith commented that this was the first time he had seen evidence of the kind of dogged determination which enables Bill to get projects off the ground and finished against seemingly insurmountable odds."[10]

Baggs' main issue was letting Nick Briggs direct. BBV after all was essentially all about Baggs creating audition tapes that showed off his talents as a director. However it was some of the decisions that Baggs had made when directing previous dramas that had made Briggs even more determined to direct this film "because I'd been frustrated, being on the set of a lot of Bill's directing of my scripts. With him doing, from my point of view, all the wrong things — and adding in scenes that weren't required. So I said 'this script that I've written, you can have it but this script comes with a price attached, which is me directing it,' which Bill flatly refused to start with."[11]

Eventually Baggs relented and an agreement was reached that he would let Briggs direct, and Barnfather sold Baggs the rights to the production. Briggs recalls the moment Baggs gave in with much hilarity. "Bill was incandescent with rage about it. I remember his voice going all shrill and tense when he said, 'Why are you being so unreasonable?' But the truth was, that I felt sick and tired of my scripts being largely badly directed by Bill. I thought to myself, 'If I'm going to go through this torture again, I at least want to be the one responsible'. To be frank, I thought I'd be better at it than Bill." [12]

Once the deal was done, Baggs decided to turn the production into the first part of a trilogy. The July 1997 issue of *DWM* carried the announcement that *Auton* and *Auton 2* would be filmed back-to-back, with the second film being written by newcomer Tim Saward, entitled 'In The Blood', to be directed by Paul Vanezis. Perhaps because of his difficult experience on the previous two *P.R.O.B.E.* films and the unsatisfactory reviews they received, Baggs wisely abandoned this idea soon after it was announced and decided to concentrate on one film.

With production scheduled to take place in late June, the BBV team set about assembling all the required pieces. However, just under two weeks before production was scheduled to begin it was announced that Nick Courtney, under the advice of his doctors, was to pull out of the production due to stress and overwork. Briggs now reveals, that the star had, what he describes as "cyclical depression," [13] with Briggs spotting the signs during the preproduction process.

"I noticed in the run up to shooting this thing, he was becoming more and more difficult about all sorts of little things." He explains further. "My wife calls this perceptive narrowing, which is when you're worried about a big thing but you can't express it, so you make a fuss about lots of little things instead. And this was what Nick was doing, I remember us having a conversation about his peaked cap and all this kind of thing and his jumper and him saying 'I'm not very happy'. And eventually he just phoned up, and I think he just left a message and he said 'I just can't do it Nick, I'm so sorry, I'm so sorry to let you down', and I said to Bill 'that's it' and this is where Bill's amazing..."[14]

After a crisis meeting between Baggs and Briggs, it was decided not to pull the plug on the project, despite Briggs' reservations. "Without the Brigadier the whole thing unravelled and Bill just said... and this is one of the brilliant things about Bill, because he wasn't really much of a writer himself, he by default trusted you to come up with something... and he just said 'come on, you can come up with something can't you?'" [15]

Briggs set about rewriting the script. "Bill encouraged my re-write whole heartedly, even managing to get two significantly different drafts out of me in record time."[16]

By not having Nick Courtney as the lead, the film had lost its only official *Doctor Who* character, but this enabled Baggs to test the water with a theory he'd had for some time. "You don't need to spend £50,000 like *Downtime*. I was looking at spending £10,000 and if you got named actors, good as they are, what does the audience want? Are they still going to buy it? What's the selling point? So I started experimenting with the monsters."[17]

In fact Barnfather recalls that even before Courtney's illness there had been some resistance from Baggs about using BBC characters or the Reeltime-owned Kate and Cavendish. "I don't think Bill wanted to afford it, he didn't want my lot in it, I think both Nick and Bill felt they could do it a lot cheaper. I would have thought having the *Doctor Who* characters within it or the *Doctor Who* related characters within it would've improved sales, but I think Bill thought he could do it cheaper without them and Nick was happy to change the script."[18]

According to Briggs, however, it was simply a case of going where the story allowed. "I rewrote it in two weeks and obviously I had to get rid of the Brigadier and so I got rid of all the other characters, which caused me a lot of grief with Miles Richardson and his then wife Beverly Cressman. I don't think to this day she will talk to me, which is a great shame because she is a very lovely person. I remember a party at Keith Barnfather's, and Beverly was there glaring at me across the room, Miles said to me, 'look I've got no problem with you, I know these things happen,' and he said 'but she's never going to talk to you again,"[19] Briggs recalls with some amusement.

Cressman herself has no memory of being involved in *Auton*, much to Briggs' relief. "I think it's because in the moment, she was told she had a job and then she was told she didn't, and I was the reason she didn't have a job. But I couldn't make the story work with two characters that were sort of support to the Brigadier." [20]

With a little under two weeks to prepare this new script, how did Briggs rise to the challenge?

"It certainly wasn't a case of just taking all the Brigadier's lines and giving them to the new lead character. What I did is take the basis of the story — the people being in the warehouse and Autons coming back to life — and then reinvent it totally around there. There isn't a single scene from the original script in the new script." [21]

Rather than being put off by prospect of creating a new lead character, Briggs actually relished the chance. "I had the freedom to create a new leading character in a science fiction/mystery/adventure story — and, in common with many leading characters in science fiction/mystery/adventure stories down the years, he would be sharp-witted, vastly intelligent, slightly mysterious and a little testy. He would be created in the image of a tradition of leading characters, of which the Doctor is only an example — albeit a masterful one." [22]

Indeed Courtney, a very insecure actor, had already expressed his doubts to Briggs that he could be the hero the Brigadier was written as in the original script. This in turn led to Briggs doubting the character. "He is a very strong, capable character superbly acted by the very talented, splendid fellow Nick Courtney — but the character just doesn't sit comfortably in the leading role."[23]

When naming his new protagonist, Briggs had to look no further than the room he was writing in. "There was one of the many French's edition plays on my shelf and I just started looking through the names of cast and characters on them. Randomly. I saw Lockwood, Margaret Lockwood, and I thought 'Lockwood that's a nice name isn't it?'" [24]

With the new script delivered in record time, Briggs and Baggs set about casting the roles. This led to Briggs recruiting a number of actors he had worked with previously, including George Telfer as Winslet and Michael Wade as Lockwood. "I didn't know anything about his involvement with sci-fi or anything like that,"[25] remembers Wade. "All I can remember happening is that, as we were leaving, on the last night of the production I vaguely remember Nick saying something to me like 'Oh well. Cheerio, nice to have worked with you and if anything comes up in any of my writings that you'd be suitable for I'll give you a call.' To be honest I put it down to what quite often happens in this business when you hear something like that. Not a lot happens. I never really paid much attention to it. We kind of kept in touch and six months to a year later, Nick called me and said, 'I've got this thing I'd like you to do.' I was available, so I went along. To be honest I didn't really understand too much about *Auton* or the *Doctor Who* spin off connection or anything."[26] What was it that Briggs liked about Wade to cast him as his leading man? "I remember he had a fantastic voice and was lovely too. I thought 'he's got that sort of look' and thought he was brilliant."[27]

Another co-star Briggs recruited was Bryonie Pritchard. "I got cast as Doctor Sal because I was working in rep theatre in Chesterfield and Nick Briggs was in the cast, busily writing the *Auton* scripts I think, in his dressing room. He asked me to tape an audition in London for BBV and there as they say..."[28] Other cast members included Verona Chard as Janice, Andrew Fettes as Ramsey and Reece Shearsmith as Dr Daniel Mathews.

Having lost his usual Lighting Cameraman after the last *P.R.O.B.E.* film, Baggs asked Andy Bell to step into the position, having previously operated the camera on the *P.R.O.B.E.* films and the final *Stranger* film. Briggs found this an uneasy collaboration. "Andy Bell was always trying to prove to me that he knew a lot more than me all the time, which was true of course because he was a cameraman and I didn't know about cameras." This lead to an uneasy relationship between the two, with Briggs feeling Bell "fought me on every shot to start with."[29]

With Baggs overseeing the production as producer, it was time for Briggs to flex his muscles as a director. Unfortunately no amount of preparation could prepare him for what was to come.

"From the first day it was utterly sunk. Due to the kind of outrageous cock-ups which always seem to befall low budget productions, there were no cameras and no tape stock on the first day. Bill instructed the crew not to tell me, because he felt it might upset me. So, there I was, watching the sets being built, talking to the cameraman about how certain scenes were going to be shot — and everyone, including the cameraman, knew there were no cameras. Meanwhile, Bill was furiously cutting a deal with the studio manager for use of his cameras. Luckily, the deal was struck; however, not so luckily, the Nestene Energy Units (those pulsing globes) hadn't been delivered, and they were required for every scene to be shot that day. I had to get on the phone and persuade actors not initially called for that day to drop what they were doing and come to the studio as soon as they could. Consequently, we were left twiddling our fingers for hours."[30]

Despite his initial reservations Baggs now says he was actually quite happy to hand over some of the pressure to his colleague. "There was some element of relief but also frustration and some pride actually, that I could do it, the very thing that I really wanted to do, I was giving somebody else a chance. The thing is, being a director on those sort of low budget things, you are doing everything, so having a director actually makes it easier because you can share the work load. If he's directing he's got some investment in the project, so you've got two people who are working their bollocks off."[31] Despite this, things were far from harmonious between the two on the shoot. "Bill was not happy and was interfering heavily on the set, which was unsettling me and upsetting the crew, who felt there should be only one chief. He further alienated himself from everyone in a meeting of the whole team (excluding the cast, thank goodness) by telling us that he'd viewed the rushes and that he thought they weren't particularly good. It was a nasty business."[32]

While Briggs was clearly offended by Baggs' interference, Baggs feels things weren't as "nasty" as Briggs makes out. "I wouldn't say we didn't get on, it's just creative tension. I mean, somebody is paying the bills, and somebody wants to spend money, so there is conflict and somebody's got to make choices. I mean, I'm sure I can be difficult to work with but I would point the mirror at him and say he can be difficult to work with too. We are all creative types so it's inevitable."[33] Though this conflict may have caused friction with the production staff, Bryonie Pritchard doesn't remember it filtering down to the cast. "I don't recall tension, because the shooting schedule was pretty tight anyway and any spare time was spent in the green room watching a video of this extraordinary as-yet-unheard-of comedy trio that Reece Shearsmith was part of. In retrospect how amazing to see the early days of Tubbs and Legs Akimbo etc."[34]

Ultimately it was Baggs who resolved the situation much to the surprise of Briggs, speaking in 1998. "Bill's solution was swift, brutal and, it has to be said in hindsight, rather selfless. He could see that, for whatever reason, his presence on set was creating tension, so he was going to keep away and let us get on with it. He also decided that his shooting schedule wasn't working and that I should take over the scheduling."[35]

Briggs pulls fewer punches when telling this part of the tale in 2016. "Luckily, I had somehow got the loyalty of the cast and the crew, and they were quite frosty towards Bill and he sensed that he was very unpopular on the set, because he was preventing things from being done because he was trying to do it his way and I was trying to do it mine. And this is what he said to me: 'well I'm going to let you make your own mistakes.' You know, he didn't say 'you know, you're brilliant and you can do this really well, I'll let you get on with it.' He was basically saying 'you know you're screwing this up, there's nothing I can do to stop it now, so I'll leave you to mess it up', so off he went." [36]

Auton was shot over three weeks during June and July of 1997 at a studio in Southampton, as Alistair Lock recalled. "Theoretically, it was a controlled environment, it was made to look like a vast warehouse, but it was the clever filming of the same corridor and boxes and so forth, so it looked much bigger than it was."[37] The studio was again part of BBC Southampton and an agreement was reached on the condition that they could only shoot between 9:30am and 5:30pm — a comparatively short day's working for video and film production. Briggs later recounted the structure of his day to *DWM*. "A typical day for me on *Auton* proceeded as follows: 8.30am arrival at studio; 10am start shooting, hectic day's work; push studio staff's patience to limit by working past the already extended 7.30pm deadline; go home; have long conversation on the phone with Bill about the previous day's rushes and where I was going wrong (actually quite helpful in some cases); plan next day's schedule and shooting script until midnight; get up at 4am to continue planning; continue planning on train to studios... It was an exquisite kind of torture."[38]

Auton lead, Michael Wade found this production unlike anything he had worked on before. "It was completely different. First of all it was science fiction, which is not something I had ever really been involved with. *Auton* was extremely good to work with because it was very efficient how they got it together in such a short time. Very concentrated. And you just had to get it right, you couldn't mess around with take after take after take, which is the way I like to work anyway. I always like to be very well prepared. I can't bear some of these actors who can't even learn three lines on the trot. And we were very professional like that. We worked hard at it in the dressing room so that when we came to do a take if there was anything the matter with the take it wasn't anything to do with the actors." [39]

It was also an unfamiliar process for Telfer. "We were almost completely in a studio. It was a completely new experience for me, I hadn't done very much screen stuff. So I did find it really interesting having come from a lot of theatre. It was brilliant to do so little and be so intense. I really enjoyed that. I really had to rein myself in because I'm a theatre actor, most of my experience had been in theatre and you know a twitch becomes a convolution on stage because I used my face a lot on stage. It was quite hard but the end results were really pleasing."[40]

No doubt because of his performance background, Briggs found all the actors easy to work with and full of ideas, being particularly impressed with George Telfer. "The character of Winslet, who's the main Auton chap? As originally conceived in the Brigadier script, he never said a word, but the old sci-fi thing of being taken over and acting like a bloody zombie is just so tedious, and I didn't want that. George Telfer, who played Winslet, came up with so many interesting ideas."[41] One such idea affected the entire scoring process of the film, recalls Telfer. "I had a clipboard and I was walking round the archive checking things off, and I said to Nick, 'why don't I just hum something as I'm walking round ticking things off' and he said 'yeah do it' and I don't know why but the tune 'Tea for Two' came into my head and then for some reason I started doing it a bit out of kilter and they used that for the whole music, those three notes in that kind off kilter rhythm." [42]

Briggs' willingness to take on board other people's suggestions also impressed Wade. "[Assistant Director] David Rowston said one day 'Y'know Nick, you've invented this character Lockwood and here we are filming him and the whole thing seems to be going very well but you haven't given him an entrance. He just sort of appears.' And Nick thought about it and said 'you're right' which led to Lockwood's entrance with the huge warehouse doors. We felt before we had it in the can that we were on to something. Nick and I did a lot of talking and developing of the original thing. And the rest as they say is history!"[43] Ultimately, Briggs relationship with his actors as a director was down to his roots as an actor, as Telfer explained. "Nick is a very fine actor so he understands the actor's p.o.v as a director, he has very clear vision of what he thinks will work."[44]

Though things were running more smoothly with Baggs off the set, Briggs reveals his producer did cause further issues, this time concerning Wade.

"Bill thought he was dreadful,"[45] recalls Briggs. Apparently after viewing the films rushes, he had harsh words about the star. "He just said 'what is this guy doing? He's ridiculous, he's terrible'. I mean can you imagine? You're pouring all your effort into making something good and you've got your boss on the phone telling you what you're doing is worthless and your leading man is terrible. I just had to think 'You're just wrong Bill'."[46]Whatever criticisms can be levelled at *Auton*, it's doubtful many would point the finger at Wade's performance as the weak link. And if Baggs was not a fan he could easily have asked for him not to return in the film two sequels.

So why did Briggs think Baggs interfered so much?

"I think he just thought I couldn't run a shoot,"[47] he theorises, before expanding further. "On whatever level, consciously or not, whether he remembers this or not, I think he thought 'I'll let Nick do this, after a few days he'll fail because he's just not got it in him to do it and then I'll come in a rescue it and everyone will say oh my goodness, Bill, you're amazing.'"[48]

According to the September edition of *DWM*, *Auton* wrapped on Friday July 4th, although, a number of pick up shots were done at Baggs' mother's house sometime after. From there Briggs and Baggs entered post production, where their less than harmonious relationship resurfaced. "The editing was even worse, with Bill and I not seeing eye-to-eye on most of the edit. At the root of it was a lack of trust between us."[49] Briggs shed more light on these disagreements in a later interview. "He promised to edit the film as I wished, then reassess it wearing his producer's hat. Suddenly, he'd pronounced over the edit suite, 'I'm short-circuiting that process'. Without dwelling on details, the net result was that there were two sequences which were not edited as I would have liked (the battle and the first zapping of an Auton — two scenes which I regard as key to the production's action based impact)." [50] The situation was a frustrating one for Briggs, who recalls further details more recently. "He did all sorts of things that I didn't agree with, but made me sit there and watch him as he did them. And I'd say 'oh you've put that scene in the wrong order, those don't make sense like that' and he'd say 'no, it works, the grammar of film making tells me that it works' and he used to say things like that and I'd say 'yes but you've now put that bit of information in the wrong place in the plot' and all sorts of things like that."[51] Briggs also cites a number instances when bloopers were left in the final film. "He left in all sorts of silly mistakes that could have been cut out. Camera shadows, a moment where Reece Shearsmith is clearly not actually holding a gun when he's supposed to be... It was most odd." [52]

Baggs later attempted to put this process and series of disagreements into perspective. "There are things that I said and would have done differently, but at the end of the day I think the bottom line is what you see on the screen, and I think the reaction to it has definitely been very good."[53]

It is worth noting that the majority of these disagreements were aired in various *Making Of* features at the time; evidently neither Baggs and Briggs felt by sharing them that they were doing either themselves or each other an injustice. However, this marks another production that ended with Baggs falling out with someone and the effects this had on their relationship would be felt later.

Auton was released in October of 1997 through mail order and specialist shops and received a re-release on the high street the following year through Reeltime Pictures, complete with a *Making Of* documentary. *Celestial Toyroom*'s Karen Davies said "*Auton* is an enjoyable, but undemanding 57 minutes. It could have been so much better had the direction been less pregnant pause and more realistic dialogue."[54] *DWM*'s Dave Owen had similar criticisms of the direction. "Briggs lingers in long shot on talking but inanimate characters," but praised Wade. "Boldly, this production features no actors who can be associated with *Doctor Who*. It does, however, promote the skills of actor Michael Wade. His character, Lockwood, blessed with the X Factor, is so superciliously smug and patronising that he demands your attention."[55] Anthony Brown of *SFX* also enjoyed Wade's performance. "Michael Wade is impressive as Lockwood. It's hinted that there's more to this character than meets the eye, and it's worth buying *Auton* just to ensure later instalments get the chance to reveal his secrets."[56]

Auton is the most *Doctor Who* like of all BBV's films. It is also the most B-Movie in its direction. To echo the sentiments of previous reviewers, shots linger for far too long — but the faults aren't necessarily down to Briggs. He later revealed that this occurred for the purely practical reason that under the tight schedule he had to drop a lot of the more intricate close ups and use the master wide shot to tell the story. In fact, it is clear Briggs knows what he wants but is let down by some poor lighting, camera work and editing. The absence of Dick Kursa is never more obvious than on this film, and had Baggs directed it, it would most likely have faced the same problems.

More positively, Alistair Lock's score and sound effects are some of the most accomplished of the entire spin-off range. The script is tight and well-paced and all the actors respond well to Briggs' direction. It's just a shame the visuals don't quite hold it together.

Bill Baggs looks back on the production with fondness "I think *Auton* is really atmospheric, though I think in the first one there could be more shocks per se to make it more dramatic and fast-paced."[57] But he is less kind about Briggs' direction. "I don't think Nick is a very good director and I don't mean this in a nasty way; he is a great director of audio but what I've seen of his [video work] on *Auton* I wouldn't ask him to it again." [58]

Original producer, Keith Barnfather, was more complimentary. "I thought they did a fantastic job, it's a marvellous film but I think a lot of that is the influence of... I wouldn't say I had, but I would say that first one there is a lot of me in that first one." [59]Despite all the challenges he faced, Briggs now looks back at his experience on *Auton* as "Largely Positive" having re-watched it recently. "It's on YouTube at the moment and I did watch it again the other night."

And his thoughts on it some 20 years later? "The funny thing is, it does sort of hold together even though it's a whole club of compromises."[60]

Chapter 17 — New Life

In a somewhat surprising move, considering *The Stranger* audios' apparent lack of success, BBV made a return to the format in 1998. Previous efforts to bring *Doctor Who* to audio had been enjoyed by fans, but led to no continuing series — the last attempt being the two Pertwee radio serials, 'The Paradise of Death' and 'The Ghosts of N-Space'. While great on a nostalgic level, they did little to prove the versatility of audio as a viable format for shows like *Doctor Who*. Indeed the best example of a continuing audio series at that point would probably have been Baggs' own AV series. Despite his previous attempts to make official *Doctor Who* audios being dismissed he remained determined to bring the characters back to the medium.

It appears Baggs may have even approached the BBC for a second time around this time, as Nick Briggs recalls. "He phoned me up, while I was at work at the Sci-Fi Channel and he said 'I've asked the BBC if I can do *Doctor Who* audios and they've said no,' and I said 'ah well, there you go,' and he said 'but I've decided to do it anyway!' That's literally what he said to me and I remember it because I was quoting it to people two seconds after he had said it to me."[1]

And so with no *Doctor Who* on the horizon in any format and Baggs not willing to take no for an answer, a new incarnation of fandom's favourite Time Lord was born. The first season of BBV's new audio venture would feature seven brand new plays under the banner of *Audio Adventures in Time and Space*, and six of them would star Sylvester McCoy and Sophie Aldred as The Professor and Ace, respectively. These plays would tread closer to the line in terms of copyright violation than any of the productions that had come before them.

Before commissioning the scripts, in fact, Baggs ensured that his lead actors were ok with the perhaps dubious identities of their characters. "Sophie bless her was up for it totally 100%, Sylvester took a little bit of persuasion because of the legal ramifications, but once he started doing it he loved it"[2] During his *Wine and Dine* interview in 1999 McCoy recalled his initial concerns. "Bill Baggs approached Sophie and said would we carry on doing it and the big mistake — and I remember thinking that at the time — was calling the character Ace. If we'd have called it *The Professor and Companion* or Professor and something else we would have gotten away with it. Professor is not a copyrighted name and Ace is, but we made them anyway."[3]

Aldred too thinks there could have been a way to do the series without crossing the line. "I think we could have got away with it, if it had been Alf. Which was Ace's initial name, so that was such a shame because Bill was a maverick and he was flying close to the edge."[4] Writer Tim Saward (who would write the third story in this season) was briefed about the copyright issue before writing. "I remember him [Bill] explaining Sophie Aldred is playing a character called Ace, but what does that mean? If she plays a character called Sophie she can never play another character called Sophie? He was very persuasive and it was all about the art of the possible and The Professor made complete sense too."[5]

The Professor and Ace it was; and Baggs commissioned several writers to pen this first season, including *P.R.O.B.E.* writer Mark Gatiss.

Gatiss' star was on the rise at this point, his comedy quartet *The League of Gentlemen* having just recorded a radio series for the BBC with a TV version just over a year away. Despite his career being on the rise, he still found time to submit several stories to the BBC's newly established *Doctor Who* Past Doctors book range. "I was skint. It's true! Everything was going really well, but there was no money coming in at all. It had been a while since I'd done one, and I put in the proposal for three thinking, 'maybe they'll commission them all!' They were called 'Fathoms of Doom', 'The Roundheads' and 'Cromwell's Dust'."[6]

Range editor Stephen Cole was a fan of historicals and commissioned the second Doctor novel, 'The Roundheads', from Gatiss, but passed on the other two ideas. Thus, when Baggs came to do his first two audio plays and asked Gatiss if he had anything he could submit and turn around quickly, Gatiss offered both to Baggs, who duly accepted. Both scripts were written within a week, with the titles being changed from 'Cromwell's Dust' to 'Republica' and from 'Fathoms of Doom' to 'Lords of Silence' and finally 'Island of Lost Souls' upon instruction from Baggs to Gatiss: "ooh it might look a bit funny if BBC Books saw them"...as if they'd care! It's a shame, as 'Cromwell's Dust' is such a lovely title..."[7]

Interestingly, *DWM 263* announced that the first two plays were to be written by Andrew Whitelock. So while Gatiss may have been sceptical in 2003 that the BBC wouldn't have cared about these productions, at the time he appeared to have been more worried and considered using a pen name.

The first two plays were recorded at Intergalactic Arts or IGA Studios, on Woolworth Road in Elephant and Castle, previously used to record three *AV* productions.

Sophie Aldred was less than impressed with the studio space. "The room we recorded it in was somebody's basement, and it was a bit damp and a bit cold. But there was Mark and there was Bill and all these people I'd known from the convention circuit. I just wanted to do justice to such an excellent script."[8]

The rest of the cast of the two plays included a host of BBV regulars — John Wadmore, Bryonie Pritchard, George Telfer, Michael Wade and — having now put their differences aside — Nick Briggs.

The first play was directed by Baggs himself, but the second release would see Briggs return to the fold after his distressing experience on *Auton*. Why then, did he return to BBV? "I was sucked in because I was working at the Sci-Fi Channel and wanted to be acting, directing, doing sound design and music! Bill gave me another opportunity to do what I loved most, bless him."[9]

"I think this was possibly my first experience of directing a script which I hadn't written. Inevitably, then, I was tempted to tamper. Luckily for me, when I phoned Mark Gatiss, who's a friend anyway, he said to me something along the lines of 'Marry him, murder him, do what you will with him...' which is me paraphrasing his paraphrasing of Sir Arthur Conan Doyle telling someone what they could do with a dramatisation of one of his Sherlock Holmes stories. Basically, he didn't mind me changing it. So, I did quite a lot of rewrites. I introduced more spooky stuff when the people in the base on Greenland start recalling the troubles they've been having. I also rewrote a lot of the Professor's lines, making him less all-knowing. I think I gave Ace more gutsy stuff to say. I completely changed the ending, making more of the big insects." [10]

Aldred was certainly happy to be back in her old role again, this being the first time she had played Ace since 1993's 'Dimensions in Time'. "I just thought it was a brilliant idea to do it on audio. I was just delighted to be working with Sylvester again and such a great team of people."[11] After his initial reluctance to sign up, McCoy too was glad of the chance to continue in his almost-Doctor role. "They're good fun, it's nice, I enjoy it because I did enjoy playing *Doctor Who* a lot and so I enjoy going back and doing it. And also you go to conventions and there was a time when people were frustrated because they weren't getting any stuff, you know they wanted more, they were hungry and they were sad that *Doctor Who* had died so it felt really good just to keep that bubble going. You give more stuff to the fans so they could enjoy it and there was more to talk about conventions so that was really pleasing." [12]

On the first day of recording, *DWM* asked Aldred if she was worried about returning to a character she hadn't played in five years. "I actually hadn't really thought about it before walking in this morning. I suddenly thought. 'Oh wow... can I still do it?' I'd almost forgotten what I did. But it was so bizarre because as soon as we started we just fell very easily into it."[13] Sylvester McCoy's feeling on the matter was similar. "The relationship is very much the same as it was before. I think it had got to a very good state by the time we finished doing *Doctor Who*. What is nice is to progress with that strong relationship. I'm enjoying playing a character that has the kind of depth that I wanted to bring to it if I'd done the fourth season. I feel as though we are now doing the fourth season."[14]

Nick Briggs was delighted to be directing Sylvester for the first time but also a little insecure. "Sylvester is a less communicative actor during a recording. He's far more likely to phone you up beforehand and talk at length about the historical or geographical accuracy of the story. This was certainly the case with 'Island of Lost Souls'. I think he'd even phoned up the Greenland Tourist Office or Embassy or whatever. He likes his 'intellectual' discussions BEFORE the acting starts. In the studio, he's very focused on his work. It's often very difficult to get him to look up from the script and talk to you while you're directing him. With 'Island of Lost Souls', sometimes I felt that he might be about to explode. I'd be making suggestions about changing his performance, and he'd be staring at the script. Being paranoid myself, there were a few points when I thought he was about to look up and say something like, 'And who the hell are you to tell ME what to do?!!'. But, of course, Sylvester isn't like that at all. He's just concentrating very hard on getting it right. But there's nothing mechanical about his performance; it's all raw energy and instinct. Consequently, you can't really guarantee what he's going to give you each time. His performance will totally change from one take to the next, whether you say anything to him or not. I find that very exciting. He's also a very warm, disarming person, and if you hit the right note with him, you can tap into his cheeky sense of humour. He can be a bit like a naughty schoolboy sometimes, especially when he knows he's got something wrong. He sort of plays this game that he's hoping I haven't noticed. But he's very clear about certain choices he makes. He's very keen not to make the obvious choice. He likes to be fascinated rather than scared in the face of danger, for example." [15]

The CDs were announced to the fan press and released in April of 1998. BBV told *Celestial Toyroom* they planned to release two CDs every other month. The first two plays went down very well with fandom. Karen Davies of *CT* said, "Both stories are wonderful. The beauty of them is that they are good, simple tales with effective characterisation. Both McCoy and Aldred are superb. McCoy especially — he succeeds in being the Doctor he should have been following 'Survival'."[16]

While fandom was happy that *Doctor Who* was back (almost), Briggs was less than pleased with his play, due to post-production issues. "Unfortunately, this was rather spoilt by some very mediocre post-production. I had envisaged huge, growling insects, lots of machine gun fire and squelchy, ghastly disembowelling going on. What I got was a few pistol shots and some strange electronic twittering which was no doubt labelled 'insects' on some sound effects CD. Also, the music was taken from *Auton* and faded up and down rather limply at certain, mostly inappropriate, points. However, despite all this, the clarity and simplicity of the story and performances communicated remarkably well and it's been just about the most popular of the CDs." [17]

The liner notes of the CD credit post production to Alistair Lock, however Briggs disputes this, believing it to have been done by someone else. Indeed, the work itself seems at odds with Lock's usual high standards. So it may be the case that Lock provided the music and was wrongly credited for the post-production work, or an early demo version was released instead of the final master.

These first two CDs would be some of the strongest the range ever produced. It is clear just from these scripts that Mark Gatiss understands the format of *Doctor Who*. His characters are well defined and his dialogue is rich. 'Republica' is a brave new take on *Doctor Who*, at least compared to its TV output. It deals with a side step into an alternative time line and wouldn't look out of place in the modern series of *Doctor Who,* while 'Island of Lost Souls' is a more traditional Hinchcliffe and Holmes type story with a sprinkle of Nigel Kneale and John Carpenter, to boot.

The third release of the season was written by newcomer Tim Saward. Saward was a recent graduate who had written and acted in various low key A-Level plays and fringe productions. In an attempt to solicit work he sent his CV to any production company he thought might be interested in his scripts, and being a *Doctor Who* fan this included BBV.

His first commission was an ultimately abandoned script for *Auton 2*, of which more later, but with Gatiss' two plays yet to be released Baggs gave Saward a basic brief. "It had to be two CDs and it had to use Sylvester for just one recording day; that was also a budget thing, so basically he could only be in a maximum of 50% of the scenes and if you think of it that way that sort of affects the balance of it."[18] With the first two plays being single discs, why was Baggs so set on this play being a double disc? "They were working on two single CDs and that was all very well," recounts Saward, "but the yield of a single CD wasn't very much so he wanted to do one that was longer and double the length. Which is a very dangerous remit to be given if you haven't really done one of those before, because that's a lot of story that you need to feed into two and half hours."[19] The script was written in two weeks and based on Shakespeare's *The Tempest*, with the finished play being almost a first draft. Baggs, of course, was notorious for giving writers quick turn arounds and perhaps as a result some of his productions suffered. Nevertheless, 'Prosperity Island' entered production shortly after the two Gatiss scripts were recorded.

Saward may have been an untested writer, but he rose to the challenge undeterred by his lack of experience, and Baggs also asked him to co-direct the play. Perhaps as a reaction to his experiences on *Auton*, where Baggs was deemed to be too controlling, he stepped back on this production and let Saward direct as he pleased "He tended to just let it happen in my case, and that also has issues in the sense that you're not getting direct feedback. I don't know if it was a very supportive relationship, in the sense that he never said 'oh don't do this' or 'well it must be like this.' If anything he was a bit more of a distant figure, in that in the recording sessions and in the writing process."[20] In casting the play, Saward approached two friends from university, Dan Riley and Clare Macmillan. Polly Pritchett was recruited as a friend of BBV's and Alistair Lock would record any additional parts himself during the editing process. Returning to the BBV fold was Peter Miles, last seen in 'More than a Messiah' along with Sophie Aldred.

Miles was happy to be back. "It was a very, very good script. It needed a bit of rehearsal but I loved doing it because I was playing Prospero [now Projoy]. There was a lovely trial scene. I love doing things to do with court rooms."[21] Saward himself took on the role of Gabriel. "It was to save money really. If you want an extra part, then the only way to get that extra part is to say 'well I'll do that one for no extra money' and then you can put it in there. The reason I needed the number of parts that I needed was because the whole thing was an allegory on *The Tempest*. so Gabriel was an allegory and you couldn't really lose that character."[22] *The Tempest* is Aldred's favourite Shakespeare play and she counted this story amongst her favourites of the time. Miles also approved, citing Shakespeare's stories as being adaptable to many genres. "Shakespeare, his plays are so real, put them into modern parlours in the 20th century or whenever so much can be adapted by simply changing the characters."[23]

McCoy also seemed to be a fan of the script, as Saward recalled in an interview with website *Megabyte Modem*. "Sylv was very nice about the script. He said it was a good one. He worked so hard that first day and he hated long speeches, especially with technobabble, and of course I gave him tons even though I'd been warned! I liked him a lot. We let him have lots of retakes, cos, hey, he's the Doctor. I was too shy to interact with him much and didn't direct him at all." [24]

The play was released in May of 1998 and received less positive reviews than its predecessors. *DWM's* Dave Owen said "'Prosperity island', the only double CD, is by far the weakest,"[25] citing the lack of involvement of Sylvester McCoy as a major flaw. Owen Morris of *Dreamwatch Magazine* also found flaws in the length of the play. "'Prosperity Island' falls slightly apart during the second CD: the emphasis switches from the emotional dynamics of the Professor, Ace and the somewhat reactant inhabitants of the island to the political intrigue and backstabbing that results because of the continent's dominant female leader disappearing.[26] Saward agrees with these criticisms. "It's not surprising really. At the time it was the first thing I'd done so I was a bit disappointed, but I think if anything it was probably quite generous. It's just too long — it just doesn't get to the places it needs to go to fast enough."[27] Saward also believes that the way the production was handled has a lot to do with the outcome. "He [Bill Baggs] gave me feedback afterwards, but it was only really afterwards. Maybe it was to do with his personality and my personality and that's it, and maybe I just gave the impression that I was really confident and knew what I was doing. And obviously I didn't and he just sort of backed off. But he was a bit disappointed with how some of it turned out and you know, so was I, and maybe it would have been better if there was bit more engagement over the content because I think we tried to do it all in a big hurry and maybe he was just focused on other things." [28]

If there is one criticism that could be levelled at 'Prosperity Island' it is one that should have been spotted earlier by the producer or script editor, and that is that it's too similar to 'Republica'. Both deal with ousted leaders trying to regain their throne. The length of the play is also an issue — while it lends itself to some great character development and never feels like it's forcing exposition on you, it simply takes too long to get between points A and B. Nevertheless, there are great performances of some fantastic dialogue, and the court room scenes particularly stand out.

During this time Baggs was still working full time at BBC Nottingham and trying to plan the second instalment of the video series *Auton*. Feeling the pressure mounting and having pushed back the release of the next CD, he asked John Ainsworth (who had had a small role in 'Republica') to come on board as assistant producer and handle the audio range. "I was effectively running the whole range. In terms of working with scripts, some of this was already in motion. Things had already been commissioned, people had already been approached so I was just getting all the scripts together and coordinating it all and getting it into studio and getting it to work."[29]

The next two plays to be commissioned were from Scotland based writer Mark Duncan. These plays were dubbed "Ace Specials" and featured very little of Sylvester McCoy, who had other work commitments at the time. Duncan had previously written for *DWM*, and had submitted a video script to BBV. "After having seen 'In Memory Alone', I submitted a script on spec in 1994 entitled 'Avatar' — a producer's dream of one set/location and six characters. Unfortunately, circumstances prevailed and it wasn't until July 1998 that Bill, looking for writers for the Audio Adventures, unearthed 'Avatar' from a box and asked me to submit some story briefs/outlines."[30]

Duncan's first play was developed as 'The Dorsai Companion' but was released under the title 'The Left Hand of Darkness' in July 1998, and featured a minimal cast with Sophie and Miles Richardson's Dorsai being the two main characters, while Ainsworth took on the role of the computer.

Apart from a short interview on BBV website little is known about Duncan, with Baggs having been sent some potential scripts from him but never meeting him. Saward — who had since started helping out BBV with the administration side of things — didn't take to him. "I knew very little about him, I still know very little about him. I don't know if he carried on with it. I just found him a bit... I spoke to him on the phone and I just remember it being a bit of a gruelling experience. He just seemed a bit bitchy to me but maybe it was me."[31] Saward concluded, "I wasn't in love with the plays. I wasn't in love with him, he was a right git!" [32]

John Ainsworth also found him difficult. "He was a very odd guy. I never met him but I did have to deal with him on the phone. He had a very grand idea about himself, he thought he was a quite important and clever writer and sort of thought he could make these sort of demands. He wanted us to make sure that all the actresses in the productions that he wrote for received a bunch of flowers, which we never did." [33]

With McCoy unavailable, Duncan had pulled selected dialogue for the Professor out of previously recorded scripts. This meant it could be inserted into the recordings to give him a small presence in the plays. However, with 'Prosperity Island' being a double disc, the release date of the 'Left Hand of Darkness' was pushed back two months. This gave BBV time to record original dialogue to be used in the plays, as Ainsworth recollects. "It would only take 15 minutes to do it because there was so little of it needed. So all the Doctor's dialogue was written by me, because I just thought 'here's an opportunity to do it' but I remember telling Mark Duncan that I'd done this and said 'look I'm very sorry you must have gone through a lot of trouble to find this dialogue' but he wasn't happy at all. I said 'but surely you can see it's better to have original dialogue than just nicking stuff from other plays?' But he didn't see it that way." [34]

'The Left Hand of Darkness' is an unconventional love story. A two-hander performed beautifully by Richardson and Aldred, the scene where Ace reminisces about her Grandmother and describes her mother as a bitch is beautifully underplayed, and in a few lines we really feel as though we know the two characters to whom she refers. Richardson delivers an accomplished performance, managing to portray an emotionless robot so sympathetically you can almost believe this robot has fallen in love.

Aldred was very happy to be given centre stage on this production and appreciated the chance to explore the character more. "I think Bill recognised that there was a lot with the character of Ace that could be done. So that was a brilliant opportunity for me to really develop the character even further."[35] Richardson, on the other hand, feels the production wasn't entirely successful. "It brought up the age old problem of how you make a robot sound interesting. I personally don't think I succeeded, but it led the way into the audio sci-fi world and I've had much fun working on those over the last 15 years or so. I think the producer was more interested in getting a semi-nude photo of Sophie for the front cover of the CD than he was in my performance."[36]

The second special was 'The Other Side' (originally 'Mortal Coil') which featured Ainsworth's then partner Jack Galagher, Jane Burke and the return of Aldred's other 'More than a Messiah' co-star, Barbara Shelley. Delighted to be working with Shelley again, Aldred found the emotional intensity of the script was enhanced by their relationship, as she explained on the day. "At certain points the energy in this tiny little recording studio was palpable, and working with Barbara, who was only 5 feet away... was a very charged atmosphere and I love that."[37]

Duncan's script gave Aldred some incredibly emotional scenes to play that helped her differentiate this Ace from her *Doctor Who* counterpart. "Well, I must admit the character is rather like me. For example, the very emotional and tense one we've just done ('The Other Side'). That one for me has been like drawing on my own personal experience really, my own feelings. Whereas in some of the others like 'Republica' or 'Prosperity Island', as soon as the character gets a bit less involved and more reactive rather than proactive I do find myself playing maybe the character that I used to play years ago."[38]

While the weaker of the two plays, Aldred is again on strong form, playing the sadness and the anger with such conviction that this play could possibly be a career defining performance for her. Barbara Shelley plays the loving and sympathetic grandmother incredibly well but it's the coldness underneath it that sells the performance as an alien pretending to be Ace's beloved nan.

The advert for these productions read "Exclusive! See more of the new Sophie Aldred Portfolio in the Ace Special CD inlays." Bill, always looking for a way to grab attention and boost sales, had convinced Aldred to pose for a series of raunchy photos. Ainsworth saw it as a clear way to appeal to the large male fan base *Doctor Who* attracted. "That was a very Bill idea, it was a blatant way of getting people to buy. There was no pretending otherwise."[39] Initially reluctant, Baggs managed to change Aldred's mind. "Bill persuaded me to do it basically. Bill's a very persuasive person and I was quite happy to do that and I thought, well, the fans will like that. I'm glad I didn't do the full Katy Manning, that was just enough for me but it was quite nice and it was all very discreetly done."[40] Baggs felt Sophie was comfortable enough with him to do the shoot. "It's this trust thing, if somebody trusts you. She understood what I was trying to do. I don't know if it actually paid off in the end but it probably ticked a few fanboy feathers." The photographs were taken by Baggs in the same recording studio in which the two plays were recorded once the rest of the cast and crew had gone home. [41]

The Ace Specials also saw the return of Harvey Summers, who had previously scored 'In Memory Alone'. He was responsible for the score on both plays and the post production work on 'The Other Side'. He found the whole process fairly relaxed. "Bill was always pretty easy to work with, we'd bounce back and forth as work progressed. Generally though, I'd get all the material together, deliver him a first draft of the final mix and then we'd maybe do a few tweaks and edits from there for the sake of tightening it up or whatever. He was happy to just allow me to interpret things the way I felt inspired to."[42]

September 1998 was marked not only by the release of 'The Other Side', but also the releases of two other *Doctor Who* spin offs not from BBV, but by some former colleagues of Baggs.

These were the *Bernice Summerfield* audios, 'Oh No It Isn't' and 'Beyond The Sun', both adapted from the Virgin *New Adventures* range. These productions featured the continuing adventures of former prose companion Bernice Summerfield and saw several *Doctor Who* alumni take on roles, including Nicholas Courtney, Sophie Aldred and Anneke Wills, while notable pro fans Briggs and Gatiss also appeared. The plays were produced by the newly established Big Finish Productions, owned by *Shakedown* producer Jason Haigh-Ellery, and the range overseen by former *AV* producer Gary Russell. Russell was asked if there was rivalry between him and Baggs. "We come from different sides of the fence. Bill's a businessman who wants to turn a quick buck, which is fine. I'm more interested in getting the quality high than the price down. It's the same argument we had doing *AV* really. But personally, we get on fine."[43]

It's doubtful whether Baggs saw Big Finish as a threat at the time; after all, his productions were the nearest thing to real *Doctor Who* you could get, while the *Bernice* range was essentially a spin-off of a spin-off — although a very well made one. However, all that would change the following year.

Returning to the new BBV audios, the penultimate release for series one would be 'Guests for the Night' written by Nigel Fairs. It had been nearly seven years since 'More than a Messiah', in which time Fairs had been busy as a jobbing actor. He had established a theatre group and also started his own amateur audio range *Pisces*.

When Baggs approached Fairs about writing a script for his new range of audios he jumped at the chance. "I just through it was really nice for the fans and it was nice for the actors. I loved working with Sylvester and Sophie amongst others, and I thought if you can't do it with the actual names then get near as. Damn it, why not?"[44] Facing a quick turnaround as usual, Ainsworth suggested to Fairs that he adapt his script from his own *Pisces* range which Ainsworth had also acted in — Baggs being at the time completely unaware of any link.

Fairs was also asked to direct the play, and cast actors he had previously worked with in various theatre productions, including Oliver Bradshaw as Webster, Julia Akerman as Nanny, Max Day as Daniel — and himself as Harold — "I was a very camp zombie!"[45] Harvey Summers was once again on scoring and post production duties, and cites this as a particular favourite. "It was set in this creepy old building that I had a lot of fun with. Very spooky and I got to write a score with lots of orchestra and choir, similar in style to Danny Elfman's score for *Edward Scissorhands*."[46]

The studio recording was another fun production, according to Fairs. "Sylvester and Sophie were a joy together and really enjoyed each other's company, and the fact they were doing it again in some form, it was such fun. The script was quite light for the most part, a bit of darkness, quite camp."[47] Of all the stories in this first season, this may be the most reminiscent of *Doctor Who* itself, as it manages to capture all the fun of the Doctor's adventures, along with the danger and the scares. Fairs explains: "That's what I like to do, I like to mix darkness with light because the one doesn't work without the other" [48]The play ends with Ace murdering the father character. Did Fairs do this to differentiate himself from *Doctor Who*? "Quite the opposite! The Doctor and his companions are always killing people, always slaughtering people, and it's never explored. And that was one of my frustrations in watching it, thinking my god, they've just murdered someone! It was a monster or it was a villain, but they still have murdered someone so that's going to have an effect on their psyche, isn't it?" [49]

"'Guests for the Night' is as strong as the first two stories of the range,"[50] *DreamWatch* reviewer Tom Conway claimed, and it's difficult to argue with that assessment. In some respects, in fact, the play is an odd creature, in that it is the most *Doctor Who* like of the season, yet isn't particularly evocative of the Seventh Doctor's era. Instead it is a strange hybrid of the *New Adventures* and Season 17 — a hybrid that just happens to feature Sylvester McCoy and Sophie Aldred.

In that respect, it is an exciting original direction for *Doctor Who* and really feels like Fairs is trying to push the series into the next millennium, while exploring the core themes of the TV show: adventure, humour and scares aplenty. While many authors tend to write *Doctor Who* as they remember it, Fairs writes *Doctor Who* as it should be and the series is all the richer for his take on it.

The final play of the season was 'Cyber-Hunt', was written by Martin Peterson (a pen name of Nick Briggs) who also starred in and directed the production. Briggs' character was essentially his Doctor from the AV range, now given the new moniker of the amnesiac, Fred.

With Briggs and Baggs in the booth together, John Ainsworth was pleased to see his AV team partially reunited. "I thought it was quite a nice idea, it was sort of nostalgic but at the same time it didn't quite feel the same."[51]

The reason for Briggs choosing a pen name was obvious. "I was very uncomfortable doing them. But this was when I thought there was no hope of the BBC doing or licensing new *Who* audio. Bill was worried about getting sued by the BBC, so he wanted to further distance his 'Who Clone' products by casting someone who hadn't been the Doctor (officially)... Me! I was very reluctant, but Bill was relentless and persuasive. I was doing *Children In Need* with him at the time. He'd given me a lot of very well paid work on that (for which I was and am extremely grateful) and consequently I felt it was almost ungrateful for me to say no. I kind of felt obliged. He would phone me very early in the morning (he was doing Breakfast TV editing), when he knew I wasn't yet up, and give me a psychological battering. He was very determined. He *is* very determined. It's his great strength — but it's a bit wearing at 7am! He told me to write *Doctor Who*, but find some clever way of making it lawyer-proof!"[52]Ever cautious, Briggs decided to write the play under a pseudonym. "I think I was embarrassed about writing something that was so close to *Doctor Who*, without being *Doctor Who*. I think the BBC legal department was talking to Bill's solicitors at that time."[53]

Considering Baggs was worried about being sued by the BBC, it is peculiar that Fred's enemy in 'Cyber-Hunt' are the Cyberons, an obvious rip-off of the Cybermen — one would think he would have preferred a more lawyer-proof foe. The plot also was not new, being a rehash of an abandoned video drama "that was like a scaled down version of 'Cyberwar',"[54] as Briggs explained some year later.

Despite his initial reservations, Briggs enjoyed his return to the role of his almost-Doctor, and being back in an audio environment. "It was great fun. Bill did the recording and I directed. We worked very well together. Bill has a very good ear for picking up on stuff that is monotonous and needs a change of pace. He was also very good at suggesting extra lines so that certain characters were more obviously in a scene from the beginning. It's a common fault with audio writers that they forget that a character is invisible if they don't speak. [55]

In casting the play Briggs brought in Andrew Fettes (previously seen in *Auton*) to play Captain Halloran alongside some actors new to BBV. Helen Bang played Olivia, Robert Boole played CyCom, Andrew James Dickens was Sergeant Grange, Stephen Franklin played Stevens and David Sax (aka Briggs) was the voice of the Cyberons.

DreamWatch's Tom Conway called the play "passably interesting,"[56] but ultimately felt the "*Doctor Who* by the back door" approach was a hindrance, concluding "I just wish the energy and enthusiasm that is going into these pastiches could be… more original."[57] Indeed, 'Cyber-Hunt' is the only real misfire of the first season of audios. Briggs' Doctor is competent, if not unremarkable, but the supporting cast are colourless in both characterisation and performance, while the cyber voices and sound design are poor. There are some nice scenes towards the end of the play where a Cyberon's conditioning fails and it remembers who it is (several years before Marc Platt's Big Finish audio, 'Spare Parts', would do something similar and more successfully.) But even here the production is let down by the cyber voices.

Despite mixed reviews, the first series of *Audio Adventures in Time and Space* was a success, selling well at conventions and via mail order. Gatiss recalls that "they went down very well. I remember Gary Gilliat saying, at the time Big Finish was starting, that if anyone wanted a model for what they should be like, it should be those two plays. Which is very nice of him. If only I'd known that 'legitimate' *Doctor Who* was about two minutes away… But that was really the end of it all"[58]

With six productions under his belt this would be that last time Gatiss wrote for BBV, but how does he view that work with them now?

"I would never be disparaging about them, principally because I got to work with Jon Pertwee, but at the same I was kind of scrambling around for a way through — it was a scattergun sort of thing. I knew what I wanted to do but how I'd get there, who knows."[59] Not only would this be the last time Gatiss worked for BBV, it would also be the last time he worked with Sylvester McCoy. The following year as part of BBC2's *Doctor Who* night, he would provide a series of comedy sketches about the programme — one of which would seriously offend both McCoy and Gatiss's *Zero Imperative* co-star Colin Baker.

Perhaps prophetically, Gatiss's two plays were narrowly beaten to the top spots in the *DWM* 'Shelf Life Awards'[60] by Big Finish's first two *Bernice Summerfield* releases. With Baggs obviously now worrying about the legal aspects of his characters, he began to search for other properties he could exploit — a wise decision as the *Doctor Who* audio market was about to change drastically.

Behind the Scenes

Inside the Yeti with Richard Landen,
David J Howe and Tony Clark © Robin Prichard

Bill Baggs, Nick Briggs
and George Telfer on location
for *Auton 2* © Patricia Merrick

Scott Fredericks and
Russell Hunter record
Kaldor City ©Magic
Bullet Productions
(Andy Hopkinson)

The cast and crew of *Unnatural Selection*

enjoy a sunny lunch © Patricia Merrick

Beverley Cressman and
Miles Richardson look
at Cavendish's keepsakes
in *Daemos Rising*
© Robin Prichard

Chapter 18 — It's Hard to Walk Tall When You're Small

While *Auton* had been another setback (drama-wise) for Reeltime Productions, Keith Barnfather was still determined to make another drama. His remit this time was simple: low budget, one location and minimal cast. Even by the standards of *Auton* this would be a small production.

Barnfather drew on his previous experience when planning his next film. "We could have only made *Downtime* as a co-production, [and] I didn't want to do that again because of all the hassle involved in it, and the time. You also get to a point, if you've done something once you don't need to prove to yourself that you can do it again. But also I wasn't going to be prepared to put my own money into it again without a return because ultimately I earn my living from this business and I cannot afford to throw my money away. So I thought, I've got to do it, I want to be in control because it's easier. So it was a question again of looking at something we could do with a decent budget."[1]

As with *Downtime* Barnfather wanted a well-known *Doctor Who* writer, but this time he didn't have to go far to recruit one. "I remember being on a train with Katy Manning and Terrance Dicks going to a convention. We were shooting *Where on Earth is Katy Manning?* (a Reeltime documentary) and we were chatting and filming some bits and pieces for it, and Katy was asking what I was going to do next and I said, 'well I'm sort of thinking about a new drama. I just want to something like a prison cell with three people in having a conversation' and Terrance just said, 'I'll write it for you' and that was it."[2]

Dicks, it seems, was not bothered by the low pay that fan productions offered. "If I had the time for a fan project or whatever, that I was sympathetic to, I would do it."[3] Barnfather had a clear idea of who the characters should be in the film, and with this in mind Dicks wrote a script featuring a Sontaran, a Draconian and a human.

Barnfather made the decision to shoot the production with multiple cameras, a method that was less common for dramas in the late 90s. As he recalls, it was done with future projects in mind. "We were seriously considering the possibility of doing a soap opera spin-off. We'd do six titles a year, do two at a time, in a studio, and it would be a *Doctor Who* kind of thing set on a space station with some monster element from *Doctor Who*."[4] The production, now known as *Mindgame*, was announced in *DWM* in August 1998 as a 50 minute drama, with Barnfather citing it as "*Play for Today* style. Acting and script are what we are about."[5]

In casting the video, Barnfather asked some old friends to play two-thirds of his trio — with Miles Richardson as the Draconian and Sophie Aldred playing the Human. To complete the cast of prisoners, and hot off the heels of his part in *Shakedown*, he cast Toby Aspin as his Sontaran. The final part — that of their captor — would be played by Bryan Robson.

Filming took place in studio M at the University of Westminster on Thursday 30th July. The call time was 6:30 am and shooting began earlier than expected at 9:15am. The idea of shooting multi-camera had two potentially positive ramifications for Keith. "One reason was it kept the costs down, we managed to find a studio at the University of North London, the same one we did *Lust in Space* at, that was really cheap. Secondly, the whole point of the way *Doctor Who* used to be shot was you could get a lot in the can very quickly." [6]

In theory this meant the *Mindgame* team could shoot the entire production in one day. Sets were designed by Keith Dunne and constructed in the studio the night before, so that when the team arrived they could begin shooting straightaway. Barnfather's plan was to shoot all the action in script order. "What I wanted to do was literally just use the cameras just to do static shots, no developing shots, except at certain points. So I made the assumption that the vision mixer could choose the points to do the cuts as we were doing it. We would run tape, they'd play the scene and the vision mixer would have the script and would just be able to do whatever they thought." [7] This presumption proved unfounded and Barnfather and his team found themselves behind schedule almost immediately. "She [the vision mixer, Julia Booth] was so used to having shots called by the director, she couldn't do it." [8]

Thus Barnfather spent the first part of the morning marking up scripts for her and the camera team, although he is quick to stress she wasn't to blame. "It was my responsibility and my fault. I should have sat down with her beforehand and just made sure. Because it's the kind of vision mixer that you are using, I should have got somebody that was more used to current affairs, who could have done it with their eyes closed, but I got somebody who had been so used to doing it by being told when to cut. I didn't need her because I could have sat there and done it myself and that's no criticism of her." [9]

With things running behind schedule, studio coordinator David J. Howe recalls the atmosphere. "It was tense but it's always tense. I think if somebody said to you it wasn't tense they are probably lying because everybody is aware that they've got to get something done in the time allotted. So let's say the atmosphere is always tense when you are recording something, because you've got to get a job done and particularly with these productions because they're very low or even no budget. So by about midday everything was running so late, Keith realised he couldn't film everything in one day. So Terrance (who was there too) was actually rewriting as they were recording it. Basically cutting great swathes out of the script to give Keith a fighting chance of finishing it in the day's recording that they had booked."[10]

For Dicks this sort of pressure and last minute rewriting was business as usual. "I had to be there and make huge cuts and simplifications to the script on the spot, which actually is the kind of thing I quite like doing. It doesn't bother me enormously, so somehow or other we got through it and somehow or another we got a show out of."[11]

During an interview for the VHS release Dicks laid out what was cut. "In the script as originally written, they eventually agree to fight but they make a deal with the alien and say that they are tired, they've had a bad time, they need food, they need drink, they need time to rest and if he gives them all that then they'll agree to fight to the death. And so there is kind of a middle act which has now gone completely, in which they sit down and chat and it's a much more kind of quieter, more reflective sort of thing. Well that just had to go. That just came out in huge chunks."[12]

While Barnfather was having issues with his vision mixer, actor Miles Richardson was having his own prosthetics-related drama. "That bloody mask. To be honest, the hands were more of a problem. The prosthetics were from the original outing of the Draconians and had perished somewhat with time. So the hands were in pieces and had to be glued on like a jigsaw to my hands. Very uncomfortable and also made me a virtual amputee. Lunch had to be liquid of course as I could only eat through a straw. I smoked in those days, but having a cigarette required an accomplice!"[13]

Aldred had a great deal of respect for her two latex clad co-stars. "That almost completely obscures what you are trying to do because it's really your facial expressions that you're working with. You can get so much subtlety, but to have none of that available to you and yet to turn in a great performance well, I take my hat off to those who come up with a believable character."[14]

Toby Aspin also had issues with his mask. Not only did he almost faint under the hot studio lights, he also had problems acting through the prosthetics. "It's not like acting, it's sort of verbal thuggery and also you can't get the words out because the mouth piece is quite small."[15]

In accepting *Mindgame*, Aldred found herself working with two people she had known for some time but of whom she was somewhat in awe. "I knew Miles but I just was blown away by what a good actor he is. I always felt he was slightly in the shadow of his father and you know his time will come, a bit like his father and so working with him was like 'he's a proper actor, I have to up my game here'."[16]

The other person she was pleased to be finally working with was Dicks. "I'd met him at conventions so I was really pleased. He came up with such fantastic scripts, so there wasn't really anything to change or to worry about. Actually the thing I was most concerned about in that whole shoot was doing justice to the lines."[17] In fact, Aldred had only received the script the week before, and due to other commitments had only read it once. She learnt the first scenes on the tube on the way to the studio and the rest on the day of recording.

Despite the initial issue with the vision mixer, the company carried on as normal with Barnfather satisfied with the momentum the production was picking up. "By two o'clock we were rolling, it really was going like a dream."[18] Over lunch he had worked out a more efficient way of working; he would block each scene on the studio floor with the actors and camera men, and then direct the vision mixing from the gallery. However, a new set of problems — all fairly standard for filming — would set the shooting back further, as Howe remembers. "It wasn't anybody's fault, with a change of wind they might have done it, but of course everything started to go wrong as it always does. Sets weren't ready, cameras weren't ready, lights weren't working, takes go wrong, people fluff their lines, all sorts of stuff and if one thing after another, after another, starts to go wrong, you just end up in this position where you kind of realise you've only filmed a quarter of what you wanted to film."[19]

With this in mind Barnfather made a difficult decision. "We were too far behind to finish it. I made a decision late afternoon that we weren't even going to bother shooting the alien control room stuff."[20] With the scenes in the alien control room being postponed, alien actor Bryan Robson, who had been in attendance all day, was finally required on set at 6:30pm to record a short scene in the cell and read in his lines for scenes where the prisoners interact with the voice of their captor. In order to get all the action in the cell set in the can, Barnfather opted to shoot all the fight scenes on a handheld camera. At 9:45pm a reluctant Barnfather wrapped the production with his film incomplete. "Terrance, bless him, he said to me afterwards 'I should have known you couldn't do this in a day.' We were too ambitious."[21]

With the bulk of the action in the cell recorded, Dicks and Barnfather went through the script and added cutaways to the alien control room. Originally due to be shot from a platform looking down into the cell, a more elaborate control room was constructed in the smaller Lime Light studio near Southbank where, a week later, a much more relaxed shoot took place to complete the film.

The final version of the film was a mere 32 minutes in length. It was released on the 14th of September 1998 and was available from retailers, along with a *Making Of* feature that did not hold back in showing the chaos of the production.

Steve Williams of *Celestial Toyroom* was not a fan of the production. "Unfortunately, it has to be said that Ms. Aldred's acting is below her usual par for much of the time; she warms up as the show goes on, but is not really firing on all cylinders here. However she is head over shoulders above Toby Aspin's pontificating Sontaran. This kind of dialogue, which could have sounded very effective if delivered in the sort of voice that makes entire parade-grounds quake, sounds empty and over done here."[22] Dave Owen also had a few negative remarks. "Originality and surprise are conspicuous by their absence in this brave synthesis of *Doctor Who*'s past," but was quick to praise the Sontaran design. "The prosthetic mask concealing Toby Aspin is the truest to the Sontaran form first seen in 1973's 'The Time Warrior' than subsequent designers within or outside the BBC have delivered, and it's only a pity that the performer cannot match his costume."[23] Overall, Owen seemed to enjoy the flawed production saying of it that an "an unambitious script receives a faultless production, with lighting and camerawork making an unsettling alien quality in the opening scenes." [24]

As an experiment, *Mindgame* is an audacious attempt to combine the production methods of yesterday with modern film making techniques, but ultimately as a film it doesn't quite hang together. The speed at which it was shot means that due care and attention simply isn't afforded to the production. Which is a shame as there is so much to enjoy in *Mindgame*: the Draconian and Sontaran prosthetics are brilliant, there are some neat camera moves considering the limited space, and the cell set is an exceptional design. Sophie Aldred delivers a confident performance while Miles Richardson's Draconian steals the show. However Toby Aspin's performance is lacklustre, to say the least, and the viewer can't help but feel he just couldn't be bothered half the time. Conversely, the set in the alien control room looks too thrown together and the laser effects coming from Aldred's guns would put K9 to shame as the gun wobbles and the laser stays still. There is just enough plot to fill the short run time and one has to wonder if the cut scenes would have added depth to the proceedings or merely added padding to a wafer thin plot.

It's fair to say the production of *Mindgame* offed a new challenge for Barnfather, who by this point had been running Reeltime for 12 years. "It was an obvious learning curve. I would now probably not direct multi-camera myself. I would try and find a director who is really comfortable with it. It's unlikely that I would do anything like that again, it was just a moment, a very interesting moment though."[25] Richardson also agreed that it was a difficult but educational process, even if he ended up appreciating it for a very different reason. "It was a learning curve for Keith and he learned to cut his cloth a bit more efficiently after that. The most rewarding bit for me, literally, was the out-take of me in my oversized costume attempting to go through a door half my size. The clip did the rounds of *It'll be Alright on the Night* for many a year and paid me about 20 times more than I got paid for the initial filming."[26]

It's quite possible that the inclusion of *The Making of Mindgame* on the VHS release was intended to soften the blow of the shortcomings of the actual film. Did Barnfather worry about showing the audience all the problems that befell *Mindgame*?

"I'm never worried about showing what happens. I know there was quite a lot of comments on the internet, once people had seen it saying 'how crap he was at organising the whole thing' and 'he should have known better' and they're right. I'm not going to argue the case. I should have known my onions before we went into the studio, but I don't mind people seeing that."[27] At this point, thanks to the internet, there was more interaction between spin-off makers and their audience and so Barnfather had to get used to a new level of criticism that wasn't present on his previous outings as director. "At that point you've got more people putting their head above the barrier saying they could do better or they want to do the same kind of thing or whatever and I think *Mindgame* had its detractors. For me I put my head above the parapet, so I had to be prepared to have it shot off, unfortunately it's just the way it is. The people I have no respect for are the people who are sitting next to their computer at home always critiquing everybody else and never doing anything themselves. That doesn't mean they don't have a valid opinion but it does mean their voices shouldn't be considered as loudly as those that do."[28] While it must have been off-putting for Barnfather to receive this negative feedback, he does agree that it's par for the course. "It's human nature. *Doctor Who* fans have and always will be terribly proprietorial and there will always be people who think nobody should have the tenacity [sic] to do anything with their sacred cow."[29]

As touched on with *Wartime* it was Barnfather's dissatisfaction with on screen *Doctor Who* that spurred him on to want to produce drama, and it's a shame that none of the audience who were so critical of *Mindgame* ever thought to enter the market themselves. Maybe they would have found out just how difficult it is to produce low budget drama.

Chapter 19 — The Will to Power

Auton had proved a modest success for BBV, even if the reviews were less than favourable about Briggs' direction. As was announced at the time, *Auton* was planned as a trilogy by Baggs, though his initial plan to shoot the first two concurrently didn't pan out. Nevertheless, Baggs was keen to push ahead with a sequel even if Briggs was initially resistant to the idea. "The reason for my long hesitation over committing to the sequel was, in short, my experience on the first film. Although it had been extremely enjoyable, I had finished work on the whole thing feeling frustrated by the paucity of the budget and especially the lack of any significant control over the editing process." [1]

By this time Briggs was also busy with his day job as Press and PR Manager at the Sci-Fi Channel and so Baggs turned to Tim Saward, who had written a second *Auton* script entitled 'In The Blood' when *Auton* was still in its infancy. Of his original script, Saward recalls writing a somewhat ambitious story. "He wanted to do a sequel and so he said 'could I write a second one?' and not really having much guidance I just wrote something I thought would work and it turned out that it would have called for a massive budget and wouldn't really have been within Bill's type of resources."[2] This original script, much like the first draft of *Auton*, was set to feature both Kate Lethbridge Stewart and the Brigadier. But with *Auton* rewritten hastily and new characters introduced, when Saward returned for his second attempt, he was asked to incorporate Lockwood and tone down his ideas. "There was another one which I also wrote, which was much more practical and based on four or five locations. It was quite snappy actually, but didn't make a lot of sense reading it back." [3]

While Saward was redrafting his script Baggs and Briggs were also in somewhat delicate negations over whether Briggs should return to the fold as Briggs discussed in his *Auton Diaries* article for *DWM.* "I eventually wrote him a letter telling him that if he couldn't increase the budget and couldn't stop interfering, I wasn't really interested at the moment. This was followed by a phone conversation with Bill, which I was forced to have at my Sci-Fi desk within earshot of several colleagues. Suffice it to say that, by the time I'd put the phone down, they were making raucous comments along the lines of 'Woah! I wouldn't want to get on the wrong side of Briggsy!'. However, Bill and I seemed to reach some sort of understanding, which basically involved him apologizing a lot. But we still hadn't reached any agreement on *Auton 2*."[4] Ultimately, Briggs was persuaded by Baggs to return to the project — initially just as the director of the Saward-penned sequel — but as Briggs later recounted, "I'd created the characters (aside from the Autons, naturally) and had started them off on their fictional journey. It was a journey I wanted to continue."[5] Plus he was not a fan of Saward's interpretation of the story. "I didn't much like it, I mean I thought it was ok. It was very old fashioned and very ploddy and full of those sort of things where people explain things to each other that they should already know. Which is always the hallmark of the sort of writing that needs a bit of help, you know, very obviously explaining things."[6]

Saward's script was eventually abandoned completely and Briggs began work on his own *Auton* sequel.

Nick Briggs' original script for *Auton 2* went through several drafts and stories and according to John Ainsworth, initially owed a debt to the second televised Auton story. "Nick's original idea was that it was all going to be set around a radio telescope and I said 'the trouble is that you will inevitably get comparisons with 'Terror of the Autons', why not take a completely different route?' and I think I actually suggested the religious power and there actually being something under the ground or under the church and Nick obviously sort of ran with that."[7] Originally called 'The Rapture', *Auton 2* would become known as 'Sentinel' (a title and a setting Briggs had originally intended for the earlier, abandoned Cybermen video), after seven drafts of the script.

One last-minute change would have a huge impact on the script, when — much as before — Briggs had to recast his lead after Bryonie Pritchard got a job in the West End. "I wasn't in the second *Auton* very much as at the time of shooting I was playing the female lead in *The Mousetrap* in London for a year, which clashed obviously, and so my shots could only be done on a Sunday, just one day. It was great that they could find a storyline to accommodate that, so Dr Sal had a presence."[8]

Briggs was forced to create a new female lead to replace Pritchard. "Bill warned me of the perils of scheduling a shoot around the scant availability of one performer. He'd done it with Colin Baker in the past and it had proved to be a logistical nightmare. He warned me, 'You'll just spend all day worrying about when she's got to leave! You won't be able to think about anything else!'"[9] — and so, after two months away from the script, Briggs created a new scientific advisor to work alongside Lockwood. "In the end, it turned out to be the ideal solution. I'd always wanted Sal to be emotionally closer to Lockwood in the second one. I didn't want all that bickering. I wanted it to be clear that time had passed and that these two people had grown to like each other and work well together. I could now have this 'comfortable' base come into contact with a new character who had a somewhat antagonistic agenda. Hence, the arrival of Natasha Alexander and a whole 'conspiracy' plot line."[10] To play this new lead, Briggs brought on-board Jo Castleton, who brought more than just her acting abilities to the role. "I enjoyed putting my own costume together for it, borrowing a real old authentic flying jacket from a friend. My car got to feature too — an old red 2CV. Hopefully it helped to give her a quirky edge!" [11]

Also absent from the sequel was Reece Sheersmith's Dr. Dan; this was for two reasons. "In a rush to rewrite the script after Nick Courtney's departure from the project, I felt that I'd rather failed to give Dr. Dan a defining scene in the first film, leaving the character a bit colourless — which is a shame, because Reece is such a fine actor. More importantly however, Reece was not available, having won the Perrier Award at the Edinburgh Festival with the superb comedy group *The League of Gentlemen* and was consequently busy and writing and starring in their new BBC 2 series."[12]

With Dr Dan out of the picture, a new supporting character was created in the form of Colonel Wilson, played by long time BBV collaborator John Wadmore. With Michael Wade and Andrew Fettes returning as Lockwood and Ramsey, George Telfer completed the cast, reappearing as the villain of the piece. "I was originally only to be in the first one," recalls the actor, "but Nicholas Courtney became ill and they had to kind of re-address the whole plot really, because obviously he was a really main player in it and Graham Winslet just went from being in the first one to being kind of the main villain throughout the three of them."[13]

With Dick Kursa now long departed from the BBV stable, Baggs decided that he would take on the role of Lighting Cameraman. After their less than harmonious relationship on *Auton*, this could easily have been a bad decision and placed more strain on the friendship between Briggs and Baggs. However, this time around it seemed to work, as Briggs mentioned in his behind the scenes article for *Celestial Toyroom*. "To everyone's surprise (including ours), this created a near-perfect working relationship between us. Being a director and editor, Bill was able to work quickly and efficiently with me, offering instant solutions to problems which threatened to foil my shooting plans."[14]

Baggs' new role may well have been a way for him to gain more creative control over the project without treading on Briggs' toes. "To be honest, we both directed it," Baggs claims, "which is not to downgrade what Nick did because I was filming it. I was directing, which was a great asset because we had two people on set who were totally focussed on production. So suddenly my burden was relaxed because he was doing the actors and I was thinking 'ok how are we going to film it'."[15]

Briggs agrees to a point. "Bill very much wanted to shoot *Auton 2* his way, but left me to deal with all the acting stuff,"[16] although he wasn't going to relinquish the director's chair too easily. "I remember us having really interesting arguments," he recalls vividly. "If someone was running along and I wanted to do a tracking shot with them, I always wanted the tracking shot to be in front of them and to go in reverse. So they are constantly running towards the camera, so that the scenery was shooting past them, so that we could see their face. Bill never wanted to do that, as he was frightened of tripping over and we said 'well we will put someone behind you,' but he just wouldn't do it and he said 'no it's much better to go from behind' and I said 'then you can just see someone's bum and their heels' and it was little arguments like that we had all the time."

But there were there any large scale problems this time?

"I have no recollection of any appalling rows. I mean the experience of working with Bill is always odd..." [17]

This new, more peaceful collaboration was as much for the film's sake as it was their relationship. "You realise you have a responsibility, once you've amassed this army of people to make something, you have a responsibility to get on with it, so you have to find a way of working together and it was pretty harmonious. There weren't any major upsets."[18]

Despite occasional small disagreements, Briggs is still full of praise for his Lighting Cameraman on this second *Auton* outing. "Of course he was working at the very limits of his ability because he wasn't really a cameraman. But I think he did phenomenally well, I think he got some really beautiful shots considering the small amount of time we had and the low level of technology back in those days. We were helped by the freak amazing weather, so I do look back on them with great fondness but they were very tiring times." [19]

Patricia Merrick was on hand playing Charlotte and helping out on the production side of things, and found the relationship between the two of them to be an agreeable experience. "They were both very enthusiastic and energetic directors. On *Auton 2* they had, as always, gathered together a great group of actors, who were happy to spend entire days in a quarry having clods of earth hurled at them and copious amounts of smoke directed at them. Happy to trek two miles along a shingle beach after a long day's filming and happy to spend evenings down the pub having a few pints and playing pool."[20]

Jo Castleton was impressed by the entire production. "We had a fantastic crew and cast and that made for a very happy time. Nick is an excellent director and knows exactly what he wants and Bill was doing the camera work and they were a great team."[21] George Telfer cites his experiences on the sequel as the standout moment from the series. "The second one was probably most fun for me. I really had a ball with that. It was just fun being out and about."[22]

Initially due to commence principal photography during February of 1998, production finally began on May 9th. The first scenes to be shot were those staring Bryonie Pritchard at The Rectory in Alderbury near Salisbury, which was doubling for the U.N.I.T. containment HQ. Production then moved on to the Hurst Spit part of Christchurch Bay, which extends out into the Solent. Here the team would shoot action involving the U.N.I.T. soldiers arriving by boat and the Autons submerging into the sea. With seven different locations on *Auton 2*, Briggs would ensure he was mucking in with the rest of the cast and crew. "I like to lead from the front and by example, so I was always the first at the location — usually posing on my deckchair, smoking a cigarette and scribbling furiously on my schedule just waiting for everyone to turn up so that I could impress them with how long I'd been waiting there. Of course, the result was that I was totally exhausted by the time we had finished shooting at 8pm."[23]

The next few days saw the crew move to a woodland area just outside West Grimstead. For Briggs, this shoot was very much drawing on locations he knew. "I went back to my roots for *Auton 2*; to the sea and the countryside near where I'd been brought up, in Hampshire and Wiltshire."[24] In the woodland, various shots involving Wadmore and his paramilitary team were filmed, with his unit being made up of some rather over excited extras "He got a bunch of pseudo squaddie types and they brought their own guns and uniforms with them. Some of them slept in ditches just because they wanted to."[25] While the production was relatively plain sailing and the weather stayed dry, location filming brought up a new set of problems that Briggs hadn't encountered on the first film. "We were plagued by sound problems — the idyllic countryside suddenly turns into a cacophony of tractors, traffic, combine-harvesters and airplanes the moment you shout 'Action!' — and the fatigue factor is sometimes overwhelming." [26] Even moving into nearby fields didn't alleviate the sound problem, as the team were beset by a fleet of tractors!

The final few days of the production were spent filming at the local St. Mary's Church, which was the home of the parents of First AD David Rowston, who kindly let the crew shoot and stay there. Rowston was a stalwart of a number of BBV productions and was invaluable help to Briggs. "Bill left first assistant director David Rowston and myself to sort out most of the logistical problems of the shoot. Bill took a back seat, just constantly checking that we were proceeding according to some sort of plan."[27] Briggs continues to praise Rowston years later. "David Rowston worked miracles to get it all organised and done."[28]

The scenes at the church saw the inclusion of a number of extras, sourced from an advert placed in *Doctor Who Magazine*. Pleasingly, as fans they were only too happy to be involved, as Briggs recollects. "They were marvellous. They never complained and always did as they were told. A truly great bunch who didn't so much as fidget when they had to sit and wait for the complex lighting setup to be completed in the church."[29]

Overall the shoot for *Auton 2* was a lot more hassle-and drama-free than some of the more recent BBV productions, as Briggs himself later explained. "I know it sounds corny, but there really was a minimum of stress and heart-ache. I think the only disaster occurred when I hit a tree trunk while driving my car up a country track and incurred damages costing in excess of my fee!" [30]

Once production was complete, an extensive post-production period was needed. At this point, Briggs' and Baggs' rocky relationship once again surfaced, with the former unhappy with some of Baggs' choices. "[Bill] managed to do all sorts of bizarre things. There's even one shot that includes people who at that point in the story, had actually died!"[31] Baggs' also continued to play with the story. "He also cut a lot of plot in the final edit, so the story ends up not making sense." [32]

As well as the editing and scoring process, *Auton 2* would feature a large number of digital effects — a first for a production of this kind. The computer generated effects were provided by Ben Smith, a recent graduate of Bournemouth University, according to Bill Baggs. "Bournemouth is famous for its animation and Ben had contacted me with a demo reel. So I said 'we are doing this film do you fancy doing these bits?' and it was just about being available to what's going on at the time and I think a lot of people were impressed by it."[33] Smith created the FX in Lightwave 3D, a piece of software than had been used successfully on popular US sci-fi show, *Babylon 5*. The effects in question included the falling debris inside the church, the Auton gun projectiles (which had previously been done using pyrotechnics) and the Nestene creature that straddles the church in the film's climax.

Smith discussed his involvement with Simon John Gerard in a 1999 edition of *DWM*. "What they wanted was this 'octopus' thing, and I said it was probably alright to do, so they kept it in the script. The thing was, I'd been trying for ages to convince Bill of the quality of effects that were possible, without drowning out the story."[34] As written in the script, the Nestene creature was a hologram but Smith convinced the BBV team that it would add more "presence" to the creature if he created the full creature, although matching up his creations and the footage did cause some minor problems. "Most producers try to have their effects shots take place in night scenes or out in space. The advantage is that you can hide matte lines or edges in the dark! We had to create a living creature that was moving around outdoors on a sunny day, so you can't get away with smudging the edges so that no-one will see!" [35]

Auton 2 is unashamedly a 1970s *Doctor Who* homage, from the use of U.N.I.T., to the landscapes of the British countryside, the villagers and the final battle in the church. All the exterior filming is well executed and

Briggs makes great use the local scenery, the shots of the Autons walking through cornfields feeling suitably ominous. The Nestene creature is a competent enough effect for its day and Telfer's Winslet makes for a malevolent villain, even if the character is a bit too close to the Master in 'The Dæmons'. Castleton makes for a good foil for Lockwood, and Wade once more steals the show, playing a harsh and sarcastic role with just enough warmth to make him likable even if you don't trust him. *Auton 2* feels like drama that perfectly straddles the divide between its *Doctor Who* origins and contemporary science fiction.

Reviews for *Auton 2* were far more positive than the previous *Auton* outing. *DWM's* Dave Owen was particularly impressed by the CGI. "The Nestene creature is stunning, and sums up in a single image the fact that BBV has grown up and is now capable of producing drama which in writing, performance, music, and appearance actually eclipse the television series which inspired them."[36] *Celestial Toyroom's* sister publication *TARDIS* contained a review from Tom Paine which, despite a few minor gripes, was also favourable. "Nick Briggs's direction is very good and the battle sequences are well realised. There are also some moments of real tension. The plot always moves along well."[37]

Auton 2 was released in October of 1998 through mail order and specialist outlets before receiving a rerelease on the high street courtesy of Reeltime Pictures the following March. The video also included a short 'Making Of' feature which had appeared previously on the Sci-Fi Channel. In June 1999 *Auton 2* was voted best spin off video in the *DWM* Shelf Life Awards, beating *Mindgame* and a number of special documentary releases from Reeltime. Despite its general plaudits, however, Nick Briggs later revealed that the video's sales performance was less than stellar. "It's all very well people saying that they enjoyed *Auton 2* much more than *Auton* and that we should do another one, but the fact is that nowhere near as many people bought *Auton 2* as bought *Auton*. I'm not telling people to buy stuff. I'm just politely reminding anyone who'd like to listen that your spending power has a direct and very tangible impact on what happens in this very small market. Only the unfolding future will let us know if there's too much out there for people to be able to afford. I hope everything does survive, but then I would say that, wouldn't I? Because I love doing it all."[38]

After a rocky patch during the previous film, it appeared that Baggs' and Briggs' relationship was back on track and that working together they had managed to produce a well-received film with high production values. Looking back on *Auton 2* Baggs said, "I'm very proud of the production and it's got loads of locations and lots of shots so you can get quick cuts which is what was lacking in the earlier ones."[39] After baring all to his audience about the trials and tribulations of *Auton*, Briggs conjured up a much more positive summary of *Auton 2*. "I do these productions because

I want to make films and this is the best and most satisfying way to learn which has presented itself to me so far. I'd love to make all kinds of films ranging from gritty emotional drama through to outrageous fantasy. But at the moment I'm involved with this kind of project because it's actually happening. The entertainment industry is bulging with unfulfilled dreams and promises of projects which never see the light of day. But, because Bill and I can share a passion with our audience (that's *Doctor Who*, by the way), we're in the fortunate position of having enough of a potential market for what we want to do to make it just about financially possible. That's why we freeze to death, swelter, choke, have terrible arguments and work until we drop. For the rest of each year I try to spend my time financially and mentally recharging my batteries, slogging away at something else; but I will certainly return to the land of the Autons as long as enough people enjoy the stories I want to tell.[40]

A mantra that, more than anything else, sums up what these films are all about.

Chapter 20 — Have-a-go Merchant

By the time BBV came to its second series of *Audio Adventures in Time and Space*, they had an expanding roster of writers, directors and sound designers on whom they could call. The team had also developed a good working rapport, with Bill looking after the business side of things, Ainsworth overseeing the production and script development and Tim Saward looking after the admin, website and online presence. "I was phoning up Robert Holmes's widow to get the rights to the Sontarans and Robert Banks Stewart to get the rights to Zygons."[1]

Baggs felt his team were performing at optimum efficiency. "It was a very organised, well-oiled machine. It's funny because doing the audios kind of galvanized the whole thing and everyone was really puckered up."[2]

Between this core team they would run BBV as a profitable business venture that to the outside world looked like a professional production company — although as Saward reveals things were a little bit more amateur behind the scenes. "His mum and dad sold the stuff from Southampton, that's how he had his retail outlet it was very shoestringy. But I kind of respect that and from his point of view that's a step up from things like the *Audio Visuals*. It was always going to be hard for him to get that leap up because you need some sort of venture capital. Big Finish had Jason as a commercial head in it and we saw Bill as ours, because he was always trying to save money, going off to conventions and doing his own stalls all that sort of stuff, he was sort of entrepreneurial but without the capital."[3]

By all accounts the money at BBV wasn't great, but Baggs would often give emerging writers, directors and actors a chance to have professional product released. BBV would accept unsolicited scripts and successful applicants were asked to write something as opposed to pitching ideas. Writers, actors directors etc. were paid a one-off fee and no royalties were negotiated.

Planning for the second series of *Audio Adventures in Time and Space* began before the first series had finished recording. In order to give themselves a little breathing room, Baggs and assistant producer John Ainsworth launched the second season with a re-release of the two *Stranger* audios, 'Eye of The Storm' and 'The Last Mission'. These were re-mastered and available for the first time on CD, though the release of the latter caused more friction between Baggs and one of his stars, according to Briggs. "When Lis Sladen's agent phoned up to complain he'd released her *Stranger* audio as a CD and the contract had said cassette, he literally said to her agent on the phone 'tell her to get a fucking lawyer' and I know that's true because Bill told it to me in triumph and Lis Sladen told it me from the opposite point of view, and she said 'do you know what he fucking said?' and I said 'I know, he told me that' and she went 'what a little bastard'. She hated him."[4]

A number of changes were on the cards for this second season, firstly the range would be diversifying from the Professor and Ace titles with a number of new releases featuring old adversaries and friends of the Doctor licensed from their creators. The second change would be at the insistence of John Ainsworth, which was to brand each of the releases in accordance with its own range rather than the overall banner of *Audio Adventures in Time and Space*. "Bill was just releasing things one after another, in some unconnected series. I said 'we need to brand these series as separate productions' and I got the designer Paul Vyse to make logos for all of these."[5]

The third and most radical change came as a result of intervention from the BBC over BBV's use of the legally dubious Professor and Ace. Baggs feels that the BBC was aware of his productions but initially weren't interested. "I paid the price for that, but it's only because a certain person rubbed their nose in it. They didn't give a toss but because somebody at the organisation, who wasn't really part of the organisation, was stuffing it in their faces saying 'look there is this guy doing this' they actually got uppity about it. But it never came to it anyway, there was a letter and that was it and I just changed the names."[6]

Baggs wouldn't name the individual in question, but Nick Briggs has no such qualms. "I think Andrew Beech (*Downtime* producer and convention organiser) was making a lot of fuss about the legality of these things."[7]

Hilariously, Baggs attempted to take his revenge on Beech, when Briggs was choosing his pen-name for 'Cyber Hunt'. "I bet Bill's forgotten this, but Bill wanted me to do it under the pseudonym of Andrew Beech and I said 'that's just provocative'."[8]

With the likelihood of *Doctor Who* returning to the air seemingly slim, it was perhaps a case of a number of fans vying for control of the show?

"That's a very good way of looking at it." says Baggs "He had resentment issues. He was working for BBC Worldwide at the time and I think he probably wanted to produce the audio series. So the irony of it was he didn't get it anyway. So the bizarre thing is not only did it back fire for him but it fucked me over as well."[9]

Steve Cole, who was in charge of the *Doctor Who* range at the BBC, thinks that it was part of a larger overhaul of the brand and its licenses. "It was the BBC Intellectual Property Department that handled these affairs. At the time, the BBC were hoping to make new *Doctor Who* with a partner, as they had with Universal, and as merchandise rights are an important and lucrative part of any TV deal, it was felt important to demonstrate that the BBC would act to protect its intellectual copyright — also to ensure that merchandisers who had paid for the rights to make official *Who* product wouldn't see that other firms were targeting the same fans without a license. It wasn't just BBV and Reeltime, I believe other unofficial merchandise producers were also sent cease and desist letters, as part of the ongoing management of a brand."[10]

And so reluctantly BBV continued its range with its two leads renamed the Dominie and Alice.

The first release of the season was part of *The Time Traveller's* range entitled 'Ghosts' and written by Nigel Fairs, who recalls the commission came almost straight after his previous attempt. "We were just about to go in to the studio to do 'Guests for the Night' and he asked me to do one without Sylvester in it because we only had Sylvester for half a day. So I had to write one based on Sophie's character."[11]

It seems likely that the sparing use of McCoy was once again down to Baggs' cost cutting, with Aldred costing considerably less that McCoy.

As before Fairs was asked to direct the play and so cast people he knew in the roles. These included Caroline Burns-Cook as Jacquos, Jackie Skarvellis as Betty Durham, Joe Young as Saul, John Cormack as Alistair Briggs and Toby Eddington as President Maxington.

The instruction to change the name of the two leads was not given to Fairs until the day of the recording, as he recalls. "Bill came in and said we've got to change the name. It was Sylvester's idea to call him the Dominie because that's Scottish for master or teacher or something like that. And then Ace becomes Alice; that was my idea because it sounded like Ace." [12]

The play is a fitting send-off for the series in this form, dealing as it does with themes of death and rebirth, though Fairs admits "it's completely coincidental but what a lovely way to look at it." [13]

Sound design and music was once again handled by Harvey Summers. In conversation with Justyce.org Fairs recalled his working with Summers. "I really enjoyed 'Ghosts', although I think it's been sadly unappreciated, I was really pleased with the way it was edited, by Harvey Summers in Bexhill, and I went down there, it was the first time I saw all the digital stuff."[14]

Overall, in fact, Fairs was happy with the final product. "In 'Ghosts' I tried to put in that emotional nuance, that I think works well in audio. The final scene of 'Ghosts' came across very well at the recording." [15]

DreamWatch magazine's Owen Morris said of 'Ghosts' "there's a lot of good ideas floating around, but somehow they don't quite gel together."[16]

While this may be true, there is still plenty to enjoy in the production and Sophie Aldred once again delivers a strong performance. Fairs' script is a cracker, delivering a political thriller in the guise of a murder mystery that tugs at the heart strings in the right places. 'Ghosts' is rather like *Doctor Who* for grownups, in that it takes itself seriously without falling into the trap of using breasts and swearing to announce its adult status. The biggest issue is the lack of McCoy. After two Ace specials last season, it seems an odd choice to start the season with another Professor-lite story.

The next release was a second outing for Nick Briggs' Fred character, with the range now called *The Wanderer*. Initially, a second script entitled 'Jihad' and then 'Warlord' was announced through the BBV website and *Celestial Toyroom* respectively. This was again to be written by Briggs under the alias Martin Peterson. Whether these ideas ever got past the pitching stage is unknown, but when the second Fred release materialised it was in the form of the Tim Saward-penned 'Vital Signs', which would be directed by John Ainsworth, who brought on-board the CD's main guest star in the form of Mike Yates actor, Richard Franklin.

"I knew him from doing the *Myth Makers* and seeing him occasionally at conventions. It was just an opportunity to have a little bit of a guest star."[17] The other cast members consisted of Jack Galagher as Kevin, Louise Morrell as Phoebe, Will Warrior as Murphy and Gerda and Andrea Newland as Andora and the Receptionist.

Saward was again present at the recording of the play.

"I'd had the discussion beforehand about what is the protocol of the writer in the room. I knew perfectly well that the writer doesn't interfere or undermine the director, yet some perverse desire in me started making suggestions and saying things unsolicited without being asked. I apologised to him afterwards because I'd been completely idiotic and he said 'well buy me a drink and that will be fine' but it all came out right in the end."[18]

Conversely, Ainsworth doesn't remember any animosity between the two of them. "We got on quite well and I actually saw him a lot in person. I think we must have met up a lot and talked about things and it was quite a good script."[19]

Ainsworth was clearly a fan of the script but how did Saward feel about his direction?

"It's really hard to say that sort of thing because if I felt like I'd done the most amazing, wonderful script for it I could have said this will really need a really brilliant director to take it to the next level. The thing is I didn't really, so I think he did what he could with it. It was at least shorter this time, it didn't need cutting on the fly by the editor afterwards." [20] Ultimately, Saward felt his second outing was an improvement on the first even if he wasn't 100% happy with it. "'Vital Signs' was another one that was a bit rambling and slow, but it had a clearer plot. I found it harder to write, and in particular I found it much less easy on that one to create personalities for the incidental characters, except Murphy and Kevin Kelly. Basically, I like to write the overstated characters, but it can get a bit monotonous."[21]

Although he was a fan of the script, Ainsworth felt the post-production let the play down. "The wolves in it are terrible, they just sound like purring poodles. They never actually growl or attack anyone or sound like they are attacking anyone, it's a shame really. It was otherwise quite a nice little story, very much spoilt by the lack of good post-production."[22]

Briggs on the other hand was completely dismissive of the entire production. "A very over-wordy script and terrible post-production work. I gave up listening to it because it was so... mediocre."[23]

Saward was at least marginally aware that Briggs was unhappy with the script. "He did take the piss out of the dialogue I think, probably because I was being a bit silly in the rehearsal. There was one character who was a classic sort of *Star Trek* type and there was a 'you know of the Sandermiens' sort of line and I think he took the piss out of that saying that's such a *Star Trek* line." [24]

'Vital Signs' does little to excite, but isn't a bad play either. Owen Morris' nonchalant review in *DreamWatch* called the play as "a pleasant mystery"[25] and that about sums it up. There is some competent characterisation, some duff dialogue and all the actors deliver satisfactory performances. The post-production work manages to suck out the little tension the script provides. Briggs' performance is a lot stronger than his previous attempt, and he actually feels like a Doctor in this play.

'Vital Signs' would be the last outing for the Wanderer, although Saward remembers there being talks of at least one more play. "I vaguely recall it was talked about one more time, but we were pretty much on the eve of the announcement that Big Finish had actually got the rights to do the real thing so I think the idea of doing those at least with Nick would have been dashed."[26]

As discussed in Chapter 18, Briggs felt uncomfortable playing Fred but nevertheless came back for the second play. "I did it because I'd promised Bill I would. Perhaps it would have been wiser not to do 'Vital Signs', but a promise is a promise. I enjoyed the studio session though, because I just turned up and did my lines. I had great fun being just an 'act-tor, darling!' and not having to worry about anything else."[27]

When Baggs is asked about Briggs' reluctance to do these plays, he takes a while to answer, as if trying to gather himself and it is the only time during the interview he raises his voice and appears visibly angered. "He never particularly expressed that to me. I think when somebody is getting paid, the vibe I get is they are more interested in that, I never got the impression that he was uncomfortable doing them, and if he was that uncomfortable doing them, he wouldn't have done it, so it's very easy for him to say that now of course." [28]

As mentioned previously, things were about to change drastically for BBV. Both 'Vital Signs' and 'Ghosts' were released in March of 1999. In the same month it was announced that the BBC had awarded Jason Haigh-Ellery's Big Finish Productions the licence to produce brand new audio *Doctor Who*, starring past Doctors including Sylvester McCoy's Seventh Doctor. Baggs had previously attempted to get the licence himself and it was this rejection that had spurred him into action with his *Audio Adventures in Time and Space* range. It's possible that by drawing the attention of the BBC to his activities, Baggs may have shown the BBC there was a market for this sort of production. However, John Ainsworth is of the opinion that his actions would prevent him from ever getting the licence.

"By doing that, he would have ruled out any possibility of being involved with producing them officially. So I think his main concern was what it would do to the sales of the BBV titles, because of course people are going to choose the genuine *Doctor Who* thing over the not so genuine."[29]

Sylvester McCoy certainly feels there would be no Big Finish without BBV. "The BBC weren't interested, but then they decided to make audios when it was proved they could work. I mean the thing was Bill Baggs proved that these could be successful, then the BBC thought 'we could somehow make these'. So they were approached by someone else, you know for the rights to make *Doctor Who* as an audio and I think that's when they [BBV] stopped, as this was slightly illegal."[30]

Tim Saward can recall the announcement vividly. "I think he had an idea it was coming, the implications were obvious instantly. however, it was going in terms of BBV and *The Time Travellers* and all of that stuff. I think it was obvious to everybody that there wasn't really going to be a long term future in that, particularly with Sylvester and Sophie, if they were going to be involved in the Big Finish thing. If the one product is earmarked by the BBC and it's actually *Doctor Who*, then we are talking one level down from the DVDs and the VHSes."[31]

For Baggs it was a testing time. "I was filming with Louise Jamieson, the short film that Pip and Jane Baker wrote for me, *The Last 28*, I was on the set of that and I had a message from Gary to say that they'd got the licence and my heart sank. I knew what was going to happen, it was one of the worst moments of my life."[32] Not only was this a huge problem for Baggs, but it also helped widen the gap between him and some of his former colleagues, as Gary Russell later suggested. "They [the BBC] were quite forthright however that we didn't get Bill involved in our stuff as a director, which was an idea we had mooted with them at one point. It wouldn't have been very sensible to employ someone who they'd initiated some sort of legal action with. Bill seems to have taken this as a personal snub from me and Nick, which is odd because he's not dim and must have foreseen the problems that would arise if you go to the BBC, ask for a licence to do something, get turned down and then effectively do it anyway. That's why we couldn't involve him in the 'Talkin' About My Regeneration' *DWM* CD cover mount. The Beeb had to approve that as they do everything we produce, and wouldn't agree to us involving someone they had a disagreement with. A shame as Bill's involvement in getting us where we are today should never go untrumpeted, but that's the realities of life."[33]

Despite the impending arrival of officially licensed *Doctor Who* audio adventures, BBV still had the upper hand in one respect, as Big Finish were still a number of months away from releasing anything. This gave them the chance to wrap up *The Time Travellers* scripts they had already committed to, and look for new properties and areas to explore.

The first release after the announcement was from newcomer Mark J. Thompson. Recruited by Ainsworth, Thompson was a writer and director who specialised in training and promotional videos and who had also written, produced and directed the self-funded *Ghostlands* pilot, which starred, amongst others, Sylvester McCoy. Thompson was the first writer tasked with writing for the newly renamed Dominie and Alice. "I know there was a massive copyright issue, but I tried where possible to make it as *Doctor Who* as possible. So I had them 'in the ship' and featured the swimming pool. I kind of thought personally it was pointless making them completely new characters when it was clear they were the Doctor and Ace, despite the copyright issues. I think I avoided using the name Alice where possible too. Omicron the shape changer was originally supposed to change into the Brigadier but copyright issues meant we couldn't sadly, so he became Samantha from the Professor's past."[34]

Thompson would also direct the play and in doing so cast a number of actors he had worked with before. Joining the regulars were a hugely experienced cast of Jo Phillips-Lane as Samantha, Sammie Winmill as Vixxy, Peter Dean playing Reg and Gary Hailes in the role of Karsius.

In both production and writing Thompson took the play into some very dark areas. The opening sees the "Ship" land in a living "Meat City." For Thompson this was part of the process of writing something that couldn't be achieved on a television. "Audio allows you to do the unimaginable. The more horrible the idea, the more to town your mind can go! As many have said before — you can forget budget when it comes to how you want it to 'look' with audio!"[35]

Thompson also drew on his favourite eras from the show's past, in order to create this macabre tale. "I love darker original *Who* (Pertwee's 1st season, Tom's 1st, 2nd and last season and Colin's 1st season). I think everyone enjoys it more — the scarier it is — look how fantastic 'Blink' was and has become a television classic. *Doctor Who* always works best when it plays into the things we fear, like any good story. Silly childish romps always bored me within the series and weakened it for me. I love good twists, and cannibalism is just one example." [36]

Continuing this theme, Thompson had little foreknowledge of what had been done with Alice/Ace in the previous plays and instead drew direct influence from *Doctor Who*'s 26th Season. "I really wanted to explore what had been going on back at home for 'Ace' which was vaguely hinted at in the TV series. Sophie really enjoyed acting out the emotional abuse scenes. The CDs were aimed at a more adult audience, so you could delve into topics you couldn't on the TV series." [37]

DWM's Vanessa Bishop was in praise of McCoy's performance and his conflict with Alice, but was not a fan of the play over all. "Never quite finding its tone, voiced with guttural evil and the tinny treated chirpiness of clichéd science fiction, BBV's latest 'Dominie and Alice' audio play jars unevenly with the darker patches it later makes space to explore."[38].

While 'Only Human' certainly crams a lot into its short run time, it doesn't feel as uneven as Bishop suggests, though you can't help feeling it would have made for a great double CD. The scenes on Omicron's home planet provide one of the most alien planets that *Doctor Who/The Time Travellers* have ever visited. The conflict between Ace and her stepfather packs a hefty emotional punch and goes into some of the darkest territory the series has ever ventured into. Vixxy the android plays like a psychotic Kryten and the reveal that she is a murderer, driven mad by her own orders is a brilliant twist. Not to mention the powerful climax of Alice berating the Dominie for his reluctance to break the Laws of Time. Thompson offers a gripping tale that incorporates so much great stuff, it is shame he never contributed more the range. He pushes the audio medium and the *Doctor Who* format to the limit, delivering a very human tale in such alien surroundings.

'Only Human' would be Thompson's sole contribution to BBV but he would go on to produce his own range of science fiction audio plays entitled *Soldiers of Love*. "I had planned to release one every other month on the months when BBV didn't release CDs. Unfortunately, BBV slowly faded away as Big Finish got the BBC licence to produce *Doctor Who*"[39]. However, he looks back on his one outing with BBV fondly "It wasn't too bad! There were areas I would like to have sharpened up, like some of the characters' portrayals and especially with post production. Would be great to do it for TV! It would also have worked better expanded over a couple of CDs so you really got to know the characters before their demise. Sophie was outstanding though in her dramatic scenes! Also would have worked better with the Brigadier as planned." [40]

With *The Time Travellers* ending, an attempt was made to create a new series that would sit comfortably alongside Big Finish's output, John Ainsworth hit upon an idea of using the character of K9 as the star of his own series. Tim Saward was charged with contacting Bob Baker and Dave Martin, the creators of K9, to get permission.

"There was a bit of suspicion on that side from the agent, as to what we were trying to do, because K9 was a product that had some currency at the time, and they were trying to make a TV series"[41] Even so. they eventually agreed and Ainsworth was then tasked with coming up with the basis for a series.

"I talked to Mark Thompson and he said 'how about we make a sitcom out of K9?' So it would be in some *Coronation Street*-like setting and him sort of living with some lady. He had in mind an actress called Anna Karen who used to be one of the regulars in *On the Buses*. He thought it could be her and K9 and their sort of deliberately comedic adventures a very domestic setting in a normal northern town. Which I think is actually quite a fun idea, It's the more sort of radical non-*Doctor Who* style."

The alternative idea and ultimately the one accepted by Baggs (who had a natural aversion to comedy) was "the obviously *Doctor Who* thing of K9 and Romana and their adventures in E-Space, after the Doctor left them at the end of 'Warriors' Gate'."[42]

While the first idea would have clearly angered some *Doctor Who* fans it is certainly the more interesting of the two and it would have been fascinating to see it play out, even if the idea probably wouldn't have had the legs to carry an entire series. It's also doubtful that this would have been the series that cemented BBV's place in the market in a post-Big Finish world.

The only issue with the chosen direction of this new series was that it would require the presence of Lalla Ward to play Romana. Ward had given up acting seven years previously, and only made the occasional appearance on the *Doctor Who* convention scene.

Undaunted, and with John Leeson already signed up to reprise his role as K9, Ainsworth got Ward's number from a convention organiser. "I talked to her on the phone. I made it clear. I said 'look this is not the BBC do you have a problem with it' and she said 'no'. It was mainly because John was doing it. It was quite a big thing for her to come back and act." [43]

With Ward tentatively agreeing, Ainsworth and Baggs went to meet her at her home in Oxford, which she shared with her then husband, scientist Richard Dawkins. Although Baggs had some initial reservations about recruiting Ward, he was won over by her immediately. "She was adorable and she was very approachable, and very interested and engaged with me very well." [44] Ainsworth recalls the meeting in more depth. "We just wanted to sit down and talk about it, and what the character could be called, because she couldn't be called Romana. We suggested various things, we suggested maybe she could be the Princess and Richard said he didn't think that would be a good idea, because princess was an American Jewish name for someone's daughter, so we ended up with The Mistress." [45]

With the two leads in place BBV commissioned a script from Nigel Fairs, who was given a week to write it. Both Baggs and Ainsworth had very strong ideas about the tone of the script. "We wanted it to be very hard, proper science fiction — not too fantasy. I think Nigel found that a little bit difficult, to keep it in that sort of style but he wrote it anyway." [46]

Fairs, who was more than capable of writing hard science fiction, also recalls this clash of styles.

"When John came to me with the idea I just thought 'oh fantastic, it's going to be hilarious and light and frothy' and then he said 'no, Bill wants it to be gritty in-your-face drama'," Fairs says, howling with laughter. "Which when you've got a tin dog is really difficult to do. So that was a real challenge."[47]

With Fairs' hastily written script in hand, a read through was arranged at Ward's home. In attendance were Ward and her husband, Fairs, K9 actor John Leeson and Ainsworth who was given a lift by Leeson.

"John didn't know who Richard Dawkins was, and on the way up in the car he said 'Lalla's husband is some kind of scientist isn't he?' and I said 'yes that's right'. I didn't explain about the whole atheism stuff and then we were sitting round their kitchen table and John decided to start telling a ghost story which of course isn't going to go down well with Richard Dawkins. I half suspect at the time Richard thought John was deliberately baiting him, Richard really quite briskly put John down about it and just dismissed the whole thing as nonsense, and Lalla was a bit embarrassed."[48]

Fairs also found the read through uncomfortable, but for very different reasons. "We read the first draft and they loved it. But I remember sitting at the table saying 'oh my god this doesn't work, it just doesn't hang together' or 'there's not enough of it' so I went away and rewrote it. I think I happened to watch something about World War II prison camps or something like that, and thought 'I'm going to bung that in', because that's the ultimate grit. So I put that in and pumped it out a bit with that but I'm still not convinced it worked. But just the joy of hearing the two of them together was lovely."[49]

The range was named *Adventures in a Pocket Universe* and Fairs' script was entitled 'The Choice'. Fairs was on hand to direct the production and managed to pull together a credible cast from his contacts including 'Time Flight' star Keith Drinkel as Emperor Lukor, Oliver Bradshaw as The Court Historian, Bernard Kay as Burns, Maggie Stables as Lenora and Neil Bull as Nathanien.

The studio that BBV usually used was unavailable on the required recording dates for 'The Choice', so Ainsworth was tasked with finding a cheap alternative. "I eventually managed to find one that was in East London somewhere. It was all a little bit dodgy and we got there and the studio manager wasn't there and we couldn't get into the building." [50]

Eventually the studio manager arrived and led them into a tiny basement studio, where the ensemble huddled around a tiny heater in the freezing cold green room. Further complications arose when a buzz in the background of the studio couldn't be removed for the recording. Much to Ainsworth's amazement, Ward took this all in her stride. "Lalla seemed so enthused and delighted that she was acting again, that she seemed quite oblivious to the fact it was freezing cold and there were all these problems with the place. She just seemed so thrilled and exited to be doing it, which was great and I think she had a great time." [51]

Harvey Summers was once again on music and post production duties, including writing a new theme for the series. "I LOVED writing the K9 theme, I was just starting to score orchestral pieces at the time and I had this madcap idea for a theme that would be jaunty and fun! Of all the work I produced over the years for Bill and Big Finish, K9's theme and K9's lament are two pieces I still occasionally see on my royalty statement from PRS."[52] Summers' enthusiasm for the score can be heard in a rip-roaring theme that wouldn't be out of place on a CBBC show today.

But did he find it more challenging to come up with a signature piece, which would be heard again and again compared to incidental music which will only be heard once?

"I would say the challenge is equal but different. A signature tune has to be pitched exactly right — it needs to be instantly recognisable and I always believe a strong melody helps make it memorable. However, the underscore work is so important too, as you're really setting the atmosphere and emotional tone for the scene. Sometimes you go against the emotional curve and that's more poignant, e.g. having a happyish sounding piece under a very sad scene can be more melancholic than going with the obvious. If you ever watch a movie or listen to an audio drama where the music has been removed, you'd be amazed at how flat it all seems!" [53]

Vanessa Bishop said of 'The Choice', "it's appropriate to align 'The Choice' not with Seasons 17 or 18, but instead with the escapades contained within a World Distributors annual. Echoing their brisk air and boundless energy, it's almost as wonderfully meaningless."[54]

This is perhaps down to the issue Fairs and BBV had with wanting differing tones. The play is enormous fun, with both the Mistress and K9 being well deserving of a series. Harvey Summers' post production and music echo these sentiments and help create a world that is leaps and bounds beyond just another knock off of *Doctor Who*. The issue comes with the more serious side of the play and the dark, emotional turn it takes at the end. It jars with the nature of the story and the characters and proves a mistake to try and turn it into a more mature drama.

It's telling that when K9 did reappear on TV, it was in a TV show that was aimed at children rather than adults.

Chapter 21 — Three

Despite the production chaos and lukewarm response to *Mindgame*, Keith Barnfather felt there were further stories to tell for the three characters in the film. "I was so frustrated about how crap *Mindgame* was and I wanted to put something out relatively quickly afterward to show I could do better. Also, you almost want to know what happens to the three people when they all disappear."[1] Rather than trying to force a second meeting of his unlikely trio, Barnfather chose instead to tell three different stories in the portmanteau style, their only connection to each other being the impact of the events of *Mindgame* on the protagonists.

In order to give each of the films a different feel, Barnfather elected to have a different writer for each section of the film, with Nick Briggs acting as script editor on the project.

The first chapter of the film would be written again by Terrance Dicks, who chose to concentrate on how the collaboration with his fellow captors had provoked a change in the Sontaran. "It sort of shakes the whole Sontaran's worldview," recalls Dicks, "because cooperation with another species is not a Sontaran thing. If you meet them, you kill them and I think the Sontaran was trying to work out how something that was opposed to all his beliefs, could perhaps be true. Because it did work and he gets tragically killed before he can tell anybody. So the Sontarans go on in their bloodthirsty way."[2]

This was the script that Briggs had the most input in, saying "there were lots of little thing I wanted to change"[3]. He and Dicks had a conversation where they were speaking at "cross purposes",[4] according to Briggs. "I was trying to say to Terrance 'I'm really sorry but I would really like to change some of the bits of your script', thinking he wouldn't want me to. And he was trying to say to me 'I'd rather you just did all the rewrites', thinking that I would want him to do them." However an understanding was reached. "So eventually Terrance, the old solder that he is, said 'look, the things is, Nicholas, if you want to change it, you just change it, however you want and when everyone says it's brilliant you'll just have to grind your teeth knowing you really wrote it yourself, because that's what used to happen to me all the time on *Who* you see'." [5]

The next writer came in the form of one of the previous film's stars, Draconian actor Miles Richardson, who pitched his idea over a few bottles of wine on a social occasion at Barnfather's house. "My involvement came from the simple realisation that sci-fi was a medium in which anything is possible, as there are no rules as to what goes on in space and time. On set, when you're not filming, you have time to muse and during the initial *Mindgame* I thought that the Draconians were quite intriguing types and not just your run of the mill green aliens. So when Keith first suggested a sequel, I immediately suggested that I write my own segment. To my surprise, he agreed without question. The writing itself took very little time, as I had the idea buzzing in my head anyway. I think it only took me an afternoon. Some will say that it looked like it as well!"[6]

This segment of the film would go untouched by Briggs, much to his own amusement. "I had nothing to do with Miles' one, 'Prisoner 451'. I think I read it and thought 'oh my god that's absolutely impenetrable' but he's doing it so never mind."[7]

The final segment, based around Sophie Aldred's human, was written by Roger Stevens. A long-time collaborator of Barnfather's, he had written, directed and produced a number of the Reeltime documentary releases. Briggs added his touch to this section. "I did some re writes on Roger's, I think I might have done a little bit of massaging of the script." [8]

Once again Aldred and Miles returned to play their respective parts. The Sontaran however, was recast, under advice from Briggs. "There were many things wrong with *Mindgame*, which I told Keith about and he said 'don't be so mean', but one of the main things wrong with it, was the chap who played the Sontaran was terrible, he really let it down I thought. So I said to Keith 'you should have got my mate John Wadmore to do it' because he can do a great Sontaran voice." [9]

With Toby Aspin's performance receiving a critical mauling. Barnfather replaced him with Wadmore.

Having learnt his lesson on the previous film, Barnfather chose to film each of the stories single camera. "I suppose it was a reaction to the multi-camera shoot for *Mindgame*. I thought, I want to do something simple. In a way it's kind of talking heads, I know that you've got a bit of movement in your Sontaran story but even then he's there in his fox hole."[10]

Shot at the London based Lime Light studios in early 1999, David J. Howe was once again on hand to help out. "It was structured in three parts, because they could all be filmed independently of each other. We filmed at Keith's own studio so he didn't have to pay any hire fees or anything like that."[11]

The first of the stories to go before the camera was Richardson's 'Prisoner 451' (a nod to the dystopian Ray Bradbury novel, *Fahrenheit 451*). Set entirely in one location, a simple prison cell was constructed by Tony Clark the night before. Richardson feels the singular location and the presence of only one actor was beneficial to the production. "The strength of the piece was having a solo performance, which meant it was easier to film and Keith's big enemy — time — wasn't such a problem. It was also an example of what Reeltime can produce with enthusiasm and commitment and a budget so small, it wouldn't buy a round at the BBC canteen. Also, Keith is lucky that he can call on a number of dedicated creatives who, like himself, do their job out of love rather than financial reward."[12]

Barnfather had absolute faith in Richardson to deliver the goods. "The thing with Miles is I knew he was perfect, I mean the takes were difficult just because we wanted to tweak it a bit and do this that and the other. I was quite confident we would finish it in time so I could indulge with Miles quite a bit."[13]

Despite there being only one set and limited room in the tiny studio, Barnfather still found plenty of ways to make the shooting interesting, utilising tracking shots and mounted cameras acting as CCTV.

While 'Prisoner 451' was shooting, Clark put the finishing touches to the cockpit of the spacecraft for the next story, the Aldred-led, 'Scout Ship'. With the Draconian adventure scheduled to wrap at lunch time, the team would strike the set and replace it with the spaceship.

Beset with delays and issues on the previous film, did Barnfather ever worry about filming two short films in one day this time round? "No, because we knew what we were going to do. Each of them was 15 to 20 minutes, it was single camera and it was in a set. We knew exactly what we were going to do with each set constructed. The prison was ready, I had all my shots worked out, they weren't particularly complicated, it was a straight forward run through it. I knew Sophie's was two cameras so we didn't have to worry about the camera, I had a couple of shots I did from a distance, no problem."[14]

Barnfather's confidence was justified and 'Prisoner 451' was wrapped at 2:30, with cameras rolling on 'Scout Ship' roughly an hour later. Although pleased to be returning, Aldred found the working conditions a little difficult. "The lines were a real pig to learn and we were filming in a very small space in his very small studio. It was very kind of cramped and hot but that kind of added to it."[15]

The script called for Aldred to deliver a sensitive performance, and she was more than up for the challenge. "It's a gift for an actor to be given a script like that. It's a great chance to sort of show off the range really. I mean, good lord, not many people have a chance to do a monologue like that, fantastic." [16] Barnfather was impressed with Aldred's performance and commitment to the script. "She loved it, she really was up for doing that and she put a lot into it I remember the studio for that and the atmosphere was quite tense. I actually think as a director I was getting there too. I was beginning to get directing actors well."[17]

And so by 8 o'clock, the second of the two films was wrapped.

The final instalment, 'Battlefield' was filmed a few days later at Harrison's Rocks in Kent, previously used for the *Doctor Who* story 'Castrovalva'. The crew arrived at sunset, set up base at the rock face on the side of the road, and dressed the area to look like a futuristic No Man's Land. In the time that elapsed between shooting the first two segments and the last, Barnfather had become ill and so called in some help for the shoot. "I wasn't feeling that good while we were doing that, I can't remember what was wrong but Nick came out to help me with that and basically he was sort of like my mouthpiece." [18]

Briggs remembers little of his role while there. "Just giving John a few pointers. When Keith said things to John that were massively unhelpful to actors, I would translate it to John to something that would help him."[19]

By 7:30 it was dark enough to start shooting, and Barnfather talked the action through with his lead, John Wadmore who had done some preparation for the part. "They'd made one before and the guy that played the Sontaran they didn't think was much cop so they said 'would I do it' and I said, 'I don't know anything about it, what is it?' but actually, I knew the character; I'd seen it, I'd watched *Doctor Who* when I was younger. He gave me some clips and stuff of Sontarans so I could get the voice right. It was quite an interesting challenge to get the part and get the voice right more than anything."[20]

Shooting was taking place across the road from a local hotel, which kindly lent the crew the use of the bathroom, where Wadmore's make-up and costume were applied. "I had panda make-up with black eyes and then just got the helmet on. It's not until you actually see it back that you realise the effect that it has with costume and gloves and the sort of helmet thing." [21]

One slightly controversial aspect of the production for fact fans was that the Sontaran had fake blood applied which was red although it had previously been established that Sontaran blood is green. This was simply a confusion with the make-up artists, who had seen blood written in the script and assumed it was red. When the question of whether Sontaran blood was red or green was posed to Barnfather on the M*aking of Mindgame Trilogy* extra, he tactfully responded that "it depends which faction you belong to, there's the green faction and the red faction in Sontaran genetics. No one knows about this yet."[22]

The shoot completed without issue and despite his illness, Barnfather was delighted with how it went. "That one went down perfectly, we started as soon as the sun went down and shot through to about two o'clock in the morning. We all knew it would be that sort of time scale, loads of tea and coffee, went home. And a night shoot looks great."[23]

Mindgame: Trilogy is all round a better production than its predecessor, with all three actors offering capable performances which play to their strengths. Wadmore's brutish thug coming to terms with the realisation that the Sontaran way of life may not be correct, adds more depth to the race than any previous outing, while Richardson offers his best cod Shakespearean Draconian, exploring an alien society and culture through his musings. Finally, Aldred's vulnerable side is once again on display as she comes to terms with her own death.

Mindgame: Trilogy is well written, well directed and makes good use of CGI to make the stories appear bigger than they are and remains near the peak of the spin-off ranges.

That said, Vanessa Bishop called *Mindgame: Trilogy* "[a] video sequel that struggles to offer more depth to the characters in the original drama"[24] — a curious observation, considering the obvious differences between the two productions. Of the leads she notes Richardson's performance is "full of eye-rolling and fussy tuts of a comic Olivier."[25]

Bishop also had issues with Aldred's work "because of the angst which the actress is asked to display — it is, for all the wrong reasons, the most uncomfortable to view."

In fact, she only really has time for the Sontaran segments of the film. "The bellowing smoke, flashes of far-off explosions and night-lit location enliven and widen the frame, ensuring this part is the tapes visual showpiece." [26]

Richardson was quick to respond to any critics of his endeavours. "Though some of the reviews for the piece seemed to suggest that it was the stronger of the tryptych, I read somewhere that me writing and acting in it was the very worst vanity project, which it probably is, but if you can't write yourself a good part, don't write."[27]

Despite this damning review, Keith Barnfather is still proud of *Mindgame: Trilogy* "A lot of what I've done has been experimental. That was, an experiment to see how that kind of thing would work and actually I really like *Mindgame: Trilogy* I think that it's one of our better dramas and the acting is superb."[28]

Although Dicks was fond of his contribution, this would be the last spin-off production he wrote. 'Having got involved in that sort of thing I found it a bit hard to get out of it. Because they weren't lucrative and as I say I made a little money on *Shakedown*, but none of the others ever made anything. I think it was bit of soft heartedness on my part, wanting to help the fans." [29]

In spite of the apparent death of the three leads, Barnfather recalls there were plans for one more film, provisionally entitled *Mindgame: Trinity*. "You don't know that anyone other than the Sontaran was actually killed and even though he falls over and goes 'arrrgh' you don't actually know he's dead. So I planned on taking them to Cyprus, where there's some absolutely amazing locations. My wife Anastasia is Greek Cypriot, so we've got family and houses and all that out there. I'd spoke to Sophie, Miles and John and they all said yes. I don't know if we ever wrote a script, but we had some outlined stories, but in the end we just had to can it, as there was never going to be the money to do it."[30]

A further *Mindgame* film never materialised and in fact this would be Reeltime's last drama for five years. This may be down to the fact that with the advent of Big Finish and BBV concentrating on audio, the direct-to-video spins off were a market in decline. However, while their drama output was non-existent, Reeltime continued to release Myth Maker tapes, securing interviews with less prominent *Doctor Who* alumni including Tristram Cary, Andrew Cartmel, Philip Segal and David Brierley.

Chapter 22 — Wonderful Sometimes

The next release from BBV's audio range was May 1999's 'Blood Sports', which would be the final outing for *The Time Travellers* as a duo (although the Dominie would have a solo adventure the following season). The play was once again written and directed by Fairs, who had no idea that this was to be the last of Sylvester and Sophie's BBV adventures. "It's a shame, as I didn't like 'Blood Sports'," [1] he now says. The script, which was another adaptation from Fair's *Pieces* range, tackled some big issues, mainly that of racism. "I think sci-fi can be very weak if doesn't explore those themes, because I think that's what sci-fi is, it's like the best fairy tales. It's actually there to put human things in a different setting." [2]

The play saw Jackie Skarvellis return as Betty Durham from 'Ghosts' and also featured roles for Keith Drinkel and Bernard Kay who had just been in 'The Choice'. Joining them was John Cormack as Zagess and Jo Castleton as Djala.

'Blood Sports' was the soleouting for Graheme Wilson on post-production and music duties, and if Fairs' opinion of the play is anything to go by, it's not hard to see why he was never hired again. "Whoever he got in to edit that should be shot. I was so bitterly disappointed, as the cast were great in the studio, Sylvester said this was a really good script; everyone was really up for it. Scenes cut, scenes without sound effects, music that sounds so distant it could be coming over the PA, dreadful. I haven't been able to listen to all of it, I was virtually crying when I heard it, I couldn't believe that was going out with my name. Such a shame."[3]

Vanessa Bishop was similarly unimpressed with the release. "The plot may aspire to the pace and power of a runaway locomotive, but the overall lack of tension ensures that the play remains uninvolving. A weak entry in a series that, by offering a unique sideline to *Doctor Who*, is more special than it seems, at present, to believe it is."[4]

While this is true, the lack of tension is almost entirely down to poor sound design; the awful music fades in and out at random intervals, sound cues are missed entirely (the train hurtling out of control is done with no sound FX at all!), the sound effects are generally poor and the release really should have been remastered by someone else before its release. All this is a shame as the story and the performances are of a high standard and Fairs' dialogue sparkles in the hands of an experienced cast. McCoy and Aldred once again bring their A game, with the former delivering a beautiful speech about the lack of rules in the universe as the end title music fades in.

In May 1999, the newly established BBV website exclusively revealed that BBV had acquired the rights to use the Zygons, Sontarans, Krynoids and

Rani. In the news piece, Bill Baggs explained the reasoning behind the choices. "These stories will create a really dramatic finish for our second season, and just go to show that there are still inventive ways of using these creations. I think we've shown with *Auton* how popular these elements of the past can be, and we undertook lots of research to discover which monsters people wanted back the most. The Zygons and Sontarans came out on top, and with their distinctive voices, they're ideal for audio."[5]

With the impending arrival of Big Finish's *Doctor Who* range it was a smart move on the part of BBV to bring out the big guns in terms of second tier *Doctor Who* monsters, and judging by the success of the *Auton* films it seemed there was a market for it.

One series that BBV hoped to get off the ground was a range centred around the Daleks.

So was Baggs trying to get his hands on things before Big Finish?

"Yes, we were exploring lots of things, we were mopping up lots of rights."[6]

Tim Saward was involved in the brief negotiations with Terry Nation's agent. "Roger Hancock, who was never going to say yes anyway, basically just sort of said 'no this isn't a licensed product and you can't do anything with the Daleks, sorry'. They had obviously done this a lot before."[7]

One thing that prevented this from happening was the complicated rights situation between the BBC and the Nation estate. While the concept of the Daleks was owned by the Nation estate, the design was entirely the BBC's as Saward explains. "Even with the permission of the estate of Terry Nation, you'd need the BBC's permission and [the Nation estate] said the BBC had to be involved and we said 'but you can't see the Daleks on audio' but they weren't having that."[8]

In 2005, this relatively informal arrangement was codified, prior to the launch of the new series of *Doctor Who*, and rights in both design and concept were split 50/50 thereafter.

A Dalek series certainly would have put BBV on something approaching an equal footing with Big Finish, especially as there were no Daleks present on the early Big Finish schedule. However, by May 2000 not only had Big Finish successfully negotiated the rights to use the Daleks but were also planning their very own Dalek spin-off series, *Dalek Empire.*

The first release from this new range of monster audios would be June's Zygon adventure, with Baggs giving the same brief to two different writers, Tim Saward and newcomer Paul Ebbs. Each writer came up with a different approach, and it was decided to produce Saward's first. For Saward this marked a significant advancement in his proficiency as a writer. "Bill sort of finally got through to me that you just have to do short scenes and make it move at a reasonable pace. I did that well to an extent, in that I tried to do something that had literally ten lines of dialogue in a scene rather than 200. The whole thing just felt like it was moving and while I think that was progress towards what I think makes a successful script of that type, I was bored by it and actually didn't enjoy writing it."[9]

When pushed for an answer as to why he didn't enjoy it Saward is honest. "Maybe I didn't enjoy writing it because it was harder to do. If I'm honest I remember being way over deadline on it, hating every second of what I was doing and thinking this is not really a good position to be in, when you are writing something you are hoping other people are going to enjoy. With this and what was going on at my life at the time, it just exhausted me and in the end I was pissed off with the whole fucking thing and so I killed all the characters.' [10]

'*Zygons*: Homeland', as the play was called, would go out under the pen name of Paul Dearing, as Saward was also unhappy with the final script. It was directed by Nick Briggs who also starred as the Captain and did the Zygon voices under his old AV alias, David Sax. Other cast members included John Albasiny as Guy Dean, Andrew Fettes as The Colonel, Kirsty Yates as Julie, Daniel Gabriele as Andrew Molton, Susan Travers as Morag and Kenneth J. Bentley as James.

While not a fan of the performances, Vanessa Bishop found the story a compelling one. "'Homeland' proves to be an effective and surprisingly sombre continuation, managing to wring out a new story from creatures with very singular aims."[11] Indeed, the play is Saward's best. The characters are well fleshed out, even if a couple of the performances are lacklustre. Rather than the typical Doctor and Companion clones being a hindrance in this play, Saward uses it to his advantage, having all of the leads sacrifice themselves at the end, and thus doing something that its parent show could never do. The scene in question is beautifully written, as three people play out their last minutes without heroic speeches and noble gestures but with fear, anxiety and the realisation of what they have done.

'*Zygons*: Homeland' would be the final time Briggs worked for BBV and marked the end of his troubled relationship with Baggs. "He could sense that I was moving away,"[12] explains Briggs, who feels the Fred plays were Baggs' way of trying to keep him happy, with the offer of the lead part. "I remember John Ainsworth saying to me, that Bill was totally mystified at my waning amount of interest in me working for him." [13]

But for Briggs the reasons were generally straight-forward. "I put up with all the pain of working with Bill — because it was always difficult — I put up with that pain, in order to do the things I loved. Then when I got the opportunity to do the thing I loved — and they really were the things I loved, and not just pretend versions of it — and didn't really have any pain associated, I clearly was going to do that."

So were Big Finish worried about Nick's continuing relationship with BBV?

"I don't think Gary Russell ever said to me 'you really shouldn't be doing these'. I think I pre-empted any concerns because Bill had already been warned off by a legal letter from the BBC. So I said to Gary 'I promised Bill I'd do this, so I'll just do this and that'll be an end to it.'" [14]

The next CD to be recorded was the second in the *Adventures in a Pocket Universe* series. The script was developed by the enigmatic Mark Duncan under the guidance of John Ainsworth, though once again Duncan was a difficult subject to deal with. "I had to force him to take out all these lines, that he'd stolen out of *Blake's 7.* Which he blatantly admitted and he said 'it's a good line' and I said 'it is a good line but it's not your line.' He was a funny character."[15]

This second volume was entitled 'The Search' and would be one of the few audios Baggs directed himself. The play had a minimal cast consisting of the two regulars Graeme Du-Fresne as Kimmel & Vulich, Mike McCormack as Caloyer and Autons, plus Bryonie Pritchard as Jora, who relished the chance to work in audio. "It's a medium I love working in. On radio you can create so much more."[16]

Ainsworth wasn't in attendance for the studio recording, but did attend a signing and launch for the play at Forbidden Planet in London. "Lalla and John were there, and I just remember for some reason she'd got it in her head that I'd directed the first one. I don't know why, because I didn't, but they clearly hadn't had a good time on the second one. Lalla said to me 'oh you were missed' which a very nice of her but I don't really know what went on." [17]

The reason for Ainsworth's absence at the studio recording was simple — although the K9 series had been his brain child, he had unexpectedly left the project and BBV just before recording. "At that point Bill rang me up and said 'I think we shouldn't work together for a while'. I must have annoyed him or upset him, I don't quite remember why. Actually, I was partly relieved because it was slightly unrewarding in every sense. He never completely gave me a reason." [18]

While Ainsworth remains unsure of why he was let go, Baggs seems to think the decision was mutual, even if he apparently didn't explain it well. "I think there was an understanding. We both knew that Big Finish had had an impact because he was on a salary essentially. I couldn't afford to pay him anymore and he knew that, so it was never going to be an on-going kind of thing. His value for what we were doing was no longer needed really, and I couldn't justify paying him."[19]

Vanessa Bishop described the release as "a weightier episode than the series' debut,"[20] enjoying Ward's performance in particular, but going on to question if the characters were suitable for this sort of adventure.

If 'The Choice' fought against Bill Baggs' wish to make serious drama for the Mistress and K9, then the 'The Search' embraces it wholeheartedly. The results of which are ultimately unsatisfactory, however.

The first third of the play makes for an atmospheric opener, with a score and sound design that underpins the mystery of the drama. However, once the characters arrive on the scene, the play descends into a series of badly thought out sci-fi clichés, excessive exposition and technobabble which confuses the listener and seems to bore even the actors, performing in it. The play reaches an unsatisfactory conclusion and the listener is left wondering what actually happened with K9 and the computer. 'The Search' ultimately lacks the sense of adventure and humour that is needed to convincingly sell a story about a robot dog and his time-travelling mistress.

'The Choice' was with retailers by September of 1999, by which time Big Finish's first CD, the multi-Doctor adventure, 'Sirens of Time', had been released and their schedule revealed to fandom.

With a line up that included Doctors five, six and seven, Big Finish had gathered up the actors who Baggs had relied on to push his projects over the last decade. Big Finish also boasted two of BBV's most reliable writers, Mark Gatiss and Nick Briggs, as well as well-known *Doctor Who* novelists such as Justin Richards, Stephen Cole and Jonathan Blum.

The impact on BBV was almost instantaneous as Baggs admitted. "I sold thousands of 'Republica' and 'Island of Lost Souls'. By the time John left we'd be lucky if we sold a thousand."[21]

Big Finish had made its mark on the *Doctor Who* audio market and put a halt on any more K9 adventures, despite Ainsworth planning a series. "Certainly the intention was there would have been more Lalla and K9 ones, but after the second one it just wasn't selling enough."[22]

Baggs was still (somewhat desperately) hoping to find his place in the market. "That whole era is about searching for something to move forward with. You knew what Big Finish were offering and it diminished the desirability of what I was doing with Sylvester and Sophie. So I needed to find what I was doing and I was playing [with] different things to see what would stick." [23]

As previously discussed, Baggs had given the go ahead to two writers to come up with workable stories for the Zygons. With Tim Saward's '*Zygons*: Homeland' already on the shelves, the second release — Paul Ebbs' '*Zygons*: Absolution' — would now take centre stage.

Ebbs was a newcomer to BBV, but was a prominent name on the fan fiction circuit, having written for the critically acclaimed Season 27 audio range. Ebbs was brought in by Tim Saward, who was impressed by his previous audio output. Ebbs discussed the differing takes on these classic monsters on the BBV website. "The idea was to give two writers the same basic brief and see how different the results could be in two separate pairs of hands. I think the contrast is intriguing. It is remarkable how different they turned out: thematically, and in the style of storytelling."[24]

Initially, it was hoped that 'Absolution' would be directed by Nick Briggs, a role that eventually went to Tim Saward. Presumably Briggs was busy working with Big Finish and with Briggs and Baggs' relationship on the rocks again after *Auton 3* it is no surprise that direction moved in-house, even if Saward's only previous directing experience had been as codirector of 'Prosperity Island' at no extra fee. "I was bit surprised actually, I remember Bill called me when I was at the hairdressers to ask me if I would direct it and I was quite floored actually."[25]

The main guest star for 'Absolution' was Peter Miles, who had previously worked on Saward's 'Property Island'. He later told the BBV website what attracted him to the part. "There's no Doctor or 'spin-off Doctor' in it. I liked doing the part I had in 'Zygons' because it had what I call in the theatre world genuine melodrama. It was dramatic and bordered on the melodrama that is something I love personally."[26]

Saward found being reunited with Miles an enjoyable experience. "Lovely Peter! He was really nice and it was just effortless... because when someone's that experienced they can just turn up in a studio and do the first scene pretty much right the first time. He was cast well because he was playing a sort of fanatical nutty character and that's what he does very well. He was very of the old school, very polite and didn't make fuss about anything and had obviously been a successful jobbing actor because of that."[27]

The rest of the cast was drawn from the BBV regular cast. Saward himself took the park of Hyrstic, Alistair Lock played Nik with Paul Ebbs as Turner. They were joined by Bryonie Pritchard as Justine and Patricia Merrick as Vetes.

Directing the play produced a whole new set of challenges for Saward, who had to work around actors' schedules, including one having an audition in the middle of the day. He also overheard one of the actors being rude about his directing skills and had a brief panic at the end of the day when they thought all the recordings had been wiped. "It was really tricky and it was so completely out of sequence, because of those demands of the actors. So it was quite hard to direct it a coherent way."[28]

Richard McGinlay of *DreamWatch* called 'Absolution', "Enjoyable fodder, though hardly innovative,"[29] but it actually does feel like a breath of fresh air, after a number of releases that lacked in one area or another. Paul Ebbs builds an interesting and believable world that is inhabited by three dimensional characters. Saward's direction, along with Michael Neilson's score creates a taut atmosphere while Peter Miles delivers a harrowing performance as a man suffering a psychological breakdown which, despite its animated nature, stays just on the right side of scenery chewing.

'*Zygons*: Absolution' was released as a double disc with the CD case also containing the next release '*Krynoids*: The Root of All Evil'. Saward believes this was done a cost saving exercise. "I'm pretty sure the cause of that, was he had all these unsold copies of 'Prosperity Island', that he wanted to reuse the cases. He only had to do the printing, it was really bad. It was a bit desperate."[30]

'The Root of All Evil' was written by acclaimed *Doctor Who* novelist Lance Parkin, who recalls the initial brief.

"I may have been given a choice from the various monsters Bill had the rights to. But that would have been the sum of the brief, I think: tell a story with the Krynoids in it."[31]

Despite being an established and successful writer of prose, audio was like learning a new discipline. "The first play was the first audio I'd ever written, and it was fun figuring out what strengths the medium had, what worked and what didn't. It's not the most complicated story I ever came up with, and it's a little too close to 'Seeds of Doom'." [32]

Parkin also drew from his previous writing experience to help formulate the story. "I'd just finished working at *Emmerdale*[33], and it's basically Krynoids killing everyone on Emmerdale Farm. I'm not sure the Krynoids are the most versatile *Doctor Who* monsters, to be honest. On audio, you can't really do much more — or at least I couldn't do much more — than have people going 'oh no, you're turning into a plant'." [34]

The play was directed by Paul Ebbs, with post production and music from Steve Johnson. The relatively small cast included Catherine Church as Eve, Mark Donovan as Karl, Will Warrior as Jeff, Neil Bull in the role of Martin and Holly King playing Sally.

Paul Winter of *Celestial Toyroom* said of the release, "[t]he performances are fine. The narrative is solid and moves along at a good pace without wasting any time. As with all good audio, you can easily imagine the pictures in your mind."[35]

'The Root of All Evil' should be one of the strongest plays of the season. Parkin delivers a simple but effective horror story, the characters are well written and the more gruesome aspect of the Krynoid creature is well utilised. Unfortunately the play is let down by some sub-par performances that make this more closely resemble an amateur play than a professional production. Like a number of plays recorded at this time, this lacks a sufficient soundscape to make this seem like anything but a crowd of people acting in a room.

The final script for Season 2 came from another newcomer, Peter Grehan, who would pen BBV's first adventure featuring the Sontarans.

Grehan worked in the arts and did freelance writing on the side, but also had a BSc (Hons) degree in Science and Science Fiction and an MA in

Scriptwriting. His pitching of ideas was part of a much larger scheme to tout for work. "I had been sending speculative stuff to various producers and publishers without any luck. I had even tried sending a couple of speculative scripts to *Star Trek* at Paramount without success. I sent a speculative Ace and Professor, *Cyberon* script (which was after all just a thinly disguised *Doctor Who* Cyberman series). I didn't have much success to give my submission any weight, so I mentioned that I had submitted some *Star Trek* scripts although they hadn't been that well thought of. I hoped they would realise I was serious about being a writer that way."[36]

Initially called 'The Sontaran Way', the play was eventually released under the title 'Sontarans: Silent Warrior'. it was directed by Tim Saward and starred Paula O'Grady as Sylvia Tanner, John Wadmore as Field Major Starn, with Polly Pritchett playing Sentinel and Michael Wade playing the very Doctor-ish part of Alex.

Grehan elaborates on whether this was a conscious decision. "A little, as was the fashion in those days, but I also had an idea of an advanced race (rather like the Time Lords) using androids to police the time lines. I think androids would make logical investigators in more senses than one." [37]

Saward was particularly fond of Wade's performance in the finished play. "He was really good. I suppose it was a little bit like that Fred persona, so it was a little bit understated and sort of retrained. I thought it was quite interesting. He did a Yorkshire accent for it, which Paul Ebbs told me he thought was the most stupid idea he'd ever heard and I disagreed with him, but I think Paul was thinking in clichéd terms of everybody has to be RP because that's how *Doctor Who* was in the 70s."[38]

Vanessa Bishop described 'Silent Warrior' as "a superior entry into the BBV range,"[39] — a summary that's hard to argue with, as the play finishes the uneven season on a high. Despite a small cast, the script and direction manage to give the play an epic quality. The stakes are high and the tension is felt from the get go. Wade once again delivers a top notch performance as the android cum pseudo-Doctor (with a northern accent years before Eccleston made them cool) and John Wadmore gives his best Sontaran. It's just a shame we didn't hear more from Alex or indeed Grehan again.

'Silent Warrior' was released in December of 1999 and would be Grehan's sole contribution to the range. He looks back at it with fondness, even so. "I loved the music, it's very atmospheric. Always strange when you hear (or see) something you've written in its final production. When you hand over a script you're sort of giving up ownership of it for others to put their creativity and vision into, so it can be different to how you saw it in your head, but overall, I was very pleased with the production values of 'Silent Warrior'."[40]

'Silent Warrior' would also be Tim Saward's last contribution to the range, as in early 2000 he would get a job at the Millennium Dome, which prevented him from contributing further to BBV. "That was a proper responsible job, which meant I was literally working from seven in the morning to nine at night most days, so I just wasn't doing any writing and didn't have any time at all."[41]

He looks back on his time with BBV with mixed emotions. "I remember it reasonably fondly, I had a very difficult time in my life in general at that time, for various other unconnected reasons, so I don't look back at anything with any fondness, so it would be fair to say it falls in that category. I get the impression of how I came across in the whole thing, that I was a very awkward, a bit Asperger's, kind of person. Oh you know one acquires social skills as one goes on, and I was very shy and very unconfident so I suspect most people probably didn't even notice me. I just wasn't a presence in the whole thing really." [42]

While Saward may try and play down his importance in BBV, Baggs was gratified by his presence. "Tim was brilliant. He was well organized and talented."[43]

The other person making their final appearance in the BBV range was Wade, who had been one of the regular stable of actors for the last three years. At the time of writing this book, preliminary research seemed to point to Wade being dead. His Wikipedia entry up until early 2015, stated he died of a brain haemorrhage (although this has since been removed), his IMDB page states he died on May 22, 2004, while the Canadian Movie Database[44] lists an actor of that name dying of brain cancer on that date, with the same credits as Wade but a different photo.

Baggs remembers "there was some confusion over whether he died or not,"[45] and many of his co-stars seemed to think this was the case, although his *Auton* co-star Telfer has a different tale to tell. "There was confusion as to whether or not Michael Wade was alive about 8 or 9 years ago. Then he turned up to see me in a play and he was absolutely fine. But I don't know, I'd love to be back in touch with him but I just don't know where he is now. He always said to me 'I've got a clear credit card with a credit balance of £40,000 and if it all goes wrong I'll just fuck off to Brazil' so he may just have fucked off to Brazil."[46]

Nick Briggs is able to shed more light on the situation. "I got an answerphone message from him, in which he told me he had cancer and that it was very bad and that he didn't expect to live. That he was going to Brazil because he knew a doctor there, who was a specialist and he was going to try and work some magic, because he didn't have much hope and he said 'please do ring me before I go' and I got the message late, I didn't ring back and it was a source of real regret to me. I spoke to mutual friends about it and we were all very depressed. So I did this thing of being scared of death, so I didn't investigate any further, in my mind he had gone to Brazil and had died."[47]

While Briggs tale initially seems to corroborate the previous information, the story doesn't end there. "Years later we were auditioning for the part of Lucie Miller in Big Finish. We had a load actresses in and one of the actresses said 'I have a friend who was involved in some *Doctor Who*-ey thing.' I said 'oh yeah, what was that?' and she said 'I think it was called *Auton*' and I said 'oh my goodness' and then she said 'Michael Wade' and I was taking to her about someone who in my mind was dead and then she said 'the other day on the phone...' and I went 'whaaat?' Because for a number of years, in my mind he'd been dead and so it was like he'd come back to life."

It seems the treatment had been a success, which Briggs describes as "something of a medical miracle" with the tumours shrinking, and while the cancer is still present, he is alive and well and Briggs has since been in touch with him. "He emails me from Brazil occasionally. I heard from him within the last couple of months." [48]

Season two marked a turning point for the BBV range. While the effect of the Big Finish announcement was undoubtedly a blow to the company, the acquisition of new monsters was a step in the right direction. While not all the releases were successful, it does feel as though BBV were looking for a new direction. It's a shame, however, that they didn't pursue some of the ideas generated in the better of these releases.

Season Two also showcases something that would become an unwelcome hallmark of BBV, that of substandard products being rush released onto the market, with a 'that will do' attitude. If Baggs wanted his audience to stay with him he should have been fighting hard to present them with high quality products; instead he seemed more intent on getting a large quantity of products released in order to sustain his place in the market.

In the long run, season 3 would see a new direction for BBV — as such, this second season feels more like a transitional period rather than a range operating at full capacity.

Chapter 23 – Exit Wounds

Despite the sales figures of *Auton 2* not being as high as those of *Auton*, BBV still sold enough copies to make the final instalment viable. And so Baggs commissioned Briggs to write the third script, which once again would be directed by Briggs, with Baggs acting as director of photography. However just before shooting Briggs left the project; the reasons behind this were never discussed in public or indeed with the BBV team. The disagreements over *Auton* were made public and Baggs' interference in the script writing process on other productions is documented throughout this book. So Tim Saward assumed it was one of their many fallings out. "They had a very chequered history, from what I gather. It was a very, very love/hate relationship."[1]

Many years later Baggs is happy to discuss the issues but doesn't go into specifics. "There was just a falling out. I think what it boiled down to was, when you are a producer and in charge of the finance you end up being quite a control freak and I think it just got a bit too much for him."[2] Baggs does, however, hazard a guess that it may have been down to crewing problems. David Rowston (who AD'd the first two *Auton* films) was unable to do the third film and therefore Briggs brought in a replacement, as Baggs explains. "There was this woman, a stage pal of Nick's, and she decided to not do it and I think very soon after Nick decided to not do it." [3]

Despite Baggs not recalling the specifics, he continued to discuss the implications of Briggs' departure. "It was obviously a huge blow. I mean, I still don't understand why because we fought and things happen and you say things that you wish you didn't and it comes from both sides. It's like a very fragile negotiation process; specifically when you've got somebody directing and there is a producer there and when there is fuck all money. There is tension and stresses. They kind of show up most of the time. I can't even remember them because it's just a normal part of the process, you just get on with it. So why Nick decided to fuck off I don't know, but in the end it basically pushed me back into directing."[4]

Throughout this book, Briggs has talked openly of his frustrations of working with Baggs and now tells his side of the story in great detail. "We'd been through several drafts, I'd written the final draft and we were due to shoot it in a week's time and everything was being organised and then he phoned me and said, 'look, I've sent you a version of the script, I think we can get another full draft out of this,' but he hadn't sent me a version of the script, he'd sent me the script where he'd outlined all the problems. And it's sort of like he'd put notes in like 'this needs to be changed' and 'these people shouldn't be in this scene' and things like that. He hadn't re-written it, he hadn't done anything helpful, he'd just smothered it in notes saying what was wrong with it from his point of view and it was just masses and masses of red type all over it."[5]

Feeling this was an impossible task in such a short time, Briggs refused, and eventually put the phone down on Baggs, feeling the producer had ulterior motives. "The reason he'd phoned me was to try and make it sound like it wasn't much to do. But I thought 'do you really think it's not much to do or do you think it's a lot? and you're trying to fool me or if you don't think it's much, that really means you don't understand anything', because it was basically throwing the whole thing out and starting again."[6]

Briggs feels that root of the problem was something that had been bubbling under the surface for some time. "I felt, rightly or wrongly, that he had a fundamental lack of understanding about storytelling, and I think that he thought the same about me." [7]

Ultimately Briggs was relieved to be done with their relationship. "I realized I'd had enough of Bilbo the Bastard Baggins. Life was too short to suffer another nonsensical conversation. So I resigned and took my name off it." [8]

With the film coming out two months after Big Finish debuted their *Doctor Who* range, it gave Briggs the perfect excuse to sever ties with BBV. "I had other fish to fry, I could see brighter and better days ahead. And I was carrying on with *Auton 3* because I'd said I would, and when he just threw this last massive problem in the way I just thought 'do you know? I've had enough of this, I don't have to put up with this anymore.' I think I was looking for our professional relationship to evolve and I just felt he was taking me around the same mulberry bush again. I thought 'oh gosh, he will never change will he?' I thought 'you will always do this,' and I think it's unnecessary and I have another option on the table. I mean if I hadn't had another option on the table, I wonder what I would have done? I probably would have gone to see him and we would have had a massive argument for about three hours." [9]

The script for *Auton 3* called for the story to be told on a grander scale than its two predecessors and in order to realise it BBV needed to secure extra funding. This came in the form of $10,000 from Who North America, with whom Baggs had previously worked. "I approached them about *Auton 3*. Basically what they were buying were the broadcasting rights for the first two. What they were buying ... was the right to broadcast the third one in advance, because if you can spread the load in terms of finance, it's always a good decision."[10]

While this extra finance helped, and Briggs had given permission for his finished script to be used by Baggs, the producer still wanted a number of changes made to the script. With Briggs unwilling to cooperate, he asked Paul Ebbs, hot on the heels of 'Absolution', to make a few changes, as he discussed on the rec.arts.doctorwho group. "I'm really proud of the work I did on it (it was the first time I'd seen anything I'd written filmed). The script is still basically Nick Briggs' (under a pseudonym) with some new sequences from me that Bill asked for late on in the day. It's definitely the darkest of the three films IMHO and not having the traditional happy *Doctor Who* ending really underlines that."[11]

These new sequences would include the early hospital scenes featuring Lockwood as well as a few scenes towards the film's climax. Of his commission, Ebbs is unsure why he was chosen, but Briggs would eventually take his name off the script and the writing credit be given to his long time alias Arthur Wallis, with additional material by Paul Ebbs. Even so, the July 1999 issue of *DWM* would state that the script was the product of Briggs' hand.

One potential issue that Baggs could have faced upon Briggs' departure was the possibility of a coup on the cast front — the majority of whom were recruited by Briggs and could have left with him. Baggs, however, found they were loyal to the production. "What I was delighted with was all of the cast stayed. All of the regulars in that series: Lockwood, Ramsey, Natasha and Sally were friends that Nick had brought to the table and what was very reassuring was none of the cast dropped out. Because when a director pulls out of a project at such short notice, you kind of begin to question yourself a little bit and I did have this huge sinking feeling, but because of the cast I thought maybe it's not as bad I was thinking, they were all very reliable actors."[12]

Briggs in part, confirms his former colleague's fears. "I suppose part of me hoped that with me leaving it, it wouldn't happen and that all the actors wouldn't want to do it without me and I certainly spoke to them, but then I realise it was work for them and they all did it."[13]

With Briggs leaving the director's chair empty, Baggs decided to take on the mantel himself also in addition to acting as DOP and Producer. In order to ease his workload he called upon long-time friend and collaborator Patricia Merrick, who had AD'd a number of films for Baggs, as well as directing two short films starring Caroline John. Merrick discusses how the relationship worked. "Bill concentrated on the 'look'/shots whilst I concentrated on the performance side. I do recall one of the few visual inputs I had was when Bill was lining up a shot of a deserted street through a bicycle wheel, and I suggested it should be spinning!"[14]

Bill Baggs, on the other hand, downplays her involvement somewhat. "I just took control really, and I mean how cheeky is this? I don't even remember that she was co-directing it, but she was certainly good moral support. I just kind of do my own thing anyway."[15] Despite not having strong memories of her contribution Baggs was still glad of the help.

"Whatever Trish did, she was great. There are people you can rely on and Trish is one. I remember having lots of fun doing that one." [16]

Auton 3: Awakening was shot on Digital Video, over two weeks in July of 1999 in Southampton and Leatherhead. All the principal cast from *Auton 2* returned and a larger part was given to Bryonie Pritchard's Dr Sal, now free from other working commitments. Joining the regulars was Graeme Du Fresne who had previously been in the K9 audio 'The Search' and was also the long-time partner of Pritchard. He played the part of Ross Palmer, which Briggs had written for himself, as Du Fresne later told Paul Griggs. "Initially, Nick was going to do it, but then he withdrew for reasons that I don't fully understand, so Bill asked me to do it which was very nice of him because apart from the audio play he didn't know much about me."[17]

This was the first time the couple had shared the screen together and much to their amusements featured a scene where Du Fresne had to kiss Jo Castleton's character. "That was the best day's filming. 'Bill? Can we do that again please? What do you mean it was alright? No, no. I'm sure it wasn't'."[18]

Du Fresne was also in admiration of the scale of the production. "For instance, locations. When I first saw the script I thought, 'What lunatic has written a story which is set in a deserted city centre?' So we were continually trying to find deserted places in the middle of Southampton in the summer. Not an easy task. So half the time is waiting for traffic noise and airplanes and god knows what."[19]

Due to the nature of the shoot they were beset with problems when filming in public spaces around Southampton, from drunk people screaming "Weyheyyy!" whenever action was called to planes flying overhead. No matter the time of day, Pritchard said they found problems. "Even at six o clock in the morning you think this is nice and quiet, but there's people watering flowers and dust carts and people who haven't gone to bed and all sorts of things."[20]

With two new directors behind the camera there was a change in atmosphere. "The third one was very different feel to the other two"[21] remembers Telfer, who found Baggs to be a less confident leader. "I think perhaps he didn't have quite the through line in his head for the third one, that he might have done. I think he may have kind of had to think on his feet a bit, as to where the third one was going. I do seem to remember thinking 'are you sure you've got a hold on this?' Which was very unlike Nick Briggs, because he had it all mapped out from day one, he knew where he was at and where he was going."[22]

Pritchard on the other hand expressed her admiration for Baggs' work ethic on the shoot. "It's very tight, especially the one we've just done this summer. I think it was incredible to see Bill work, because he is incredible at organising everything. And when he's got the scope to do it that's when he really shines. Which he did have this time. I think other years he had a bit of, not necessarily difficulty because everyone had a valuable contribution to make, but I think he felt he had much freer rein because he was directing."[23]

For Telfer it was this shoot where he and Wade cemented their friendship, sharing most of their scenes together. "My friendship with Michael really got big in that one. I used to mimic Michael which was rather cheeky. The memories are lovely of that, he was a really good mate and I really enjoyed his company." [24]

Thanks to the success of the CGI work in the previous film, *Auton 3* featured more CGI than any other spin-off production. It was a process that Michael Wade found difficult to work with. "To be honest, I only had a rough idea when we were filming. When I saw the finished article there were certain scenes where no one was more surprised than me with all these effects that were later added. It was very good experience to just get it right in a short space of time and trust that it was going to work and I think the results speak for themselves." [25]

In late 2014 Pritchard summed up her memories of the *Auton 3* shoot. "I remember lots of location stuff on that, e.g. early morning confrontations with the Autons on the empty streets of Southampton. Fabulous hospitality from Bill Baggs' mum and family and a generally creative atmosphere, though you had to very adaptable." [26]

During the script's development, Baggs had insisted that more CGI elements be added. Returning CG artist, Ben Smith, told *DWM* that "Bill wanted to take what we had learned in the previous film and add to it. To be honest, after having just one big effect in *Auton*, they've gone absolutely nuts in this one!"[27]

Well over 50 effect shots were created by Smith in little under a month, the workload in the end proving a little too much for Smith. "I did feel slightly that they'd written in a bit too much, and I simply wouldn't have time to get it all done to meet their deadline, so Bill re-thought sections of it." [28]

It was during the editing and post production that Baggs began to notice some flaws in the story he hadn't picked up on before. "I quickly realised — and this is going to sound awfully like sour grapes — but it was the worst fucking script that he'd written. But if you write as much as he does you aren't going to be writing at your best all the time are you?"[29]

One issue that Smith recalls involved a scene where the characters retreat from a group of Autons, having just figured out how to kill them. "We couldn't work out why the main characters would then run away from another lot! As Bill was editing the scene, he realised there was no good reason for them to do this, so he wrote in a direction that 'the Autons appear with a massive cannon'! I wasn't sure about this, so I thought about it and suggested that thousands of Autons are beamed down, and we've stuck with that. The only problem now is to work out how the Nestene creature gets all these Autons in the first place!"[30]

One effect that was done by computer on this occasion was the Auton's signature hand-concealed weapon. "I made a 3D model when it was decided that they weren't going to use the 'prop' hands. They filmed the actor's hand 'live', which I then made a very simplistic model of. You then 'map' the original footage of the actor's hand onto it, so it looks just like a real hand — which it is — but, because it's a model, I can move the arm around, shift the position of it to the background, and come up with something that's entirely new. Seeing the effect is very odd, because the 'real' hand can suddenly split and you can have the fingers drop away to reveal the weapon!" [31]

Despite this heavy reliance on CGI Baggs was still keen that it not become the focus of the story. "We've tried to pace the effects throughout the film this time to give the audience more excitement, so what you get this time is something at the beginning, the middle and the end..." [32]

Auton 3: Awakening is a mess from start to finish. It is essentially a run around for Ramsey, Palmer and Sal as they go from one special effects set piece to another, while Lockwood mumbles to himself and Winslet eulogises on behalf of the Nestene. While there are some eerie scenes of the Autons on deserted streets early on in the film, the direction on the whole is stilted and poor. There are too many static shots and too little coverage to build the pace the film requires in the edit. In one scene, Ramsey and Sal fire their new energy weapons at an Auton and kill it. They then stop to congratulate each other while two more deadly Autons just stand and watch. In a later scene a confrontation between Palmer and Natasha sees the former strongarm the latter in a wide shot that looks so unconvincing as to be laughable, and the same can be said of what should have been a heroic death scene for Natasha. Which is not to mention a scene where Ramsey is supposedly killed and then shows up again unharmed a few scenes later! If handled more skilfully, this could have been a nice little trick to play on the audience but as it is, it just looks like a mistake. And the less said about the Auton serving Lockwood tea in bed the better.

All the characters deserve better than this and it's a shame the entire thing peters out without any real tension. The actors do their best with the material provided but they too deserve better after the strong work they put in in the first two films. The only saving grace of the film is Telfer, who puts in a performance on a par with the great *Doctor Who* megalomaniacs. Overall, though, the film suffers from an underdeveloped script and lazy direction that seems to rely on special effects to plug the gaps left by a lack of vision in shot choice.

Auton 3: Awakening was released in September 1999. Richard McGinlay of *DreamWatch* called it "powerfully realised and performed, this is an excellent conclusion to the trilogy."[33] *DWM*'s review was more searing, however. "Continuing a story arc shamelessly cribbed from *The X-Files*, *Auton 3* is an addendum to a trilogy which perhaps attained maximum effect a story too early."[34] The review went on to be critical of the writing and Baggs direction. "Dispensing with *Auton 2*'s zippy direction and showy editing, this chapter is a sluggish one, displaying little of its precursor's verve and none of its clarity."[35]

Co-writer Paul Ebbs was quick to jump to the defence of the film when it was criticized by David J. Howe on the rec.arts.doctorwho forum. "Well I haven't seen any pro-reviews yet, but the one screening I have attended and talking to Bill about the screening at Battlefield it seems to have gone down quite well with most people. I think you're a little harsh about the effects being the *only* good things in it. George Telfer is wonderful throughout IMHO and gives a very strong performance as both versions of Winslet. If I'd have had more time with the original script I think I would have given Lockwood much more to do ... and as for there being no plot ... well, I know there's one in there, which *Auton 3* were you watching? Sure it shows it's [sic] limitations in places, but what spin-off hasn't?" [36]

While the final film may not have been the triumph some fans expected, it still did healthy business for BBV — but Baggs too felt let down by the final film. "*Auton 3* in my view is probably the weakest of the three in some ways. It's more adventurous than the first one which was set in one place, it's bigger in ambition but there's not much story. It's more set pieces." [37]

And did Nick Briggs ever see the film? "I think I watched it once. I think I found it an extremely upsetting experience. I couldn't believe it, I didn't understand it, I didn't know what it was about. It seemed to me to be the embodiment of everything I expected of an unfettered Bill Baggs thing." Is it a case then that the script was unrecognisable? "I think there was something of the basic sort of thrust of the story, that was something like it. But I suppose it's a bit like *Thunderball* being remade as *Never Say Never Again*."[38]

The film also caused a rift between Briggs and another member of the BBV stable. "Paul Ebbs and I have never really got over that experience in the way that we relate to each other. He has what I would interpret as a massively difficult, offensive, aggressive attitude towards me. But maybe that's what he's like anyway and then he desperately tried to work for Big Finish, which was quite difficult because he was the man who took the poison chalice and Bill's shilling to do that."[39]

The video received two premieres on either side of the globe. The first was at the Coventry held convention Battlefield 3 in October 1999, which

Baggs and Michael Wade attended. The second was at the Gallifrey convention in America in early 2000, with George Telfer and Jo Castleton in attendance. The reception was quite overwhelming for the film's stars recalls Telfer. "It was very flattering for me. When you are selling photographs of yourself it feels pretty good and they were very, very interested in Winslet and how Winslet came about and all the background."[40] Castleton remembers the general response to the film to be a successful one. "We had a very positive response at conventions, I think really because at the time there weren't any other *Dr Who* related films being made."[41] Wade told the BBV website that he thought he was prepared to be inducted into *Doctor Who* fandom. "I can remember doing a tour with one of the main actors from *Neighbours* [Stefan Dennis aka Paul Robinson] and he would be mobbed in the streets and people would call him by his *Neighbours* name. Nobody had a clue what his real name was. And when he would say to them, 'no. My name is Stefan, mate,' they just stared at him blankly. Quite extraordinary. So I suppose that in a way I am a bit prepared because from what I've gathered sci-fi fans are a bit like that in large doses. Ad Extremis." [42]

BBV were regulars at all the major conventions as it was a chance to interact face to face with their fan base, promote their wares and sell product. Baggs found the fans at these events very responsive. "They were always very welcoming, I was amazed that people wanted my autograph and wanted their photograph taken with me."[43]

Baggs found the response in the United States even friendlier than in the UK. "I went to Chicago several times. It was Visions before Chicago TARDIS and then at Gallifrey people were very interested in what was coming up. Very eager to express what they thought, whether they liked it, whether they didn't like it.; and that's a good thing about *Doctor Who* fans — you always know where you stand." [44]

Tim Saward went to a number of conventions with Bill Baggs and manned the BBV stall in the dealers' room, and also found the fans agreeable. "People were very nice, they came up to the store and Bill was doing his hard sell thing. He'd even do that mystery shopper technique, where he'd walk up with a fan next to you, not knowing it was Bill Baggs and he would start going 'oh that looks interesting, what's that?' and he would start to sell himself his own merchandise."[45] As well as selling CDs, Saward also found himself doing panels at these events. "They were obviously a great ego boost. People listened very politely and asked questions and some people were genuinely interested in these particular products." [46]" Saward was also pleased to be asked to go the American conventions. "I went with Bill's wife and her friend, who were doing the sales and I was just helping. Gallifrey was fun because I got to hang out with people like [*DWM* Editor] Garry Gilliat and I met assorted *New Adventures* authors people like Keith Topping and Paul Cornell." [47]

The response at conventions went so well that Baggs briefly toyed with the idea of putting on his own convention — the one day event, BBV-Con. Announced in the April 1999 edition of *DWM*, the event had Sylvester McCoy and Sophie Aldred headlining and offered fans "a chance to watch, and maybe even take part in, the recording of the latest *Time Travellers* audio drama."[48] Also booked were Lalla Ward and John Leeson.

Despite the convention offering something a little different to normal *Doctor Who* conventions, the announcement of its cancellation appeared in the following issues of *DWM*, due to lacklustre ticket sales. "I bottled it, putting on a conventions is quite a challenge," Baggs admits. "I think I realised at a certain point that if I didn't have enough attendees it wouldn't work. I thought that it would have been quite good, but it was probably a bit ambitions and so somebody talked me out of it."[49]

BBV Con or not, the response at the Battlefield convention was positive and while *Auton 3* would be the final chapter in the series, Ebbs told the rec.arts *Doctor Who* group that he hoped that there would be a future for the human stars of the film. "I think Dr Sal from the *Auton* series or Lockwood and his team would make good on-going characters. Whether or not the audience at the end of the day would accept something as removed from *Who* as that I'm not sure. At the end of the day BBV is not a public service (certainly not now there is so much official *WHO*) and has to make a profit to continue."[50]

Ebbs' hopes for a continuation would never come to fruition, although there would be another outing for the Autons, when the VHS release featured a 7 minute spoof entitled *The Auton Diaries*. Written by Paul Ebbs and Arthur Tretheway, the comedy short chronicled the life of a down and out Auton who, after reaching the dizzy heights of success in 70s *Doctor Who,* finds stardom in the new BBV productions. It's a harmless enough piece that provides a few chuckles on the way and after much resistance proved to be BBV's first attempt at comedy.

The troubled journey of *Auton 3* to screen was another difficult chapter in the BBV story and with Briggs parting ways with the company, it left a hole that wouldn't be easy to fill. A cynic might argue that Briggs departure was in fact another nail in the coffin for BBV, and while it was certainly a huge blow and a sign to fandom that all was not well behind the scenes at BBV, they still had a few aces up their sleeve. The market place was changing and the next few years would see BBV experience more creative highs than lows, but Baggs' business practices would once again come under question.

Chapter 24 — Doing the Unstuck

While 1999 had been a trying year for Baggs and BBV, they faced the turn of the millennium with a renewed sense of optimism. "What we realised was, we had to kind of compliment what [Big Finish] were doing. We had to find our own kind of niche."[1]

With a new story editor in the shape of Paul Ebbs, BBV began planning a third series of audios to launch in February of 2000. Although, as it happens, Ebbs was never formally made script editor, but instead fell into the role. He also came up with the series new tag line "Familiar Faces — New Adventures."

Baggs was pleased to have Ebbs on side, as he brought a new pool of talent to the table. "Paul was very immersed in the writing talent, I hadn't immersed myself in the same authors' world as he had. My strengths were in directing and other areas, so he brought a lot of experience, interest and enthusiasm for the writing and brought a lot people on who I was very grateful for."[2] Ebbs laid out his intentions for the range on the rec.arts.doctorwho group, as people lamented the loss of the Dominie and Alice. "I guess it's all a matter of taste and whether or not people will accept stories without *Doctors* in, now that BF are doing what they're doing. Personally I'd like to bring a kind of *New Adventures* mentality to the BBV audios in the next season, so that we are making stories that although connected to the *Who* universe sufficiently push the envelope enough to justify their continued existence."[3]

The first release under the new script editor was originally intended to launch in December of 1999, with a double CD featuring 'Revenant', written and directed by Paul Ebbs which the author told the BBV website was a "sci-fi time travel odyssey with a twist in the tale." The play was scheduled to be recorded in October 1999 and feature Colin Baker in the lead part — his first BBV production in nearly five years. The second CD would be another Ebbs' penned and directed adventure, 'Cybergeddon'.

This double CD never came to pass and 'Revenant' was never recorded, to Ebbs' disappointment, although a script was written, which would have been a single-hander for Baker, with the odd robot voice thrown in. However Baggs was unable to agree terms with his former leading man. Instead BBV launched the season with the release of three different titles, the first of which was 'Cybergeddon' and featured the return of the Cyberons.

Ebbs had previously directed a number of his Season 27 Audios and was keen to do more, and as such took up the reins on this production. He cast Barry J Gordon as Corrigan, Jack Gallagher as Christian, Kerry Skinner as

Emily, Mark Donovan as Duncan and Ebbs himself played the part of the Cyberleader.

If season 3 was about change and carving a new identity for BBV, why then did they choose another of their *Doctor Who* knock offs to open the seasons? Baggs responds, "we were just having fun and being a bit irreverent, and a bit sticking two fingers up at the whole licensing thing, we were just kind of having fun with the idea." [4]

The play is a strong opener for the season, even if it is an odd choice. *Celestial Toyroom*'s Paul Winter described it as "both well written by Paul Ebbs and well put together. The plot moves along at a steady pace and builds to a nice climax at the end."[5] A sombre mood permeates every aspect of the play and makes the Cyberons a formidable opponent, offering some truly horrific sound design during the conversion scenes with bones cracking and harrowing screams; although the creatures voices are a little hard to understand at times. There are shades of *Blade Runner* to the plot, the music and the general tone and despite being part of the *Who* universe (sort of) it shares little of the feel of a *Doctor Who* story but instead offers a hard sci-fi/horror production that could easily have been turned into a big budget feature. The play is a bold starting point for this run of releases — but doesn't necessarily represent where the rest of the season will go.

Alongside 'Cybergeddon' was 'Punchline' by Jeremy Leadbetter, now better known to *Doctor Who* fans as Robert Shearman. This release would see a surprise return from Sylvester McCoy's Dominie, this time flying solo. Ebbs, who was also directing the play, felt Shearman's approach was very much in line with what he wanted for the new season. "Where I want to take season 3, is a completely different direction to the way BBV had been perceived in the past, and set it up and give it its own identity. The notes I gave to Jeremy were to do that, to be as wild as you like, let's make this a wild fantasy, let's do whatever you want to it. There was a point where I was going to be writing the script before Jeremy came on board and my ideas was not totally dissimilar to this. It was to be putting The Dominie into a game show and it was coming from those sort of ideas, a game show, sit-com. and Jeremy went away and came back with this wonderful idea, which he ran past me and I said 'yeah, go with it'."[6]

The script for 'Punchline' was written in one day and was Shearman's first dip into the world of *Doctor Who* scripting. Of the play's background he told Baggs, "I've always been a big *Doctor Who* fan and I was also a big seventies sit-com fan and this links the two in a way" going on to say "so trying to put them together was something massively nostalgic and watching it being recorded today is... I just feel like I'm 14 years old again." [7]

The comedy element of the play came from Shearman's admiration for McCoy. "I wanted to write something which was a comedy, because I happen to love comedy and when I was asked to write something for Sylvester... Sylvester I've always thought is the most comic personality I can think of and I just thought actually I'd like something which can give him a chance to show that off. And I always thought it would be really fun to get Sylvester for a real complete comic science fiction non-*Doctor Who* type story."[8] McCoy would return the compliment saying of the play, "I think it's the best *Doctor Who* script I have ever done"[9] a sentence that was plastered all over the adverts for 'Punchline' although to avoid courting any more controversy the quote was change to "...it's the best script (of this genre) I've ever done."[10]

Alongside McCoy as Dominic/The Dominie, Susan Travers played his wife June, Barry J. Gordon portrayed Sir and Neil Bull was Kevin. The play was recorded in a single day and due to the small cast was done entirely in script order. Although the day did not start perfectly, as when the crew arrived at the studio, there was nobody there to let them in and so they went to the cafe below to do a read through, much to the amusement of the customers.

Shearman hasn't heard the play since the recording, so has nothing to say retrospectively on the matter. But he was due to have his first official *Doctor Who* title released through Big Finish later in the year. "I think he was a bit anxious," Baggs recalls. "He'd also written something for Big Finish at the time and it was about being sensitive. But I don't think Rob Shearman's name at that time meant anything anyway."[11]

Reviews were generally positive, although the official magazine did not review the CD. *DreamWatch*'s Richard McGinlay, however, concluded that "This is just the kind of off-beat narrative that these single-CD audio dramas do best."[12] Indeed, if 'Cybergeddon' was a move towards a more dark sci-fi edge, then 'Punchline' is a complete departure from anything that had been seen in the BBV range or indeed *Doctor Who* before. It is a triumph of scripting, directing and acting and is the crowning jewel in this season, maybe even the entire BBV catalogue. The story is a meta look at the nature of *Doctor Who* and radio drama itself, with the climax exploring what makes the show unique as well as its own imposed story telling clichés. By being a spin-off, this play allows Shearman to explore themes that the parent show would never and perhaps should never do. As the last *Time Travellers* play it is a fitting finale and with official *Doctor Who* audio starring McCoy and Aldred now out it manages to finish on a sombre note that holds the promise that the Dominie's adventures live on somewhere.

The third release of the season would be written by newcomers Simon Gerard and Colin Hill. Gerard was a writer in commercial radio, writing topical comedy sketches, features and news reports. He also went on to write for *DreamWatch*, later becoming the co-editor and was also the partner of second Doctor assistant Wendy Padbury. Hill was an old school friend of his from Crosby in Liverpool. Wanting to try their hand at *Who* related fiction, they initially considered writing a novel for the third Doctor which was never completed.

They were asked by Baggs to submit a script for the range and got the choice of using Zygons, Krynoid, K-9 or the Sontarans. "Colin and I would have really long phone conversations and kick ideas around," Gerard explains. "The first thing we came up with started with a diplomat in the UN giving an address and breaking off to plead for sanctuary or something; he shimmered, changed and was revealed to be a Zygon... For whatever reason, we changed to using the Sontarans."[13]

Over the coming weeks, the two writers fleshed out the idea. "During one conversation, Colin had the idea of a Sontaran, sitting in deep shadow next to a fireplace — a bit like Roald Dahl at the beginning of *Tales of the Unexpected*! We liked the idea of this creature being somewhat urbane and wearing a smoking jacket. I'd been thinking about the Rudolph Hess situation, with him being kept at Spandau Prison and a different member country of the UN taking charge of him for a year at a time (I'm not sure if that's exactly how it worked with Hess but it seemed feasible). So we knew that he'd been kept prisoner for a very long time, and that his confinement had caused him to adapt." Gerard found that Baggs gave them a certain amount of freedom when developing the story. "Bill's approach was to tell you to write whatever you wanted, then gradually inform you it had to be changed to fit in with schedules, budget, whatever." [14]

Although initially the play had a larger cast, with the Sontaran having a butler, it ended up being a two hander between Brak played by John Wadmore (who also directed the play) and Wells played by Sally Faulkner (who had been a guest star in the Troughton era story 'The Invasion'). Gerard wanted to give the Sontaran an almost polar opposite to play off. "Bringing in Captain Alice Wells of UNIT was something that seemed to work well. She was a pen-pusher as far as Brak was concerned, so he didn't initially have a lot of respect for her. As he says, her gender is of no interest (not even if she has a weaker thorax) but he is testing her limits and seeing if she's got the heart of a fighter. Wells also gives Brak the opportunity to show off, exhibiting his knowledge of literature and culture. But even as he's doing it and testing her, he's starting to show cracks in his own facade." [15]

Indeed, the play reveals Brak had been in captivity for some 80 years and the two writers had a very clear idea about how that changed him. "One of the images we had early on was a beast in an opulent cage (which I think we gave as a line to Brak in the finished story) so there was an almost Hannibal Lecter vibe about him. Here's this creature, bred for war, suddenly being visited by Archbishops, Prime Ministers, officials... what does he do? He could have snarled and ripped their heads off but, like Lecter, we wanted to create that sense of never really knowing how thick this veneer of respectability is. Can a creature like that exist for 80 years and still remain, recognisably, a Sontaran? So all of these questions made it interesting for us to keep prodding him and seeing how far you could take it before he revealed himself. Obviously that meant we needed a sparring partner." [16]

Vanessa Bishop was certainly a fan of this production, and in *DWM*'s first review of the season she said, "With dialogue crammed in as tight as a Sontaran in a polo-neck jumper, fans of the potato-headed ones will find them done much honor."[17] Indeed the play is once again amongst the strongest the range had produced, one which is packed with lavish dialogue that is performed beautifully by the two cast members, creating an evocative mood. It explores the psychology of the captive Sontaran and its broader native culture, while drawing parallels with humanities own conflicts. This is perhaps the finest outing the Sontarans will ever receive from a spin-off or indeed the main show itself.

While there are things Gerard would have liked to have changed about the play — "The ending needed more work" — he was happy with what the two actors came up with. "Sally and John worked brilliantly with the material. They give Alice and Brak a relationship rather than just a conflict, so it's not just a back and forth argument which would have been a bit one-note and without nuance." [18] Baggs too was happy with the final play: "I considered making that into a film actually. Very evocative, very moving, very moody. Brilliant!"[19]

With 'Old Soldiers' turning out well and being a relatively hassle free process for Baggs, he quickly commissioned another play from the two writers as Gerard remembers. "Colin and I only refer to it as 'the bank robber play'! We knew it was a rush job so probably weren't feeling overconfident about it. There was a scheduling problem with another script and Bill asked if we could do something quickly to fill the gap."[20]

The basis for the play was the same plot as the abandoned pitch for their unwritten third Doctor novel, *Infidel's Comet*. Perhaps as a statement of intent for the new direction BBV was taking, the play featured no actors from *Doctor Who* and no monsters, save for some brief cameos. Instead it was straight science fiction drama. Although nobody can recall whose choice this was, Gerard offers the opinion that this route was possibly a mistake. "We may have been a bit arrogant in thinking that two unknowns could follow up a Sontaran story with something so off the wall. It's a shame." [21]

The play was directed by Jo Castleton, who also played the part of Kate Spencer. Also featuring in the play were Kieran Smith as Jimmy, Paul Ryan playing Henry, Adam Stafford as Haworth and Gary Barber as Terin. "*Infidel's Comet* was fun," recalls Castleton, "as I was able to use friends from a variety of theatre jobs who I knew would be fantastic."[22]

Gerard was present at the play's recording, although reluctant to get too involved. "Other than offering a few comments, I sat quietly. Jo did an amazing job of directing it and played a blinder with her role as 'Kate Spencer, EBC News'. The cast did a great job and I'm forever grateful to Jo. Poor Jo, being lumbered with our bloody weird script though."[23]

The play is notable for featuring the line "compared to the terrible big finish everyone was expecting, this a great relief." Asked if this was a cheeky swipe at BBV's newly established rivals, Gerard confirms, "The bank robber play is full of such 'hilarity' and I freely admit to having a Lennon-esque pop at our rivals. It wasn't intended to be nasty, just cheeky." [24]

BBV released *Infidel's Comet* in April 2000. The release also contained a second disc, featuring the music from the play which Gerard suspects was "to give it a bit of a boost for anyone unsure about parting with their hard-earned cash." [25]

Upon its release *Celestial Toyroom*'s Paul Winter said "the presentation of this play is first rate" but he did not rate the script, going on to say, "[a]s it stands, I am not sure whether this succeeds or not." [26]

The play is a strange one, reminiscent of the movie *Independence Day*, only done in the style of a 1950s American radio play. The actors deliver capable performances and the direction is solid enough. There are cameos from various *Who* monsters and even K9 and the Mistress make for entertaining distractions from a fairly predictable and mundane plot. *Infidel's Comet* is ultimately an uncomplicated and unremarkable release.

Baggs doesn't look back on this play with as much fondness as 'Old Soldiers'. "*Infidel's Comet* was a disaster. I mean, it was ok but it was utter nonsense. It was a mistake I made as a producer. When somebody writes something as strong as 'Old Soldiers', when they come up with another idea you kind of think, well they are good writers, but it doesn't necessarily follow through that a script from someone who is a good writer is actually going to produce something that was malleable so that was a lesson I learnt."[27] Castleton found out first hand from a fan that the play wasn't that well received, when she was doing a signing. "A guy came up and said 'oh you directed *Infidel's Comet*, didn't you?' Yes, I said, smiling. He replied, 'I hated it. I wanted to smash it, smash it, smash it!!!' Guess you can't please everyone."[28]

Despite this perceived misfire, Gerard and Hill were asked to work on a number of other projects for BBV. "There were also a couple of BBV film scripts that we worked on for Bill but time and money scuppered them,"[29] as well as a follow up to 'Old Soldiers'. "Colin and I had started working on

'Old Soldiers II' which was set prior to the first one. It was set in the early Sixties and would have tied in to 'Old Soldiers' quite a bit. We were going to release a teaser trailer for it, and Mike Tucker [BBC FX supremo] was offering to create a CGI opening section which you would have been viewed on the BBV website. Yes, we were so far ahead of our time at BBV! Sadly, it never got beyond the page (although I do have the audio trailer) and it was probably at the time that Bill was seeing Big Finish getting the licences for so much of the Whoniverse. He moved over to producing the splendid *Faction Paradox* plays and the *Doctor Who* monsters went back in the box."[30]

Ultimately, their only produced contributions to the range would be 'Old Soldiers' and *Infidel's Comet.*

The month after *Infidel's Comet*, BBV released another non-*Who* related CD, titled *The Pattern* written by Marc Duncan. Gareth Preston who did the post production on the play, sheds some light on why he thought Bill was branching out "I think Bill had had some feedback that there was a demand for original audio SF in the USA, where I believe *The Pattern* sold well. Plus, I'm sure as a creative person he wanted to create original work because it's very satisfying if it is popular."[31] Ebbs too confirms this, stating that Baggs was interested in seeing if non *Doctor Who* related ranges would sell, even if ultimately this proved not to be viable.

The Pattern was directed by Ebbs, although he didn't commission the play. Ebbs cast Susan Travers as Logan and her Orb, Peter Yapp as Coleridge, Catherine Barker as Chase, Carlos Amsell as Mac and Brett James as Easton.

Although he didn't attend the recording, Preston recounts the somewhat troubled post-production process. "The recording had already been done in London. So I was sent the raw recordings on CD-ROM and a copy of the script and worked from there. I enjoyed post-producing it a lot. It's got some of my most sophisticated work in it. The only downside was that I had a major hard disk failure at one point and so missed my original deadline, which meant it was not ready for a US convention Bill was attending. I felt very bad about that and in fact I waived my fee. Getting Orb's voice right was a challenge. At first Paul Ebbs felt it was too human, but then I think I went too far with the effects and if there had been a sequel I would have pulled it back. I also supplied the dying scream of a character but I don't think anyone noticed the change in his voice. "[32]

Preston was a fan of the script. "I liked it. The electrical alien anticipated the Wire [in the David Tennant story 'The Idiot's Lantern'] and the movie *Virus*. There was plenty of scope to develop Logan and Orb and I even wrote some notes to pitch a sequel myself, set on a ramshackle space station." [33]

Baggs was also happier with his second *Doctor Who*-free release. "I was much more pleased with this second one. I like *The Pattern*, it's very gentle but I like her character [Logan]. it was nice to have a female Doctor in a sense, so that was the experiment there. And we could have done more with that, except Paul Ebbs didn't like Marc Duncan as a writer."[34]

This would be the last of four scripts Duncan contributed to the range, but did Baggs think he was as odd as his co-workers claimed? "If his scripts were anything to go by he probably is! He used to hard type his scripts and they never arrived in file format."[35]

Kathy Sullivan said of *The Pattern* "This is an excellent story, with believable and likable characters, good science, fast paced action and nice suspense."[36] However, perhaps because it had no links to *Doctor Who*, the CD failed to receive a review in any of the major high street genre magazines — though equally this may simply be because it wasn't very good. *The Pattern* is perhaps the most unexceptional play of the season, possibly even the entire range. The direction is competent and the performances are agreeable but the script lacks pace and the threat never feels very palpable. The twists and turns are all too obvious and the listener can't help but feel that this has been done before, and much better.

The next release would be a second play penned by Lance Parkin. *I Scream* as the play would come to be known would feature The I, a race of giant insects featured in the BBC *Doctor Who* book 'The Seeing I' by Jonathan Blum and Kate Orman, which had been published in 1998. Both friends of Parkin's they gave him their blessing to use their creations and Parkin began developing the script. "I was just picking up on the idea of a creature that was always there, but just out of view, and had been there throughout human hist— huh... like the Silence. Hadn't even noticed that. The I were just quite a nice concept, and I had an idea for a planet that was given over to making just ice cream, with the title being a pun on that, and that title also dictating it had to have some sort of horror element."[37] In Parkin's script, Baggs found exactly the sort of story that he was hoping to champion with his third season of audios. "The reason why I picked this and was very keen to do it, was that it was a very different sort of style and that's how BBV is making its mark., In the sense that it's doing something that the other companies can't really do, it doesn't fit in to a particular formant."[38]

The CD's lead, known only as the narrator, would be played by Lisa Bowerman, who had come to prominence in fandom for her role as Bernice Summerfield for Big Finish. Bowerman had already had one encounter with Parkin's work, when she appeared in an audio adaptation of his New Adventure novel 'Just War', and Parkin was keen to work with her again. "I'd met her at a Big Finish launch party and basically decided she was a brilliant person and actor, and so built the story around her. It's not a foolproof script, though, it needs to be quite carefully judged. I knew Lisa could keep the lead character sympathetic, sell the choices that her character makes without making her look idiotic." [39] Other cast members included Peter Yapp as the Eyescreen, Andrew Fettes as John and Jo Castleton (who also directed the play) as Sol.

I Scream was recorded in May of 2000 at Mike Nielson's home studio, aka his spare bedroom, in North London. Peter Yapp found the process enjoyable despite the less than perfect working conditions. "This is a very creative studio because it takes terrific daring to record audio plays in a spare bedroom without any particular sound proofing on a flight path and occasionally somebody building a conservatory next door!" [40]

Parkin was also on hand to see his script recorded. "The cast and crew of 'I, Scream' were all great and it was a fun day recording it. I like that script. It's kind of an SF horror short story, a little bit *Twilight Zone*-y, I guess. I was pleased as punch when Jo got cast as Scoblow for Big Finish's 'Venus Mantrap', and she and Lisa got to be all camp and bitchy at each other. I'd thought about writing something for them as a double act, had a sort of crime/spy thing in mind where they'd be Steed and Peel, or two Peels, or two Steeds." [41]

James Potter of *Celestial Toyroom* called *I Scream,* "well-made, well-written science fiction drama that tells an entertaining, thoughtful tale featuring characters from the world of *Doctor Who*, but freeing them up and allowing them to stand as original creations."[42] Which is as apt a description of the play. Lisa Bowerman makes for an excellent lead while Peter Yapp provides an electrifying performance as the sinister I. Additionally, the soundscape is genuinely unsettling in places, making for one of the creepier productions. After two relatively lo-fi productions *I Scream* is a triumph for all involved.

Chapter 25 – Ambitious Outsiders

Despite being an already crowded market place, the *Doctor Who* audio scene was to see another company enter the arena in the latter part of 2000 (although the first play wouldn't be released for another year). Alongside the struggling BBV and the ever growing Big Finish Productions, Magic Bullet Productions would, it turns out, offer a viable alternative to what both the other companies were offering.

The driving force behind this new venture was Alan Stevens, a *Doctor Who* and *Blake's 7* fan who, as well as organising numerous conventions and writing for *DWB* and *TV Zone*, also had a Higher National Certificate in radio programme making and had produced content for local radio. He was also responsible for three *Blake's 7* related audio productions, alongside Alistair Lock, who he had previously met at a *Doctor Who* convention in 1987. The first of these was a docu-drama entitled 'Travis: The Final Act'. which Lock put together on a fairly basic set-up. "All I had then was a four-track cassette deck and two identical cassette decks. To assemble the piece, there was lots of starting and stopping of both the four-track and the cassette machine, which played in either interviews or sound effects. It was a long and laborious process. If I made a mistake, I had to erase what I had just done and try it again. Music was recorded separately onto cassette. The final master cassette was produced by playing back the four-track, through a simple mixer. The music was cued manually through this same mixer from a normal cassette deck, and the final mix recorded onto a second normal cassette deck. But that was the start of my work with Alan."[1]

With 'Travis: The Final Act' proving a success, Stevens and Lock created two further *Blake's 7* dramas, in the form of 'The Mark of Kane' and 'The Logic of Empire'. For Lock these plays represented a significant increase in the technology available to him to produce audio drama. "I brought a DAT machine with my redundancy money and the whole thing was assembled on my Akai sampler. because I still didn't have a computer powerful enough to run more than two stereo tracks without glitching. I couldn't multi-track dialogue or FX, so the whole thing was carefully edited on my sampler. I triggered all the individual lines of dialogue and sound FX with midi from my computer and recorded the audio onto DAT. This audio was then recorded back into the computer. The next phase was to compose and record the music. This was also played out onto DAT, then recorded back into the computer as audio. The computer was powerful enough to play and mix the scenes and music, and the final mix was played onto DAT tape. I can't remember if the DAT or a master CD was sent to the duplicator."[2]

These unofficial full cast dramas featured characters and cast from the world of *Blake's 7*, including Gareth Thomas, Brian Croucher, Peter Miles, Paul Darrow, Jacqueline Pearce, Peter Tuddenham and also featured Ian Reddington and Trevor Cooper. The plays, which were made available on a not-for-profit basis, were sold via mail order and at conventions. It was while selling these that Alan first encountered a young fan and aspiring writer named Jim Smith. Smith recalls, "I met Alan at Manopticon, which was an event that took place in Manchester town hall in 1993. Alan was wandering around the dealers room (he didn't have a table) with a small cassette box that contained copies of his tape 'Travis: The Final Act'. He was carrying a piece of paper that just said '*Blake's 7* audio play. Five pounds' and, as I actively wanted a copy of 'Travis: The Final Act,' I went up to him and asked him for a copy. He later said it was the easiest sell he'd ever made." [3]

Smith had submerged himself in *Doctor Who* fandom at an early age and was a regular on the convention scene. He was also quite the fan of spin-off media, noting he had purchased "All of them. Literally all of them. I was a *Doctor Who* fan — I am a *Doctor Who* fan — and someone had taken away *Doctor Who*. I needed my methadone! There are a very, very small number of VHSes and so on, at the fag end of the 90s and after, that I didn't get, but in earlier years I did literally get the lot. All the BBV videos, all the New Adventures, the Missing Adventures, Reeltime dramas, Myth Makers videos. All of them." [4]

The two kept in contact, and later Smith acted as script editor on 'The Logic of Empire'. According to Smith, after the success of the previous releases, Stevens was keen to produce more audio drama but wanted to do something a little more adventurous. "Alan wanted to do something that would appeal to *Blake's 7* and *Doctor Who* fans, but which he could sell for a profit, and which also didn't tie him down to a previously established continuity. Something that could stand on its own." [5]

With this in mind, Smith approached BBV about the possibility of producing a series. "Jim met Paul Ebbs in a pub," remembers Stevens. "At the time Ebbs was working for BBV. The following day, Jim rang me up and told me that BBV would be willing to produce an audio series of our devising." [6] Between them, the two talked over some ideas to pitch to BBV. Smith can recall at least one other concept they considered. "We had another idea at the time which was much more humorous. It was a violent, contemporary, black comedy about some gangsters. We thought one could be played by Paul Darrow and the other by Brian Croucher."[7]

Stevens sheds a little more light on the idea. "The two gangsters were called Birastropthe and Dinsdale, but it was just some daft bit of nonsense we'd come up with one drunken night while I was staying at Jim's London flat. I don't think we ever seriously considered doing it for BBV. As far as I remember, Jim had approached Ebbs with idea of doing the 'Corpse

Marker' spin-off series, and it was this that Ebbs was giving the green light to." [8]

'Corpse Marker' was a BBC Books novel by Chris Boucher, featuring the Fourth Doctor and Leela. Not only was it a sequel to Boucher's TV story 'The Robots of Death' but it also features the character of Carnell, who had appeared in the Boucher-scripted *Blake's 7* episode, 'Weapon'. With this in mind Stevens made an approach to the writer. "I called up Chris Boucher, and I said to him, 'would you be interested in doing an audio drama CD series called *Kaldor City*?' and he asked me what I had in mind and I told him, and he said, 'go off and write a script, and if I like it, you can go ahead with a series'."[9]

Stevens and Smith set about writing the first script for the potential series, hammering out the entire thing over the telephone, which was a fairly amicable process for Smith. "We just talked it out, we just played the characters and worked it out."[10] Stevens too found it a harmonious affair. "I enjoy writing with other people, because I like bouncing ideas back and forth. I remember explaining some plot idea to Jim and he said, 'oh, yeah, Occam's Razor,' and then I thought, 'that would be a good title'."[11] Smith believes the main thrust of the plot was influenced by a comic book he had read as a child: "The idea of somebody committing a series of murders, waiting for a brilliant detective to impose a logic on them, when in fact the murders are completely random and there is no logic, is in fact what I thought was going to happen when I was halfway through reading the *Batman vs. Predator* comic, but in the end is not the plot of the comic."[12]

Stevens, on the other hand, remembers the storyline having a different origin, even if it is still firmly rooted in comic books. "Years ago, around 1988, I had this great idea for a story about this 1940s detective who was a paranoid psychotic. That, while investigating some case about a possible cheating husband, he alights on some massive conspiracy, but it's actually all in his head. Then one day I walked into a comic shop and found the first issue of a comic called *The Bogie Man*, about a guy who thinks he's Humphrey Bogart. I picked it up and began to flick thought it, and there was my story! God, that pissed me off."[13]

With the ideas being drawn from Boucher's creations, Stevens made sure Boucher was kept informed of developments. "We were always talking about stuff and had known each other for about 10 years at that point. When I finally got back to him with the script for 'Occam's Razor', he loved it; he suggested a few minor changes, and that was about it, really."[14]

With the script now complete, they again approached Paul Ebbs, but things did not work out as they had expected, as Stevens recounts. "When we got back to BBV with the script and the cast we wanted, they weren't too interested; I think they thought it would be too expensive. Big Finish then showed some interest, but one thing led to another and I eventually decided to do it myself and set up my own company."[15] And so Magic Bullet was born.

With the first script ready to go, Stevens decided the economical thing to do would be to record two plays at a time. So he approached Boucher about writing the second episode. "He was always going to write episode two, because it was necessary to get his input in as quickly as possible. Your first two episodes are basically the springboard for everything else." [16] Boucher's instalment was entitled 'Death's Head' and although this is his only script for the series, he was credited as Creative Consultant across all of the releases. "After he'd written his segment we had a long chat as to what was going to happen next. It was his idea that we should just have Blayes working for the Tarenists, and not bother showing the mechanical process that lead up to it. Chris's argument was that if you explained everything, you'll eventually bore your audience, so it's better to imply. As the CD series continued we explained less and less, until by the end we weren't bothering to explain anything at all." [17]

Content with his initial scripts, Stevens went about casting the two plays. Russell Hunter was asked to reprise the role of Uvanov from 'The Robots of Death', much to the actor's surprise. "I couldn't believe it. And it's such a walloping big part. It's fun in that studio with my own little script-stand, bellowing at Paul Darrow!" [18]. Scott Fredericks, who portrayed Carnell in *Blake's 7*, was also needed. "I contacted Russell Hunter through a friend called David Bickerstaff,"[19] recalls Stevens. "I knew of the connection because I'd met Russell Hunter myself in 1990 at a convention Bickerstaff had organised. Scott Fredericks was more difficult to track down, as he now lives in Southern Ireland. I eventually contacted him through BBC Residuals, who forwarded on the script and an accompanying letter."[20]

Fredricks was initially unsure about reprising the role after such a long period. "I was a bit nervous when first approached, and so I had a quick look at the video, just to be on the safe side. Of course the great thing about doing it for audio all these years later is that I don't have to look the same!"[21]. But his fears proved unfounded. "I'm so glad I was asked back. If someone else had taken the part I would have hated it. I wouldn't like to relinquish that character. It's really been a pleasure." [22].

For the part of anti-hero Iago, Stevens approached Paul Darrow, for a part that bore more than a small resemblance to his role as Avon on *Blake's 7*. Stevens had known Darrow from the *Blake's 7* convention scene and through working with him on 'The Logic of Empire', had written the part specifically for him, although if Darrow had turned it down Stevens would have approached Alexis Kanner.

Other cast members included Trevor Cooper as Rull (who was suggested by Boucher), Brian Croucher as Cotton, Peter Miles as Landerchild, Annabel Leventon as Devlin, Peter Tuddenham as Strecker,

BBV regular Patricia Merrick as Justina and David Bickerstaff as Kyle. The latter, according to Stevens, had a big impact on the overall casting. "David Bickerstaff kept coming up with more and more well known actors he knew on first name terms and who would be available for us to use. That's how Nicholas Courtney ended up in a small part as a newsreader. And then Russell Hunter and Brian Croucher started suggesting people, and that's how we nearly ended up with Tom Baker. It was very tempting, but we realised that if we did get him in, he'd be expecting to appear in a massive part. Eventually, Jim and I came up with this story idea where the opening scene would feature Tom Baker suddenly turning up in Uvanov's office, saying "hello there!" and then being promptly shot dead by Iago, and that this would go on throughout the story, with Tom continually turning up and getting executed, until finally Uvanov had all these dead Tom Bakers stacked in his shed like cord wood. The idea would have been that they were the manufactured physical representations of the mad Xoanon computer from Chris Boucher's *Doctor Who* story 'The Face of Evil', but we'd never actually state that, and, as far as Iago and Uvanov were concerned, it would just be this complete mystery. Well, we thought about putting the idea to Chris, but Fiona [Moore, co-author of the third *Kaldor City* audio] advised us not to."[23]

In the end, 'Occam's Razor' features an impressive cast that totals twenty individual voices. With the average BBV audio CD normally having a total cast of five (usually including one or more of the crew) with only one star name, it seems obvious why BBV turned down the series.

The first two releases were announced in the September 2000 *DWM*, stating that recording was currently taking place. With the two plays being recorded back to back, Magic Bullet were able to maximize the use of their actors, as Smith elaborates. "They were recorded as a block, which is why they sort of share cast. You'll find that whereas one actor features prominently in one CD, they will appear in a smaller role in the other and vice versa. This is all down to budgeting, actors were paid by the day, and you wanted to get all their stuff done in one day. So Peter Tuddenham's character is a major character in 'Death's Head' but only has a few lines in 'Occam's Razor'."[24]

The first two instalments were recorded on the 22nd and 24th August and 12th September 2000 at Skylight Studios in London. The plays were co-directed by Stevens and Alistair Lock. "To be honest, the calibre of actor we were employing was so high, we mainly just let them get on with it,"[25] recalls Stevens. "I do remember when Russell Hunter did his first scene as Uvanov, he was playing it very stern and hard, and I asked him to lighten it up a bit. Paul Darrow was very keen on playing Clint Eastwood, and would say all his lines very slowly. So we were continually saying to him 'faster, Paul, faster.' Luckily, he took it all in good humour. Really, the secret to getting through a production like that is not to record it in scene order, but to instead write up a document where all the scenes featuring particular actors are grouped together. That way you haven't got people walking in and out of the studio every five minutes, which can really slow a production down. If you're recording out of sequence, however, you've got to ensure that your actor knows exactly where they are in the script and how the scene they are doing now relates to those around it." [26]

According to all involved, the recording was hard work, but went smoothly. Smith was also on hand as production manager. "I can honestly say we didn't have a single cast member who wasn't delightful and that's really true. Paul Darrow is enormous fun; funny, witty intelligent, just a nice man, and hardworking. Russell Hunter is an absolutely delightful actor; enormous experience, full of anecdotes and interesting stories. Constantly smoking absolutely filthy-smelling French cigarettes, in a way you could do in those days inside a studio and just can't now."[27] Peter Miles was also in awe of the cast Magic Bullet assembled. "I'd never met Russell Hunter before in my life, I just knew how good he was. He was a joy to work with, but the poor man was chain smoking himself to death."[28] He was also pleased to be reunited with his 'Doctor Who and The Silurians' co-star. "Paul Darrow is a great character and takes the mickey out of himself, and is more modest than you would believe. He's got the goods." [29] As an old associate of Stevens, Miles relished the chance to work with his friend on the project. "His knowledge of sci-fi is immense and he's a very clever script writer, book writer and a good director." [30] Hunter later told *DWM* he found the recordings an enjoyable experience. "There's always a lovely atmosphere in the green room. And we even have sing-alongs. Well, I do anyway! Everything's up to date in *Kaldor City*."[31]

Kaldor City is a welcome addition to the spin-off scene. The world presented in 'Occam's Razor' is rich in detail, with its intricate political system and social hierarchy presented in a way that feels natural and not shoehorned in. The characters are both brilliantly cast and brilliantly written with the superlative dialogue being delivered with such vigour it's impossible not to adore even the most minor of characters. There is a dry humour that runs throughout the script which enlivens this well structured murder mystery and the plot keeps you guessing right until the end. Darrow and Hunter are the main stars in this play with the manic mannered Uvanov working perfectly in conjunction with the razor sharp charm of Iago, whose performance stays just on the right side of ham. Throw in Fredericks' insidious and calculating Carnell and the testosterone-propelled Rull and Cotton and you have some of the best characters ever to have appeared in the extended *Doctor Who* universe all in one place.

The second play is a lot less gung-ho than its predecessor, but that isn't to say it drags in any way. So enamouring are the characters that just hearing the actors get their teeth into the seductive dialogue is enough to leave the listener satisfied. The choice to have the CD narrated through a one-sided conversation from Carnell is a neat bit of misdirection and the reveal that the actual culprit is a series of multiple characters is a pleasing twist. Only in *Kaldor City*, where everyone is equally as conniving and callous as each other, could this sort of resolution be possible. Once again the Magic Bullet team deliver a grade A production, in which you don't even realise the Voc robots, which you think would be one of main pulls of the series, are barely featured.

Despite being recorded together in late 2000, 'Occam's Razor' wasn't released until 1st September 2001, with 'Death's Head' following on 20th April 2002. The reason for this delay was because Alistair Lock, who was handling the post production work, had other commitments. *DWM*'s Vanessa Bishop called 'Occam's Razor' "entertaining," while describing it as "ultraviolent and hard-nosed," and was suitably amused by Darrow's character: "...his performance starts from the crotch and radiates outwards."[32]

Her review for 'Death's Head' lacks any major criticisms or praise, and instead concentrates on the underuse of the robots and the titular city, saying "Boucher has taken its air of vitriol and murder, but none of its finery and decadence,"[33] going on to say that "of all the future worlds in *Doctor Who*, none is so razor-tongued as Kaldor... It makes Chris Boucher's tale, touted as 'Chandleresque suspense', fun — Paul Darrow's cold tones could make the line 'I love you' sound like 'you sack of shit'."[34]

The first two *Kaldor City* releases proved that there was still room within the audio market for a Doctorless drama. It also showed that audiences were still willing to try out new products if the concept, casting and production was of a high enough quality. While BBV may have been struggling to adjust to the lower sales figures of their later releases, Magic Bullet was born into a post-Big Finish world and could tailor their approach accordingly.

Chapter 26 — My Little Underground

Following *I Scream* would be another Sontaran adventure, in the shape of 'Conduct Unbecoming' by Gareth Preston. Preston was brought on board by Paul Ebbs, the two having crossed paths previously on the fan audio scene. "He liked my writing a lot and encouraged me to send my Fine Line *Doctor Who* script "Trick of the Light" to Bill as an example. Happily Bill liked it too."[1] From there a commission wasn't too far away. "Paul rang me up and told me to write a Sontaran story and suggested making it about the science of cloning. It was as simple as that. And since like most writers I hate looking at a blank page, it was actually quite helpful to have that as a starting point." [2]

To help formulate his story, Preston watched all the previous *Doctor Who* stories to feature the Sontarans. "It struck me that here was a dichotomy between what the Sontarans boast about — their dedication to their race and their thousands of super soldiers hatching at once — and what actually happened, since all the ones we met have personal agendas and styles. And where there are different people, there are politics and self-interest. The other factor that really leapt out is how funny they are." [3]

The brief was to feature no more than six cast members, which Preston adhered to. The play featured John Wadmore (once again on directing duties) as Bestok, Anthony Keetch as Drell, Tom Chadbon playing Forrest and a Sontaran, Amanda McKay in the role of Maria and Paul Griggs as Kreel. Preston was impressed with the cast. "I'd seen/heard John Wadmore in other BBV stories so I knew that Bestok would be in safe hands. I was really pleased about Tom Chadbon, not just for his *Doctor Who* connection, but for his reliably good work in a host of other shows. I think I might have geeked out a bit talking to Tom Chadborn. He was a bit surprised I could recall details so many of his guest appearances in the likes of *Between the Lines* and *Midsomer Murders*. He had arrived to play the duplicitous Forrest, but readily agreed to play the part of the old Sontaran on the day." [4]

Anthony Keetch was another fan turned professional actor who had been recommended to BBV by Lisa Bowerman. Keetch did have some trepidation taking on an iconic villain. "I was worried beforehand as I was playing a Sontaran, and feared doing the voice all day would strain the throat, especially as I had a massive great speech. We actually recorded that last and I just went for it. One take, I think, although whether that was because I was good or we were just all knackered, I don't know. Tom Chadbon was charming and seemed unfazed by the bed-sitness of it all."[5]

The play was once again recorded in Mike Neilson's spare room, with Preston present. "I'll be honest and say I was disappointed. I had gone to London expecting to be in a proper recording studio. Recording in the bedroom was something I did for my fan audios! However Mike did a great job on the production and graciously put up with the fact that I'd arrived at his house an hour early due to a mix up in the times. The recording seemed to proceed very smoothly, with fairly little debate over the script and I think just the occasional retake over a line. It was done rehearse-record scene by scene. In fact I can only remember stepping into the room once to correct a pronunciation of one of the alien names. Once the recording was finished around four, myself, John and Paul went into the room to record the behind the scenes podcast and I think I was on my way out of London by five." [6]

'Conduct Unbecoming' is a political thriller in the guise of a space opera. Vanessa Bishop enjoyed the play, saying "this BBV drama has a satisfying sting in the tail," and noting that "writer Gareth Preston plays [to] the strengths of the Sontaran Empire."[7] It's an interesting exploration of Sontaran culture and provides an expansive history to the Sontaran cloning process. While it is another quality entry in the BBV catalogue with a fine script from Preston, it is however slightly let down by the two human characters with even the mighty Tom Chadbon failing to deliver a convincing performance.

The penultimate CD of Season 3 was perhaps the most high profile of the range. It saw the return of the Rani and was written by the characters creators, 1980s *Who* writers Pip and Jane Baker. This would signify the first and only time Baggs had a release authored by bona-fide television *Doctor Who* writers, although Baggs had known the Bakers for a number of years before the commission came about. "Colin introduced me to Pip and Jane years before that and Jane adored me. They offered me several film scripts they had written in the past and for various reasons they didn't get made. I'd go round for tea and they'd say 'we've been having this Gary Russell phoning us from Big Finish and we haven't said yes.' There was this loyalty thing going on, they wouldn't work for him because they were friends of mine and they knew about the history of it, and they felt I'd been unfairly treated. I can't remember if I asked them to write a Rani script or if they offered to do it, but it was a logical step."[8] Originally called *Resurrection of the Rani*, the title was later altered to *The Rani Reaps the Whirlwind.* The CD saw a rare appearance from Baggs in the director's chair and starred Anthony Keetch in the dual roles of Urak and Dean. Edward Cory, a friend of Keetch's, played Sam and Vorag; Patricia Merrick was Lucy/Pivor; Brian Knight played Arbitus and, of course, screen legend Kate O'Mara returned as the Rani.

Baggs and the cast headed to O'Mara's home in Taunton, Somerset where they assembled for a read-through they day before recording. As Patricia Merrick recalls, the cast were in awe of the former *Dynasty* star. "Working with Kate O'Mara was a wonderful experience. When we all arrived at her home for the read-through of T*he Rani Reaps the Whirlwind*, I think we were all a bit nervous/over-awed by the idea of working with such a star, well I know I was. Kate had prepared a delicious meal, which gave us the opportunity to socialise before we started the read-through. We had lots of laughs — I had a line 'look at her she must have ice water running through her veins.' There was a pregnant pause as we all waited for Kate's line and she looked up and said serenely 'oh, I'm terribly sorry I was busy focusing on the ice water running through my veins.' Much laughter ensued. Kate's portrayal of the chillingly egocentric Rani was in a class of its own."[9] Keetch also remembers the read-through due to the Bakers' unique style of writing "The script was... interesting. I seem to recall that at the read-though the night before, at Kate's cottage, there was a certain amount of suppressed hilarity at particular lines."[10]

While there may have been the odd snigger at the dialogue, O'Mara appeared to be an admirer of the script. "It's so vibrant! Pip and Jane have terrific imaginations and they've managed to use some really clever analogies — which as a vegetarian, I find particularly interesting."

With the read-through complete, the crew retired for the night to a local guest house, although according to Keetch the sleeping arrangements were less than satisfactory. "Bill, naturally, stinted on accommodation so all four of us — Bill, Edward Cory, me and Patricia Merrick — were booked into the one room of a B&B! Luckily, there was an annexe so I suggested Patricia sleep there — which she accepted with alacrity." [11]

The play was recorded on Wednesday 20th September in a studio at local radio station, Orchard FM. Cory wrote about the experience for *Celestial Toyroom* shortly after recording. "Anthony was isolated because he had to have his voice treated to make it more 'alien.' He was also isolated from his packet of Boasters much to his annoyance. Recording was speedy, and in just over four hours it was 'in the bag' The grunts and snorts Anthony and I were making as Tetraps sounded like something out of a late night Channel 5 film, and even more worrying I was beginning to take on a Tetrap 'pose' while reading my lines. At least I wasn't playing the Creature from The Pit!"[12]

The Bakers weren't present at the recording due to illness, but as Keetch recalls their presence was still felt. "Pip'n'Jane weren't at the recording but there was a debate at the read-through re the pronunciation of 'Tetrapyriabus.' Being a good dedicated actor I had watched 'Time & the Rani' in Day-Lewis-esque preparation so I was pretty sure I was right, but Bill called the Bakers, and I ended up chatting with Jane on the phone. I don't think she knew how it should be pronounced."[13]

DWM were not fans of the play saying, "Pip and Jane Baker's best *Doctor Who* work has not involved the Rani, and this play continues the trend,"[14] before going on to call it "annoyingly lightweight." Indeed the play is typical of its authors, in that it presents a series of unrealistic characters with clunky dialogue. The plot contains some fairly typical sci-fi tropes — the mad scientist carrying out experiments, kidnapped prisoners and blood sucking monsters. The cast do the best they can with the material provided and it's wonderful to hear O'Mara back as the Rani in all her hammy glory. The sound design is some of the best the series has to offer and Bill Baggs' direction is the most adept it has been in some time.

The Rani Reaps the Whirlwind was released in November of 2000 at a slightly higher cost than that of the normal CDs (£12.50 up from the usual £11.50) as the BBV website explained. "We regret to announce that it will be released at a slightly higher price than our usual single CD releases to accommodate the necessity of a higher budget, but with interest for this CD higher than anything so far released we feel sure that you won't mind going a little further to be part of Kate O' Mara's return to the fold."[15] The CD garnered a larger than usual amount of publicity for BBV, due to its high profile guest star, including a signing at the Tenth Planet shop in Barking and an article in *DWM* by a young Benjamin Cook, the first article a BBV audio play had received in the publication. Again it was hoped there would be more Rani audio CDs from BBV, and O'Mara was only too eager to appear in them. "Absolutely! I think these audios are fantastic, I really do. I think BBV should go for it and do as many as they like. I'm sure that there's a market for them and I think they should exploit the market."[16] Once again though, the sales failed to justify cost, although this wouldn't be the last time the cast worked together, as Keetch remembers. "Kate was fantastic, and all of the cast of *The Rani Reaps*... were offered work with her theatre company at the Brewhouse Theatre in Taunton in the following months. Patricia, Brian and I were in 'The Crime At Blossoms' in Jan 2001, and Edward was in 'The Dresser' in Sept 2001."[17]

The season would finish as it started with a story written by Paul Ebbs. 'Wirrn: Race Memory' was initially due to be recorded and released in late 2000 but wasn't recorded until 4th January 2001 and released the following month (the same month that Big Finish was gearing up to release their first Eighth Doctor adventure). Recorded in the North London flat belonging to Mike Neilson, the play was once again directed by Ebbs and featured Keith Drinkel as Parker, Mark Donovan as Charles, Nigel Fairs as Joshua, Steve Johnson as the Wirrn Queen and making her BBV debut, Sarah Sutton as Sarah.

As the title suggest, the play once again featured a familiar *Doctor Who* monster. "It's a sequel to 'Ark In Space'," Ebbs announced on 'On Web' (the

BBV web series), "the old *Doctor Who* story which is definitely one of my favourites and one of the best *Doctor Who* stories they ever made."[18]

Paul Griggs was once again present and wrote about his experience for *Celestial Toyroom*. "While it involves a great deal of effort and work from the cast and crew, there is also always a sense of camaraderie and fun. The running joke for 'Race Memory' seemed to be that Nigel Fairs was the only person in the entire universe that hasn't watched *The League of Gentlemen* and thus various references such as 'Hello, Dave!' and 'Twelve-ty' were sent spinning way over his head."[19]

The production is one Ebbs remains proud of — "great cast and we had a fabulous day recording it."[20]

Vanessa Bishop called *Race Memory* "an excellent sequel to 'The Ark in Space',"[21] in *DWM* and was in full praise of the play, which much like the majority of the season is exemplary of the very best BBV could offer. The play is steeped in a dark atmosphere, with rich characterisation and sharp dialogue that push this sci-fi/horror tale through to a tense climax. All the cast are excellent with Sarah Sutton giving a better performance here than she ever did as Nyssa. The sound design and score are first rate and add an extra edge to the action-packed ambience.

As well as the continued releases of *Audio Adventure in Time and Space* BBV also took a side step into the audio book market in April 2000 with the release of a reading of Tom Baker's novel *The Boy Who Kicked Pigs*, read by the author. Notoriously unpredictable, Baker had declined the opportunity to return to the role of the Doctor for Big Finish so even if it wasn't a *Doctor Who*-related project, Baggs won a small victory over his former colleagues. Baggs later explained how he came to work with the fourth Doctor actor. "Tom had found this guy he'd toured the book with, I don't understand where this guy had come from but he'd given him the rights to do the talking book. He contacted me and Big Finish but ended up doing the project with me, so that was another feather in my cap at this time, because at the time Tom was refusing to talk to Big Finish about doing any *Doctor Who* stories."[22]

Initially intended to be a one CD release, the reading was too long and so was spread over two discs with a bonus interview, much to the delight of Baggs. "I kind of secretly wanted it that way and I spent a whole afternoon with him interviewing him and socialising with him. Because he was my Doctor, it was like a bit of a dream come true."[23] With the CD proving a success and Baggs having struck up a good relationship with Baker, a line of communication was quickly re-established between Big Finish and BBV. "They had become a very successful distributor, so at one point I rationalised I could produce something and they could distribute it. So there was talk that I could direct Tom and that was how they would get Tom Baker."[24] This collaborative project did not come to fruition and it would be 12 years before Baker eventually signed up for Big Finish.

This brief collaboration would lead to one more project that failed to get off the ground from BBV, involving the elusive star. Author Lance Parkin was set the task of writing the unusual story. "I put together a sort of meta thing that was about Tom Baker making *Doctor Who* in the seventies, reality bleeding into fiction, that kind of thing. It had a part written for Sarah Jane, but K9 was in it, too, so there was a sequence with the fourth Doctor, Sarah and K9 together, which was kind of fun and a thing you have to remind yourself never happened on TV. I really enjoyed writing it, and I got a handwritten note from Tom Baker with some suggestions, including some great dialogue and general riffing on what I'd written."[25]

Baggs too recalls the script with fondness. "Lance wrote a very lovely script, based around [Tom's] era in the show. It was quite risky and he got off with some fans and has sex with them. So it's quite irreverent but it's kind of like him behind the scenes, him as Tom Baker playing *Doctor Who* behind the scenes."[26] So why did this play never happen? "I realised that although I got on with him very well, Tom was very slippery," explains Baggs. "He was up for it and then for some bizarre reason... he was on/off/on/off kind of thing. I think he is quite deeply insecure, so that's why you kind of get this indifference."[27] A further play by John Miller was also announced for Season 3 but never produced.

After the troubled events of the second season, the third is a more assured, more daring and ultimately more well-rounded season, the only real misfires being the two non-*Who* related titles and *The Rani Reaps the Whirlwind*. Baggs and his team managed to lead BBV out of a creative cul-de-sac of *Doctor Who* knock-offs thanks, in no small part, to Paul Ebbs, as Baggs concedes. "I think that Paul would probably admit that his script writing wasn't as good as it is now. He's a very verbose character but what he had is, he had quite strong ideas about what he wanted do, where he wanted to go and what was dramatic and what was interesting. So what we are looking for is things to peg a sale onto and that's what drives it. It's all about telling stories, because we all enjoyed telling stories, because we wanted to make a living out of it, so therefore, in order to make a living out of it, it has to fucking sell so you are looking for things that are going to capture an audience's imagination. And one of the things I remember quite distinctly at that point, certainly coming from Paul, was that we should chose the writers very carefully, and go that route and use writers from the *New Adventures*."[28]

The third season's sole contribution from a NA/BBC Books' author was from Parkin, but at least two more were on their way. The season was a creative high point for BBV but it was now a question of whether the current output was sustainable in an already overpopulated market, one that was about to become even more crowded with the release of Magic Bullet's new plays.

Chapter 27 – Shake the Disease

BBV's next direct to video drama had a long and convoluted journey to screen that stretched back to 1994 when Bill Baggs was intent on making a Cyberman film.

With the initial Briggs-penned *Cyber War* and then 'Sentinel' scripts abandoned, Baggs turned to Tim Saward to come up with a story. "There were going to be three of those to begin with,"[1] recalls Saward. "They were going to be actually Cybermen. I pitched something that was going to be done in chapels I found in the Essex countryside. It was going to be set in the Georgian riots, because I'd just read *Barnaby Rudge*. It would have probably been impossibly expensive."[2]

Always one to hedge his bets, it is likely Baggs also approached a number of other writers to come up with ideas for his cyber trilogy. As Baggs remembers it, the Cybermen weren't the only *Doctor Who* villain he was looking to bring to the screen. "I was trying to get this thing with the Cybermen, but if we didn't get them, then we'd flip it to the Mandragora so we had two scripts and we were shooting for two different scenarios at the same time."[3] But, as previously discussed in chapter 14, Baggs was never able to get the go ahead from the Kit Pedler and Gerry Davis estates.

Never letting something as simple as copyright get in the way, Baggs ploughed on with his cyber project, starting afresh with a new script written by Lance Parkin, who recalls the brief came the day after the recording of his audio play *I Scream*. "Bill and I chatted on the phone the next day to slap ourselves on the back. He wanted to do a video that summer, but didn't have a script he was happy with."[4] Despite sharing a name with the creatures that appeared in *Audio Adventure in Time and Space* the Cyberons of *Cyberon* have nothing to do with their audio counterparts and even less to with the actual Cybermen (confused yet?). It was Parkin who wanted to distance the production from the audios. "I was keen that they weren't just Aldi own brand Cybermen, but wanted to keep some of the body horror stuff, and setting it in a hospital was an efficient way of doing that, and I knew that would mean a pretty easy location to find and shoot in. I don't think there was much of a Cyberon mythos or anything like that to trample over."[5]

While Parkin may not see this as an issue retrospectively, at the time he was keen to differentiate the three races in *Celestial Toyroom*. "For those that keep track of these things, 'Cyberon' in this story has nothing to do with the 'Cyberons' that have appeared in a couple of BBV's audio stories. The video isn't a spin-off from those, there's no need to listen to them to get up to speed. Anyone expecting a Cybermen story, or who assumes this video will feature monsters just like the Cybermen, but with a slightly different name, will be in for a surprise, but hopefully not a disappointment."[6]

When developing the script, Parkin was keen to keep things straight forward. "The story was quite a simple one, with a 'too good to be true' drug being tested. Jo's character gets the moral dilemma stuff that it's helping people, and she's fallen for the guy peddling it, but she's clearly having her doubts." [7]

Cyberon would be a first for BBVs video range, in that it not only featured no actors from *Doctor Who* but also no *Who* monsters at all. Parkin didn't feel this would have an effect on the core audience, however. "I wasn't worried about alienating the *Who* fans — yeah, sure, if it was a Dalek thing more people would have bought it, but Bill and I were known to *Doctor Who* fans, BBV was well known. It was enough of a connection that if people were interested, they'd give it a try. And I think Bill wanted to make something where he wasn't trading on it being an actor from *Doctor Who* or an old monster." [8]

So what was it that appealed to Baggs about the project? "It was having something that would appeal to the core audience, but if 'Terror Game' and 'Breach of the Peace' was pushing the Stranger away, this was me going as far away as I could because it's about relationships."[9]

Cyberon would feature Baggs' new leading lady, Jo Castleton, as Lauren Anderson, alongside P.J. Ochlan as Tom Mordley. P.J was an American actor who had previously appeared in *Space: Above and Beyond* and had a regular role in *Police Academy: The Series*. Other cast members included fellow American — and P.J.'s partner — Camilla Aitken as Denise, Oliver Bradshaw as George Cooper and David Roeciffe as Ray. A number of BBV regulars had small cameos in the film including Nigel Fairs, Jackie Skarvellis, Patricia Merrick and Paul Griggs (the film is also notable for featuring cameos by both of Baggs' parents).

While he wasn't featured in the film, actor Anthony Keetch was also briefly involved early in his association with Baggs. "I think the first thing I did was read-through of *Cyberon*, playing the lead. I'm not sure if I was ever intended for the role, or if I was just a useful male voice for the read-through. *Cyberon* at that point was going to be filmed in America, 'guerrilla-style' according to Bill (which meant no visas, etc.). I wasn't keen on this as I was visiting the States quite regularly at the time and didn't want to cause any problems for myself."[10]

By this point Baggs had found his American audience to be very responsive and it's possible by shooting in America and casting an American lead, he was hoping to cash in on this market and perhaps carve a niche there. Indeed, his stars (remembering this is a relatively mobile free period) took three days to get to England, as they drove from California to the other side of America and then flew onto Paris — panicking Baggs and the BBV team when they couldn't be contacted.

The film was shot in Surrey and London in June 2000. Paul Griggs was on hand to help out on the production side of things. "It was the first time I'd ever worked on something of this scale, and it was the hardest week's work I'd ever done. Don't think for a second it's easy, it's not an easy ride. But even though it was up at six, bed at midnight, six hours sleep if you're lucky and then working solidly, it was also the most fun I have had in my entire life."[11] Nigel Fairs later told Justyce.org about his brief cameo. "I played a detective in a very short scene. I'm a great friend of Jo Castleton, we go back a long way and she was playing the lead, and I went down to play the detective, to Leatherhead, and because I had such a good day I said to Bill 'can I stay on for the afternoon?', so I got be a walk-on, and I stayed on for the next day as well, because I enjoyed myself so much in the afternoon, I'm walking on in about four or five scenes, as different characters."[12]

With no star names attached to the project, the cast and crew found the whole experience a much more collaborative process than normal. As Ochlan told audiences at that year's Gallifrey convention, "we would have days where we were scrambling for a location, and en route, putting scenes together and saying 'well this doesn't quite work because we are going to be here, then we need that little bridge in between and how are we going to make this work?' And we were just drafting these new ideas in cars on the way to new locations. It was a very exciting process, because in all my experience I've never had something so... it wasn't even just the pace of it necessarily, but just the creativity was such a daily situation, every single day you had this intense creativity from every person."

Aitken, who was on the same panel, concurred. "It was wonderful watching everyone work in that collaborative environment. I felt very safe for one thing and it was really, really great to be part of so many different parts of it. When you are an actor, you go do your scenes and that's it, you go home. I was able to be involved in every day of shooting."

While the cast no doubt enjoyed the process, they seem to be putting a positive spin on the hectic nature of low budget film making, with Baggs often demanding a quick turnaround, logistical and script problems that might otherwise be avoided can present themselves. One such problem arose with the script as Baggs explains. "He'd [Lance Parkin] missed a whole chunk out, so we went back and we inserted a whole sequence towards the end of the story, that wasn't there in the original. So that's my editing skills coming in, so I could see that there was no jump or leap in the story that would be a problem." For Castleton the ever fluid script and schedule was something she was used to working on BBV productions. "We were learning those scenes quite quickly, we'd often chop and change things just before we shot them, so you are kind of trying to remember it — you just kind of did it and hoped for the best and hoped you made the right decisions and you were in the right place."[13]

While the cast of unknowns were enjoying the freedom the production provided them, Baggs once again put out the word in *Doctor Who* fandom for extras to appear in the film's club scene which were to be shot at the Po Na Na night club. One of these extras, John Isles, wrote of his experience on the BBV website.

After a delayed start due to an over running crew and an oversleeping club owner, the shots were filmed in three hours. Of his experience, Isles wrote, "I was impressed with the speed and skill that Bill and his crew set up each shot, also how Bill consulted PJ & Jo on how the shots looked when he was setting them up. I think one of the best things you can do as a director is listen to your cast — don't let them make every decision for you, but it does sometimes help to bring in a different perspective on something." The scenes were recorded with no music ("I felt very self-conscious dancing to no music") and minimal extras, although Isles was impressed with how Baggs dealt with this. "Another trick employed to make the club look busier (remember there were only about five extras at this stage) was to have the girls walk occasionally back and forth in front of the camera. I'm sure watching the finished scene you won't notice (I hope!)."[14]

The Cyberons themselves were designed by Terry Cooper and their design is something of a mixed bag, with a well cast fibreglass helmet, but a body suit that showed the limitations of the budget. In order to hide these limitations CGI FX were added in post, much to the relief of Castleton. "I thought that they worked better as a visual effect rather than the scenes when they were there in their boiler suits and crates!"[15]. The FX were created by Steve Johnson and BBV were so impressed with them that they used them as an advertising point for the film. The additional FX meant that *Cyberon*'s release was delayed from September to December 2000.

Cyberon is an entertaining enough film that deals with the limitations of low budget film-making by concentrating on character rather than special FX and action. The script keeps things simple, although events are wrapped up a little too swiftly and the ends lacks the dramatic punch that the script requires, but this once again is more down to the direction, which for the most part is pedestrian and more soap than sci-fi. At the same time, a lack of any correct care being given to the lighting means the entire picture has a very flat feel to it. It is the first of these films that actually feels like it's set in the real world thanks to Parkin's dialogue, which is very natural and the actors handle it with confidence. The special effects are much subtler than those of *Auton 3* and the film benefits from it immensely. The biggest let down of the film is the Cyberons themselves, whose spray painted overalls make them look like bad cos-players rather than menacing monsters.

Upon release, the BBV website boasted the video was "The most anticipated BBV release of all time." The film received a public screening at the LA convention Gallifrey 2001 in February, where Baggs, Griggs, Castleton, Fairs, Parkin, Ochlan and Aitken were in attendance. Meanwhile, drawing the short straw, Paul Ebbs and Steve Johnson presented the film at Battlefield V in Coventry on the same weekend.

With no *Doctor Who* link, the film received no review in *DWM,* but Ian Atkins of *Starburst Magazine* stated that "the direction creates wonders from what is clearly a tiny budget and the special FX are astonishingly well used," while *SFX*'s Stephen O'Brien said "*Cyberon* is a compelling and polished production."[16]

Looking back on the film, Baggs is very positive. "I'm probably, of all of those films, the most proud of *Cyberon.* Even though it's not lit as nicely as some of the early ones, it's shot well, the script is interesting, the performances are good and it's a clever story."[17] Parkin too is fond of the finished product. "I think for the time and the budget, it was pretty good," he said in 2014. "I'd have gone a little bolder, if I'd had my time over again, and I guess now it would be faster and darker. We thought it would be the first of a series — not necessarily with the same characters or story, or that I'd be writing them all, or anything."[18]

In producing a film that had no obvious link to *Doctor Who,* Baggs could be seen to be either taking a wild gamble or once again penny pinching. The truth undoubtedly lies somewhere in the middle. Baggs had always laid out his intentions to move away from *Doctor Who*-related drama, but if he wanted to do that, perhaps a bolder move would have been to drop the pseudo Cybermen altogether (there is no given reason why the Cyberons should be called that or appear like that, beyond the obvious *Who* connotations), which undoubtedly brought in a few viewers expecting something more in line with BBV's knock off *Who* range. But Baggs had also already noted the shrinking market and with less money available a star name may not have been viable.

While seemingly a critical success, the fact that its follow up would feature a *Doctor Who* monster is perhaps a sign that the sales did not reflect the company's desire to move away from its core audience. Never the less, it was successful enough to spawn a sequel that would become one of the most notorious *Doctor Who* spin-offs for all the wrong reasons.

Chapter 28 — That Joke Isn't Funny Anymore

Despite having previously shied away from comedy, apart from a brief flirtation with *The Auton Diaries*, BBV's next release would be an all out comedy that would poke fun at both *Doctor Who* and the spin-off media it had inspired.

Do You Have a Licence to Save This Planet? as the video would be known, was conceived by Paul Ebbs in collaboration with Baggs and Gareth Preston. "I was egged on by Paul Ebbs who thought a spoof would make more money, and I thought why not?"[1] Baggs told Mike Harberfaner. "Actually, my first spoof was *The Auton Diaries*, a ten minute short for a company involved with the *Auton*-films, which I thought was quite funny, so I thought why not do something a little longer. It was also an opportunity to try out some heavy duty CGI-stuff." [2] Preston was brought in by Baggs, thanks to the success of his previous release. "He and Paul felt that the humour I had put into 'Conduct Unbecoming' made me a good choice for a collaborator, plus Paul and I were good friends and had a similar sense of humour. We tossed a few ideas about and one that was on my mind was the way that Bill's spin-off videos, particularly the first few *Stranger* ones, had flirted so close to being *Doctor Who* in all but name."[3]

Once again this was Baggs' way of attempting to find a new niche within the *Doctor Who* market. "I'm playing against what I normally do and I'm exploring new territory for me, as a director and as a producer. We'd done *The Auton Diaries* before, so it was an extension of them. It's about seeing if there is a market there, what does the market want? What do I want to do? And throwing something in the pond and seeing whether it swims."[4]

After this initial conversation, Ebbs and Preston wrote the script via email, turning in eight drafts. Bouncing ideas between them, they came up with a rule that helped the collaborative process. "If one of us deleted a line, the other could not re-insert it," explains Preston, "which I think is a good strategy for any collaboration. Ironically, one of the most successful jokes I came up with was added as an aside at the bottom of an email rather than put in the script initially — 'I'm not that kind of Chiropodist, you must look after your own feet.' Paul put it in and it always seemed to get a warm response." [5]

As well as *The Stranger*, Preston was also inspired by another of Baggs *Doctor Who* knock-offs. "The Cyberons, which were so obviously imitation Cybermen, I was amazed Bill got away with those two audios. That got me wondering what the Cyberons themselves thought about it? Could it be they might have an insecurity about it and were envious of the merchandising that the Cybermen enjoyed?" [6]. To cast *Do You Have a Licence to Save This Planet?*, Baggs once again called on some of his ever reliable regulars, with Mark Donovan playing The Salesman, Nigel Fairs as Geoff/The Licensor and Joe Castleton as Gloria, plus cameos from Nigel Peever, Gareth Preston and Paul Griggs. The lead character, The Foot Doctor, was originally due to be played by George Telfer, as Preston recalls. "We envisaged him in Victorian clothes and the original few scripts were more verbose, reflecting our audio drama backgrounds." [7]

However, at a very late stage the role was taken by Sylvester McCoy, much to the delight of Preston. "It was a pleasant surprise to have Sylvester McCoy along instead. Bill pushed us to make the comedy a lot more visual. The Foot Doctor's coat was actually Sylvester's own." [8] Baggs was keen to use a name that would help sell the video and felt it was a part McCoy could play to his strengths. "Whether you like Sylvester or not as an actor, what he has is a wealth of experience and he gets tired very quickly given his past [in Ken Campbell's Roadshow], but he's an excitable inspiration when I'm not asking him to be serious. It was a really interesting experience."[9]

Unsure that this new venture would sell and with ever decreasing sales, Baggs had ordered the writers to keep the budget tight and chose to film the production predominately in and around his house in Surrey. Filmed over two days in January 2001, the shoot was attended by *DWM*'s Benjamin Cook, who spoke to McCoy. "We've been filming outdoors and I'm absolutely freezing! Working in the cold expends so much energy. It's hard enough to keep alive, let alone string a sentence together!"[10].

According to Preston, McCoy was in a "subdued mood" throughout the shoot. "He was a bit under the weather and I believe had some back pains. I don't think he really understood our script or where the comedy was coming from. I remember him saying that jokes should have an inner logic to them and I suspected he felt a lot of our jokes were lacking that. But he did his best and he did come up with some funny adlibs."[11] Despite his mellow demeanour, Preston is quick to stress that McCoy was never anything less than professional. "He wasn't awkward or unpleasant but I did get the feeling he was there to do a job he wasn't enthused about. I was there for the second day's filming and there was a slightly disorganised air about it. I'm used to working against time on various fan films and this had a similar atmosphere, which surprised me for a BBV production."[12]

Paul Griggs was also on hand. "It was great fun and it was an absolute pleasure and privilege to watch Sylvester work. I've said it before — comedy genius!"[13]

Castleton and Fairs were once again delighted to be acting together, as the former recalled. "That was great fun playing silly comedy cameo roles — I just remember laughing a lot!"[14] Fairs too enjoyed the humour that the roles required, as he later wrote on the BBV website. "It's a freezing cold Monday morning in January, my face is covered in tomato ketchup, a piece of raw bacon is being carefully placed on my left shoulder and I suddenly have a dreadful feeling of deja vu."[15]

Although Preston wasn't a huge fan of his performance — "Nigel Fairs is a great actor (and director and writer) but I was disappointed he played the next-door neighbour as a nasally comic character, when I intended the part to be a really normal bloke to contrast with the weirdness of the others. Having said that he played the villain excellently and he came up with the best line in the whole film — 'Or should I say — the Gynaecologist?'"[16] — Fairs relished the chance to play an OTT version of the Master. "I think that was a rather good Anthony Ainley myself but that wasn't the best thing, was it? I loved doing it because I was with Jo and we were giggling and having a lovely time. It was a lot of fun to do but not so much to watch."[17]

The shoot again was very much a collaborative effort with things being rewritten on location and people pitching in ideas. Even by BBV's previous standards, the *Do You Have a Licence to Save this Planet?* script was fairly fluid, according to Baggs. "With straight drama you've got the script mapped out and although there are moments where you do develop the script as you're shooting it, with this you're kind of developing it all the time, the script is literally just a starting point."[18]

Unfortunately, this method of working wasn't always successful, as Preston later admitted. "Paul was there too and Bill was asking us to come up with some jokes to put in it. This led to Paul, Sylvester and myself sitting that evening in the bar of the Freemason's hall where we were filming the climatic scenes, trying to come up with a new scene on the spot and failing miserably. So I felt bad, feeling I wasn't pulling my weight as a writer and worse Sylvester was sitting there watching me fail, clearly just wanting the filming to be over so he could go home. So that was the low point but there was some good banter during the day."[19] McCoy too was able to put his wealth of comedy experience to good use and suggest some changes, as he told Cook. "Bill doesn't give up until he gets what he wants, but at the same time, he's open to suggestions."[20]

This input extended to the comedy timing between McCoy and his co-star which impressed Preston no end. "It was good to watch Sylvester and Mark Donovan at work. Their partnership was to me the highlight of the whole film."[21] Fairs too made some suggestions on how he should play the villain. "I decided that if I was going to play the Master as a sort of Anthony Ainley, I was going to have one of the most over the top costumes ever. So I got hold of a selection and I think Bill misunderstood me and I had this Camp-o-meter where I changed costume every two minutes or something and it just got more and more extravagant."[22]

Once shooting was complete, to counterbalance the cheap and domestic setting, Baggs asked Steve Johnson to add several CGI elements to the film, much to the surprise of Preston. "We were asked to keep the budget fairly tight, which is why I was surprised to see a Krynoid appear, something that wasn't in our script."[23]

Do You Have A Licence to Save this Planet? looks cheap and rushed. The main sensation when viewing it is that cast and crew are having a great time even if the viewer isn't. While the plot is thin, there are some decent jokes that are let down by Baggs' substandard direction and editing. McCoy and Donovan have a great chemistry and really make the material work, while the rest of the cast seem unsure how to play the material and appear to send it up rather than play the comedy. You can't help but wonder if Baggs was too concerned with simply getting stuff in the can, rather than working with his actors. Or perhaps comedy just isn't his forte.

Upon its release Vanessa Bishop wrote a disparaging review in *DWM*. "The answer to the titular question is 'no' — and I'm afraid this sci-fi comedy isn't going to change things,"[24] before going on to pose the question "it's silly — but is it funny?", and finally concluding that'[i]rritating is probably the kindest word to use. *Do you have a Licence...* might be a hoot with anyone longing for a new series of *Rentaghost* — but for the majority, the pratfalls and clumsy cartoon humour will raise only thin smiles. "[25]

Preston was understandably displeased with this response. "It was disappointing, particularly since *DWM* was going to be practically the only magazine that would review it. However I'd already had some bad comments from others. I remember Mark Wright telling Paul and I that he 'actively loathed it'!"[26] If Preston was upset with the *DWM* review, the response at that year's Battlefield convention, where the film debuted, must have lifted his spirits. "The reaction was actually quite positive on the night, especially for the references to other shows. The *Blake's 7* materialisation effect in particular got a huge cheer. But maybe it was the convention atmosphere that helped because I never had that kind of positive response at any subsequent showing." Baggs also premiered some early footage at that year's Gallifrey convention and was somewhat nervous about the response, as he told the crowd. "With the straight videos you're actually much more confident that people will enjoy it, whereas with [comedy] it's still kind of very precious and raw and it is fascinating to hear what people laugh at." [27]

Preston understandably has mixed feelings about *Do You Have a Licence to Save This Planet?* "In retrospect the concept of *Doctor Who* spin-offs and their legitimacy was probably a bit too niche to base a whole video on. It was a sketch idea stretched to breaking point. Ultimately, it would have been better received as an extra to *Cyberon*, rather than a release in its own right." [28] Some of the negatives he blames on his own inexperience, as well some of the production problems. "The editing is where it often falls down. The ends of scenes sometimes linger and it all feels a bit flat. I know

Bill was under pressure to get a lot of filming done in a short time, so the actual direction is fine."[29]

He does, however, have more positive memories. "There are some jokes that work very well. I think Mark and Sylvester make a good team and Nigel's performance as the villain is excellent."[30]

Bill Baggs has a more novel way of looking back on the project. "Purist fans might find the parody sacrilegious, but there is the whole aspect of fandom that likes doing these things. With *Licence* you either love it or hate it, but if you watch it after having had a few beers with some of your mates, it is a bit funnier than when you watch it stone-cold sober."[31]

Despite ultimately proving a bit of a disappointment for those involved, and the audience not taking to the film, there was briefly talk of a follow up film. "Buoyed by the good audience reaction to 'DYHAL'," recalls Preston, "Bill did ask myself, Barry Williams and Rupert Booth at Battlefield V to write another SF comedy. We did come up with a script called 'Time and the Fans' which involved two SF geeks being recruited by a glamorous agent from the future to stop a new race of super-soldiers. It was in the style of Channel 4's *Spaced* but not nearly as good. But the ultimately bad sales of 'DYHAL' put paid to that."[32] While this sequel sounds interesting, part of the appeal of *Spaced* lay in Edgar Wright's individual directorial style and it's doubtful that Baggs could have pulled off anything approaching that with his then work ethic.

Do You Have a Licence to Save This Planet? suffers from what is now a familiar Baggs trope, that of quantity over quality when recording. By cramming a thirty minute film into two days, the film undeniably lacks due care and attention. Where Baggs once strove to create showreel material, his remit now seemed to be to get a product out as quickly and cheaply as possible

Although he was unaware of it at the time, *Do You Have a Licence to Save This Planet?* would be Baggs' last video release for the foreseeable future. As such, it is perhaps fitting that it is in many ways a tribute to the cottage industry it helped create, as well as featuring some of BBV's more memorable faces in McCoy, Fairs and Castelton, as well as the Cyberons, Sontarans and Autons.

Chapter 29 — We Hate It When Our Friends Become Successful

2001 marked the tenth birthday of BBV and, as it transpired, it would also mark the beginning of the end for the company.

To celebrate this milestone, BBV launched its new website, offered any of the single CDs from its first two seasons for just five pounds each and began its fourth season of *Audio Adventures in Time and Space*. The releases in Season 4 would be in flux for much of the season's long duration, but BBV promised scripts from Pip and Jane Baker, Dave Stone, Iain Hepburn and Lawrence Miles.

The first release of the season was from the pen of actor Anthony Keetch, who had appeared in a number of BBV plays. "On the way home from the recording of 'Conduct Unbecoming', I pondered some ideas for audios I could write. I knew Bill used the Zygon and the Krynoids, so I came up with ideas for both of them. I was going on holiday to the USA a couple of days later. I bought a notebook in the departure lounge, and spent the whole holiday making notes, even writing scenes. Completely unsolicited. It was a rare instance of a script almost writing itself. I then submitted the completed thing to Bill, and he accepted it in the same phone call that he offered me *The Rani Reaps*... It was another six months at least before we recorded it."[1]

In crafting the macabre tale, Keetch drew influence from a number of places. "I'm of the generation that grew up watching Hammer films, the Hinchcliffe era of *Who*, plus lots of BBC period stuff. I'm steeped in that fake gothic Victoriana. (Those foggy London scenes were actually written on a hot beach in Maine). I'm also not a huge SF fan, more a horror buff. I only like SF when it has a scary component."[2]

Entitled *The Barnacled Baby* the production was directed by Paul Griggs and starred Nigel Peever as Jethro, Kerry Skinner as Doris, Clive Merrison as Sir Frederick Maltravers, Deborah Watling as Queen Victoria and Anthony Keetch as Toby and Henry Bruge credited as Bobby aka Demeris the Zygon. Although this may have been Keetch under an alias, with him taking on the part as a budget saving measure but had always had himself in mind for the role. "I wrote the Zygon for myself, and soon learnt that it's a terrible idea to give aliens lots of dialogue, and in particular, long speeches. The Zygon initially had a couple of great monologues, but they were a bugger to do in that voice, and even more painful to listen to. This is why Daleks aren't given soliloquies."[3]

Richard McGinlay of *Sci Fi Online*, called *The Barnacled Baby* a "clever and darkly witty spin on *The Elephant Man*"[4] — an apt summation of this macabre affair. Keetch's script is an unusual beast, that feels more like an extended scene from *The League of Gentlemen* than anything that had been attempted in the *Doctor Who* universe before and that is probably why it is so successful. In taking a *Doctor Who* monster and placing it a different type of story, it enables the Zygon to develop its character further than any of the previous outings have. All the cast are excellent and deliver Keetch's epigrammatic dialogue with aplomb.

Despite good reviews, Keetch was unhappy with the finished production. "I was a bit miffed at the time about the end result of *Barnacled Baby*. The script was rearranged in post-production, my carefully thought out structure went for a burton, and important scenes were dropped and filler I had been asked to write to go on in the background was brought to the fore. I haven't listened to the CD since its release. I'd probably be more sanguine about it now, although I'll be very self-critical of the script and my performances."[5]

The next two releases from BBV would be the start of a brand new range of adventures from fan favourite, the occasionally controversial, Lawrence Miles. Miles had been behind some of the most popular *New Adventures* and BBC *Doctor Who* books, including 'Christmas on a Rational Planet', 'Interference' and 'Alien Bodies', which introduced readers to Faction Paradox. It was Faction Paradox that Miles would bring to BBV.

At first, Miles was aware of, but not familiar with, BBV's work. "When I started on the *Faction Paradox* job, BBV offered to give me some of their CDs to listen to, but in the end I thought it'd probably be better if I didn't know what the form was. When you think about it, the only reason CITIZEN KANE ended up as such a seminal movie was that Orson Welles didn't know you weren't supposed to be able to do that kind of thing in the cinema. Because obviously, THE FACTION PARADOX PROTOCOLS is at least as important a cultural landmark as CITIZEN KANE. Look, it was just an example, that's all." [6]

Miles was brought into the BBV staple by Paul Ebbs, who had met the author at the Fitzroy Tavern. Ebbs was full of praise for the first script, citing it as the best he'd ever read, and Bill Baggs was only too happy to have him join the BBV roster of writers. "I must admit, I think that was a really neat move, because it was very successful. I mean not so successful that I could continue with it, but it was certainly the thing that BBV could focus on."[7]

In spite of this, Baggs admits that he had very little to do with Miles personally. "I never met him. I think he's someone who needs a very good editor. But in terms of genius and originality he was great. I'd be fascinated to know where he gets all his sources from, it's very rich and kind of spiritual." [8]

Initially conceived as rogue Time Lords in the BBC book 'Alien Bodies' (although there is a casual reference to them in the New Adventure

'Christmas on a Rational Planet') Faction Paradox had to be reengineered for a Doctor-less and copyright infringement-free spin-off outing.

Miles later discussed the premise of *Faction Paradox* and its extensive history with Brent Keane. "The Faction's universe is on the surface an SF universe, but it works on the same principles as traditional folklore. It's all very feudal. There are, or were, 'people' who ran history — 'history' being a way for us to deal with the world around us... and these 'people' are generally nameless and faceless, but with the attitude of an aristocratic upper class. Ruling Houses, in effect." He went on to discuss the mythology and history of the universe. "At some point these Houses engaged in a war with an equally inscrutable enemy, and the war intersected — still intersects — human history like a biblical War in Heaven, impacting on humanity but without direct human involvement. Usually. So that makes *Faction Paradox* a Prometheus among the Titans, it's a splinter-group halfway between the elite and humanity, which believes in (a) introducing its principles to the 'collaterals' caught in the crossfire — that's us, essentially — and (b) interfering in the plans of the Houses whenever possible."[9]

Elsewhere, Miles told the BBV website about his delight at seeing his character being brought to life on audio. "For anyone who knows *Faction Paradox* from my books, this is where the characters take centre-stage. There aren't any limits on them this time, they're in their natural environment, they finally get to be the heroes. Well, as much as they ever can be. For anyone who doesn't know *Faction Paradox*, the story's basically a great big gothic voodoo space-time opera." Lawrence seemed eager to hear the finished product. "This is the first time the Faction's been anything other than an abstract... I mean, Cousin Justine's got a proper voice now, which is scary... so the whole thing's meant to give the characters a decent world of their own. And then blow large chunks of it up." [10]

The two interlinked plays were recorded on July 14th and directed by Nigel Fairs, who also handled post production, composed the music and played both Lord Ruthven and the Sontaran General Kine. Fairs discussed how he came to have such a large influence over the plays with Chris Dueker. "Having edited audio drama for about 25 years by then I was keen to do some for Bill, and he gave me *Faction Paradox* as an 'audition' of sorts. To be honest I had no idea what they were about, really — I'm not a huge sci fi fan and I had NO IDEA they were all about the Time Lords etc (though of course I recognised the Sontarans and tried to do an impersonation of the brilliant actor who played Lynx for the first two). But I thought they were well-written and quirky audio dramas." [11]

The two main protagonists were cast via auditions, and came in the form of Suzanne Proctor as Cousin Justine and Emma Kilbey in the dual roles of Cousin Eliza and Godmother Quelch. With a limited budget, Fairs had to rely on colleagues from various theatre productions to bulk out the cast. "I had to rope in friends I'd worked with in the theatre, promising them that though the money was rubbish, I'd cook them a nice lunch and we'd have a drink afterwards!"[12]

These other cast members included Caroline Burns-Cook playing Lolita, Ellis Pike as Godfather Morlock and Linda Bartram playing The Voice. The plays went under the banner of *The Faction Paradox Protocols* and were released in November of 2001 under the titles 'The Eleven Day Empire' and 'The Shadow Play'.

In an interview with Nigel Fairs for the BBV website, Proctor discussed her hopes for the future of her character. "I think that as time progresses Justine should gain a lot more confidence and be able to confront her fears. She should be able to make more decisions without the help of Morlock, but I think she will always respect his judgement. It would be really nice to see Eliza and Justine getting a little bit closer, as at the moment Justine seems to be holding up a barrier between them, maybe, not sure!? And it would be great to have a massive fight scene at the very end where Eliza and Justine kill Lolita, or turn her into a rancid turnip or a smelly cabbage or something similar!!!"[13]

'The Eleven Day Empire' takes the BBV range to uncharted terrain, and while Vanessa Bishop called it "tense and edgy," she did note that "although its dark moods swirl about to give the impression of something happening, not a lot actually does," and concluded the play was "intriguing and confusing."[14]

Indeed, the world that Miles has created is rich with mythology — and though the play crams in all the exposition it needs, it contrives to do so without sounding too cluttered. The first release sets up an interesting scenario for the forthcoming series, although the production does lack pace, taking its time getting to where it needs to go. It is also let down by the recording, the mics sound distorted and although the sound design does its best to disguise it, there is no escaping the amateur feel that this gives the entire production. The theme tune for the series is also a little too 'my first Casio keyboard' for comfort.

Bishop generally enjoyed 'The Shadow Play', saying "accomplished performances and excellent production keep you dug in until the end,"[15] although she was not a fan of Proctor's performance.

This second CD is an enjoyable continuation of the events set up in the first instalment, even if once again things are a little too drawn out and convoluted. Lolita makes for an auspicious villain with promise that there will be much more to be learned in future outings, though the demotion of the Sontarans to mere henchmen undermines the species' initial power and their development within the BBV universe. As such they feel a little forced into the play as a selling point and connection to *Doctor Who*, rather than being needed in the story.

On the acting front, Suzanne Proctor plays Justine with a detachment that serves the characters well and Eliza makes for a more grounded co-star. However, the feeling that one would rather hear more from Qulech and Morlock than the two survivors of the Empire, doesn't bode well.

Responses were generally favourable for both releases, and Fairs was mostly happy, although some of his favourite scenes ended up on the cutting room floor. "Sadly, the first couple overran and Bill decided we should cut quite a lot of my favourite sections (all of which are on CD somewhere); mostly character monologues which gave them a bit of style, made them stand out I think. But he was the producer and it was his choice, quite rightly, to push the story on."[16]

The next release would be from the pen of Zoltán Déry, who had written a number of articles, reviews and short stories for various fanzines. Déry initially submitted a script for BBV's short lived *K9* series entitled 'The Liberator', and although the script was rejected, Déry had done enough to impress BBV. "It was a very good rejection, asking whether I had any other scripts, and if so, they would like to see them. And so I inflicted *The Green Man* upon an unsuspecting world."[17]

After an initial conversation and the delivery of a synopsis, the script was written and recorded in little more than a week. *The Green Man* had a medieval setting, which Déry chose for a number of reasons. "Firstly, I can't believe that I was the first to draw a link between the Krynoid and the Green Man motif seen in so many medieval churches, but I seem to have been the first to write it into a script. Secondly, the adverts for the BBV audios called them *Adventures in Time and Space*. Yet most of the audios were futuristic, with the rest seeming to be contemporary. No historicals sprang out at me, despite the popularity of the 'pseudo-historical' stories in *Doctor Who*. This was the sort of story I wanted from BBV, and I hoped that others would too, not least Bill Baggs. After all, I reasoned, perhaps no one has submitted such a script yet, in which case mine might stand out. And lastly, I had been reading a Role Playing Game supplement about Robin Hood with more than a hint of *Robin of Sherwood* about it, and I thought that such a setting with overt monsters might be interesting."[18]

Recorded in January of 2002, the play was once again directed by Nigel Fairs who was also on post production and music duties. Fairs also played Osbert with Arthur Bostrom of *'Allo 'Allo* fame playing Earl Godfrey (who was also writing a book on the Green Man legend at the time), Saul Jaffe as Henri D'Arree, Keith Drinkel as Moses of Tyre and Michael Chance as Alfred.

Fairs recalls the recording with fondness, even if it is perhaps for the wrong reasons. "That is one of the funniest days I've ever had in my professional life, because the whole script was unintentionally loaded with double entendres. So I said 'we don't normally do this, but we are going to have a read through,' and we sat there and were literally crying with laughter when we read through because of all the double entendres, that the poor writer hadn't realised were there 'it's so huge, it's so green' all that sort of stuff. I think it turned out alright but it was very funny."[19]

Vanessa Bishop described the release as "an enjoyable medieval version of a 1950s monster flick,"[20] and it's hard to disagree. The central premise of the story works well, even if the script is, as Fairs notes, littered with double entendres. The production is marred by bad recording and poor performances, and there is also an air of camp that the actors bring to the table which makes it impossible to fully enjoy the play. This is a real shame as taken more seriously, this could be just as scary as Fairs' score tries to imply.

Déry was a huge fan of the BBV range, but is unable to listen back to his own contribution to the range. "I know that it is traditional for writers to blame others for their failings, but there is one section of the audio where even I can't tell what is going on, because someone chose to take out about a page of dialogue. (It is the part where the human's cunning plan goes badly wrong. Alas, the part where the plan is explained is missing. Ho-hum.) Whinge over. The problem I have with it is that all I could hear when I listened to the CD is all the places where I should have made cuts or done things differently."[21]

Although this was Dérys' only contribution to the range, he did also pitch one more script to Baggs, entitled *Bring me the Head of Sabalom Glitz*, which would have seen the popular sixth and seventh Doctors' associate become the most wanted man in the galaxy. The proposed script was a humorous endeavour, which really captured the essence of the Glitz character. But a change in direction for BBV meant the script would never be recorded. "BBV seemed to become a Lawrence Miles factory after that, and who can blame them? I would rather listen to new Lawrence Miles plays that anything by me." [22]

While Big Finish seemingly had the official *Doctor Who* audio market cornered, the BBC's *Doctor Who* website joined the party in February 2002 with the webcast of *Death Comes to Time*, a five episode *Doctor Who* story that continued the story of the broadcast BBC4 radio pilot of the same name.

The audio series, with accompanying illustration, was written by Director/Producer Dan Freeman under the alias Colin Meek, and starred Sylvester McCoy, Sophie Aldred, Nicholas Courtney, Jacqueline Pearce, John Sessions, Anthony Stewart Head and Stephen Fry as the Minister of

Chance. While *Death Comes to Time* stands as something of an anomaly in *Doctor Who* history, seemingly killing the Doctor and taking creative liberties with the series' folklore, it would not be the last we will hear from the Minister of Chance or Dan Freeman.

After the success of *The Boy Who Kicked Pigs*, BBV released a further talking book, in the form of *The Killing Stone*, written and read by Mike Yates actor, Richard Franklin. The reading in question has a long and convoluted history.

It first began life as a novel, which Franklin was eager to publicise in his *Myth Makers* interview in 1989. "It's what happened to Captain Mike Yates when he left in 'Planet of the Spiders'. It was to have been published by WH Allen but unfortunately they've discontinued the series, because the ratings have dropped and so I'm going to publish this separately, privately myself. I'm kind of going to do what Dickens did, I'm going to produce one edition, one chapter each month for eleven months."[23]

Whether this initial approach to WH Allen was a commission or simply an idea that he hoped to pitch is unknown. But ultimately neither this nor a self-published version ever materialised.

The next sighting of *The Killing Stone* would be as a one-man show at the Edinburgh Fringe in August 2000, with Franklin performing an abridged version at The Claremont pub in the city. *DWM*'s Dave Owen wrote a cutting review of the performance, in an article entitled 'Franklin Flops at the Fringe'. Observing the audience on the day he visited was in single figures, Owen remarked, "As the hour wore on, it became clear that nothing of consequence was going to happen to Yates, save a series of disjointed flashbacks and reflections," before going on to share a number of embarrassments for the performer including the fact that "his stage manager hadn't bothered turning up, leaving Franklin's costume changes embarrassingly devoid of linking music. Attention was instead focused on his prose — which had, very obviously, been combed neither by a knowledgeable *Doctor Who* fan nor by a script editor."[24]

Despite the book remaining unpublished for a decade or more, and the Fringe performance being badly received, Franklin nevertheless saw further life in *The Killing Stone* and pitched the book to Bill Baggs, who recalls, "Big Finish turned him down so he came to me. I'd worked with him before."[25]

While other BBV releases were treading a fine line between a cheeky knock-off and copyright infringement, *The Killing Stone* is, strictly speaking, illegal. It features appearances by Sarah Jane Smith, Brigadier Lethbridge-Stewart, Sergeant Benton and the Doctor himself, but this didn't seem to worry Baggs.

"I think he'd cleared it with the BBC — but no it didn't bother me because they were his interpretations. And I think that's fair. And although it wasn't the best story ever, it certainly had charm and a certain cachet."[26] Baggs was only too happy to welcome Franklin into the fold, saying of him, "[he was] very friendly and eccentric. I loved his enthusiasm. His characterisations of the Doctor and the Brig were very funny. When Richard puts his mind to his craft he's very talented." [27]

The story was released on a single disc, with a further disc containing an interview with the actor turned author. To fit the story onto the CD Franklin had to edit the manuscript. "*The Killing Stone* was originally intended to be read as a novella. Bill Baggs produced the CD and said it had to be 55 minutes and cut it, it had to be cut quite savagely, literally in half, there is more than half the book that has never been seen."[28]

Released in May 2002, Vanessa Bishop was kinder on the CD release than Owen had been of the show. "This is a diverting reading of what sounds a whimsical novella," she stated, although she did take issue with his characterisation of Benton and the play's ending. "The conclusion, however, descends a tad too much into farce (Benton undercover in a dress) and would, I feel, work better staged than read."[29]

While Bishop goes easy on the release, listening back to it now the entire thing screams of desperation. The CD is either a massive joke on the part of Franklin, or the product of a deluded narcissist, who believes Yates was a pivotal character in the history of *Doctor Who*. The plot pushes credulity to the limits, taking a series of mundane autobiographical incidents and attempting to weave them together into an exciting plot. Yates' character and ego are at complete odds with the character we know from the Pertwee era and Franklin makes for an unconvincing lead. The other characters fare just as badly, with Franklin reimagining the Brigadier as a pompous idiot, the fourth Doctor as an angry snob and Benton as a comedy idiotic yokel. This story is an insult to the era of *Doctor Who* it represents and everything that made it successful.

The Killing Stone would finally be published in novel form by Fantom Films in October of 2012 under the title *Operation H.A.T.E.* The new publishers however, took none of the risks that Baggs had, as Franklin explains. "A lot of it is *Killing Stone* but 50 percent of it is actually new and unseen and actually all the names have to be changed because the BBC copyright situation is rather tougher now than it was when I did *The Killing Stone* but it's quite recognisable." [30]

While the release rate of CDs had slowed down rapidly by mid-2002, Baggs began taking advantage of the relatively new DVD format and commenced on a release programme for the company's back catalogue. The first release for the range was *The AirZone Solution*, announced in July and issued later in the year. The DVD was presented in a remastered format and jam packed with extras including out-takes, deleted scenes, behind the scenes footage, an extended Peter Davison interview and a trailer. It was also advertised as containing a commentary, although this didn't appear on the final release.

The next release would see BBV again diversify their monster range to include the Sontaran's enemies, the Rutans. The play was initially entitled 'All the Little Boys' but was later renamed *In 2 Minds*, and was written by newcomer Iain Hepburn. Hepburn was a journalist writing for various regional and national newspapers as well as being a digital editor for *SFX* magazine. Despite his background, this was his first attempt at writing any fiction. "I knew at the time I'd never write for Big Finish, for various reasons, and I didn't have a book in me or anything, but the idea of doing an audio seemed interesting at the time. Since I'd seen and heard some of BBV's output while at *SFX*, they seemed the obvious place to try."[31]

Even so, when the commission actually arrived he found the task a daunting one. "When I got an email back asking for a script, I was stunned. I kind of struggled with writing it — it was the first time I'd written anything like that. I had the first act worked out, and knew what the ending was, but couldn't get the dots to join in the middle, as it was. Then the web publisher I was working for went bust, and I was redundant. Funny how the need to make some money focuses the mind, really." [32]

It took Hepburn six months to complete the first draft, although there were only minor tweaks made after that. He found that Baggs gave him free range in his approach — the choice of villain was his and he decided to take the play away from its *Doctor Who* roots in favour of a conspiracy thriller. "I definitely didn't want it to be a straight up and down *Who* rip-off. I had in my mind the story I was trying to tell, and the structure just came from that. In the midst of writing it, of course, came September 11, which made me stop for a bit and rethink, although it didn't make much difference in the end. Initially in the script I'd skirted round mentioning it, with Tommy at the end saying the jets are on alert 'due to recent incidents'. The production team made that a bit more explicit, and ultimately I'm glad they did since it sells the time and place of the story a lot more." [33]

Nigel Fairs returned to direct the play and was also responsible for post-production and music in addition to playing the part of Hall. The rest of the cast consisted of Martin Broad as Foley, Ashleigh Gray as Nicola, Nigel Peever as Wight, Jackie Skarvellis in the role of Liz, Joe Young as Dunne, Mark Greig as Tommy and Richard Stemp playing various roles. Fairs saw this as one of the stand-out plays of the later range. "I really like that one. I thought it was quite sort of modern and gritty and Richard Stemps [is] in that one and he's brilliant."[34]

After delivering a disappointing final production with the *The Green Man* script, Nigel Fairs delivers a far more well rounded production with *In 2 Minds*. Vanessa Bishop seemed to enjoy it also, noting that "BBV stick to the 'small cast, small focus' approach that always serves them well" and saying of the performers that "Ashleigh Gray, as hack Nicola, is a stand-out."[35]

The story is a political thriller that gives the actors an interesting plot, well formed characterisation with which to play and a couple of hilarious one liners. The most striking thing about *In 2 Minds* is how real it feels, and while the Rutans may be a little generic (through no fault of the writer), the characters are some of the most realistic BBV have ever done. In fact not since 'The Terror Game' has BBV attempted and succeeded in presenting such a gritty drama.

It's a shame then, that the ending feels a little rushed and lacklustre but with so much else to enjoy it's impossible not to like the play.

As before, Baggs was hoping for a series from this first Rutan outing, as Fairs recalls. "That was meant to be setting up for a series. I remember I had to compose a theme tune that would be used for the series."[36]

However, Hepburn was not asked to contribute any further ideas. "I wasn't asked, and I didn't have any inclination to do it anyway. I had a vague notion of pitching a sequel, which would have been to do with the Rutans and Scottish independence, but I'd struggled pulling the first one together so much that I figured I'm not a natural fiction writer and stuck to my day job instead."[37]

Along with *In 2 Minds* September 2002 also saw the release of David A Mcintee's *The Quality Of Mercy*. Mcintee had authored numerous Virgin and BBC *Doctor Who* related novels, and this play resurrected a character from his 1995 *New Adventure* 'Sanctuary', the knight Guy de Carnac. "I always wanted to do more with that character," says Mcintee, "and there was always meant to be more novels, which will finally appear next spring... I don't recall, though, whether it was myself or someone at BBV who actually originally suggested doing an audio with him. Especially since I mostly had Gabriel Byrne in mind to 'play' him while writing him in prose."[38]

The Quality Of Mercy much like *Faction Paradox* before it, has a tenuous link to its parent show. But while *Faction Paradox* had the Sontarans to strengthen its *Who* connection, *The Quality Of Mercy* features a character who only had one outing in a novel, essentially becoming a spin-off of a spin-off.

With Big Finish now in full swing, does Mcintee think that moving further away from the source material was the only way BBV could compete? "I don't think they were really in a competition, or at least they shouldn't have been — it would make far more sense for them to expand into original creator-owned stuff, and that's what they did, to at least some degree. I think, really, that trying to stay linked to *Doctor Who* elements held everything back, to be honest. They could have gone really wild with creator-owned genre projects rather than trying to appeal to a tiny fraction of an existing limited audience."[39]

With Fairs back behind the boards he cast himself as the Sailor, Joe Young as Guy, Jackie Skarvellis as the Woman, Martin Broad as the Merchant, Nigel Peever as Brother Reynard, Richard Stemp as Father Baldwin and Mark Grieg as Priest. Mcintee was pleased with Fairs' handling of his script and although he didn't get his dream casting, he was happy with the performer he got, calling Young "fantastic" and going on to say "[he] totally won me over right from the start, and I wish we could have heard more of him in the role."[40]

The Quality of Mercy is a much subtler release than many of those that preceded it. The script boasts exquisite dialogue that is superbly delivered by a well-chosen cast. The direction is faultless and the score underpins the drama of the piece without being too over powering. It is a simple story that relies on well-developed characters to hold the listener's attention as opposed to simple action. It's a shame that this is McIntee and Guy's only outing with BBV as this, more than any of the recent releases, would have made for an excellent series had all the releases been of this exceptionally high standard.

Behind the Scenes II

Deborah Watling and Nicholas Courtney on location for *Downtime* © Robin Prichard

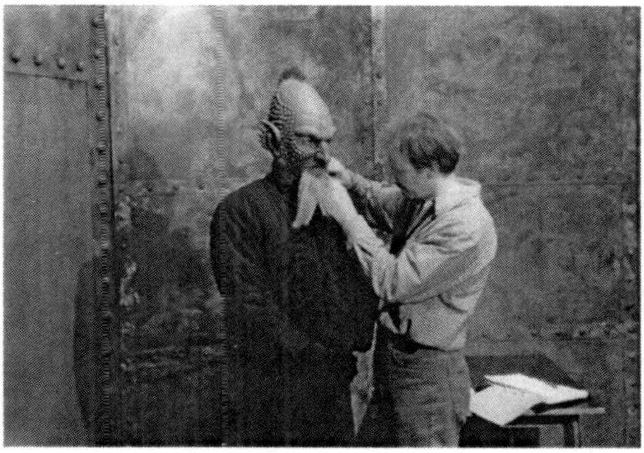

Keith Barnfather making last minute adjustments on the set of 'Prisoner 451' © Robin Prichard

John Levene, Nick Briggs and Mark Ayres enjoy a wet day on location for *Wartime* © Robin Prichard

Chapter 30 — Going Up

While BBV were busy cutting costs and corners in order to deal with the stiff competition of Big Finish, Magic Bullet took their time to ensure their releases were of the highest standard. Despite an uncertainty about the potential success of the first two releases, Alan Stevens had planned the entire series out from the start.

"It was broadly there in my head as to how things would pan out, and, as more episodes got written, the more concrete those ideas became, although I did build a few trap-doors into the series just in case an actor turned out to be unavailable. For example, a new character played by Philip Madoc would have filled the Poul/Paullus role if David Collings had not been available, and I remember mapping out some kind of background for him. As it turned out, however, I got everyone I wanted to get, so it wasn't a problem. Things also changed a bit as we went along. For example, in my original outline, Cotton really did suffocate Rull to death and I think he survived to the end. There was also a thing where Cotton took a security team down into the Sewerpits in search of Blayes, but I think it was dropped as one plot element too many."[1]

The third play in the range would be written by Jim Smith and newcomer Fiona Moore.

"I met Alan Stevens in 2000, when he made a guest appearance at the *Doctor Who* fan group I was involved with at Oxford University," Moore reminisces. "I'd given him my phone number, and, much to my surprise, he rang me up a while later — the President of the fan group had given him a copy of our club 'zine, and he'd liked an article I'd written for it, and he wanted to know if I'd be interested in writing a piece or two for *Zenith*, a *Blake's 7* magazine he was editing at the time."[2]

Moore would become a close friend of Stevens, having input into the development of the series, attending the recordings of the previous two plays and even providing the voice of the lift in 'Occam's Razor'. On *Kaldor*, Stevens found Moore a stimulating collaborator. "Fiona is a very clever person with a doctorate in Social Anthropology from Oxford. I remember having a lot of long and complex discussions with her about the social setup of Kaldor City, the nature of the Fendahl, and how they would all interrelate."[3]

Having written the first play in the range with Stevens, Smith found working with Moore a contrasting collaborative operation. "That was a completely different process, in that Alan and I wrote speaker to speaker. With Fiona it was a question of me writing scenes and giving them to Alan with his producer's hat on, and them going to Fiona and her giving scenes to Alan with his producer's hat on and them all coming back to me. So every scene in 'Occam's Razor' feels like it's mine; I'm not claiming to have written all of it, that would be ridiculous, but I feel a sense of ownership over every scene and line because every scene and every line rolls out of a conversation that I was in, whether I actually wrote the words or not. Whereas there are scenes in 'Hidden Persuaders' that I didn't write and that's not wrong, it's just a different way of collaborating, and I'm very proud of the play that exists, but it is just a completely different collaboration. There are scenes I wrote all of, there are scenes I wrote bits of, there are scenes I wrote none of."[4]

Moore too recalls the process with Stevens acting as the go between: "There wasn't a lot of overlap; Jim wrote some scenes, and I wrote others, with Alan acting as a coordinator and filling in other parts as needed."[5]

Stevens feels the play, much like the rest of the series, was the brainchild of a larger group. "'Hidden Persuaders' ended up as a kind of four-way writing experience with Jim Smith and Boucher providing the initial ideas, then Fiona coming in and writing all the Carnell/Uvanov scenes, Jim dealing, for the main, with Rull, Cotton, Blayes, Iago and the Tarenist stuff, and myself supplying the basic plot mechanics, while also revising, with help from Fiona, the Iago/Uvanov and Iago/Blayes/Manzarek scenes. A lot of the humour was Jim, a lot of the violence was Fiona. In the end I decided their contribution was greater than either Chris's or mine, so I just gave them a joint writing credit. People were making contributions to all of the scripts, and the crediting finally came down to who had made the greatest contribution."[6]

On the day of recording, Smith discussed with Douglas McNaughton some more details of how the writing was divided and certain influences he utilised with the dialogue. "There's a section in the middle, the siege element, which I found tremendously difficult to even imagine, and Fiona did some terrific work on that. I was much happier working on stuff like the opening funeral scene, all the bitchy one-liners and the interplay between the characters. That's the sort of thing I like doing really, the contrast between the 'court' i.e. Uvanov, and the 'rude mechanicals' shall we say, i.e Cotton and Rull. It's all ripped off from Shakespeare and his contemporaries. I'm very enamoured of — I'd say influenced by, but that's a bit pretentious really — people like Middleton and Webster and Marlowe. Alan is too, actually."[7]

The next two plays, 'Taren Capel' and 'Checkmate', would both be credited solely to Stevens, although as with the rest of the series it was a collaborative effort. "As I remember, Fiona did have some input into dialogue for Vance, Packard and Carnell," Stevens confirms, before jovially adding, "but as I had gone uncredited for my extensive work on 'Hidden Persuaders,' I thought she owed me!"[8]

'Checkmate' saw the return of another Boucher-created *Doctor Who* foe, the Fendahl. Stevens is quick to point out that the writers had been planting hints about its return throughout the previous scripts: "The

Fendahl is right there in the *Kaldor City* CD series from 'Occam's Razor' onwards. That's why a pentagram appears on Justina's wall in the first story; that's why a skull appears in the second, and becomes an obsession with the Tarenists from story three onwards. That's why a painting of a giant supernatural snake appears on Uvanov's wall in story four."[9]

The Fendahl and the world of Kaldor City don't necessarily seem like the most natural fit (beyond the obvious creator credentials) but Stevens felt the two worlds could be interlinked easily. "The idea was that there was this huge power influencing Kaldor society, but that it was so enormous, the majority of the population were completely unaware of it, and the only ones who could even glimpse it were the insane or somehow out of kilter, and only then if they possessed a certain genetic compatibility. The possible exception to this was Carnell, and this was because he was a psychostrategist, who had lived in Kaldor City for some years. So the appeal wasn't so much crossing 'The Robots of Death' with 'Image of the Fendahl', but crossing the Fendahl with Carnell." [10]

The three plays were recorded together on 4th, 8th, 9th and 12th August 2002, at The Moat Studios in London. The leading cast from the previous two plays returned to continue the series, and they were joined by David Collings playing Paullus (later to be revealed as Poul, the character he played in 'The Robots of Death'). Stevens had met Collings at Panopticon 2000 where he was helping to launch the DVD release of 'The Robots of Death'. Approached about reprising the role, he was only too happy to do so. "It's always nice to have somebody ask you back to play the same role, it means they must like you," Collings told *DWM*. "I'm very pleased with what's been done with the character and I think it's a very clever twist on what has gone before. No more sobbing and hiding under tables. Poul's much happier now — as he's gone completely mad."[11]

David Bailie also returned to his role as Taren Capel in the play of the same name, albeit as a series of archive recordings. In an interview for the *Kaldor City* website, Stevens asked Bailie how he found recreating a role he had originally played some 25 years before, and if he had revisited 'The Robots of Death' in preparation. "No. I took my performance from the *Kaldor City* scripts, which I thought were very good. Sometimes you'll read a part and instinctively you know you're there, and it's wonderful when that happens. I also found the production side very interesting. I remember getting the scripts and thinking, 'Jesus, there's a lot of writing in this!' but then I've never done radio before, and really it's completely different to film, theatre and television. With an audio play you have to rely almost entirely on words, as words are basically all you have. I found the experience quite a challenge, but also very enjoyable. Taren Capel has returned, and I am more than happy to once again give him a voice."[12]

The play saw Carnell play chess with V31. Prior to writing that section of the play, Stevens, along with Sarah Egginton, worked out the entire game including the details of how the moves on the board corresponded with the action within the play. They also worked out the moves for strategies that were not heard within the story.[13]

'Hidden Persuaders' was once again co-directed by Stevens and Alistair Lock. The two then took solo credits for the final two plays, with Stevens directing the fourth instalment and Lock taking credit for the fifth. "We actually co-directed really," admits Lock. "We just decided we'd take alternate credits on the later ones. We'd discuss the scenes between us, then deliver the information to the actors. Perhaps on the final two, it was more from Alan on one and more from me on the other, but we were still effectively co-directing."[14]

Stevens expands on this thought. "The credit as sole director and writer is an affectation. The CDs were recorded out of order, so you'd have a scene from 'Hidden Persuaders', followed by perhaps a scene from 'Checkmate' and then from 'Taren Capel' and so on, so in reality, *Kaldor City* was all co-directed with Alistair Lock (except when he was playing Hume). We just decided that for two of the *Kaldor City* CDs we'd give ourselves individual directing credits."[15]

Once again, proceedings were a joyous occasion for all involved and Stevens recalls them vividly. "I remember Brian Croucher and Trevor Cooper were always doing Tommy Cooper impressions, and Scott Fredericks asking Russell Hunter for his autograph, and that whenever you had to get Paul Darrow back into the studio, you always knew where he would be — outside in the car park smoking cigarettes with Patricia Merrick and his PA Maureen Marrs. I also recall Russell Hunter doing a ventriloquist act with a stuffed toy penguin." However, there was also a tinge of sadness. "I remember Russell Hunter telling me that he had leukaemia. At the time, I didn't fully grasp what he was saying, however, in retrospect, it's now clear that he was telling me that his days were numbered."[16]

'Hidden Persuaders' was released on the 30th November 2002. By this point, Vanessa Bishop was eager to see what the story was building up to. "Each play has given up storm mines of information, where the fuller picture seems to be as thought-out and considered as the plot in hand," she noted, closing the review "as dark as *Kaldor* is, I find myself interested to know what's next."[17]

The third instalment of *Kaldor City* builds on the good work of the previous two entries. It presents a cutthroat world full of grimy characters, who are all too used to stabbing each other in the back and resorting to violence. This is a darker side to the *Doctor Who* universe than we have seen before, but it is still recognisably a world that exists within those confines. It's a testament to the writers that even secondary characters such as Rull and Cotton are written with panache and vigour, and so it's not surprising that they have attracted such high calibre actors. Cotton in particular is on fine form and gets some truly hilarious moments. The political intrigue really steps up a gear in this chapter and there is a sense that the series is building to something truly spectacular. While many series have highs and lows, *Kaldor City* continued to produce output that remained on a constant high and which was a delight to listen to.

'Taren Capel' followed on the 15th March 2003, with Bishop full of praise for the project. "This is the strongest *Kaldor City* of the series so far, maybe because it can be easily viewed as a sequel to 'The Robots of Death' — and a far better one than Chris Boucher's 'Corpse Marker' novel." [18]

'Taren Capel' ramps up the tension to 11 and even for a *Kaldor City* play the atmosphere is taut and the stakes are high. The script cleverly confounds the listener's expectation by having Capel's presence felt without bringing back a clearly dead character. Having his message manipulated by the Church to make him the poster child for everything he hated is just the kind of amusing satire one has come to expect from these plays. The final twist, that all the characters who have tried so hard to outmanoeuvre one another are themselves being manipulated by something not even Carnell can comprehend, makes for a satisfying revelation. Finally, ending on a truly perilous cliffhanger, that presents the idea that several million robots are now about to wage war on Kaldor City is a terrifying prospect.

'Checkmate' made its debut on 20th of September 2003, causing Bishop to note that "as *Kaldor City* has grown, it's become clear that it's best viewed as one long serial rather than as collection of individual stories, and previous elements that first appeared throwaway or a distraction have later been successfully worked in."[19] Indeed, she found herself hoping that the series wasn't soon going to end. "I sense *Kaldor City* coming to an apocalyptic end — characters are disappearing and getting killed — but I hope not quite yet, and not without more from its 'creepy mechanical men'."[20]

Iago being outmanoeuvred is a fitting end for the series (at least in this guise), as is the ambiguity of what has happened (did he change the past/future or is the Fendhal creating an illusion?). There are so many plot strands tied up neatly in this play that leaving a question mark over the power that has been controlling them all this time seems apt. The use of the Fendhal is a brilliant plot thread, weaved subtly throughout the previous releases, making it seem all the more dangerous when it is finally revealed. The play is once again a tense and gripping production, and the sound design is of epic proportions, with the Fendhal genuinely scary.

Over the years some listeners have speculated that maybe a full scale robot massacre should have played out over the course of the production and that maybe a further volume should have overseen the complete collapse of Kaldor City at the hands of the Fendahl.

However, Stevens goes some way towards addressing this issue in his 2009 interview with Chris Dueker. "There's a scene in 'Checkmate' where Blayes goes back and has a shoot-out with Iago. If I'd been doing that as a T.V. production, or a film, I would have done it as a huge *Scarface*-style shoot-out, with security forces storming the house and Iago fighting them off with automatic weapons and all that stuff, but that wouldn't transfer to audio. It's a good idea not to have more than two or three characters in a scene, because it can be very confusing for the audience. You've got to be more intimate and clever when you're writing for audio."[21]

The end of the series left some doubt as to the motives of the Fendhal. Stevens told the writer Dale Smith that this was because the Fendhal's intent would be indecipherable to the mortal population of Kaldor City. "This was a prerequisite from Chris Boucher, that the Fendahl was ultimately unknowable. Therefore, what we have at the end of 'Checkmate' is an overlap between Justina's human mind and the alien mind of the Fendahl. Are her motives simply to save Iago? Or, following her discussion with Carnell about confusing love with pain, was she trying to test him? Was it really Justina talking to him, or was it the Fendahl, and if so, then why was it talking to me, and for what purpose?"[22]

Six months after the release of 'Checkmate', Russell Hunter passed away after a battle with leukaemia and lung cancer. In an obituary on the *Kaldor City* website, Stevens remembered his colleague. "During recording breaks, Russell used to keep all the other actors entertained with his outrageous stories and wicked sense of humour. His ventriloquist act, performed without a dummy, had to be seen to be believed! He told me that he loved the part of Uvanov and the story of 'The Robots of Death'. He was very familiar with it and jumped at the chance of playing the part again. He also got invited to a number of *Doctor Who* conventions and signings on the back of his *Kaldor City* work, which he found great fun. He must have known that he was living on borrowed time, but seemed determined to live life to the full right up until the end. He was a smashing actor, a great man, and finally a very courageous human being. I'll miss him very much."[23]

While the series seemed to have come to a close with the events of 'Checkmate' and the passing of Hunter, Trevor Cooper found his association with the series did not end there. "I was doing a tour for the Royal Shakespeare Company where we did *A Midsummer Night's Dream* with an orchestra, and one night we came out and these autograph hunters were only interested in me, and there I was being asked to sign copies of *Kaldor City*. It was the same kind of thing when I was appearing in the West End. The other actors would say, 'What's so special about you?' and I'd say, 'Look, if you do *Star Cops* or *Doctor Who* or anything like that then there are going to be lots of people who want your autograph' [laughs]."[24]

The *Kaldor City* releases had proved that there was still room for a new *Doctor Who* spin-off in the audio market and that Big Finish and BBV had some stiff competition. The creative team assembled produced some of the finest audio productions the market would ever see, and it is a testament to all involved that they got a cast that never gave less than 100%.

Kaldor City remains an impressive series and, while this was the end of the story in its current format, this wouldn't be the last time listeners would visit its world.

Chapter 31 — alt.end

By late 2002 BBV releases were becoming more intermittent and Baggs was becoming somewhat disheartened with the prospect of continuing the range. While things weren't over yet, they were in state of flux.

Tellingly, a number of projects were announced but never made it to the recording studio. A brand new *P.R.O.B.E.* audio release entitled 'Drome' was commissioned from Virgin and BBC author Dave Stone. "It was rubbish," Baggs recalls of the commission, although he quickly reins in his criticism. "It wasn't rubbish, it was Dave Stone's style and you know he produces a particular product and you know that's what he does. It was riddled with his character, it was nuts. So I read it and part of me at the time thought this is great, but this is so not me."[1]

Once again the issue of budget played a part in Baggs' decision to pull out of the project. "It was this thing again of, if you have a *Doctor Who* actor in it, it's at least 500 quid to the star rather than 50 quid or 100 quid so would it sell, was the question?" [2]

Anthony Keetch also wrote a follow up to his play, *The Barnacled Baby*. "I cheekily decided it would be part two of a trilogy," Keetch recalls. "I'm not sure if it ever had a title. Maybe 'The First Zygon on the Moon'? Bill wanted me to direct which I thought was unwise as I was writing and appearing. I suggested Patricia Merrick and I co-direct."

According to Keetch it was scheduled to be recorded a number of times. "It kept being delayed, then Bill offered Debbie Watling and Clive Merrison only £50 each to return, and they both, quite rightly, said get stuffed. Finally, it was going to be recorded just before Christmas 2002 in Brighton, directed by Nigel Fairs. I emailed him a couple of nights before recording to see if he was happy with the script, and got the response that it had been cancelled. I was very miffed." [3]

Iain McLaughlin who had recently written 'Eye of The Scorpion' for Big Finish also pitched a number of ideas. "One was about a news crew in an area controlled by South American guerrillas. There was a Zygon in the mix — maybe more than one. I also pitched one about time distortion and one about an Egyptian cult but the Zygon one was the one Bill was interested in."[4] McLaughlin's plays were entitled 'Kill or Cure' and 'Precis'. While the scripts were never completed, full synopses for both stories were produced. These can be found later in this book, reproduced for the first time.

Jonathan Blum also wrote a follow up to Lance Parkin's *I Scream*, featuring his creation The I. "Bill liked it, but he wanted me to cut it down — I'd made sure it was CD-length, but he wanted 60 minutes rather than 70-75. And while I was trying to figure out how to simplify it — it's a pretty complex heist story — the whole line basically shut down."[5]

A press release for the CD touted the story as follows. "They're mad, they're bad and they're dangerous to know and they're going to pull off the heist of the century in an attempt to learn the secrets of the mysterious alien 'I'. This is definitely no 'self-preservation society...' Featuring the 'I' from his novel 'Seeing I' and the follow up BBV audio *I Scream* from 2000."[6]

David A Mcintee was also asked to write an audio incorporating a character from one of his *Missing Adventure* stories. "Baggs wanted to try an audio thing featuring Anthony Ainley as a variant of the Koschei character from 'The Dark Path', investigating stuff in, if I remember rightly, which I might not, a sort of *Sapphire & Steel* or *Omega Factor* type vein. Obviously I was definitely up for that! Sadly I only had a brief outline of the first story when Ainley died, so that never came to pass, for the obvious reason."[7]

Gareth Preston also remembers discussing a number of ideas with Ebbs for the fourth season. "I'd had ideas for sequels to *Race Memory*, *The Rani Reaps the Whirlwind* and *The Pattern*. The former would have involved a new generation of children with mutant Wirrn-derived powers and how the older people reacted. The latter two were essentially the same scenario of a hippie space station community under threat. But nothing came of them."[8]

In November of 2002 BBV announced via *DWM* that they had begun shooting a new video project whose cast included Jo Castleton, Daniel Harcourt and Keith Drinkel, although the article stated "at the time of writing, the identity of the antagonist is under wraps."[9] Said project would not emerge for a number of years as we will see later.

When BBV did return with more audios, in February 2003, it was with two more *Faction Paradox* releases. 'Sabbath Dei' and 'In The Year of The Cat' were once again overseen by Nigel Fairs. "It was Bill just handing it over. He was selling them and he had a hand in script editing the *Faction Paradox* because they were hugely overwritten, so he would cut them basically."[10]

Fairs admits he may not have been the best person to run the range. "I didn't understand them, but they had a kind of atmosphere to them. I think if you just followed the story it was quite fun but there were so many references that went way over my head." However these two remain his favourites from the range. "The middle two I really liked. It was like a grown up *Harry Potter*, because it was all about magicians and things." [11]

The two-part story was designed to interlink with the forthcoming *Faction Paradox* comic, according to Miles. "Originally I thought the comic would be out before the audios, and I wrote Volumes Three and Four as a kind of 'prequel', so that if you'd read the comic series then the audios would explain how things got that way. But then the comic got pushed back, and I'm just... not really sure it works as well this way round. I think there's a risk that the comic will end up looking like a sequel, so in a lot of ways people who buy the audios will be getting the jump on everyone else. But they're two sides of the same continuity, certainly."[12]

While it was very much business as usual on these plays, Fairs did make an alteration to the theme tune, which he had composed. "I changed the theme because nobody liked the original version!! I think Lawrence thought it sounded too jolly, which, on reflection, is quite right. I think, because of the quirky nature of the monologues and Ellis Pike's character (Morloch?) in the first episodes, I thought it was meant to be a *Hitch Hikers Guide to the Galaxy*-style thing. I mean all that stuff with the swearing witch woman and the Sontarans and the Servalan-type character was all a bit camp!! Of course I later understood that it was meant to be darker than that and tried to change the music accordingly." [13]

However the rest of the music was something Fairs was proud of. "I was pleased with the score — a lot of harpsichord I think, and a Chinesey-kind of theme for the robots. And the cast was wonderful, we laughed such a lot recording that one. Saul Jaffe and Jo Castleton in particular are terrible gigglers. My cat was in it too!!"[14]

The two plays shared a large cast that saw Suzanne Proctor back as Cousin Justine, Michael Chance playing Lord Sandwich, Emma Kilbey once again as Cousin Eliza, Jackie Skarvellis as Mistress Culver, Eric MacLennan in the role of King George III, Caroline Burns-Cooke as Queen Charlotte, Saul Jaffe as Sabbath, Mark Grieg as the Earl of Bute, Linda Bartram in dual roles of the Lady and Annabel and Jo Castleton as The Sieur d'Eon a role with which she was not enamoured. "The *Faction Paradox* ones — I hated having to be French and I think that is why I have wiped it from my memory, although working with Nigel Fairs is always a pleasure and Bill would spend most of his time trying to stop us giggling."[15]

With money and resources in short supply, Fairs had to create this alien sound scape any way he could, which led to some innovative solutions. "I had VERY limited equipment and effects, so I was literally hitting things and twiddling knobs and seeing what they sounded like! The shadow weapons were me bashing an oven tray and a frying pan together and then putting a reverse echo on it!!!!" [16]

However, for Fairs it was all about the characters. "The scripts were very, very filmic, which sometimes worked and sometimes didn't. I thought the best thing about them was the character interaction and the overall character storylines. But that interests me more than monsters and space battles anyway!"[17]

Vanessa Bishop gave 'Sabbath Dei' a glowing review, noting that "its mix of history, science fiction and black magic is intoxicating and so gloriously dark, twisted and bloody, it's a pleasure just to drink it all in."[18]

This is a view not without its merits, as the play is a more well rounded production than the previous releases. The recording and sound quality is of a much higher standard, the two leads are better written and more assured as actors, the guest cast is on fine form and the opening theme is much more atmospheric. However, as events unfold the listener can't help but feel that you are just being given the set up for a relatively simple story, stretched out either to fit the CD's length or just to embellish the world for no given reason. Often the mythos of *Faction Paradox* is explained to the point of tedium. While there is always room for world building and character development, 'Sabbath Dei' feels drawn out and over written, even if, when the story does unfold, the events are for the most part exciting.

'In The Year of The Cat' was released in April 2003 and predictably, Bishop was a fan of this follow up.[19] "Lawrence Miles' fourth play hides some good surprises, the best being a shock revelation about the royal family. The play also benefits from the show-stealing return of the wickedly arch Lolita, who delights in meddling with Earth's history as much as she did destroying her own Homeworld."

In retrospect, while this is a stronger release than the first CD, with the cast bringing the script to life with an air of confidence, 'In The Year of The Cat' has the same issues as its predecessor. Once again the narrative is over long and overindulgent. Miles' world is so rich and full of interesting little details that it is possible to get too bogged down in with it all. It feels like the author believes every little thing referenced needs to be explained fully, which ultimately weighs the play down with its own continuity. It is also overcomplicated and when you realise the story of these last two plays is essentially the trial of Justine, which it takes a play and a half to get to and is dispensed with in 15 minutes, you are left wondering if it really was worth the two hour ride it took to get there, no matter how enjoyable the trip may have been.

During this period BBV still continued to re-issue its early output on DVD. March saw the release of the first two *Stranger* titles on DVD. Although given a warm review first time round, *DWM* gave the DVD version of 'Summoned By Shadows' a less than glowing write up. "Overall, 'Shadows' appears rather weighed down with the feeling it's got something to prove, whether it be Colin giving a subtler performance than he was allowed as the Doctor or Bill Baggs showing he can cut it as an interesting director — hence all its little avant-garde weird-for-the-sake-of-it moments."[20]

This change in viewpoint clearly signified a changing attitude towards BBV in the fan press.

In June 2003 BBV announced via their website that they no longer accepted unsolicited scripts. "Due to changes in the structure of our product lines, BBV is no longer accepting unsolicited script submissions for the Audio Adventures range. Apologies for any inconvenience or disappointment this may cause."[21]

The July issue of *DWM* (released at the same time) contained an advert that saw massive reductions on the majority of BBV's output. Branded as a summer sale, it was hard not to see this as BBV selling off its surplus, unwanted stock.

In September 2003 the BBC announced that *Doctor Who* would be returning to screens for a brand new series.

Although Baggs' inner fan boy was pleased, there was a sense at BBV and within the fan community that this was the final nail in the coffin for the company. Interestingly, it was Baggs who accidentally leaked the identity of the enemies in the first episode of the new series. "[The BBC] didn't know who had the rights, so before the first series, Julie Gardner phones me up saying 'do you own the rights to the Autons?' So she was basically telling me that it was going to be an Auton story and to keep a lid on it. Then I happened to mention it to my wife, who that weekend was flying to Gallifrey with Nigel Fairs. She was just working for me selling stuff and she mentioned it to Nigel and he of course then knew it was an Auton story for sure. So then I get another phone call saying 'we are very disappointed in you'. But then it was flattering in a way that they knew about my stuff."[22]

In the same month *Doctor Who*'s return became national news, BBV announced that the next two *Faction Paradox* releases would conclude the elongated Season 4 and would also see a change in focus for the company. "Season 4 also wraps up BBV's audio output for the time being, with the exception of the *Faction Paradox* range, which will move to a separate audio series in their own right. For the foreseeable future BBV will focus on visual media with the continuation of our DVD releases plus other video projects."[23]

The final two releases for BBV would be another two-part *Faction Paradox* story, consisting of 'Movers' (which arrived in December 2003) and 'A Labyrinth of Histories' which was released two months later in February of 2004.

Fairs once again assembled a cast of reliable colleagues. Suzanne Proctor was back as Cousin Justine, with Ellis Pike as Godfather Morlock, Keith Drinkel as Godfather Sabbath, Kate Dyson as Demetra Kein, Linda Bartram as Shuncuker, Lena Rae as Emma, Matt Kelly as First Ordinary Selvynkesh, Chris Manville as Second Ordinary Keeble, Emma Kibley as Fiora and Scott Craig as Mr. Smith.

The play called for a new villain in the form of Demetra Kein, a character Fairs was particularly drawn to. "Demetra is quiet, controlled, determined and most of all professional: she comes from a culture in which assassination's an everyday event and empire-building's a way of life, so as a leading member of a self-made semi-aristocratic family she knows about being clinical and detached."[24]

By this point Fairs was more comfortable with the range and tried to express that via the score. "It was all based round a piece of classical music that was written in the year the flashback (to Justine's childhood) was set. I remember a bit I was really pleased with when the girls were romping in the fields at the beginning. And also another cue at the end — by then I'd understood that the whole thing was meant to be a sweeping epic and intended to slowly take the style and scores into more filmic territory."[25]

'Movers' was released in December 2003. Although personally not keen on dream worlds, Vanessa Bishop was still very much in praise of the release. "The production, though, is as full, rich and beautifully crafted as ever, Nigel Fairs, directing and suppling the music bathing the whole thing in the thick and grisly atmosphere that characterises the series. If you didn't know better, you'd think this was a film soundtrack."[26]

The dream world actually works incredibly well and serves to further extend the mystery of *Faction Paradox*. While the previous two stories contained a lot of padding in the guise of world building this genuinely feels like part one of a two-part story, complete with a cliffhanger. This play is also the most overtly sci-fi, with the prison world resembling *Doctor Who* more than anything else in the *Faction Paradox* plays, while the juxtaposition of the dreamworld running smoothly alongside the prison makes for an interesting contrast. The acting and characterisation are uniformly excellent and a genuinely intriguing mystery is built up about the newcomers, Kine and Shuncucker. This is by far the most well rounded of the *Faction Paradox* range.

Bishop felt this final chapter, 'A Labyrinth of Histories', continued the strong tradition of the range. It was "funnier," she noted, and "dialogue wise, this is one of Lawrence Miles' best."[27]

'A Labyrinth of Histories' rounds off the series in exceptional style. Offering twists, turns, scares and humour in abundance, every intricacy of the story serves as a valuable plot point in the final moments of the play and there is little in the way of padding. Nigel Fairs' direction, post production and score are the best they have ever been and everyone involved gives a top drawer performance. Miles crafts a tale that makes the listener truly understand the nature of *Faction Paradox* and their relationship with time, as seen through the eyes of a young Justine.

The play is complicated and epic in equal measures but never once is anything less than enthralling. While this is a fitting finale for the BBV audio range, ensuring it goes out in style, it is a shame that the adventures of Justine, Eliza and the others aren't allowed to continue in this format.

Despite his waning interest at the time, Baggs remains proud of these last two releases. "*Faction Paradox* is weird, there is something you can grab hold of. It was very rich and I like that. I thought Nigel did a very good job of directing and realising it and casting it and just presenting it so that was nice."

Fairs on the other hand felt he hadn't been fully briefed when working on the series. "Somebody told me years later that they were supposed to be Time Lords, which I never knew. I wish I'd had a handbook or someone had told me right from the start as I might have geared it in a different way." In fact he later told Chris Dueker that he now can't listen back to the plays, due to the poor production quality (the plays having been recorded in his bedroom). "I can't bear to listen to them now really, as the quality of dialogue recording is so poor. But they were invaluable to me as far as experience went and I really enjoyed the scripts, I thought they were very different. I'd love to have known what happened next, and had something to do with them, but I understand Alistair Lock did a superb job, so that's brilliant. I used him several times on *Sapphire & Steel* and love his work."[28]

Lawrence Miles, on the other hand, later admitted he *never* listened to any of the *Faction Paradox* CDs.[29]

Despite initial plans for further *Faction Paradox* titles, 'A Labyrinth of Histories' would be the final BBV audio release as, after 40 releases, BBV discontinued their audio range.

Did Baggs find this a difficult decision? "Not at the time no," he later claimed. "It was diminishing returns, I did um and ah about whether to continue with *Faction Paradox*, but it was lot of work; it was a combination of things, but it had had its day. Big Finish was a machine and I couldn't compete and I had nothing else to offer."[30]

Despite there being a new series of *Doctor Who* on the horizon, Baggs made one last effort to produce some more *Doctor Who*, this time within the BBC.

In February 2003 *DWM* revealed that Baggs, along with the editor of *South Today*, Lee Destry, would be producing a project made by BBC South. "BBC South is planning to mark *Doctor Who*'s 40th Anniversary with a special project which will air in the spring, although it is all very much in the planning stages, the hope is to produce a special *Doctor Who* drama of about 20 minutes' duration. This will probably be split into 5 four-minute episode to be broadcast over the course of a week. The current plan is for it to be transmitted on BBC1 on *South Today* in its 6:30 slot, but there is the possibility of a broadcast outside of that."[31]

The article went on to say they were negotiating the rights and a script had been written, but that they also planned to shoot some mini documentaries about locations used to film the series in the area.

According to Nick Briggs this was simply Baggs up to his old tricks again, trying to get new *Doctor Who* made before BBC Wales intervened. "He was going to make it and do it as a little celebratory thing, even when the TV series was announced as coming out and Alan Cumming and him were as thick as thieves and he was going to play the Doctor."[32]

This bizarre project was finally put on hold by *Doctor Who*'s new executive producer. "Eventually Julie Gardner phoned up BBC South and said 'no' but it took that. He was going to go with it and how he didn't get the sack from BBC South for fibbing to them all..."[33] Once again Briggs is bemused by the sheer determination of Baggs. "He's amazing, he just keeps going until you build a brick wall in front of him."[34]

While there was still the promise of new video output from BBV, the company limped on for number of years in various guises. By April 2004 the BBV website was hosting fan art and still regularly releasing DVDs of its back catalogue. Although — much like the productions themselves — as time went on these appeared to be produced with a more slap dash approach. While the early releases would feature a wealth of extras and a well designed product., the final releases were DVD-Rs with nothing but the main features on them.

As 2004 made way for 2005 and BBV slowly faded into oblivion, a redesigned website promised more content, but it never materialised. The articles and reviews from the old website were no longer online and all that was available to buy was the last remaining stock of BBV's back catalogue and the newly issued DVDs.

On March 26th 2005 *Doctor Who* finally made its return to TV screens and became a titan of the broadcasting industry, garnering critical praise, awards and mainstream success — and new fans. Suddenly merchandise was in supermarkets and toy shops across the nation, as tie in books, annuals and comics proliferated. Away from the news series, Big Finish provided fans of classic *Doctor Who* with an avalanche of product, and in all this there simply wasn't room for a home run enterprise weaving in and out of copyright loopholes.

It is undeniable that the arrival of Big Finish had a massive impact on BBV and the return of *Doctor Who* must have only compounded that. But do those involved in these productions feel Big Finish killed BBV?

"Yes, they must have done," John Ainsworth opines. "Especially as Big Finish's production expanded with more titles every month. You're going to spend your money on real *Doctor Who* rather than an imitation of *Doctor Who*."[35]

Nick Briggs seems in no doubt about the situation. "I suppose it must have done. That's not what we set out to do. But, as I say, Bill was doing sort of pretend *Doctor Who*. We were doing the real thing. So it would have been odd if the market had preferred the 'fake' version, wouldn't it?"[36] Writer Peter Grehan feels it was a combination of factors that killed the BBV range, and highlights one crucial advantage, the legitimacy conferred on Big Finish. "Once Big Finish was officially sanctioned by the BBC to produce official *Doctor Who* stories I think BBV couldn't compete whatever they did. With that as their flagship production they could diversify into a lot of other series, *Sapphire & Steel*, *Judge Dredd*, *Survivors*, *Blake's 7*, etc.. They had the credibility to get the licences for other productions. I think what might have hurt BBV more, with regard to irritating the BBC, was their thinly disguised *Doctor Who* stories, like the Cyberons, who were a bit too much like Cybermen, and Alice and the Professor. With the return of official *Doctor Who* there was no real demand for ersatz *Doctor Who* niche audio/video productions anymore."[37]

Iain Hepburn, however, believes it was more to do with the attitude towards BBV in certain parts fandom at that point. "Back in the day, yeah, I think (Big Finish) they probably did for BBV — in fact, more than that, I think they did a lot of damage across the board. Look at *Death Comes to Time*, for instance. Now, it's got its flaws, undoubtedly, and Dan probably didn't do himself any favours, but it was a bold, ambitious attempt to try and do not only new *Doctor Who*, but to use the web in an interesting way. And it has a hell of a cast. I mean, if someone put together a cast with Len Fenton, David Soul, John Sessions, Tony Head, Kevin Eldon and Stephen Fry for the TV series now you'd think, blimey, that's not bad. But it got absolutely slaughtered, just buried by the *Monthly* at the time, which dismissed it as meaningless and a distraction from Big Finish's 'pure' work. There was a lot of whispering and briefing against it. I mean, you just have to go look back at the editorial when *DC2T* came out by, I think, Alan Barnes. Just brutally dismissive of a project which just about toppled the BBC servers, such were the demands from folk trying to stream it. And of course the author of that editorial just happened to write regularly for Big Finish as well. So you had this little clique which was tied into the books, the *Monthly*, the audios, and for some of us it left a bit of a bad taste frankly."[38]

Hepburn is quick to point out that despite this he is a fan of Big Finish's more recent work, but is adamant that it was a clique of fans that had a negative agenda against BBV: "when you've that kind of 'you scratch my back' relationship going on, it means stuff on the outside doesn't get much of a look-in. So *DC2T* gets dingied. BBV barely got a sniff. Plus, when you've the official books, the official audios, the official magazine, it narrows the field for unofficial projects to make much impact. BBV was always going to be a struggle once Big Finish came along, since as I've said it's a spin-off of a spin-off, effectively, and one with very limited distribution channels compared to its larger 'official' competitor." [39]

According to Simon Gerard, there was nothing so premeditated behind the decline of BBV. "There was rivalry, but Bill had been one of the people to keep the spirit of *Doctor Who* alive when nothing at all was being produced; no TV show, no audio... There were the book ranges but BBV meant you could hear Sylvester, Sophie and many others in a world that was sort of almost like *Doctor Who*. Once Big Finish was able to offer the real deal, BBV was bound to take a knock."[40]

Big Finish producer Gary Russell thinks BBV shutting up shop was more probably due to external factors. "It probably had more to do with Bill having more interesting and new things in his life, plus four kids and stuff like that to draw his focus."[41]

David A Mcintee is blunter. "I think Baggs totally losing it killed BBV."[42]

It's worth considering a for a moment, how different *Doctor Who* fandom would have been, had Baggs been running an official audio range. "Big Finish were much more conservative," Tim Saward opines. "I think that's because they understood their market. Peter Darvill-Evans was doing the *New Adventures* so that was anything outlandish and new. They understood their market was geeky conservative fans, basically people who like the idea of traditional four parters, traditional stories."[43]

Paul Ebbs also discussed this with Mark Simpson in late 2004. "Baggsie gave me my first real break and I owe him a great deal. He's a really underrated bloke, who really should have been the head of *Doctor Who* audio production, but it was not to be. Shame really. I think the whole landscape would have been more daring and interesting if Baggsie had got the licence. He never ran BBV like a mates club, and would always encourage the new writers (which BF have finally done this year, *after* all their mates have written stories you'll notice. Bwhahahahahahaa!)."[44]

The landscape of *Doctor Who* fandom would indeed be very different place had Baggs got an official licence to produce *Doctor Who*. While he was always keen to give new writers a chance and would have no doubt continued to discover some interesting talent. Perhaps a lack of quality control would have meant the range had little of the consistency of the early Big Finish plays. The lack of budget would also have hampered the chances of BBV getting as well rounded casts as Big Finish did. Ultimately, what Baggs needed was a financier to give that initial injection of cash to start the range proper and get away from the DIY mentality his productions resonated.

BBV was to all intents and purposes dead, despite a promise to the contrary on the website. "There are currently no new projects in production. But, just for the record, this isn't the end ov [sic] BBV!"[45]

A final update in May 2005 saw an unusual request from Baggs. "Apart from the DVDs, there are no new releases planned for the immediate future. I have devoted my time recently to Emotional Energy Healing. I am looking for Case Studies to work on so if you're interested in a bit of self analysis and want to improve yourself awareness then drop us an e-mail."[46]

By 2006 the BBV website had regenerated once more and was now selling a broad range of *Doctor Who* merchandise, not just BBV releases. "It was simply business," Baggs recalls. "We were just experimenting with different things but it wasn't successful. I took a lot of the merchandise to conventions with me and it was selling there and there were certain products that sold very well, but my heart wasn't in because it wasn't creative."[47]

BBV had clearly had its day. Bill Baggs had gone from being a prominent name in fandom, who produced some impressive low budget productions with high profile casts, to a character who was starting to get a name for dubious business practices and releasing amateur sounding productions, loosely based on *Doctor Who*. And so Baggs stepped away from fandom to pursue other interests. But the BBV story wasn't quite over yet.

Chapter 32 – Once More with Feeling

While BBV were winding down their audio output and Magic Bullet were preparing their next venture, Reeltime Pictures (who had been predominately concentrating on their corporate work) made a surprise announcement in the September 2003 edition of *DWM*. For the first time in four years they would be returning to the spin-off arena with a new film, *Daemos Rising*.

Keith Barnfather admits to being inspired by *Doctor Who's* approaching birthday. "*Doctor Who*'s 40th anniversary was coming up when I conceived the idea. It seemed like a great idea to commemorate *Doctor Who* and also get some new drama made."[1] The film would be a sequel to the Jon Pertwee tale 'The Daemons', and feature two characters who had previously appeared in *Downtime*: Douglas Cavendish and Kate Lethbridge-Stewart, played by husband and wife team Miles Richardson and Beverly Cressman.

Barnfather's initial inspiration for this low key drama was not *Doctor Who*, however, but one of its competitors. "I'd always been a great fan of *Sapphire & Steel*, a seventies TV series which essentially had two main characters in it who were always in a confined space in the programme itself and I liked the idea of developing that. I wanted to do something similar because I think it can really add drama when you have two good characters."[2] The writer for this sequel would be David J. Howe, who had approached Barnfather about writing for him on a previous production. "Like everybody I can be a bolshie bastard," remembers Howe, "and when he did the *Mindgame trilogy* I said to Keith 'why didn't you ask me to write one of these, you know I write?' and he said 'oh you know, Miles wanted to do the Draconian one and Roger wanted to do the Sophie one'. He'd already promised them, but said 'but next time I will ask you'."[3]

Sure enough, when the possibility of doing a new film came about Barnfather approached Howe, though with a number of stipulations. "I was very, very, very happy with the casting of *Downtime*. I thought Bev was consistently good and Miles was just a great actor and underused in *Downtime*. I had logged, shall we say, Bill's point that you don't need *Doctor Who* actors to do these kind of things, as long as you've got a good strong connection to *Doctor Who*."[4]

Another caveat Barnfather had was the location. "We agreed, what we were going to do with this, was shoot it at Miles' mother and father's cottage down in Cornwall. This was Ian Richardson's hidey hole away from London, so I knew we couldn't really have a regular *Doctor Who* actor down there."[5]

With the characters and location in place, the piece needed a villain, although initially Barnfather had asked Howe to use a different Pertwee era adversary. "The original idea was that he wanted to use the Sea Devils," Howe recollects. "That was the monster he thought he could get the ok to use in it, and I know he wanted to film down by the sea." So how would this story have panned out? "There was some genetic thing going on, where humans were being turned into Sea Devils in a cottage by the sea and UNIT were involved, hence Captain Cavendish being involved."[6]

After this draft was submitted, however, Barnfather discovered he was unable to get the rights to the Sea Devils, according to Howe. "Keith discovered the estate of Malcolm Hulke wouldn't allow him to use the Sea Devils. I think part of the reason for this was around that time, the BBC had been going out to all of these rights holders and saying to them 'if you will work with us we'll make sure you're ok and if you want to license these to anyone else, that's fine but you need to ask us first' kind of thing. So the BBC were trying to grab control of as much of *Doctor Who* as they could."[7]

As this was on the eve of the announcement of the return of *Doctor Who*, does Howe think the two could have been linked? "There were definitely moves afoot within the BBC to try and be more aware of their rights and what they owned, and to make sure they could use it if they wanted to use it. I think this might have been borne in part out of the 'TV Movie', where Universal ended up owning half the rights and the BBC was a bit hamstrung over what they could actually do."[8]

With his first choice of villain unavailable, Barnfather hit upon the idea of using the Daemons from the *Doctor Who* story of the same name. "I knew Barry [Letts, writer of 'The Daemons'] well and I knew Robert Sloman [Letts' co-writer on the serial], so it was easy to get the rights."[9]

With this new enemy in place, Howe went about scripting this alternative version of the story. "We still had the same restrictions, we still had the cottage, we still had the filming on the beach or cliffs or something. So I kind of melded all my ideas together and came up with this sort of sequel to 'The Daemons', where the Daemons are coming back for a third time because they said they would. There's quite a lot of elements of a horror film called *Suspiria* in there, which is one of my favourite films."[10] Howe was even able to cross it over with another *Doctor Who* spin-off series, Telos' range of novellas, *Time Hunter*: "Because of the Daemons and the way they work, I used some of the *Time Hunter* elements, the idea of time sensitives and time channelers."[11]

Despite both Barnfather and Howe being happy with the script, it was given to *Downtime* scribe Marc Platt to give it the once over. "Marc did a proper script editor job on it,"[12] Howe recalls. "I knew the script was underrunning slightly and Marc's a very experienced writer, absolutely knows what he's doing and so he came up with some really good ideas. In fact, strangely it was Marc that came up with the idea of all the artefacts in the garage, and he was absolutely spot on. There were various other suggestions all the way through, which I was quite happy to go with as they all made sense and if they didn't make sense, then we had a discussion and we came up with something else. It was all good input from Marc because we had to extend it by about 5 or 10 minutes."[13]

Daemos Rising features only three major cast members, with the spotlight cast firmly on Cavendish and Kate, although as Cressman reveals, things weren't all great behind the scenes. "To be quite honest, *Daemos Rising* was personally not a great experience for me, simply because it was the start of the collapse of my marriage to Miles. So doing a film opposite your husband, who clearly may leave you at any moment was not great. I would have pulled out if it had not been for my loyalty to Keith and the logistics of getting the film together."[14] Despite this, the two took to the filming admirably and if there was any tension, there is no sign of it on the behind the scenes footage that accompanied the DVD release. In fact during the shoot the couple celebrated their wedding anniversary.

The part of the Ghost, the third member of the cast, went to Andrew Wisher, son of spin-off regular, the late Michael Wisher. For Barnfather it was a simple decision to offer the part to Wisher. "I'd known Andrew for a long time (obviously as he grew up — as I knew Michael very well). He presented Michael's re-edited *Myth Makers* and we'd always hoped to work together one day on a drama. When *Daemos* came up he was the perfect choice."[15]

Securing the use of his parents' cottage was not the only contribution Richardson made to the production process, as he also secured the services of his father, Ian Richardson, as the Narrator as well as bringing a new Lighting Cameraman to the project. "I would suggest that my main contribution was to bring in the services of Neil Oseman as cameraman. Though Keith had often been his own operator, he wanted to up the game with this project. Fortunately, I had just had the misfortune to find myself involved with a project called 'Blood Relative', which was a real case of a vanity project if I ever saw one. The main advantage was the producer had brought in Neil as cinematographer and I immediately saw his potential and got him in on *Daemos.* He immediately upped the game with dolly shots, crane shots, stedi-cam, lots of things Keith would have liked to have used if his old enemy Time hadn't been in the way."[16]

Barnfather too was full of praise for Oseman "I didn't need to put any energy into the relationship with Neil, sometimes with cameraman you are geeing them along, like you want them to achieve something and you are trying to get them to go there, but with Neil he was there before I went there. We were talking about shots and I was saying 'I want to do this shot outside' and he would put the camera where I had conceived of putting it before I said a word to him. He was very fast and very efficient and just did his job and I found that really rewarding."[17]

Of course, things weren't all plain sailing. Oseman's van, which was transporting the crew to the location, broke down en route to Devon, stranding everyone at the side of the road. Despite this, shooting began on Wednesday 17th September 2003. The day shoot consisted of Kate's arrival at the train station and surrounding areas., while the evening saw the first lot of filming in Kent's Cave between 5pm and 12am, with all the cast present, including several supporting artists playing monks.

Thursday found the crew filming various external scenes of Kate and Cavendish with the statue of the gargoyle (the gargoyle in question having been built over eight days by prop maker Philip T Robinson). The crew then returned to the caves that evening, where they stayed on until 3am.

The third day saw the team film the scenes within the shed/garage at the cottage which featured an array of *Doctor Who* props including an 'Earthshock' style cyber chest unit, an Auton doll from 'Terror of the Autons', a Dalek gun, an Auton head and a giant maggot in a glass case from 'The Green Death'. The props were also provided by Robinson and some of them are still extant today, as Howe reveals. "I've still got the maggot in the glass. Keith kept the book, the grimoire. I wanted to keep it but he thought he might want to use it again."

Cressman also crossed paths with one of the props after the film. "After the shoot, the one gargoyle statue was left in the garden there and it used to really scare my children when they were young."[18]

The next three days were spent at the cottage doing the interior and exterior shots until shooting was complete.

The shoot was a predominately fun affair, with a minimal crew enjoying a week's away working. Rosemary Howe provided lunch for the crew, while Richardson would cook dinners back at the cottage. Howe recalls the occasion with affection. "It was very enjoyable, we had a great time, it was a very nice crew. We had great fun in the caves with some gun maker thing and filling the caves with smoke, smoking everybody out. We had lots of lovely meals and it was just a really, really friendly, nice shoot."[19]

Even so, there were a couple of accidents, with Cressman spraining her ankle when a stool she had to stand on buckled underneath her. Howe too found himself in need of medical attention. "Miles had his dog there which was a black Labrador, and this dog got very, very excitable and there was one moment where the dog raced up to me and I bent down to go 'hello how you doing?' and the dog jumped up at me at exactly the same moment and we basically cracked our heads together and my nose bled. I'm fairly sure it actually broke my nose, and I had to sit down with an ice pack on and all sorts of stuff. I got dizzy and it was horrible."[20]

Richardson was pleased to be there and was more than happy that Cavendish had been given more depth since his appearance in *Downtime*.

"As to Cavendish. Well, he had been a simple UNIT operative before. But by now the writers knew me and my work and thought we could, perhaps, go quite deep with him. This was aided by the fine cinematography and to a certain amount of freedom I was given to alter the script as I felt it needed. With approval I might add. It's a shame that Beverley didn't perhaps, stamp her foot a bit about the somewhat two dimensional qualities of her character. But I would suggest that sci-fi is the last club with a predominantly male membership, for whatever reason and female parts are often poorly served. That's just a personal opinion which might be slammed as terrible generalisation."[21] Despite what was going on in her personal life Cressman enjoyed herself too, although she isn't very pleased with her final performance. "We filmed it at my ex parents-in-law's house in Devon which was a treat. Keith was a good director but I think Miles and I were doing two different performances. I underplayed it too much and I was obviously rather distracted. I do not give a good performance in this at all and I wish I had done a better job. I let my personal life interfere which is a lesson in itself."[22]

With *Doctor Who* due to return to screens the following year and BBV seemingly closed for business, it appeared that *Daemos Rising* would be the last production of its kind, a sentiment stressed by the review in *DWM*. "If the video spin-off is to vanish in a puff of smoke. *Daemos Rising* ensures it goes out in moderately good style."[23]

Daemos Rising is well directed, well written and a well acted piece. Aligning itself with a style that sits comfortably in between classic *Who* and the post 2005 reboot, its self contained setting and limited cast work in the film's favour, while the production values are high despite some CGI that doesn't hold up too well today. The ending feels a little tagged on and there could be a little more tension when the Daemon expels the Solidarity but ultimately, the film ensures Reeltime exited the *Who* spin-off market rather better than BBV had done.

Barnfather's feelings on the final film are slightly mixed, however. "I'm happy with it as piece of direction, I'm so pleased with the first 35 minutes of that. I love it, I love the camera work, I love the acting, I love the way I composed the shots. The problem with it is the end — it's simply too much CGI and that's a huge problem — and its budget.

"What would make that story work brilliantly, would be to have a bunch of UNIT guys turn up to kill the monster, run into the caves having this wonderful battle scene with bullets flying and them all being wasted. While the Daemon is concentrating on the UNIT guys, Kate and Cavendish come in and do the deed, and then we would have cut down on the animation and I can see that looking fantastic. I don't remember if I felt it at the time, I think I might have had it going through my head and I just decided I couldn't afford to do it and it wasn't in the final script."[24]

Richardson is in high praise of the work of the film. "I would suggest that *Daemos Rising* is one of Keith's finest works to-date. Mainly because a lot of factors just seemed to fall into place at the right time."

Much like Barnfather, Richardson can see issues with the film's final moments. "If the piece has a flaw, it is in the climax. Having achieved so much with the human characters, the CGI devil seems a bit of a let down. But given the date of the piece and the limitations on budget and the advances in CGI since, it was not a bad effort."[25]

Released in March 2004, the video would be the last non-BBC *Doctor Who*-related drama for four years.

With so many changes in the market since his last release was Barnfather ever worried it wouldn't perform as well as some of his previous titles?

"We made it on a very really tiny budget and so we weren't so desperate for it to perform and it actually did very well."[26]

Howe was certain that a market would exist for the film. "I knew it would find its own market because fan things always do. Remember I'm a fan, I was brought up with the show, I did my first fanzine in '76, I've been doing fan things for as long as I've been breathing and there is always a market for them. So it never worried me because when I saw it, I knew it was good enough, I knew it was good and that people would enjoy it and they would buy it and they would hopefully appreciate it. You do these things because you want people to like them, because they are fun to do. You're not doing them for the money, you are doing them for the love, so I wasn't worried at all that it wouldn't find a market."[27] Howe feels the success of the film is a testament to Barnfather's skills as a producer and director. "As with all of these, all kudos goes to Keith because he's the guy that pulls it all together, he's the guy that makes it happen, he's the guy that worked out all the filming, the shots, the locations everything that needed to be worked out. He got the cast together so as always it's down to him that that thing is as good as it actually was." [28]

At the time there were plans for a further outing for Cavendish and Kate, and Cressman was eager to see them reunited. "I would have liked to have seen the characters of Kate and Cavendish continue. I certainly would not have had any problem working with Miles again!! All that aggro is long gone!"[29]

Howe was again tasked with writing the script, having been given some ideas from Barnfather. "He found a castle in Crete he wanted to film in. So he wanted it all set in this castle and along the shores there, and so him and Anastasia, on one of their trips out to Crete, took a load of photographs, they then set me to work."[30]

The script was duly completed and featured the return of another familiar *Doctor Who* monster. "It was called 'The Face of the Fendahl'. It was basically 'Masque of the Red Death' meets 'Image of the Fendahl'. Same limitations as before, limited cast, limited locations, doubling people up. So lots of sort of similar ways of managing it all. I was very, very pleased with the script." [31] Although the film was never made, the script is available in Howe's book *Talespinning*, from Telos Publishing.

Richardson feels there were a number of reason the film never happened. "I think the re-emergence of *Doctor Who* on the television put a halt to many of the projects that were in the pipeline, not just for Reeltime. It would be impossible to compete with the BBC budget. I also got very busy working in other mediums, mainly stage, which gave me little time for filming. Beverley and I divorcing didn't help! Though I would say we are on friendly terms these days."[32]

Howe feels there are other contributing factors. "I think in a nut shell Keith got diverted into lots of other stuff and of course Beverly and Miles split up, so it put a bit of kibosh of them working together on something else and so basically it's never been done."[33]

Daemos Rising is a fitting finale to the direct-to-video spin-off saga, with a story that riffs off ideas presented in a classic *Doctor Who* story without getting bogged down in continuity, a simple premise that can be achieved on a modest budget and featuring two characters that the spin-off genre created. Not to mention a production by the man who started it all, Keith Barnfather.

The CGI lets the film down a little, but it is within the spirit of these productions and indeed *Doctor Who* as we knew it that ambition often outweighs budget — and ambition is what these videos were all about.

Chapter 33 — Every Time is the Last Time

Following the catastrophic events portrayed in 'Checkmate', and the real-life passing of lead actor Russell Hunter, it seemed the *Kaldor City* series had come to a natural end.

However, according to Stevens, it is a misconception to believe that, had Hunter lived, there would have been further adventures for Uvanov. "Hunter died on 26 February 2004. He told me he had leukaemia on 8th August 2002. If I had wanted to use the character again, I would simply have written some more scripts featuring Uvanov, booked a studio and recorded his scenes all together in one day. I didn't do this because, as far as I was concerned, Uvanov's story was over and there was nowhere else for the character to go. Indeed, 'Checkmate' was all about systematically destroying the series by exposing the hidden alliances, killing off a number of the major characters and bringing everyone's story-arc to a conclusion. The manifestation of the Fendahl literally brought death to the show. That's not to say that there weren't any plans for a sixth full-length CD, but the intention was to go in a completely different direction and, as far as I was concerned, the only hanging thread I thought worth addressing was how the robots fitted into the Fendahl master plan, which consequently brought up the idea of the Fendahl being both a destroyer and a creator of life."[1]

However, the next Kaldor City production would show up in an unlikely place. The short play 'The Prisoner' would form part of 'The Actor Speaks: Volume 4 —Paul Darrow', an interview CD released by MJTV.

The story was written by Stevens and Moore; the latter recalling the commission as follows. "[Mark J Thompson] was planning [an interview CD] for Paul Darrow, and asked if Alan and I would like to do one of the fiction segments, ideally something *Kaldor*-related. Now by this time 'Checkmate' had come out, so we opted to do something rather metaphysical, reflecting the direction the series was taking, with Iago being interrogated by Landerchild, but what seemed to be a straightforward prisoner-and-captor situation turning quite strange by the end of the story."[2]

Stevens was keen to push the abstract nature of the story, which was a twist on the political thriller elements of the previous plays. "We were also working with the idea that what was happening may well have been a process taking place within the mind of the Fendahl, and possibly even that the being had manifested two hundred years prior to 'Occam's Razor', so it had been game-over right from the start, and everything that was now taking place was either a dream or a thought experiment."[3]

Although he wasn't involved in the 'The Prisoner', Jim Smith did read the script and made an unusual suggestion. "I proposed that they record it twice and get the two actors to swap, because it exists in the Fendahl gestalt anyway. The idea was that maybe you could trim some of the character identifiers off, so they would do the version that you've got now and then do a version where Peter plays the intruder and Paul plays the householder. And that would have fitted in with the atmosphere of the series at that point."[4] While Stevens was keen on the idea, it was never put into action, most likely for budget and logistical reasons.

'The Prisoner' was recorded on the 10th of February 2004 at Soundmagic Studio in Essex and released on the 24th of April that year.

The play is a diverting little piece, with both actors chewing up the make believe scenery in typical *Kaldor* fashion. The premise is an interesting one, with Iago manipulating his line of questioning so that he eventually becomes the interrogator. The play can be viewed on a number of levels: either it is an amusing skit that makes for an interesting look at the two characters with a metatextual ending, or, as Stevens suggests, the scene takes place within the mind of the Fendahl, following which a whole series of possibilities open up as to what is actually happening.

The final full-length instalment of the series came from the pen of Daniel O'Mahony. O'Mahony was an old friend of Stevens and Moore and had previously written for both the Virgin *New Adventures* range and the *Missing Adventures* range. "When 'Checkmate' came out in 2003 I'd assumed that was the end of the series. It ends on a fairly conclusive note and, of course, Russell Hunter died soon after it was released. I hadn't during any of this time thought of writing for *Kaldor City* at all, though when it had first been announced I'd made a jokey pitch to Fiona for a story — based on the film *The Baby of Macon* — about a troupe of Dum robot actors. I had this perverse urge to try to make a pitch like that work on audio!"[5]

Around this time Magic Bullet were considering an anthology release, provisionally entitled *Tales from Kaldor City* that would feature short plays, around twenty minutes in length, that centred on different characters from the series. Several ideas were conceived by Stevens, Moore and O'Mahony, as the latter recalls. "Fiona and Alan and I would knock about lots of story ideas and concepts in general, though not necessarily with the intention of taking them any further." It was one such idea that formed the basis of the final play 'Storm Mine'.

"I was very keen to write for Blayes, who struck me as the most interesting of the supporting cast," says O'Mahony. "She's the one who most obviously changes and develops across the course of the series, and I also had the idea of putting her aboard a Storm Mine with amnesia. So that was the basis of my 20-minute pitch, which Alan felt could and should be expanded to a full length play. (With hindsight I realise that the script seems like a parody or inversion of 'The Robots of Death', but that wasn't my conscious intention when I wrote it.)" [6] O'Mahony was then asked by Stevens to produce an hour-long version of the story. "He outlined his ideas and it clicked with something I also had in mind, so I told him to send me an outline. I think, originally, Daniel was only planning to do a 20-minute short like 'The Prisoner', but I was angling for a full-length story, and that was what we eventually ended up with."[7]

O'Mahony had concerns that the play would not fit with the series as a whole. "I worried that it couldn't really be a 'proper' continuation of the series because it had been conceived after the fact and seemed so divorced from what had gone before. But eventually Alan and Fiona persuaded me to give it a go as a full-length script. I made a stab at writing a 20-minute draft only to find that it quickly went over that limit, at which point I conceded!"[8]

One stipulation made by Stevens was that Paul Darrow's Iago, a character absent from the initial pitch, would appear in the expanded version. "As usual I was resistant to changing that for the final play, even though it should have been obvious to me that they'd need to have at least one of the stars of the series in 'the next story.' We discussed it at dinner one evening and hadn't come to any conclusions, but later as I was waiting at a station platform for my train home, I suddenly worked out how he could be fitted into the story, then spent the next two and a half hours frustrated because I couldn't email Alan and Fiona about it straightaway!" [9]

As the final official instalment of the series, was Stevens ever tempted to write the closing play himself? "Not really. I just wanted what was best for the series. Daniel had a very interesting take on the series and so I gave him the go-ahead."[10]

Despite handing over the reins to a new writer, the script was once again a collaborative process, with O'Mahony finding both Moore and Stevens easy to work with. "Generally, I found that Magic Bullet were very receptive to the ideas that I came up with, and they ended up being integrated into the final storyline. For instance, I suggested the Zen elements which Fiona was very keen on and developed further, and the use of a genuine chess game in the story came from me as well. I used the second game of the 1997 rematch between Garry Kasparov and the supercomputer Deep Blue; specifically the one that prompted Kasparov to make an allusion to Maradona's 'Hand of God' (implying that IBM were cheating and using a human player behind the scenes). Off the top of my head I think that was on either 4th or 5th May, but I can't recall exactly."[11]

With the story sketched out, Stevens and Moore then left O'Mahony to his own devices. "They left me alone to flesh it out with the dialogue and characters, which is fine by me. Plotting is one of my weak areas anyway so that wasn't a problem. The only serious area of dispute in the actual script was over John Leeson's death scene. *Kaldor City* is quite a ruthless series and I tend to be not quite so ruthless in my writing, so I softened the way the scene played out in dialogue. Alan wasn't keen on that and we were at loggerheads for a couple of days. He wrote his own version of the scene, and we haggled over some changes — mostly me trying to introduce ambiguities — and eventually reached a happy compromise. My natural reaction to editorial advice is usually to dig my heels in regardless of how sensible it is, before capitulating — with caveats — a couple of days later. That was definitely the case here!" [12]

The script for 'Storm Mine' featured a smaller than usual cast for a *Kaldor City* play. The main cast consisted of Paul Darrow as Iago, Tracy Russell as Blayes, John Leeson as the Chief Mover and Philip Madoc as the Commander, a role that had been specifically written for him at the request of Stevens and Moore. "I believe he was someone they'd always wanted to cast, but hadn't had the opportunity to before,"[13] recalls O'Mahony. For Madoc it was a chance to play against type. "The Commander is interesting, and the lines he has to speak have a lot of style to them, it's a very good part to play, but I'm also wondering what it was they saw in me, that made them choose me for it. I'm intrigued, as it's quite unlike many of the roles I am usually offered. Maybe, when I hear the finished production, I'll discover the answer."[14]

Once again Stevens shared directing duties with Alistair Lock, and a number of smaller parts were played by Magic Bullet regulars including Lock, Mark Thompson, Wanda Opalinska and Patricia Merrick. The play would also feature a further alumnus from 'The Robots of Death': D84 actor Gregory de Polnay, as a new robot, V23.

The proposition came as a complete surprise to de Polnay. "I was working with a group of American students, because I direct and teach for RADA, and I got this message saying, 'Will I phone this number?' and so I rang, and Alan Stevens, the producer, answered and said, 'I've got something that might interest you.' He wanted me to play a new robot called V23. So, I looked at the script and I thought it was very intelligently written, and this character V23, although they wanted the same kind of voice, was a much more advanced robot than D84. V23 has a very interesting mind, very interesting."[15]

For the recording, the Magic Bullet team returned to The Moat Studios on the 11th of October 2004. O'Mahony was present and spent the majority of his time in the green room with the actors. "I remember Tracy Russell saying how unusual it was for her to spend so little time in the green room — I'd definitely given her a lot more to do than usual. Mostly I remember being overawed by the actors, particularly Philip Madoc — who was very friendly and approachable and enthusiastic. Alan had told him that the script had been written specially for him, and I think he appreciated that!"[16]

For de Polnay it was a chance to get back to his roots. "It was great fun. As I've said, I spend all my life now teaching and directing, so it's great fun when I do a bit of acting again. In fact, after this I'm going on to do a movie. I'm glad I'm not a full-time actor anymore. But I love it."[17]

For Leeson, the recording was a chance to cross paths with some old friends. "It's an extraordinary thing, you work in this business, very intensely, sometimes, with actors for a short period of time, and then you don't see them again for years and years. It's been years since I worked with Philip, it's been years since I worked with Paul. And, first thing, you fall into a conversation you finished twenty years ago, twenty-five years ago and the rapport is instant. Marvellous, absolutely marvellous."[18]

The CD was released on the 18th of December 2004 and, although Vanessa Bishop enjoyed the play, she was somewhat confused by it. "Despite multiple listenings to the last quarter, confusion still reigns over exactly what O'Mahony's play is all about," she says, going on to conclude, "although intense and claustrophobic, 'Storm Mine' doesn't quite make its quota."[19] However, *Celestial Toyroom* reviewer Marilyn Burge seemed more in tune with O'Mahony's script. "There are no instructions on how to assemble the pieces of the puzzle that is 'Storm Mine', or what to make of the result. Interpreting this story is the listener's responsibility."[20] This sentiment is echoed by Luca Signorelli on the Doctor Who Ratings Guide. "*Kaldor City* has already established itself as the best *DW* audio spin-off ever... But 'Storm Mine' takes this series through a qualitative quantum leap."[21]

In some ways 'Storm Mine' returns to the parent series' 'The Robots of Death', with its claustrophobic action set on a Storm Mine, and its small human cast. But it soon offers a chilling conspiracy that is more supernatural than science fiction.

Some fans may have been disappointed that the fall of Kaldor City was not presented in an action-packed finale but Daniel O'Mahony's script chooses instead to look at the fall though the perspective of outsiders and survivors, and is all the more successful because of it.

The play's main strength is that is can be interpreted in a number of ways; are these events really happening, or are they taking place on some spectral dreamscape? The play also implies that Blayes may be something more than just another pawn in the game; the Fendhal calls her an enigma and it is typical of *Kaldor City* to take a supporting character and place them centre stage. While not the finale some would expect, this thoughtful and ambiguous narrative is a fitting end for an unpredictable series.

Despite good sales and strong reviews, Stevens felt *Kaldor City* had come to an end with 'Storm Mine'. As he told Chris Dueker in 2009, "retailers told me when I ended Kaldor, 'you're insane, why don't you do more?' And I replied, 'well, it's a six-part series and now it's finished. There isn't any more to say.' In fact, people sent scripts in for Kaldor City 7; Fiona and I even wrote Kaldor City 7 ourselves, and then threw it away, because it just proved to us that the show had come to a natural end with 'Storm Mine'."[22]

Although never completed, a partial script exists (totalling some 8 pages) written by Stevens and Moore, entitled 'Kaldor City Part 7: Kaston Iago'. The script opens with the final scene of 'Checkmate', where Iago goes back in time and kills Justina as a way to avert the series of events that lead to the collapse of Kaldor City, as brought about by the Fendahl. The scene then starts again, but this time ends with Iago taking a different course of action. Stevens explains the motives behind the script: "I was interested in what would happen if you were taken back to a point in your own timeline where you vaguely remembered what had taken place... what would you do? Try to mechanically act out the events of 'Occam's Razor'? Or just go nuts and throw everything out the window in the hope of somehow changing the future? Guess what happened?" Needless to say, for Iago it would have been the latter.

The script sees Iago researching the origin of the pentagram painting. Throughout his investigations, he can hear Carnell's voice in his head, and converses with it. Iago calls Cresswell, the chief of Uvanov's personal security force, into the office and breaks his neck, before going out to the concourse where the entire Guard Squad have been assembled, and shooting them all down. Stevens explains where the story would have gone next: "having requisitioned an Armoured Personnel Carrier full of Z9a explosive packs, Iago drives to Carnell's office, blows up V31 and kills Carnell. The invisible Fendahl Core/Carnell disappears and is replaced by an invisible Fendahl Core/Justina.

"Iago returns to the Carrier and next crashes it through the front of the Company Central building. He sets the timer on one of the Z9a explosive packs and throws it in the back with the others. Iago fights his way up to the Operations Gallery where he shoots Rull and Cotton and then fights his way down to the Divisional Archive where he finds the painting of a snake (which has previously featured in the episode 'Taren Capel').

"Meanwhile, the primed Z9a explosive pack aboard the Carrier detonates, causing a chain reaction that brings the entire building crashing down on top of Iago as he admires the picture.

"The story subsequently loops back to its beginning with Iago standing with Justina in front of the painting of the red pentagram. Iago once again says, 'you'll have to get rid of that painting...'

"It is then revealed that Iago and Justina are images on a monitor screen which has been plugged into a weatherbeaten decapitated Voc head. These images are being observed by two more Vocs. One turns to the other and says 'Do they never do anything else?'"

Ultimately, though, Stevens felt the story wasn't quite up to scratch: "...basically it doesn't go anywhere and it certainly isn't something you could use to build further episodes. It also relies heavily on action sequences, and I very much doubt the story would have stretched to 54 pages, the average length of a full *Kaldor City* script; perhaps 20 at most. Finally, it doesn't really say anything about Iago's fate that can't already be discerned from the final scene of 'Checkmate.'"

A further story was also submitted by Jonathan Blum, running to 56 pages: 'Silent Partner'. This script acted as a prequel and a sequel to both *Kaldor City* and 'The Robots of Death', centring on Poul, who is tasked by Landerchild to protect his daughter (Vydia) from a serial killer. Ultimately it is revealed that Vydia and her friends were manipulated into killing each other by Psi-V9, a psychiatric Voc that was treating them. The play also shows the first meeting of Poul and D84 and features Taren Capel and Cotton.

Stevens explains why the story was not produced. "The detailed twelve page storyline Blum originally submitted was very intriguing, in that although it appears to take place sometime prior to 'The Robots of Death', the possibility existed that it was also happening simultaneously within Poul's head and that of the Fendahl gestalt entity. However, when Blum came to write the full script the story began to collapse, as it soon became very clear that Poul was not a lead character, but rather as originally developed, a facilitator for other characters and events.

"Consequently, Boucher had written Poul as a walking mystery, made up of various contradictory elements. To make Poul into a lead would require you defining a set of character traits as being Poul's true self, but paradoxically, that meant that Poul was no longer Poul, but someone else, which would then bring the character, through the prequel element of the story, into conflict with his portrayal in 'Robots of Death", and the first six Kaldor City plays.

"Kate Orman then did her best to rescue the project and we had a long and detailed email exchange that covered many aspects of the Kaldor City series. Unfortunately it didn't help Blum's script any, in that the more we explored the contradictions within Poul the more redundant Blum's script appeared to become.

"Poul is a Company agent who denies he's a Company agent, who becomes a Tarenist who denies he's a Tarenist. Poul clearly wants to reject the Company, the robots, and the society he lives in, but everything he does is supporting some aspect of the system. There's a lot of complicated layers here, but if the Fendahl reflects who you are, then it must reflect him, and as the Fendahl itself is a mystery, then through its very existence Poul is going to be thrown into a personal hell of everlasting and irresolvable doubt."[23]

Another pitch came from Dale Smith, a fan of the series who had written a review of 'Storm Mine' for *Celestial Toyroom*. "I asked if Alan was looking for anybody to write the next *Kaldor City* story. He wasn't... but if I had a good enough idea, he might be convinced otherwise."[24] Smith and Stevens discussed a number of ideas, but had several integral difficulties they had to conquer first, as Stevens recalls. "The situation you faced came down to this. If you chose to write a script that's set between 'Checkmate' and 'Storm Mine', then you are placed in a position of answering a question posed by the Fendahl which, by definition, cannot be answered. And if you try and write a story set after 'Storm Mine', then you do so without having any narrative lifeline to lead you back to something that can be understood." After initially giving up and withdrawing his pitch, finding the task too difficult, Smith eventually stumbled upon an idea. "In looking at the two threads left hanging by the series, I realised I'd focussed on the wrong one in trying to work out why Kaston Iago was sent back in time. I should have been thinking about the robots."[25]

Although never recognised as part of the official scripting of the series, Dale Smith went on to write a story concerning Carnell's survival, which can be found on his website.[26]

Kaldor City proved that there was still room for a well-written, well-cast and well-produced *Doctor Who* spin-off that could compete against Big Finish. If BBV had paid attention, it is possible they also may have been able to salvage their range. The people behind *Kaldor City* look back on the series with great fondness. "I'm happy with the one I wrote," says Jim Smith. "I'm happy with the other ones. Part of my Production Manager job was reading the other scripts and commenting and talking, you wouldn't call it a script editor job, but just having input. I'm real proud of all of them, I'm proud of my involvement I think they are very good."[27]

Alan Stevens agrees. "My overall memory is that it was just a really great experience doing it. One of those rare occasions in your life where everything just comes together and works like clockwork." Fiona Moore concurs. "I'm very proud to have been a part of it. I still sometimes get people at conventions coming up to me and saying how much they enjoyed it, and I've even been approached by co-workers at the university telling me they've heard and liked the series!"[28]

Chapter 34 — Never Enough

When BBV discontinued their audio range, Magic Bullet was their obvious Doctor-less successor, and as a result Alan Stevens found himself being pitched a number of abandoned BBV scripts. "Some of them were excellent,"[1] he recalls. One such message came from the creator of *Faction Paradox*. "Lawrence Miles sent me an email couched in the kind of language you'd expect to get in letters from the RSPCA when they are trying to find a new home for an abused pet. I'm still not sure why he came to me, because we didn't really get on. Lawrence used to hang out with Ben Aaronovitch and through that association he'd become a Stalinist. As a consequence, Lawrence and I kept having arguments and fallings-out over Stalin's collectivisation policy and 'Remembrance of the Daleks'... Once the proposition was put to me, however, I did do some research, which basically amounted to getting hold of Lawrence's *Doctor Who* novel 'Alien Bodies', and then borrowing copies of the BBV *Faction Paradox* audios off Daniel O'Mahony."[2]

Stevens' opinions on how the property had been exploited in the two genres varied wildly. "I thought the book was good, but I was less keen on the audios. Nigel Fairs is a hugely talented individual, but he has since openly admitted himself that he really had no idea what *Faction Paradox* was supposed to be all about, that the budget he'd been given to work with was tiny, and that the equipment he was using at the time to produce the audios was very limited."[3]

In order to launch the range afresh, Stevens requested a completely new series that featured no returning characters, but Miles refused and insisted on the return of Cousins Justine and Eliza. With this in mind, Stevens went searching for Suzanne Proctor and Emma Kilbey, who had played the respective parts in the BBV range. "At the time, I couldn't find anything," remembers Stevens. "I even contacted the actor's directory *Spotlight*, but they knew nothing about them at all. I was also concerned because, from reading 'Alien Bodies' and Lawrence's character notes, it seemed to me that the casting of Justine and Eliza was the wrong way round, plus Justine had been given this peculiar Lancastrian accent."[4]

Concerned, he called up Miles to get his opinion. "He said he had no idea, as he hadn't listened to any of the *Faction Paradox* CDs. So I said, 'can you go away and listen to one now', and he said 'no', and I said 'why not?' and he replied 'because I don't want it to fuck with my brain'. Apparently, he had created this model in his head as to how everything should be when writing the scripts, and so he never listened to the CD versions because he thought it would ruin all of that. I then asked him if he'd listened to any of the *Kaldor City* CDs, again, 'no', came the reply. 'So why do you think I'm the best guy to do your *Faction Paradox* series?' 'Well, a few months ago I was in Forbidden Planet, got one of your CDs down off the shelf, read the back and saw you had this tremendous cast list! And so I thought you could perhaps do the same for me.' I said, 'In your head model of *Faction Paradox*, does Justine have a Lancastrian accent?' 'No', said Lawrence, 'that would be completely wrong'. And that's when I made the definite decision to recast."[5]

This new series would see *Faction Paradox* involved in the affairs of the Osirians, most notably Sutekh, last seen in the fourth Doctor story 'Pyramids of Mars.' This was a lifelong wish of Miles', according to Stevens. "He told me that since he was a child, he'd always wanted to write a series based on the Egyptian Pantheon, and he'd been planning it for ages."[6]

Stevens was keen that the series should have some connection to *Doctor Who*, as it was becoming increasingly hard to sell an original product, even with an extensive advertising budget. "If you do a completely original show, it won't sell. Because people think, 'What's this? I'm not going to take a chance on this.' And even if it has got actors from *Doctor Who* it won't really sell, because people think, 'Well I want Sarah Sutton playing Nyssa, not Sarah Sutton playing Cathy, or whatever.'"[7]

Once again, an impressive cast was gathered together by Stevens with the help of David Bickerstaff, although Stevens admits it was a more difficult process this time round. "I'd already used up my full complement of actor contacts with *Kaldor City*, forcing me to step outside of my comfort zone."[8]

Stevens initially approached Ian Richardson, who proved too expensive, and Bernard Kay, who couldn't commit due to a schedule clash. He also reached out to screen legend Julian Glover to play Upuat and Gabriel Woolf to reprise his role of Sutekh. "Julian Glover refused my initial offer, but after we'd chatted a bit and I'd pointed out that the money was coming out of my own pocket and Magic Bullet wasn't this huge corporation, Glover relented. It was the same story with Gabriel Woolf who, of course, was crucial to the production, as he had played Sutekh in the *Doctor Who* story 'Pyramids of Mars'. As it turned out, both chaps were very nice, understanding people and were great to work with."[9]

Indeed, Glover suggested his wife Isla Blair to play Zab-Amira Merytra Ellainya, much to the delight of Stevens. "I thought she was outstanding in the role."[10] Wanda Opalinska took over the part of Cousin Justine, while Jane Lesley took on the role of Cousin Eliza, although, as Alistair Lock (once again on co-directorial duties) reveals, this wasn't always the case. "Initially, we had actually cast them the other way round, and then it was decided that it made far more sense if we reversed it, it worked so much better, because you had Wanda being very calm and regal and with this wonderful sort of solid and centred presence, and then Jane being the more sort of fiery one, which suited them and made for a better dynamic."[11]

Other voice actors included Peter Miles as Anhor, Alistair Lock as John Pennerton, William Johnston as the Captain, David Bickerstaff as Abelard Finton, Francesco Calabretta as Don Escuro, George Birtwell as Gennarino, Robin Fry as Jala, and Robert Lock as Corwyn Marne. Maria Fontanetti played a Prostitute and Patricia Merrick took on the role of Astarte Marne.

The series was named *The True History of Faction Paradox*, with the first two plays entitled 'Coming to Dust' and 'The Ship of a Billion Years'. They were recorded on 16th October and 9th December 2004 and 10th February 2005 at the Moat Studios in London.

The assembled cast seemed to relish the chance to get their teeth into such well written parts. Glover later told Fiona Moore that he found this character an appealing one. "He's lovely, he's so laconic. He's so cynical about it all. I love the idea of an Egyptian god being cynical. He's sees all these magnificent processions and says, 'Oh, god, this is so boring'. 'A sun? Who would worship a sun? Who in their right minds would worship a sun?' And you think back to the Inca civilisation and the Aztecs (laughing). Wonderful stuff."[12]

Despite his clear admiration for the script, this didn't stop there being a run-in between the star and the author. "Lawrence actually came along to at least one of the studio sessions," remembers Stevens, "and sat with Alistair and myself behind the recording desk. Well, I say sat, but Lawrence actually kept getting up and moving about. Finally, Julian Glover came up to me and said, 'who is that prick who keeps walking up and down behind the recording desk?' And I said, 'oh, that's the author', and Glover replied, 'well, tell him I think he's written a great script, but would he stop walking up and down like that, it's very distracting'. So I went back and I said, 'hey Lawrence, Julian Glover loves your script. He also thinks you're a prick, and you should sit down'. And Lawrence seemed pretty chuffed with that, and went around afterwards telling everyone that Glover had called him a prick."[13]

Glover's wife, Isla Blair, was also pleased to be taking on such a richly scripted part. "There are lots of sides to her, she can be haughty, she can be dismissive, but at the same time she's got all sorts of facets to her, and I hope that comes across."[14]

Gabriel Woolf too was satisfied with the direction in which the script took Sutekh. "At first I really was a bit doubtful as to whether they could kind of reproduce the character in terms of the dialogue, but I think they are terrific scripts by Lawrence Miles. I really do. Yes, I think Lawrence has handled the character very well. I didn't know if I could do longer speeches, because I thought that Sutekh is a god of few words, but it worked very well. And the production values are tremendous."[15]

'Coming to Dust' was released on July 23rd 2006. *DWM* wrote in praise of the rebooted series, saying "this is exciting and easy to follow, and boasts some enjoyable rich and flamboyant characterisation."[16]

As with *Kaldor City* before it, the production values of this new series of CDs are of an exceptionally high standard, although, after warming to Suzanne Proctor's Justine and Emma Kilbey's Eliza, it does take a little getting used to these new interpretations. It is also a shame the story of the *Faction Paradox Protocols*, although mentioned, isn't concluded, but this first instalment does lay some interesting groundwork for the series ahead. While Lawrence Miles' tendency to over-embellish the details is once again present, he does offer some nice additions to the mythology, particularly concerning the procreation methods of the Great Houses. The appearance of the Osirians is a welcome one and the brief glimpses of Sutekh act as an appetite-whetting sampler of what's to come.

'The Ship of a Billion Years' was released on 15th April. *DWM* was again supportive, with Vanessa Bishop writing that "Miles' script is grand and epic, and soaked in the kind of overripe dialogue that only warring deities can get away with."[17]

Although a continuation of the last story, Magic Bullet are careful to ensure each play can stand on its own, rather than take BBV's approach of splitting one play into two parts. As such, 'The Ship of a Billion Years' is another well rounded release — an epic tale complete with a grandiose soundscape and a powerful music score. The world of the Osirians feels a truly alien one in a way that perhaps has never been done before in the *Doctor Who* universe. The stellar cast are given an extra boost by the star quality provided by Julian Glover and Gabriel Woolf.

Yet again Magic Bullet pulled out all the stops to ensure the range was cast, recorded and produced to an exceptionally high standard, and instantly surpass those of the previous BBV *Faction* range. Equally, the world created is as rich, if not richer, than the best of the Big Finish range. If Magic Bullet at this point could be considered the torch bearer of independent *Doctor Who* drama, then they ensured that it burned brightly.

Chapter 35 — Bitter End

Late 2006 saw the broadcast of the first official BBC *Doctor Who* spin-off series since 1981's *K9 and Company. Torchwood* was the brain child of *Doctor Who* show runner Russell T Davies and was a more adult take on the *Doctor Who* universe, in a similar vein to some of the later BBV audio and video releases.

By 2007 the BBV website was now predominately a shop front for regular *Doctor Who* merchandise, although BBV couldn't possibly hope to compete with the larger and more established *Who* retailers such as The Who Shop or Galaxy 4, while the BBC launched another *Doctor Who* spin-off series aimed at children, the Lis Sladen-led *The Sarah Jane Adventures.*

With two officially sanctioned spin-off series on the BBC it seemed there was little place for a further independent video series. During this time BBV continued to rerelease their back catalogue on DVD, with many releases remastered and featuring updated effects (and in the case of 'Unnatural Selection' a number of especially shot flashback scenes). Later, as previously discussed, the DVDs would lose the extras and become DVD-Rs.

However the only new production that came out of BBV was actually outsourced to Gareth Preston and Westlake Films. "Bill got in touch and asked if my friends and I who made up Westlake Films would like to film a comedy extra for *Auton 3*,"[1] recalls Preston. "Initially I planned to do essentially an interview with a few cutaways but John Isles and Kevin Haley encouraged me to write a more ambitious story including a plastics factory, a visit to the BBC and a recreation of the Auton invasion from 'Spearhead from Space'. I enjoyed working with John on the script, again we had that similar sense of the ridiculous."[2]

The ten minute comedy short was to feature on the DVD release of *Auton 3* and would once again see the out of work Auton find fame in the new series of *Doctor Who*, the creatures having appeared in the revived series' first episode. The film is also notable for poking fun at Baggs' new spiritual side, which Baggs himself suggested much to the surprise of Preston' "It was actually his idea! He wanted the short to have a theme that BBV was effectively wrapping up and was more than happy to appear and send himself and his new age interests up." [3]

With BBV seemingly abandoning any new productions and Bill Baggs' interests elsewhere, it was a complete surprise,when in June 2007 an advert for a new BBV production appeared on the back of *DWM*. Scheduled for release in Autumn of 2007, it appeared that with *Zygon: When Being Me is Not Enough* Baggs was attempting to play off the success of *Torchwood* by advertising the more adult nature of the film. "Contains male and female nudity and scenes of an explicit nature. Not suitable for children. Certificate 18"[4] read the advert.

The story of *Zygon* however, stretches all the way back to 2001 and Lance Parkin's *Cyberon* script.

"*Zygon* was a follow up to *Cyberon*," recalls Parkin, "with Jo playing the same character. The original idea was that it would build on that, learn a few lessons and be a spooky standalone story that was grown up — which meant sex and violence, in this context. I wanted to make that, to coin a phrase, artistically valid, and thought that a Zygon character who could become other people would make for a great criminal — they'd appear on CCTV, leave DNA and so on, but not as themselves. So some of that became basic Ring of Gyges stuff — if you could go anywhere and get away with crimes, or pretending to be someone else, what would you do? More to the point, if you were a policeman after that guy, how would you stop them?"[5]

Parkin would turn in six drafts of *Zygon* but with BBV looking for a new direction, Baggs seemed unsure what he wanted from the project. "The brief kept changing from *X-Files*, to a more conventional detective thing. I think Bill said he wanted it to be like *Cold Feet* at one point. All of those approaches would work, but you couldn't put all of them in one script. I may have written four drafts, pretty much complete rewrites. There were some I really liked, and there was some great material in there, I thought. The project kept mutating, and BBV decided to do *Do You Have a Licence To Save This Planet?* first, and I was just busy with other stuff. As was entirely his right, Bill decided we should part ways on it. I gave it a shot."[6]

While Parkin left the project, he had a hand in choosing his successor, in the form of Jon Blum, who had recently submitted a script for his ultimately abandoned audio play *The I Job*. "When [Lance] hit a roadblock on *Zygon*, he dropped me a line and asked me if I wanted to take over," explains Blum. "Bill was agreeable, so I picked up the script after Lance's sixth draft. We agreed to split our fee."

Although he never saw the first five drafts of the script, Blum felt that a good chunk of the story was already in place. "By the time I got a hold of it there was already a fair bit of material that would survive. We had the whole backstory of Mike and Bob — the whole *Twin Peaks* reference was Lance's idea — but Mike was married to a woman named Anna, and he and his wife were trying to repair their relationship. They had a whole separate plot thread. Meanwhile Bob was interfering with Lauren's attempts to treat Mike, and convincing her to walk on the dark side. There was also a lot more emphasis on the police investigation of Bob's killings, with a bunch of other characters. The final twist, of Lauren killing 'Lauren', was there, but all the action leading up to it was different — Lauren's and Mike's story threads went in completely different directions."[7]

Blum would do a further six drafts on the scripts in order to craft the film that Bill wanted. "The first was just a quick polish of Lance's version, then I started cutting down the police plot and tying Lauren more to

Mike's side of the story. Then Bill decided that Mike and Lauren should get involved with each other, and that we should ditch Anna, which required a major rethink. Instead of building the character drama around an established twenty-year marriage coming apart at the seams, now I had to build a relationship from scratch *and* tear it down in the same amount of screen time... and make Lauren into a doctor who'd be willing to shag a patient. Which is why there's that kludgey bit about her breaking off the professional relationship before they start seeing each other."[8]

Zygon: When Being Me Is Not Enough is notorious in fan circles due to several revealing sex scenes. There were rumours that the film was partly funded by an adult entertainment company and Baggs was trying to break into that genre of film. Asked about these rumours, Blum is unsure of their validity. "I have no idea how Bill got the money, and I wasn't bothered either way — he could sell himself to anyone, as long as it wasn't *my* body he was selling! I do know that Bill was always aiming for an R rating, and he asked for three sex scenes."[9]

Baggs himself dismisses the rumour but admits he was trying to broaden the appeal, though there was never any danger of it being truly pornographic in nature. "It was just something interesting to do. Funnily enough having been to the Gallifrey convention is LA I met a whole new realm of people who were into the adult movie arena, so I thought maybe that's another thing you could be interested in. So it was just another area to experiment with."[10]

Parkin seems sure the adult nature was present right from draft one: "the original idea was that there would be nudity, I'd tried to make it ethical, part of the story. I'm not sure it's ever ethical, but in this case Jo trusted Bill, she was keen — as she was in *Cyberon* — to show her range and boldness as an actor. Asking an actress to take off her clothes... it's always exploitative to an extent. I tried to incorporate that into the story, tried to do something that felt honest about sex, something that wasn't about sexual violence as entertainment, and which was about a strong female character in control of her situation, enjoying herself."[11]

Blum took a slightly different approach to the sex scenes, compared to his predecessor. "In Lance's draft, two of them [the sex scenes] were fairly straightforward ones with human emotional elements (including one where we're expecting Mike to turn into a Zygon, but he doesn't), but I tried to come up with ways to relate all three to the question of Lauren, and her own shifting boundaries... her first night with Mike, her first time as a man, and her attempt to reshape her own body."[12]

However, the final film did contain more nudity than he expected. "In my script, there was nothing full-frontal. And there were a couple of scenes that I wrote clothed, which were played without..."[13] While the film contains plenty of full frontal nudity that is often misplaced and gratuitous, it would be wrong to describe it as pornographic, with it playing out more like a late-nineties, late night Channel Five film.

According to *DWM*, shooting for *Zygon* began on September 23rd 2002. Returning to the role of Lauren Anderson was Jo Castleton, accompanied by Daniel Harcourt (formally Mathews) as Michael Kirkwood aka the Zygon Kritakh and Keith Drinkel playing Bob Calhoun aka Zygon Torlakh. Supporting roles were played by David Roecliffe, Becky Pennick, Alistair Lock and Nigel Peever. Filming once again took place around Baggs' hometown of Southampton.

Baggs advertised for well dressed extras on the BBV website to feature in restaurant and hospital scenes. The crew also returned to Baggs' place of work as Castleton remembers. "I remember filming at BBC Southampton during the night and Keith half naked, made up to be looking pretty dead, giving a security guard the shock of his life! Not sure we were supposed to be there!!!"[14]

Having enjoyed playing the role first time round, Castelton was pleased to be returning as Anderson. "I liked the fact that Lauren was pushed to her limits and had to struggle not to give in and become one of them. I liked the love story with her patient/Zygon."[15] She was less of a fan of the sex scenes. "I wasn't so keen on some of the more graphic scenes. Daniel [Harcourt] was lovely and really easy to work with which was helpful as we all were naked at some point or other, not that Keith or Daniel had a problem with it."[16]

Castleton was also thrilled to be reunited with the villain of the piece, Keith Drinkel. "Keith is a fantastic actor and we had worked together before so it was great fun being reunited for *Zygon*, and we had some intense scenes together." [17]

Baggs seemed in good spirits on the shoot, being back where he belonged behind the camera. "I really enjoyed filming it and having a good feeling about filming. Although I realise it was just over optimistic."[18] Drinkel certainly was impressed with how Baggs handled the shoot. "I think we're able to work at quite a tight pace. The great problem with a short filming period is that you don't want to cut corners, but you want to get it right — so the demands are very much upon you and the director, to use all the time that you've got to make it work: I think Bill did."[19]

For Castleton it was also a chance to get back to a different sort of acting. "I do a lot of theatre normally, so it's really nice to do some filming. There's such a different atmosphere — a completely different process."[20] Also present for the initial shoot was Alistair Lock who was on sound recording duties for several scenes. "I was involved just for one day. There was this sort of hospital or clinic near where his parents lived, so they were shooting some stuff down there. He just asked whether I'd be interested in helping out, so I came round and recorded sound for a day.

That was the day a bed was being pushed down a corridor and I was edged between the cameraman's thighs. Which wasn't bad, as we belted down the corridor."[21]

With the majority of the film in the can, Baggs assembled a rough cut of the film (which was complete up to the point of Bob kidnapping Lauren), which he duly showed to Blum at a convention. "I thought it was coming out okay — the only bit I objected to was Jo Castleton's full-frontal flash when she got out of bed, which just looked crass. (I just want to make it clear, there were no visible genitalia in my script, male, female *or* Zygon.) I knew things were going to be tweaked a bit, but I basically felt things were on the right track."[22]

Shortly after this Baggs made the decision to scrap the project all together.

What reasons did he have for halting the project?

"Well, because it was rubbish! It was funny, it was kind of a spiral down and again, because I was just so pleased with what Lance had produced for *Cyberon* I just assumed that it would work with *Zygon*. I mean he wrote things that were probably very good, but I didn't want it and I thought he was writing something better, but the reality was I was a bit misguided. Jon can't write, well he can write, but he doesn't have an idea of how to construct a film; it's just language on a page. What Lance has got is some sense of how drama develops so what Jon produced was an audio play. Looking back, I didn't realise that at the time, I was too driven and desperate to produce something."

Castleton recalls that the news came as a complete surprise to the cast. "It was a shame not to finish it and we thought that it might not get used at all which was disappointing."[23]

And so the final BBV release would remain unfinished for the time being. Bill Baggs, once a prominent figure in fandom, all but disappeared from the public eye and rumours of bad business practice and his change in direction spread. So what was he actually up to?

Putting the question to a number of his peers evokes some interesting answers. Nigel Fairs was of the opinion he had left the country. "I think he moved to Australia. He had long hair last time I saw him and a beard."[24] Nick Briggs also came in contact with him during this period. "I remember bumping into him at an American convention years later," he recalls, "when he looked like one of the disciples, which was really weird. He'd sort of got this beard and long hair and had this far away weird look in his eyes. He never used to be like that, he used to be very definite, with beady little eyes, very concentrated, very direct and then he'd sort of become like the guru, it was really odd. It's like he must have had a nervous breakdown. And he said 'yeah I've been following your progress' and I said 'oh yeah, you stalking me' or something and he went 'oh no, no, no'.

He had no sense of humour and he went 'I'm very pleased for you and I think it's amazing what you've done.'"[25]

David A Mcintee too remembers his life taking a more spiritual direction. "He got into some sort of spiritual massage thing, started with an R, I think. (Not reiki, though, I'd heard of that.)"[26] Perhaps more through hearsay than anything else, Andy Grant seems to think his spiritual direction was of a darker nature. "I hear Bill Baggs has set up some religious cult or something." [27]

Tim Saward, however. is more diplomatic. "I think he got a bit lost at that point and it wasn't clear to him whether he was going to go off and go down the line of erotic videos — which I don't know he really would have felt comfortable with — or into the line of this emotional energy healing thing, which I think he had done for a while, but not necessarily stuck with. He just needed a complete change because he needed to leave the field of combat with Big Finish I think."[28]

George Telfer seems to think Baggs had a lot of issues he need to deal with to progress further in his life. "He's an interesting character, he was very kind of free and easy. I think maybe there were things going on with Bill that he was trying to deal with, inside himself, I'm really not sure. He had a lot of issues going on himself, that he needed to address, but I never had a problem with him. I think he's gone a bit bohemian since, I think he found religion, so I think that was his free and easy spirit." [29]

Another interviewee for this book, who asked not be named, explained that this change in direction caused friction in Baggs' personal life. "BBV wasn't working at that time, he left his wife or she left him — I don't know which way round it was — and he just went into this Emotional Energy Healing thing 110 percent. There was even some tension between him and his wife about him doing emotional energy healing on the boys. Essentially it was a sort of a breakdown."

There is some truth in all of these statements but nothing as dark as a cult was involved, as Baggs revealed in early 2015. "After *Zygon* I got very depressed from the divorce and *Zygon*. I was very unhappy and lots of things were kind of colliding, for years I'd been trying unsuccessfully to knock on the doors of various soaps and other directing things, and been knocked back and knocked back, for whatever reason the universe didn't want me to go in that direction. And I'd had enough and lost a lot of whatever it was, the energy that was driving me to do it."[30]

Which led to his Emotional Energy Healing — "I qualified as an Akki energetics practitioner, so I can treat physical and emotional problems."[31] With his personal issues mounting did he see this as a new path of enlightenment or simply a career change? "It was Spiritual. This was around about the time my marriage was breaking down and it was a very traumatic experience, and a turning point and as I discover now, you have these junctures, you're kind of open to exploring something different.

These being significant moments, terrible and horrible and depressing at the time but actually amazing in retrospect, but actually they were golden opportunities. So I started exploring, there was a technique I was into called Tibetan Pulsing Yoga and that was the turning point and I went to Australia and that kind of led to other things."[32]

While it's easy to be sceptical about these new age forms of healing (a debate over its veracity could fill several books alone) Saward feels that Baggs needed the change. "I'm a bit of a Dawkins fan and that sort of thing. I couldn't really go with him or even just humour him in that, and he was going through a whole load of stuff at that time and so that's when we drifted apart really. But I could see that there was a thing in him that this healing thing expressed, that he completely kept back from all of his engagements with everybody else. There was an emotional core that wasn't being given a vent to in what he was doing creatively. So I think he was very blocked from himself in that sense and not sort of... being able to get out into the world, what was in his head and that was great but I think it became a bit much in the end."[33]

As a result of *Zygon*'s abandonment, a further film starring the eponymous aliens, which Baggs had already commissioned, would also remain unmade. David A McIntee had written the script for this forgotten tale, describing it as a "kind of a Faustian thing about their shapeshifting ability, and people wanting to get that."[34]

At the point of commission, there was no *Zygon* script to use as a reference point, although the two films would not be related in any case. "The script for the first one was either still being written, or had just been delivered. Baggs just obviously wanted to get his money's worth out of the rights and out of whatever costumes he'd be making, by doing more than one film, which is understandable." [35]

For this eventually abandoned follow-up, Baggs had a few peculiar demands. "There was a scene where the main characters are undergoing a process, and Baggs said "can they be naked in this scene?" And I said that as he's the director, he could have them do that, to which he said, "but if I tell them I want them to strip off, they'll think I'm weird. But if it's in the script, well, what can I do...?" [36] This wasn't his only request for scenes of a more explicit nature. "He also wanted there to be a sex scene in it, and I usually find 'obligatory sex scenes' in movies to be boring at best, so I wanted to be sure that if I had to write one, it'd be totally integral to the characters and story, if possible, and so it was — it would have been very progressive as well — but it kind of means I'll never write another one because I can't really see myself getting it so right again for another set of characters or situations." [37]

With *Zygon* in limbo and Baggs' personal and work life in a state of disarray, McIntee found himself in a difficult situation with Baggs. "When he commissioned the *Zygon* script it was on a deal of 10% advance, and the rest on completion, OK. So he paid me the 10% and I got writing. After the first draft, it went back and forth through about another three, until he was satisfied. So then I was due the 90%. Which didn't appear. So I asked, and he said he was having a cash flow problem, couldn't afford the rest of the fee yet, but would give me another 10% for now. OK, so around Easter of 2004 I got another 10%."[38] When McIntee went back to Baggs to chase the rest of his debt, he was apparently given the cold shoulder. "He stopped answering emails, then, eventually, like a year or more later, when he'd pretty much gone off to do that... whatever it is, I got a message of 'Oh, I *really* meant the balance would be due when the film was released, and we're not making it now, what a pity, never mind.'"[39]

While the McIntee and Baggs feud remained unresolved, the *Zygon* film would have a happy ending of sorts. At some point during 2007, Baggs decided to finish the film that had been abandoned some five years previously. And despite the issues he felt the film had, he decided to tackle it with a fresh perspective. "What I realise now, going back and regrouping and finishing it and finding some inner strength... I thought initially I was going to be giving up on my whole drama world but what I realise now is I was going back to find some stronger place in myself so that I could come back again and not give up."[40]

Irrespective of motive, the filmmaker's return and indeed the resurrection of the long dead project came as a surprise to the cast, including Castelton. "Bill got re-inspired and we finished it! I was pleased to finish it, if a little shocked and worried if we all looked the same!"[41]

Alistair Lock was also called in help out. "I heard it was abandoned and then he came back to me and said 'I'm shooting some scenes, would you be interested in being in it?' and he dangled the carrot of having a small part and you know, would I do the music? So we went down to the same hospital again and it was nice to see Jo Castleton because I hadn't seen her in quite a while. So we recorded these scenes with me and this other girl who I kissed in one scene, it was fun to do."[42]

With all the footage finally in the can, including new scenes written by Baggs himself, a rough cut was assembled and given to Lock to score. "When I saw an edit of it, I said to Bill, 'it's too domestic.' Yes it's about a guy that's got stranded on Earth after an invasion attempt has gone wrong and he's got stuck in the form of the guy he took over, and he believes that he is the guy until he realises he's a Zygon. Even so, it's just so domestic, it needs a more global or galactic influence, so that's why we put those effects of the planet, and more visual effects to give the illusion there was a bigger budget. When I did the score I tried to do a bigger orchestral score to make it sound more big budget than it was."[43]

The rough cut was then presented to Blum for his thoughts on the near complete project. "Bill sent me a complete rough cut, after he'd shot various pickup scenes to tighten it up. I watched it with Kate and my friend Andrew... and before the opening credits, there was a full-length bluescreen tracking shot down the full frontal length of the male lead's naked body, lingering at cock-height as he presumably transformed into a Zygon... and I knew we were embarking on a strange and terrifying journey."[44]

If Blum thought that was odd then nothing would prepare him for what was to come. "The next few minutes were a blur... some of the scenes I'd written were still there, but all in the wrong order. All the build-up I'd intended to make the relationship convincing, as Lauren reluctantly opened up — gone. Out of my first 25 pages, about nine survived. And Bill's new scenes... Well, the one that began on a tight close-up on a supporting actress' boobs just left us all gaping. Jo's random costume changes between old and new material were just the icing on the cake. That and the St. Kitts Hospital sign that was just printed on a piece of paper stuck on the door."[45]

Despite all this Blum does lay a little of the blame at his own feet. "The thing is, looking back on my script, I can tell that first chunk could definitely have been tightened. There was too much dialogue, especially the way it was delivered — I'd written stuff to be fairly rapid-fire, but even then there was too much of it. But even so... there *had* to be a better way to fix it than that."[46]

After this initial shock, the script and action became more familiar to Blum but the film offered up more surprises. "Then we got into the new stuff past the end of the previous rough cut... and I saw the locations he hadn't been able to afford, the leaden filming of scenes that were meant to move fast, the actors I felt sorry for trying their best while being shot in such a clunky way, the styleless sex scenes, a couple of fully-clothed scenes which looked more like they were shot for a porn movie than any of the sex scenes, Bob being stark naked for no apparent reason, the female cop who'd been rewritten as a guy (thus missing the point of letting Lauren adopt a female shape that *wasn't* a hot babe), the baggy Zygon... the sense of the complete artlessness of it all just overwhelmed me. Partway through this, I remember looking over at Andrew, and he was cringing behind a sofa cushion, with eyes like he'd seen into one of the tackier pits of hell."[47]

Unhappy with the way the film had been handled and the insertion of new material, Blum took swift action to disassociate himself from the project. "Basically within minutes of seeing that complete rough cut, I emailed Bill and told him I wanted my name off it. He said yes, and that's the last I heard from him."[48]

The film would go on to be released without any writer credit on it. Blum would never see the finished film. "He never sent me a copy, and never paid me or Lance." [49]

The exact release date of *Zygon* is unknown, but we can put it roughly at March 2008 as the first advert appeared on the back of the June 2007 *DWM*. On July 3rd an update entitled "ZYGON' AUTUMN 2007" appeared on the BBV website, though the only words the article contained were "ZYGON — cert 18. Contains male and female nudity."

This would remain as the site's last update until 31 December 2007 when the same post was retitled "*Zygon* Spring 2008." This would be the site's final update. From May 2008 the site would read "This site is currently under construction. Please visit again soon!"

The March 2008 issue of *DWM* featured an advert on the back page that masqueraded as an article, with quotes from the cast and crew about the production. The advert stated the film had taken four years to complete and noted "*Zygon* has both a lot to live up to and quite possibly a lot to live down. Having to balance the increased visual expectations, brought about by modern standards, with the perceived cheapness of earlier films in the genre has been a complex challenge: one that has resulted in a very different kind storytelling and a very different kind of story."[50]

In the article, Alistair Lock also drew comparisons to other unnamed genre programmes — a clear indication that BBV were aiming for a *Torchwood* audience. "The film is aimed at a whole new demographic, with an eighteen certificate already given; and it can probably best be compared with current post watershed sci-fi programmes."[51]

The film was now entitled *Zygon: When Being You Just Isn't Enough* and the cover featured a topless Castleton and sported an 18 certificate. The film received little coverage from genre press, relying instead on promotion from fan sites.

Zygon: When Being You Just Isn't Enough throws up some interesting ideas about the nature of identity in relevance to shape changers and the power it would give you. Keith Drinkel delivers a brilliant performance as the scheming Bob. but unfortunately that is where the praise stops.

In fact, there is so much wrong with this film that it's impossible to go into all the details. The execution is amateur to say the least; for instance the lighting throughout is awful, with scenes moving from bright daylight in one shot to artificial light in darkness in the next. Scenes are cut together in a way that means it's impossible to tell if there has been any passage of time. Explanations are thin on the ground throughout — what are these devices that are used to transform people? Where are these greenhouse gases being released from? Most basic of all, for the uninitiated, what *is* a Zygon?

The film is badly directed and suffers from Baggs' characteristic concern with simply getting scenes finished rather than the quality of what he has shot. High (or rather low) lights include a dating montage which is so bad it's funny, and sex scenes with laughably inappropriate music (a shame, as Alistair Lock's score is otherwise great). Additionally, a Zygon costume looks awful even in brief glimpses, extras look directly into the camera, and there are sundry continuity failures.

Perhaps the market place was ready for a new more adult *Doctor Who* spin-off, maybe even filling the void that Virgin's *New Adventures* had left? If so, *Zygon* was not the solution.

As a product, it resembles nothing so much as a cash-in on *Torchwood* and consequently has a slight air of desperation about it. But perhaps given events in Baggs' personal life, it's understandable that his mind may have not been on the job in hand.

Blum sums up the film best, saying, "I do think there's a good story in there which was worth telling. But there's just so much stuff in the way of it."

Baggs doesn't think it's quite as bad as some believe. "I'm kind of happy with it now, because I rewrote bits of it but it's not fulfilling when you watch it and you compare it to *Cyberon.*' It's not so fulfilling or engaging. It should be, on paper it's quite interesting."[52] But he does shoulder the the blame himself. "It was just an ill conceived project in the first place. It was probably more down to my state of mind at the time than it is to do with anything else so I don't blame anybody." [53]

The play film also soured Baggs relationship with Castleton, as she was unhappy with putting her topless image on the DVD cover. "We didn't speak for several years after that, I rang him up and said you should have told me, it was quite embarrassing."[54]

This was Baggs doing what he always did — producing drama with ambition on a tight budget, and that at least is to be admired.

And with that BBV closed their doors for what appeared to be the final time.

Chapter 36 — Gods Will Be Gods

The True History of Faction Paradox was planned as a six-part series and, even though there would be a two-year gap between instalments two and three, it was always Stevens' intention to return and finish the story. "The BBV series had self-contained two-part releases, whereas our series is a six-part story, and characters come and characters go, but the ripples of what has happened run strongly through it all." [1]

The gap was partly due to Stevens wanting to test the waters with his new product in a post-new-*Who* world. "I wasn't sure how well *Faction Paradox* was going to sell, and the amount of sales affects the amount of money you have to spend on the series. *Faction* didn't sell as well as *Kaldor City* initially, but... it picked up a lot, and it now sells very well."[2]

In contrast to *Kaldor City*, which had a number of writers working in collaboration, *Faction Paradox* had only Lawrence Miles.

Miles was notable for his unpredictable behaviour, and has stated himself that he's been "diagnosed with what they call 'severe social phobia', which is why I don't get out very much these days... Clearly I'm not mad, or anything... but I can be a bit intense, I am on the autism spectrum... only on the lower part of it."[3]

He is somewhat notorious in fandom for his controversial outbursts, but he is also a fierce intellect with an exemplary creative talent. So how did Stevens find working with him?

"I was apprehensive, since we'd had some fallings-out in the past; however, as a work colleague he was hugely professional. I remember pointing out some plot problems with the first *Faction* story, 'Coming to Dust', and he just went away, corrected them and sent me the revised pages, with no argument. If I wanted anything clarified, he would clarify it, if I wanted anything rewritten, or cut, he would rewrite or cut it. If I suggested, for the next script, reintroducing a character, he'd put that character in."[4]

Indeed, the main problem Stevens faced was one BBV also had when dealing with Miles. "He would write far more material than was needed. Consequently, a lot of my time was spent slashing out tons of redundant dialogue, all beautifully written, but completely unnecessary to the plot. I used to ring him up and tell him what I wanted to cut, and he'd say, 'hey, go ahead.'" Then one day he said, 'look, you don't have to ring me up on this, I trust you to do it properly, just cut what you feel is necessary.' Which I thought was an extraordinary generous thing to say, but then, if he's got this perfect representative model in his mind as to how *Faction Paradox* should be, then why would he care what I did with the audios?" [5]

Gabriel Woolf once again returned as Sutekh with Wanda Opalinska and Jane Lesley as Cousin Justine and Cousin Eliza, and Robert Lock and David Bickerstaff appearing as Corwyn Marne and Abelard Finton. The first two plays, 'Body Politic' and 'Word from Nine Divinities', saw Philip Madoc cast as The War King, a role that has long been rumoured to be the Master in all but name. When asked about this, Stevens teases that "the laws of copyright infringement prevent me from answering that question, although it may also be the War Chief."

The part of Anubis was given to cult TV favourite, Peter Halliday. Another new face joining the series was Chris Tranchell, better known to *Doctor Who* fans as Andred from 'The Invasion of Time,' as Mortega. Tranchell was attracted to the script's ambition. "It's a great adventure, this sort of Boy's Own Ripping Yarn element, but the fact that you then scatter it in space, with such sophisticated scene-setting of quality and accuracy, that identifies the location and gives the right sounding relationship, it's impressive work."[6] Other voices included Tracy Russell as Nephthys and Bruce McGilligan playing Lord Ptah.

Edward de Souza appeared in the final two plays as Geb, a part which Lawrence Miles later stated he had singled out for someone else. "You know Geb, Sutekh's dad? You know David Bradley who played William Hartnell? Geb was supposed to be David Bradley, that's what Geb was supposed to be." Miles went on to discuss this in more detail. "Now Edward de Souza is a good actor but no, it was specifically supposed to be a class thing because you have this rough primal god versus Sutekh."[7]

Stevens, in part at least, disputes this. "When I told Lawrence that I'd cast Edward de Souza as Geb, he told me that he'd actually based it on the actor John Henshaw. At the time, Henshaw had been appearing in a series of adverts for the Post Office. With this in mind, I instructed de Souza to give the character a Northern accent, which wasn't a problem for him. Indeed, a year later, de Souza was playing Colin Grimshaw in *Coronation Street*. So the class thing was certainly there, which Lawrence must have forgotten, because I did tell him this."[8] Edward de Souza has a slightly different recollection on where the Henshaw influence came from. "The writer gave notes for the actor who plays Geb, and it struck me that he was supposed to be a cross between Brian Blessed and John Henshaw, and as that is what I perceived it to be, that is what they got. And for that I do not apologize."[9]

The final four plays in the series also featured a returning character from the BBV series in the form of Lolita, this time played by Jet Tattersall, although she wasn't the first actress Stevens approached for the role. "My first choice was Mary Tamm, who always had this rather unnatural, mechanical element to her acting, and therefore, I thought, would be perfect for the role. Well, that was my mistake; I found her a very difficult person, and eventually withdrew the contract."[10]

Later, Stevens elaborated upon these difficulties. "In regards to Tamm, I don't want to speak ill of the dead and in retrospect, part of the problem may have been my fault, in that you get an impression in your mind of someone based on their performance, and this can influence how you relate to them. The commentary tracks on 'The Key to Time' are also misleading in that she was with people she knew and was talking about something she was familiar with. Taken out of that context, however, she was someone else entirely. Outwardly calm, but perhaps inwardly insecure, although maybe not wanting to expose that insecurity.

"She had agreed to play the part before the scripts featuring Lolita had all been written. I'd described the character to her during our one phone conversation and she seemed very keen and friendly. When it came to recording dates, however, she started to subtly put obstacles in the way as to her availability. It could have been that she hated the part, but then she never said that, indeed, she never made an attempt to discuss the character at all, which is a tad unusual. I mean, it has been my experience that most actors want to talk their role over with you, even if it's just to tell you how they intend to play it. Maybe it was the money? Lawrence had finally included the character in four scripts, but if Mary had wanted more money, she never said so, or gave any discernible hint that this was even an issue.

"Anyway the upshot of all this was that the recording date kept being pushed back, and I was continually having to return to actors like Edward de Souza, Philip Madoc and Gabriel Woolf and ask for more dates as to when they were available. Even Madoc, who had previously asked me to pass on to Tamm a very pleasant note containing a few lines of Estonian, and which spoke of how much he was looking forward to working with her again, eventually got irritated and started calling her "Bloody Mary," which I saw as a clear prompt to either pin Tamm down to a precise date and time or recast.

"Basically my proposal was that I'd book the studio just for her on whatever day she chose and record all her lines separate from the rest of the cast. She turned the offer down flat, with no explanation. I then sent her another email which basically said 'I'm recasting the part. Thanks for wasting everyone's time. If you didn't want to do it why didn't you say so three months ago?' Her reply mainly consisted of haughty bluster about having to balance work commitments, but then she said something very curious 'perhaps if we'd communicated more, things would have worked out.'

"On the surface this seemed an odd thing to say, in that during the many weeks she'd been pissing about, we'd had a massive email exchange, but then I thought perhaps she meant I should have phoned her and we should have got to know one another on a more friendly basis, which might suggest some kind of social phobia or neurosis? Then again, maybe not.

"When I told David Bickerstaff about it he seemed totally unsurprised over her behaviour, saying that it had been a serious error to have approached her in the first place."[11]

The bulk of the recording for 'Body Politic', 'Word from Nine Divinities', 'Ozymandias' and 'The Judgment of Sutekh' took place at Slap Studios on 17th and 18th December 2007 with further sessions on the 15th and 16th January 2008. Several other sessions were also scheduled at Alistair Lock's own studio to accommodate the actors who weren't available for the main recording block, with Wanda Opalinska recording her scenes on 13th November 2007, Peter Halliday on 27th November 2007, Jane Lesley on 4th December 2007 and finally Chris Tranchell on 6th February 2008.

Co-director Alistair Lock was glad to be back for this second round of *Faction Paradox* audios.

"It was some brilliant writing and very, very good stories. It had this really epic feel to it and we were able to capture that on audio, with the sound design and music. So it was quite fun and nice working together again and we got to work with some nice people."[12]

Despite the high quality of the writing and a good atmosphere in the studio, the scripts presented a logistical nightmare for Stevens. "Lawrence's scripts were far longer than the ones written for *Kaldor City*, so we were always under time pressure in the studio to get everything done. Also, when working on and devising a *Kaldor City* script, I'd always have in the back of my mind how I was going to record it. So it was built into the series that you'd have these certain groups of characters who would always appear together, which allowed you to just bang through their scenes in the studio one after another. However, Lawrence's background isn't in audio production, it's in prose, so he wasn't thinking about how it was all going to be recorded; he was just thinking about getting his story told. The first two scripts had pretty much been a nightmare to record, so, afterwards, I told Lawrence he could only have ten speaking parts per script, that each scene could only have a maximum of three characters, and that each script could be no more than 12,000 words long. He did consistently stick to the first two rules, but by 'The Judgment of Sutekh', the word count had gone back up to something like the 23,000 mark. So, in sum, I didn't enjoy doing the *Faction Paradox* audios as much as I had enjoyed doing the ones for *Kaldor City*. However, I will also add that I did learn a hell of a lot from the experience."[13]

Unsurprisingly, Miles' attitude towards the range was unchanged from the BBV days. "I never heard any of the audios I've written. I put the script online ages ago for the BBV ones. There's loads of bits missing from the script apparently."

Despite this he seems sure that these new entries were superior. "The reason the Sutekh ones are better is because Alan Stevens actually stuck to the script."[14] A claim which somewhat undermines the role of casting, performance, directing and sound design.

'Body Politic' is the most sci-fi-centric of the *Faction Paradox* audio plays, and it is also the one that most bears the hallmarks of its influences. While *Faction Paradox* feels far enough removed from their Time Lord roots, having been conceived as renegade Time Lords, the Great Houses can't help but feel like Time Lords in all but name, with their 'Deadly Assassin' style bickering and fleet of Time Ships. The addition of Philip Madoc to the cast is a welcome one, which more than makes up for the lack of Julian Glover in this outing. Another welcome return is Lolita, albeit recast, her manipulation of rules and gods alike makes her a formidable foe and while one would expect Sutekh to be the main villain her presence ensure you are never quite sure where Lolita's influences begin and end.

'Word from Nine Divinities' is yet another tense and stylish chapter. As always, the devil is in the detail, and Miles pulls together the narrative strands and political strategies of Justine, Sutekh, the War King and Lolita in such a way that, although complex and overlapping, the various plots and counter-plots are always clearly and expertly articulated to the listener. This is in part helped by the fact that Miles has given both the Homeworld and the Osirian Court identical systems of governance, which, although perhaps straining credibility somewhat, does allow him to compare and contrast the competing characters, as they forge and break their respective alliances. Indeed, Justine's closing deal with Sutekh makes it all the more evident that this is a story not about good versus evil, but rather one concerning the ruthless application of realpolitik.

With 'Ozymandias', once again the *Faction Paradox* range confounds listener expectations. Where one would expect a courtroom drama to follow the previous play, Miles instead chooses to bring the story crashing down to 18th century Earth and reintroduces characters whose story was thought long since over, in the form of Finton and Marne. Echoing H. G. Wells' *The First Men in The Moon* (1901), their subplot is a great success, even if its relevence to the ongoing plot doesn't become apparent until 'The Judgment of Sutekh'. The bitter Northerner Geb, played expertly by De Souza, makes for an amusing god, and his contempt for his children and the Great Houses permeates every sentence he speaks. Praise should also be given to Jane Lesley and her impressive vocal/personality transformation from Eliza to Horus. With a convincing battlefield set, this episode makes for a great build-up to the series' final act.

'The Judgment of Sutekh' is an epic saga told on a grand scale, extrapolating the many seeds and strands planted throughout the six-part story and bringing them to a gratifying conclusion. The non-linear narrative is possibly the best use of time travel ever seen in a *Doctor Who*-related drama, but the play also packs in a plethora of tense confrontations and manages to give all of the cast some meaty dialogue.

Add in several emotionally charged scenes and some truly horrific ideas and as a finale this is an impressive feat and remains a perfect example of what a combination of fluent story-telling, exemplary production values and a talented cast and crew can create within the *Doctor Who* universe.

By the time 'Body Politic' was released on 3rd May 2008 *Doctor Who* fever was in full swing across the UK (at this point, David Tennant was in the middle of his triumphant fourth season as the Doctor). 'Word from Nine Divinities' followed on the 24th November 2008, with 'Ozymandias' arriving the following year on the 8th June 2009. By the time 'The Judgment of Sutekh' was released on the 23rd November 2009, David Tennant was just a month away from handing the TARDIS key to Matt Smith and *Torchwood* had recently completed its critically acclaimed mini-series 'Children of Earth'. It is perhaps no surprise then that *DWM* did not review these final plays.

Despite this, Stevens told Chris Dueker that the show's return had had no ill effects on *Faction Paradox*.

"Since *Doctor Who*'s come back it's very difficult to get advertising anywhere in the *Doctor Who* media. They're too busy reviewing the latest Cyberman-Voice-Changer-Helmet to find room for anything else. But it doesn't seem to make any difference. I think the CDs sell because they're good, and people recognize that. I've certainly been sent some lovely emails over the years, which is all very encouraging. I was expecting a drop in sales when *Doctor Who* came back on TV, but as *Kaldor City* and *Faction Paradox* are clearly spin-offs, then I suppose you have to be in a spin-off frame of mind anyway to buy them, so the return of *Doctor Who* hasn't knocked our sales at all. They've all sold very well. In fact sales have gone up."[15]

Magic Bullet were the last company standing in the once vibrant spin-off market. If the end of BBV's output had suggested that this market was no longer viable, Magic Bullet seemed determined to prove otherwise. Of course this was undoubtedly a team effort, but equally one can't overstate the resilience, passion and drive of Stevens.

He later told Chris Dueker, "If I'm interested in something I will move Heaven and Earth. If I really, really want to do something, then I will do it. If I'm not interested, you can't make me."[16] Stevens clearly had the get up and go attitude needed to make the series — and market — work. Despite little coverage from *DWM*, Magic Bullet sustained impressive sales and never compromised on quality. They didn't disappear overnight nor did they fade away through a lack of enthusiasm; they remained strong and even now represent some of the best of the spin-off media.

The company was comprised of people inspired to create by a show they loved, and in the act of creation brought into being something truly remarkable. If the independent spin-off series had to finish, then they went out in style with Magic Bullet.

Chapter 37 — Big Mouth Strikes Again

Over the course of this book there have been a number of people who have stated, quite plainly in some cases, that they feel Baggs owes or owed them money. Producer Andy Grant was very insistent about the point, saying "I know some of [the productions] were sold to the Sci Fi Channel but Bill Baggs didn't pay any of the money. I believe I'm one of many that are owed a great deal of money, which again I'm quite happy to put in the book."[1]

With this in mind, it would be remiss not to ask exactly how sound BBV's business practices were, and did Baggs unfairly exploit people?

Tim Saward recalls that he could be very secretive, often withholding information if he could. "He was very cagey, Bill. You wouldn't get a straight answer out of him about a lot of stuff that was going on with other people. I remember him paying for my fare to go to one of these conventions, and me mentioning this in front of John Ainsworth and Bill getting quite cross with me, because I don't think he was paying for everybody's fare to go to different things. So it was very cards close to the chest."[2]

Nick Briggs too remembers his unforthcoming nature. "He seemed often not to be telling the truth. He got caught up with his own enthusiasm, which perhaps meant he forgot things like sticking to the facts."[3]

George Telfer also remembers wondering where the money from these productions had gone. "I think the *Auton* videos sold quite well, although I never got any money from it, but I think they did sell quite well. But that was probably our fault, maybe we should have gone into it with our eyes open a bit more and had some sort of paper work set out, saying what was going to happen if it suddenly sells millions of copies. I don't know how many it did sell, but I think it did reasonably well."[4]

Although Anthony Keetch found a surefire way of getting money from Baggs, thanks to Patricia Merrick. "She even offered me invaluable advice about getting paid by BBV — you invoiced Bill's mum!"[5]

As discussed earlier, Baggs had offered Debbie Watling and Clive Merrison fifty pounds to appear in the sequel to his play, and Saward also found himself being asked to offer actors low fees. "Like Sally Faulkner, where he said 'don't mention my name, offer her £50 and see if you can persuade her' and I really tried. I felt awful doing it as well, but I was sort of doing his dirty work really. Initially she agreed, as I tried to charm her on the phone and then she phoned me back ten minutes later and she said 'you know what that's ridiculous, I'm not doing that, it's got to be at least 100 pounds' and I almost was relieved when she did, because I was like 'ok sanity prevails.'"[6]

David A McIntee claims he was never paid for his work on the second *Zygon* script, even though the relationship started out amicably. Citing it as "easy going at first, just chatty over email. Until he started backtracking on deals, and getting into whatever that cult massage thing he ended up doing was,"[7] McIntee clarified that "business practice went out the window. I dunno what sort of trouble he was having." The entire affair left a bitter taste in the mouth. "I'm not the only person who he did that shit to, by a long way. And you don't do that shit and still keep people working with you, so no wonder BBV died." [8]

Jon Blum, who also was never paid for his efforts, looks at it slightly more lightheartedly. "On the plus side, it was a good bonding experience with various other actors and behind-the-scenes people, at conventions and so forth, where we all had our own Bill Baggs stories![9]"

The most damning response, however, came from Nicola Bryant, following her experience on *The AirZone Solution*.

"It leaves a really bad taste when you've given, out of the goodness of your heart, somebody a start and they promise you money and they start sending you abusive mail saying 'No, no, I never promised that' and me thinking I trusted someone. [The] same is true of Colin, same is true of Nick. Nick got ripped off in the end, everybody got ripped off. That's why I was replaced, so he could take the next person and rip them off."

Bryant is visibly angry during the interview, concluding, "I really wish it hadn't happened, because it's such an unpleasant thing, and not only that, he continues to sell it and I don't see any of it."[10]

Saward also recalls another incident where one of Baggs' apparent debtors used the BBV website to air their grievances. "There was an actor who'd been in one of the *Auton* things, who just went all over this forum saying 'when are you going to pay me, when are you going pay me?' and I said [to Baggs] 'do you want me to remove or delete one of these postings' and he said 'no, no, let him play it out and we shall see,' but it was obvious even then."[11]

Unsurprisingly Briggs, who had more run-ins with Baggs than anyone else, has a lot to say on the matter. "He's broken all his contracts with us, he had long fought arguments about contracts and royalties and rights and things which he was really difficult about. But eventually we had some sort of mature discussion and agreed on it, but what he did was the same thing he did with the sex and nudity with Nicola Bryant and Colin Baker, he'd realise he wasn't going to win an argument, and he'd come to an agreement with you, but knew that he was just going to not bother to agree to it later. And that's what he's done with all our contracts. I mean were any of us able to marshal lawyers, he owes us thousands of pounds and that's why we are all a bit funny about talking about him."[12] And Briggs is aware of many other people who feel the same. "Equity ran a file on him for quite a while, I believe. People were trying to get him to pay the money they felt was due, and Colin Baker has often discussed with me the possibility of taking legal action. Mind you, I'm fairly certain Bill didn't keep good records, which would make it very difficult to actually prove anything." [13]

Mark Ayres who worked for both Baggs and for Barnfather's Reeltime Pictures feels people may have been expecting rewards that were never going to materialise. "Like all of these things, you ask various people and there have been rumblings since, about who made money off these. But you know Bill and Keith were both sort of running companies that weren't making any money, therefore nobody made any money off the back of it. We've all asked questions about quite where the money went. And the answer is, there was probably no money to go anywhere, but I know a lot of people got quite upset about it." [14] Nigel Fairs is also of the opinion that there was very little money to go around. "There wasn't any money at all. It would be 'here's your fee for the whole thing, will you write the music? Will you do the sound fx? Will you play six parts?' or whatever."[15]

Ayres goes on to discuss the nature of his agreements with both parties. "I hope that both Keith and Bill are aware that with me, I've always said, if there is some money about I'd like a share because I'm contracted to have a share, but I never expected to get rich off these. It would really upset me if I thought they were pocketing everything and I wasn't getting what's due." [16] He remains on good terms with both men. "I do still get the occasional small payment from Bill, even after all these years. And Keith and I got together just a few weeks ago, because he is now going to release a lot of that stuff on DVD and for download and we have come to an agreement on what will happen.. You do have to do the occasional bit of chasing, though!" [17] Ayres should know more than most how the finances of these productions worked, having been a producer on *Shakedown*. "I never made any money off any of them, I never made any money off *Shakedown*. Kevin and I were each on a share of the profits and there were no profits." [18]

It's important to point out that while a small group of the interviewees for this book raised the issue of finance regarding Baggs and BBV, nobody suggested any such issue with Barnfather or Reeltime.

So how does Baggs feel about this vocal group that have questioned his business practices? When the question is put to him, he takes his time to answer. "Well you can't control how people react. Business-wise, there are probably things that I regret, that I would do differently on my own moral compass, but I don't have any regrets, real regrets. I think I've been mainly fair and honest, I mean people will have their own feelings. What I strive for, if somebody pulls out of a project, or decides not to do it, or thinks that I owe them money, or whatever, I think I'm quite an approachable person. I mean I know I'm quite an approachable person, if there's something to be discussed."[19]

And how does he respond to accusations of low rates of pay? "If I offer you a rate and say 'do you want to do a play?' you have to choose, nobody is holding a shotgun to anybody's head. I would like to have been able to offer more, but I have to make some money, you have to make some money and I was providing the finance. If a project was making a lot of money, the rates would be commensurate on that basis and the audios were not making money. The early ones made a lot of money, but the later ones didn't, so what we were paying what was in relation to the performance." [20]

Nick Briggs, for one, feels Baggs' attitude is unacceptable. "I really do think he ought to regret what he did," he says firmly. Indeed, he feels his former colleague's attitude to these matters is completely unjustified. "Goodness knows what he may have done to justify the non- or under-payment of royalties. I personally think it's wrong for him to just forgive himself for that, when I believe he has done something bad. It's all very well to say you can forgive yourself and live without regret, but what about making amends if you've practiced deceit?"[21]

These problems made for a number of damaged relationships, not least with Colin Baker, who in conversation with Nick Briggs in 2013 briefly discussed Baggs. "We will gloss over the perpetrator of those videos, whose rather bizarre attitude is that 'even though DVDs were not invented then... I don't have to pay you for them. I can release them because they didn't exist when you did it, and I can take your house and your family and I can't eat them.'" Briggs seems to agree and jokingly responds, "that is his actual attitude."[22]

Baker concludes by saying "you've just reminded me, I need to have a few conversations with the legal profession about that."[23]

And how does Baggs feel about Baker's attitude towards him? "I don't know, I can hazard some guesses, but it doesn't particularly interest me. I chose to live my life without regret and to strive to see the positive and that's all good." [24]

And his relationship with Briggs? Do the pair stay in touch? "Not really, and that's with some sadness, because we were really good friends. We were very good friends and it's ever since that *Auton 3* thing and it's kind of got very amicable and pleasant, but there's no striving to keep contact."[25]

And what of Briggs' ongoing success? "What always used to tickle me was, it was me and him who made those Dalek voices, so there is a little bit of resentment there. But I'm glad that at least he got something out of it, but what I see is the effort that he has put into something has paid off."[26]

While Briggs once told the Justyce website that he and Baggs had "parted creative company over *Auton 3*, but as I mentioned... we still chat. Bill can be the most annoying person on Earth, but he's a real professional at heart and ultimately will not let working disagreements get in the way of friendships."[27]

Whatever Briggs feelings towards Baggs at the time of the Justyce interview, the effect of Baggs' alleged business malpractice, has been enough to drive a firm wedge between the former friends. When asked if they still had a relationship, Briggs' response is understandably conflicted "No. He seems to have gone through some form of 'rebirth' of his 'spirit' or something. I'm really not quite sure what's happened to him. I've bumped into him a few times and we've always been civil to each other. He has a sort of strange, faraway, spaced-out look in his eyes, which is rather odd. He seems very affectionate and full of love, which he never was when we worked together. He's a real curiosity, that Bill Baggs. I look back to that time when he was a huge part of my life, when every phone call seemed to be from him, when he was always making demands, and I get a profound sense of relief that I have nothing to do with him anymore. But, as I keep saying, in many ways I'm grateful to him too. When I think of him giggling uncontrollably about something silly, it does bring a smile to my face. Bless Bilbo The Bastard Baggins and all his madness. We did have fun."[28]

But ultimately Briggs is happy not be part of Baggs' life any more. "He's such a force of nature, and when you work with him, certainly this was the case, I don't know now and hope never to know, he tries to inhabit every bit of your life. This was the era of phone calls rather than emails and he would contact you in the middle of the night, and so you felt like you could never escape from him."[29]

Baggs is also no longer in touch with Mark Gatiss, who once stated he would never allow *P.R.O.B.E.* to be released on DVD. "One, they're not available. And two, I forbid it. Christ, for all I knew, they were the only things I would ever get to make. And I learned a frightening amount from working on them." [30]

Baggs sees resemblances in his relationships with Gatiss and Briggs. "The same with Mark really, because when you are working with somebody... I've spent days in my boxer shorts sitting with Mark Gatiss, because it's the heat of summer, banging out those things, banging at the key board and then you don't see them and there is some sadness there."[31]

But once again he is happy for his former friend's successes: "it's the same with Mark, he isn't brilliant, but what he's done is, put a lot of effort in and what's coming is the fruit of his efforts." [32]

While it is easy to get side-tracked by these negative accusations, there are many who have positive things to say about Baggs. Gareth Preston describes him in glowing terms. "He's a doer. He goes out and gets things done. As a director he's very calm and assured. I certainly wish I had had his confidence when I was younger. Plus he's given people like me our first break in the business and that is very generous. He's always been friendly and supportive in our conversations."[33]

Lance Parkin too has a certain amount of admiration for him. "Bill has always had the spirit that you just get things done, you try stretching the resources and tell the best, most ambitious stories you can."[34]

Mark Ayres is also mainly positive about their experiences together. "Bill I find great fun, a bit strange around the edges. As I say he cut the one scene in *Zero Imperative* that explained the plot, he did have very odd ideas about editing. But he was full enthusiasm, he spent a few days at our place, when we were doing the sound and making the sound fx, great fun to work with."[35]

Simon Gerard found him a very amicable person. "I always liked Bill and would welcome the chance to do stuff for him, even now. I socialised with Bill and his family sometimes and we'd meet up at conventions too. I liked him and still do. He treated Colin and I fairly and gave us opportunities, encouragement and matching camel coats with fat cigars..."[36]

Harvey Summers, like a number of people, is very grateful to Baggs for giving him his first start in film. "I don't think there were many 17 year olds around at the time scoring films & audio dramas! It was a great start for me and led on to some other great projects. I'll always be grateful to Bill for that first opportunity!"[37]

Sophie Aldred discussed Baggs' best qualities earlier, and she remains incredibly fond of him. "He was a pioneer, doing something that nobody else had taken on." [38]

While opinions of Baggs are mixed, some may have spoken of him more highly had their relationships not ended badly. But it is perhaps the people he worked with and surrounded himself with day to day that can paint the best picture of him.

John Ainsworth found him an enterprising individual with some great qualities "[at] getting things done, definitely, he was brilliant." He goes on to elaborate "He didn't exactly have a schedule, but he didn't want to stand still, so he was always keeping things moving. He was always pushing people; it didn't make him very popular but it did get things done. Which is a great quality particularly when you're asking people to do things for no money or very little money. He manges to get things done so he's a good driving force."[39] Once again though, the two did have some run-ins. "There were things that irritated me, he could be a blunt I suppose. He had very fixed ideas about scripts and drama and perhaps not necessarily be open to other people's interpretations." [40]

Tim Saward, as an aspiring writer, found Baggs' encouragement a strong positive. "In my experience, he was prepared to let people do their thing and find out for themselves what was wrong. But the downside to that was you didn't have very much guidance when things did go wrong. As a person, I just always found him very personable, always interesting to talk about ideas."[41]

Even Briggs can look back at it all with a certain degree of detachment. "What Bill achieved was remarkable, because it was against all reason and all the odds. He tried to bring a dream to life and in order to do that, against the odds and not see the obstacles and just say 'no I'm going to do it' you have to be a very particular, special kind of person and you have to have an incredible drive and some kind of charisma to take people with you and then lead them. So it was incredible, because actually it was all a completely stupid idea, it was silly to do it, but people like myself and even the people who played the Doctors on the telly thought 'well he's offering me a bit of work' and he would have offered them quite a bit of money."

Despite the conflicts Briggs is quick to point out that "it's not all bad. We did have loads of laughs, but he is odd, I mean we're all odd, we're all bonkers in our own particular way I suppose."[42]

Asked to consider why he thought people worked with Baggs, Briggs is only too happy to elaborate. "A lot of people believed, including Colin Baker, because he's mentioned it to me, that Bill was potentially going to be big news one day, and I think that's why a lot of people did it."[43]

It seems the same attitude that got Baggs into trouble latterly also allowed him to get to a decent position in the first place. "People like Colin and maybe even Nicola thought 'oh he's a young film maker, he's got a lot of get up and go' and Bill was able to marshall a lot of people, and he was much younger than most of the people he was dealing with, and I think people admired that determination and a lot of people were quite enamoured. They love that cheeky, aggressive slightly taking the mickey thing."[44]

Bill Baggs certainly ruffled a few feathers during this period, and while it seems clear that he made some bad business decisions, his role in keeping *Doctor Who* alive should not be overlooked. In hindsight, though Baggs' gift of the gab got him a lot of favours some recognisable faces, this gift could only take him so far.

When he failed to deliver on promises (promises that, at the time, he probably thought he could keep), he upset many of the people on whom he relied. By bypassing agents, contracts were not negotiated properly and deals were made hastily and exploitation rights forgone. It also seems that he allowed issues in his personal life to affect his business and there is no doubt at that point he made some rash decisions and arguably wronged a number of people.

While the sales figures for these films are unknown, if indications from Barnfather about his own output are any measure, there was little in the way of profit to share. And Baggs would also have had to recoup the large production costs and make a return on his sizable investment before sharing profits. Perhaps the presence of these films on the high street presented those involved with a false image of large sales figures and a breakout success. In fact these were low budget films that were in shops on a sale or return basis.

Whatever wrongs he has done to people, it is clear that Baggs is a different person now and that he has made peace with himself. It is now up to him if he chooses to try to build bridges and mend relationships with those who feel he owes them something.

Chapter 38 — The Landscape is Changing

In early 2011 a number of writers within the fan press community received a complimentary copy of a newspaper called Radio Static through the post. This mock conspiracy theory periodical was dated two months in the future. Among the various conspiracies the paper covered were several mentions of both Paul McGann and Sylvester McCoy as well as *The Minister of Chance*. The promotional item was a strange one and piqued the interest of a number of media outlets, not least because it gave away very little about the mysterious *Minister of Chance*.

Simultaneously, however, a website, Facebook page and a Twitter account for this new venture also appeared.

The Minister of Chance was in fact a web based audio series from Radio Static featuring a titular character who had originally appeared in the BBC online *Doctor Who* story *Death Comes to Time*, where the part was played by Stephen Fry.

This new series was masterminded by *Death Comes to Time* writer Dan Freeman, who had always planned a series based on the Minister but had failed to get it off the ground after *Death Comes to Time*.

"Given that, at that time, *Doctor Who* had long finished on the BBC, I thought it was best to do what they did with *Star Trek TNG* — to say a fond goodbye to the actual characters and to move ahead with completely new ones, but with a notional continuity — keeping the spirit of the thing. Hence, The Minister."[1]

The original idea was to have Fry reprise the role and although the actor was interested, his schedule meant he couldn't commit. The role instead went to veteran actor of stage and screen, Julian Wadham.

Freeman's first meeting with his potential star had occured some years previously. "Years ago I was working at a studio and I was in the waiting room with another guy sitting opposite quietly. There was something about him I instinctively liked. Then suddenly I shouted 'OH! YOU PLAYED PITT!' I remembered him from *The Madness of King George*, which is one of my all time favourite performances. He was a bit taken aback at this nutcase shouting at him, but then we chatted and that was it, for years. I said I'd love to write something for him and we weren't in contact for ages."[2]

When it became apparent Fry would be unavailable, therefore, Freeman thought of Wadham immediately. "There were more famous names in the frame, but we knew it would take someone with amazing acting chops to step into Fry's shoes. When Julian agreed I was delighted."[3]

For Wadham it was a chance to play a character with a different sensibility to those he had played before. "The Minister appears cold and narcissistic, lacking utterly in feeling and tact, but never in intelligence. I find him beguiling precisely because of his human-like failings. He is full of surprises."

In order to get the series off the ground Freeman needed a reliable production team to help. While a number of roles would be in flux throughout the series, the figure head of the production was producer Clare Eden, who was introduced to Freeman through a mutual friend. She later discussed her role with Steven Sautter.

"When you want to produce a series you also need a nuts and bolts person, usually with sharp pencils and a phone — he's the architect but he needed someone to help him build it and when you hear him talk about his vision it's easy to find yourself thinking, mm, I think I could help achieve that..."[4]

The first instalment of *Minister of Chance* appeared in March 2011 in the form of a nine-minute prologue featuring Jenny Agutter as Professor Cantha, Isobel Collingwood as Princess Didi, Lauren Crace as Kitty, Lloyd Hutchinson in the role of Meninm, Mark Lewis as The King and Paul McGann as Durian. This last role was originally offered to another sci-fi luminary, according to Freeman.

"I did conceive Durian with Anthony Daniels in mind," he told Greg Jameson. "He is a very fine actor with a beautiful voice, but he couldn't do it because of *Star Wars Live*, so we were very lucky to get Paul McGann. The reason is that, as my neighbour Alan once said — conmen are always nice people. Baddies very often look nice, and sound nice. They're rarely warty old hags who cackle! I like the fact that Paul is all charm and handsome, whilst he's doing terrible things."[5]

'The Pointed Hand' makes for an excellent teaser for the series. Paul McGann plays a character who at first appears to be similar to his incarnation of the Doctor but when he reveals his true intentions, his calm nature and the actor's soft spoken delivery render his performance all the more sinister. Mark Lewis's performance as the King is perhaps a little over the top, but all round the production is a pleasing start to the series.

With appetites suitably whetted, Freeman went about putting together the first episode, with the funding coming out of his own pockets. This episode would boast an impressive cast — joining McGann and Wadham would be Paul Darrow as Lord Rathen and Sylvester McCoy as the Witch Prime, with the newcomers keeping the rest of the cast amused according to Freeman. "McCoy and Darrow are great comedians so there are a lot of jokes going to and fro."[6] McCoy had met Freeman when they recorded *Death Comes to Time* and was pleased to be playing against type. "I said that I wanted to be a villain. They're much more fun. Having played a superhero for such a long time, it's kind of nice to be a nasty villain."[7]

Also on board was *Hyperdrive* star Petra Massey as Gurk, as well as Stuart Fox playing Porcher, Richard Garaghty as Match Werming, Lloyd Hutchinson in the role of Menin, Kane Sharpe portraying Rosta and Gareth Jones as Corporal Sona.

Another actor making a return was Lauren Crace as Kitty, who could briefly be heard at the start of the prologue. She was brought in to audition by Clare Eden. "Clare told me about this pretty blonde actress from *Eastenders* who she thought was great, and I couldn't have been less interested," Freeman recalls. "Then I met Lauren, and I was struck by her maturity and authority, so within a couple of minutes I took her very seriously. Then when she auditioned (along with some other incredible talent)... I remember literally looking at Clare and rolling my eyes while Lauren was talking, I just couldn't believe how hilarious and clever her performance was. She makes me laugh even though I wrote the lines!"[8]

Freeman also had initial reservations about Lauren Crace, little knowing that the actress too had doubts about doing science fiction. "I was initially a little dubious about having to read an entire sci-fi script as I'm more of a 'kitchen sink drama' girl myself, but I absolutely loved it! I was immediately hooked by the storyline and found myself laughing out loud. It's full of great characters — that's what drew me to it the most!"

With the cast now in place, recording got under way, with the initially hesitant Freeman soon finding his stride. "You're always nervous at first because you don't know how it's going to go, but again, as the recording went on we knew we were onto something good."[9]

Thanks to the experienced cast the recording session was an enjoyable event for everyone involved. "The whole cast are very easygoing and game and up for it, which is fantastic," explains Freeman. "They all get on well too, it's great to see the Macs working together because they know each other of old, and Julian and Lauren get on really, really well which is lovely to see. I can honestly say it's a really fun atmosphere."[10]

Episode One, 'The Broken World', was released in March 2011 at the download price of £1.49. Shadowlocked.com called this first instalment "lively, witty, beautifully rendered and splendidly cast""[11] — an apt description of this unusual expansion of the *Doctor Who* universe. Pitched somewhere between *Discworld* and 'Battlefield' the play poses the question of the value of magic vs science within the *Doctor Who* mythos. It is clearly aimed at a broader audience than any of the previous spin-offs, being accessible to genre fans of all types, not just those who known their Quarks from their Krotons. The world on offer is steeped in fresh ideas and colourful characters that grab the listener from the get go and presents some interesting plot threads that will be explored in further instalments.

The second episode of *The Minister of Chance* saw all the major cast returning, to be joined by *Game of Thrones* star Gethin Anthony as Sutu, Peter Guinness as the Horseman, Jay Taylor as Ilias, Luke Carroll as Private Merat, Andrew Martyn-Lewis as Private Devian and Rachel Spicer playing Kitty's Mother.

While the series was attracting a high calibre of actors, financing the production proved to be an issue, as Freeman told Mike Hickerson. "The challenges in making this are mainly financial, that's a massive hurdle. No one is commissioning these in advance. There's also the factor of being able to get a cast like that in one place at one time, luckily we have Clare Eden who could organize a tea party in a war."

Freeman went on to discuss the business model behind the project. "We made the episodes really cheap so that anyone will feel that they can buy it, so that's the main way, just buy the episodes. Audio is so easy to copy and everyone does it, so we're incredibly grateful when people buy the show. We've also got the amazing posters by Lee Sullivan and our T-Shirts, so just buying the stuff funds production. We're not like a studio or a network, we simply don't have any money at all, so people are literally buying more life for the series."[12]

The second episode, 'The Forest Shakes', was released on 13 January 2012 priced at £1.29 (with the price of the previous episode also lowered to match this). The wired.com website was in high praise of this episode saying, "The dialogue is still brilliant and witty. The soundscapes are rich, lush and elaborate; transporting you to another world, one that you can not only hear but see, feel, smell and taste. The action is fast-paced, moving forward with tremendous speed."[13]

It is fantastic addition to the series that delivers more action than its predecessor. Occasionally the action becomes a little hard to follow but that is a minor criticism. The world it creates is so delightfully prodigious, that it leaves the listener enthralled from beginning to end. And while this may be a *Doctor Who* spin-off, it isn't simply *Doctor Who*-lite. *The Minister of Chance* actually provides a compelling alternative to the show that inspired it.

For the third episode a change in the way the series was funded would have a huge impact on the success of the series. Executive producer Eden suggested utilising the fairly new platform of crowdfunding, though Freeman was initially resistant.

"I rejected the idea out of hand, I thought it seemed kind of cheap and unprofessional. But then I looked again and saw how it actually worked, and I couldn't have been more wrong. I hope I never have to use another means of funding ever again. It's FANTASTIC! It means that you don't have any interference from any studios, any commissioners, there are no interminable delays, no middle-men. It also means that you're in contact with the audience and the fans in a really important and special way. It's like building an Amish barn together. It's just amazing when someone donates, an incredible feeling.'

Eden too was pleased with the freedom that crowdfunding offered. "The commissioning process can be very frustrating and there is no doubt that it is liberating to be able to make something because we think it'll be good — and to make it the way we want to. But it doesn't mean we're not answerable to anyone, we're answerable to a heap of people who have invested their very hard earned cash into becoming Minister Moguls. It's fantastic to be in direct contact with its audience and to experience their phenomenal support, and both Dan and I feel a real sense of responsibility in making that support count."[14]

McCoy too was excited to be part of a project that had such direct interface with its audience. "I thought it was a wonderful adventure, breaking new ground. Something very new. It's getting rid of lots of middle men, and it gets you closer to the fans. They can fund it, by listening to it. That seems to me wonderful, not just for drama, but for other things. It's a great experiment, and I hope it works!"[15]

This new funding platform meant a rebranding for the series and the first two episodes were made available for free from iTunes. The series' new tagline was now "A WORLD WHERE A TIME-LORD IS A HERETIC..." This was the first overt reference to *Doctor Who* the series had made, and in an interview with *Geek Crash Course* Freeman discussed the technicalities of the copyright situation with the BBC.

"The weird thing is that there aren't any licensing issues. He's officially a Time Lord according to the BBC, but I own him. He doesn't have a TARDIS (it was revoked when he fought the Doctor in *Death Comes to Time*) and we don't use the Daleks or any properties owned by outside parties."[16]

The cast for this third episode, 'Paludin Fields', added a further star name to its ranks in the form of Tamsin Greig as the Sage of the Waves. Freeman was thrilled to have the actress on board. "She was funny, extremely easy to get on with, absolutely professional and just got on with it. She was very thorough, she quizzed me for about an hour in the studio before we recorded a word. We are a really friendly bunch and we treat the recording as a party. She was amused that the first thing we did was guide her round the various cakes we'd brought along. I was so pleased with her performance."[17]

Other new cast members included Daniel Easton as Corrio, Beth Goddard playing Sunflower, Simon Hickson as Gallichan, Frances Tomelty in the part of the Seer, Kevin Baldwin as Keep, Kemi Bo Jacobs as Estris,

George A Murphy playing Sherred the Pimp and Richard Oliver was The Executioner Duall with a surprise cameo from Sophie Aldred as Polichar.

'Paludin Fields' was released on the 20th July 2012 with *Radio Drama Reviews* describing the soundscape as "truly breathtaking in its scope, combining music, effects and echoes to create a genuinely unsettling world."[18]

While the review is right to praise the sound design, the episode does suffer from a number of sequences in which it is impossible to decipher what is happening, thanks to a lack of dialogue. Which is a shame as the story is another great continuation of the ever-evolving plot, building on the themes of science vs magic, political intrigue and the all-knowing Time Lord. The mystery behind Kitty's origins are once again brought to the listener's attention and the identity of the Horseman also makes for a perplexing puzzle. The tension within the series mounts nicely and with questions building it's impossible to guess where the series will go next.

No sooner had the dust settled on episode three, than episode four began pre-production. The fourth instalment was once again crowdfunded via IndieGoGo with the minimum budget set at just over £10,000. Fundees were offered a number of perks including the chance to say a line in the episode, signed script pages, T-shirts, posters and the chance to have a character named after them.

In October of 2012 Freeman told Greg Jameson what fans could expect from the new episode. "I've just had the script back from Jonathan Barnes (Script Editor) and Clare Eden (Exec Producer) and they said it's very fast and exciting, and shocking. Let's say that some actors aren't having their contracts renewed, which is really sad, but we've got to stick to what makes the story work."[19] In the same interview he laid out his intentions to make a feature film version of the series.

Episode four, like those before it, was recorded at RADA. Lauren Crace discussed with the *Preachers Podcast* what a typical recording day on *The Minister of Chance* consisted of. "The day normally begins about 9.30am where we catch up and scoff our faces with biscuits Dan's wife has baked. Eventually we get started (normally behind schedule), working through the list of scenes Clare has put together for that day. It's always a very relaxed process. Some scenes naturally come together very quickly and we will record them in a couple of takes and some may take longer. We always end the day with a pint or two in the local pub."[20]

Episode four, 'The Tiger', was released on March 1st 2013. Reviews were once again positive with Tony Jones of *Starburst* magazine saying "the production values are superb, the direction and acting top-notch and waiting for the final part a regrettable necessity."[21]

'The Tiger' is another strong episode that reaches a tense climax for all involved. The answers to the questions the series has presented are satisfactory and the reveal of Rathan being behind it all is an unexpected twist. However, it is in these twists that the problems lie, as the plot is basically a retread of Freeman's previous work, *Death Comes to Time* and while it may be wrapped up in a fantasy overall, it is still plain to anyone who knows it that they have heard it all before. Which is a shame as this seemingly unique series loses a little of its individuality through doing so.

The final instalment of the series would once again be crowdfunded and the team offered a wide range of new perks, including a personalised message recorded by Paul Darrow or Sylvester McCoy for purchasers' answering machines, T-shirts, baseball caps, beanie hats, mugs, iPhone cases, autographs, postcards and scripts.

Episode five, 'In a Bark on the River Hex', saw the addition of two new guests stars in the guise of *Lord of The Rings* star Jed Brophy as Pilot and *Life on Mars*' Philip Glenister as the Summer King.

"I am terrifically proud of the cast we've assembled for this," Eden explains of the tremendous collection of acting talent, "and mostly it just required a good deal of nerve! I worked for many years as an agent and one thing I held onto firmly was that my clients found it hard to resist a quality script even if it did come with a bonkers budget. So we simply thought who we'd like to be in it, I approached their agents and we held our breath. Creating audio drama for release like this is a very innovative idea and fortunately the concept and Dan's script piqued the interest of a superb cast! I was also able to introduce Dan to some really good actors that had been clients when I was an agent, and we have been able to work with several very young actors I know because they were Bursary students with the John Thaw Foundation which I run for Sheila Hancock."[22]

'In a Bark on the River Hex' was released on the 17th May 2013, with *Red Rocket Rising* describing it as having "the usual splendid set of performances from a writer who knows how to weave a legend."[23]

Sadly, while the actors all seem to be on point, the finale is once again a rehash of *Death Comes to Time*. It's hard to know what to make of it, as the episode crams a lot in yet feels too drawn out. Quite why the Summer King and the River Hex are needed beyond some brief exposition remains to be seen. As with previous episodes there are also numerous occasions where there is too little done to explain what actually is happening. Ultimately, the listener is left with the feeling that this would work much better on screen than in audio.

Shortly after the release of the final episode of *The Minister of Chance*, Radio Static announced they would shortly be crowdfunding a movie version of the series. The aim was to produce the movie in four parts, with the first instalment costing £100,000.

Despite it being four years since the series started, Crace was aware of the plans from the very beginning. "I knew it was something Dan always wanted to do. He mentioned it in my very first audition. But because of the format of this series (the fact we rely on crowd funding) means we never know what the next stage will be. I would love to take *The Minister of Chance* to the next level. The Minister and Kitty are such a great double act. I think it's time people got to 'see' them."[24]

The Kickstarter page opened funding on 1st July 2013 and raised over £15,000 in its first day. However by its closing date of October 31st the campaign had failed to move beyond the £50,000 mark, prompting a rethink in strategy for Freeman and co.

As part of this, a Prologue for the film was shot at Little Moreton Hall in Cheshire in October 2013. Based on the Prologue that originally preceded the audio series, Paul McGann returned as Durian with Tim McInnerny playing the King. Simon Bugg also featured as Major Apper, with Beccy Meany as the Spider Guard, Richard Oliver as the Spider, Scribble as Princess Didi and Lee Oulton as the Segway Rider.

Released in February of 2014, the film was initially available to view only to the crowdfunders and then to those who purchased a "cinema ticket" online, before eventually being released for free. The *Who-natic* blog called the film "very professional, very slick and very impressive."[25]

For the most part this is an accurate summary; the five minute prequel (with a further five minutes of credits) demonstrates that the *Minister of Chance* universe works well in a visual medium. The locations, special effects, props and costume design are all excellent. Equally importantly, Tim McInnery gives a much more reserved performance than his predecessors did, and the production is better off for it.

If there is one criticism, however, it is that the film is let down by its hardware — specifically, the camera used appears to be a DLSR, which leaves the film looking cheap and amateur.

Although their initial attempt at crowd funding the movie proved unsuccessful, the Radio Static Team still plan to make the move to the big screen.

In November 2014 a second audio series was announced for the following year and a new investment scheme was launched where fans could buy shares in the film for just £20 a unit. The investment scheme was spearheaded by a new Executive Producer, Rob Graham, who had previously worked on the financing of the BAFTA Cymru Award winningmovie *The Machine*.

The relaunched Radio Static website later began offering investment from £50 upwards, with Graham Associates taking care of the investment and the website stating that a large crowd funding campaign would take place once £10,000 had been raised. As of August 2015 the investment campaign had raised £10,389. A crowdfunding campaign then took place in several stages, the first two stages were successfully funded by donations via PayPal with various perks still available. Stage 3 was then listed as coming soon. As of September 2015 all efforts of the team were on crowdfunding their new audio series 'The Light of September'. Although it also saw the website advertising the tax relief options that any potential investor would receive if they invested in *The Minister of Chance* film. By December there was no mention of Stage 3 of the funding campaign on the Radio Static website, but it did offer a download and CD release of the director's cut of *The Minister of Chance* Prologue and first episode, remastered, re-scored and reworked. With the movie still touted to start filming in Spring 2016. By November 2016 the Radio Static content had moved over to Dan Freeman's personal website and while no mention of a movie was made, Freeman was now crowdfunding a novel of the series at £250 a chapter.

However as of the November 2016 the Radio Static website stated "The full movie is scripted, budgeted and scheduled, and we're looking for a producer."

The Minister of Chance offered a very different take on the *Doctor Who* universe, so different in fact it can barely be called a *Doctor Who* spin-off at all. The series is quite clearly set in an entirely different universe to *Doctor Who,* the use of magic doorways instead of a TARDIS being one of the many not so subtle changes. Radio Static may have clearly used its *Who*-related origins as a selling point when launching the series, but at its heart *The Minister of Chance* is a more fantasy heavy series, that feels more in tune with the work of Terry Pratchett than that of Terrance Dicks...

Chapter 39 — There is a Light That Never Goes Out

With the independent *Doctor Who* spin-off evolving beyond its parent show and with the original pioneers of the genre taking a leave of absence, it seemed that the industry was all but dead. However, as *Doctor Who*'s fiftieth anniversary approached some of the old guard would rear their heads once again.

First off the mark was Magic Bullet, who released a short *Kaldor City* audio play, 'Metafiction', in summer 2012. Written by Alan Stevens and Fiona Moore as a stage play, it was initially performed at the Sci-Fi London Film Festival in 2011.

The production was a two-hander between Paul Darrow and Patricia Merrick that was very well received. "The actors were picking up on the energy of the audience, and it really affected their performance," Moore reminisces. "I was initially worried because I knew we would be going in front of people who might not be that familiar with *Kaldor City*, or *Blake's 7*, but Paul Darrow and Patricia Merrick pitched it very well and so the audience understood what was going on, even if they didn't know the backstory between the two characters."[1]

It was the reception of this production that sparked the audio adaptation, according to Stevens. "'Metafiction' had received such a response from the audience at the event, I decided it record it together with two other productions I was also planning: *The Time Waster* and *Radio Bastard*."[2]

'Metafiction' was recorded at Brighton Acoustic on 14th December 2011 with Paul Darrow reprising his role of Iago and Patricia Merrick once again playing Justina. The play was released as a download only on 7th July 2012 and also featured an alternate ending that linked the series to *The Time Waster.*

Seemingly set between 'Occam's Razor' and 'Death's Head', the story sees Justina questioning Iago over his past. As Iago is telling his tale, it becomes apparent to the listener he is actually recounting the story of *Blake's 7* from the perspective of Kerr Avon. While it seems this is revealing that Iago and Avon are meant to be the same character, when Justina asks Iago what his real name is, one version of the play has him replying "Paul Darrow."

On the surface, 'Metafiction' seems nothing more than an amusing skit that pokes fun at the series and at its influences, but Iago's alternative reply of "Frank Archer" suggests something much deeper and more disturbing, as Stevens explains.

"Frank Archer is the time-travelling Detective Inspector who, in his bid to fight crime, duplicates himself seventy-one times, and, during one timeline iteration, sparks off World War Three. The fact that his wife is played by Tracy Russell and the story ends with her trying to assassinate him is no accident. If Paul Darrow is Kerr Avon/Kaston Iago/Frank Archer, then Tracy Russell can also be Sheila Archer/Elska Blayes, and even maybe Elise Kapsanis from 'The Logic of Empire'."

The Time Waster then leads into *Radio Bastard*, with both plays set in the fictional county of East Langford, and with both Frank Archer and Detective Inspector Gregory Simmons from *The Time Waster* making an appearance. Simmons is played by Trevor Cooper, who also appeared in *Kaldor City* as Stenton Rull and 'The Logic of Empire' as Kelso.

Finally, *Radio Bastard* concerns a mad scientist trying to destroy the world with killer robots, so the meta-narrative isn't just about identity confusion, but also memes, archetypes and repeated patterns. The Fendahl didn't so much destroy the world as lead us into a mirrored prism from which a new reality was constructed."[3]

Reeltime Pictures too resurfaced in the anniversary year, as Keith Barnfather announced his first drama production since *Daemos Rising*, itself a celebration for the fortieth anniversary.

Entitled *The White Witch of Devils End*, it would once again be a sequel to 'The Daemons' and involve writer David J. Howe. The project would be produced by Keith Barnfather and directed by his partner Anastasia Stylianou. It would also feature the return of Damaris Hayman, now well into her eighties reprising her role as Miss Hawthorne from 'The Daemons.'

The idea for the production initially came from several encounters Barnfather had with Hayman.

"We did an interview with Damaris Hayman for one of our *Myth Makers*, 'Flight Through Eternity'. I was just struck by this amazing mature woman, with this mind that just wants to carry on working. Then because we could have done a much longer interview with her, we phoned her up and said 'can we come and do your *Myth Makers*?' and Anastasia and I went to see her, we spent the day up at her house and recorded her *Myth Makers*. And while we were doing it, we were talking and she was just basically saying 'I'd love to do something else' and how much she loved doing 'The Daemons'. For her she feels it is the best thing she ever did."

With this in mind Barnfather and Stylianou formulated a plan for Hayman to reprise her role. "I rang her up and said 'look I've not got anything specific yet, but if we were thinking about doing something, would you be interested in doing this?" and she just said 'yes' straight away, so then it was a question of what we were going to do."[4]

With Hayman unable to walk and only having the energy to act a few minutes at a time Barnfather and Stylianou, in conjunction with Howe, hit on the idea of doing a talking heads' piece.

"He wanted to do it like the Alan Bennett *Talking Heads*," Howe reveals, "with Damaris telling stories of her life as the White Witch of Devils End. He wanted a number of different writers involved, he wanted different stories and stuff. So I discussed this with my partner, the author Sam Stone, and together we discussed the writers and we basically came up with a number of writers. All of who we knew had a good affinity for a white witch, that element of nature and the way of living and all of that kind of thing, so we contacted the authors and pulled the whole script together."[5]

The authors in question were Raven Dane, Debbie Bennett, Jan Edwards, and Suzanne J Barbieri, with final script-editing duties being performed by Big Finish writer, Matt Fitton.

The shoot took place in summer of 2013, at a cottage thirty miles from Hayman's home. The team shot one piece a day, every day for a week. Hayman seemed in good spirits, as she relayed via the films press release. "I shall retire, I think, in my coffin! Miss Hawthorne was my all-time favourite role and I was enchanted by the thought of being her again for a little while. After a lot of working together, consulting over the scripts, I'd subsequently never enjoyed filming more, and I can't wait now to see the final result."[6]

Once filming was complete they also returned to the village of Aldbourne in Wiltshire, where the original *Doctor Who* story was filmed, for a further day's shoot linking the character and location.

It was planned to film a number of illustrative cutaways, and then to release the film on Halloween 2013. However, things didn't quite go according to plan.

"This is almost like a docudrama," Barnfather explains. "Every piece, half of it is cut away drama. Half of what she says we want to visualise those things happening, or allude to those things. So there's a three to five day shoot in Aldbourne, that we have to do."[7]

Unfortunately Reeltime's heavy workload (and the birth of Keith and Anastasia's son) has meant this keeps getting postponed. "We've been so busy," discloses Barnfather. "We've just had a broadcast television series show in Cyprus [and] we are in the middle of filming another one in Cyprus. We are doing another one of our lost trains series, which we are now doing in Malta. I've got another set of videos to do for Moorfields Eye Hospital and we are trying to relaunch the entire website with all of our back catalogue, so we are remastering everything."[8] As of November 2016 *The White Witch of Devils End* is due for release in November 2017 via Koch Media, who have recently re-released a number of Reeltime titles onto the highstreet. The delay has also caused Barnfather to rethink his initial concept. Initially planned as a 50 minute film, when the first edit was assembled, it came in at two hours and five minutes.

Plans to cut it down however, did not work out. "I was going to have to really get ruthless," Barnfather admits, "and I tried... and realised we can't cut it down, because the script is the script, and you start chopping the script, it doesn't make sense." [9]

This problem led to an ingenious solution. "What we've decided to do now is to turn it into a series. So it's going to be a series of five or six episodes. And we are going to do it like a *Doctor Who*, not with a cliffhanger but with a voice over at the beginning saying 'My name is Olive Hawthorne, I am the White Witch of Devils End.' So you watch episode one, which is one little story, you watch episode two and it's another little story and actually it will probably be a lot better."[10]

Barnfather is hopeful about this new format. "We shall release one a week for six weeks on the website and then issue the DVD. And actually that might be a blueprint for things in the future. If that goes down well we might consider doing something similar."

The DVD has been available for pre-order from *Doctor Who* retailers Galaxy 4 since its announcement in 2013. The continued delay forced Barnfather to issue a statement apologising to customers.

The release is also set to contain the documentary *Return to Devils End* and a *Making Of* feature. Now scheduled for release in early 2017, it will be interesting to see how Reeltime's drama output has moved on in the last ten years and if there is still a market for this sort of drama.

While Reeltime's return to the world of *Doctor Who* drama was still in limbo, BBV also made an unexpected announcement in late 2014 that a new *P.R.O.B.E.* film was due the following year.

A full seven years had passed since *Zygon* was released and even longer since it had actually been filmed. This time Baggs would be acting in the capacity of writer, director and producer.

So what drew him back to the *Doctor Who* fold after so long? "As I said, thinking my career path had changed, in terms of going into a healing thing, well, actually the need and the urge to make another film [was still there]. I just thought, I just want to write something myself, entirely on my own rather than rewriting other people's stuff."[11]

Initially this led to Baggs going back right to the beginning. "I started by rewriting another episode of *The Stranger*. What I was going to do was re-write, start again, but with the Soloman character again. Because one of the minor dissatisfactions with 'Terror Game' was that it packed too much into too short a space. So it warranted unpacking it and doing it again, but I was unsatisfied and it didn't work, it wasn't going anywhere. So I thought how about another *P.R.O.B.E.* story? Caroline [John] had died and I just thought there was still life in that, and it would be nice to do something, kind of in honour of her and the work that we'd done. and also a bit more up to date. So it was an experiment to see if I could actually write it on my own, so I wrote it and it took me about a year to write." [12]

'When To Die' featured a cast of unknowns, with Hazel Burrows taking on the role of Liz Shaw, Georgette Ellison playing Patricia Haggard (a role previously played by Louise Jameson), Peter Ward as Corporal 7891A, Marcus Kinsella as Bennet, Neil Gwynne as Major Johnson, Clare Groome as Josie and the author himself playing Giles.

Baggs pulled his cast from several local amateur dramatics groups he had been working with in the Southampton area. "Some of the actors in there, if they wanted to, they could be professional. But for whatever reason, they chose not to, or some of them have aspirations to do that, and I just thought there is a ready made pool of actors to use and some of them are fucking brilliant. So I thought it's not going to cost me anything, certainly not upfront, because we are doing it profit share and I bought myself a camera, a new DVS HD camera, and even cast myself in it, which was a challenge filming that." [13]

The character of Liz Shaw is a BBC copyrighted character. Did he have to renegotiate with the BBC?"

"Of course," he replies with a smile. "I have a piece of paper that says I can use the Liz Shaw character." Then, referring to the initial permission he was given in 1994, he goes onto to say that "nobody has given me a piece of paper to say I haven't got the Liz Shaw character. I work on the basis that unless somebody says no... I don't think anybody cares ... When I was producing the Professor and Ace, nobody at the BBC gave a shit; it was only because somebody from fandom rubbed their nose in it." [14]

It seems that Baggs is simply taking a chance that the initial permission he was given remains valid.

Unfortunately, the film isn't the success that Baggs was hoping for, with the entire production having a distinctly amateur feel. The camera work lacks any originality and the camera on which it is filmed seems to be the sort used for news or live events, rather than drama, meaning that the images are flat and are only a couple of levels up from that of a smart phone. Any lighting seems to be entirely natural, so the images suffer even more.

If Baggs was hoping to make a statement about his skills as a director then he fails. The film really needs a decent Director of Photography and some technical know how to make it work. The cast are mediocre at best, and do little but cement the am-dram feel of the production, with Hazel Burrows' Liz Shaw doing little to convince the viewer that this is the same woman played by Caroline John. The standout performance is actually Baggs as Shaw's likeable sidekick — perhaps he may yet have a career of some merit in that area.

All this is a shame, as the script is rather good, with Baggs also proving he has some worth as a writer. Once again though Baggs demonstrates that his films are only as good as the people around him, and the people involved in this film simply don't have what it takes to make high end drama.

While Baggs' first venture back into the world of film may not have been the advancement he was hoping for, he nevertheless has further projects in the pipeline, including a return of *The Stranger* and a romantic comedy.

Barnfather too has another project lined up once *The White Witch of Devils End* is finally released "We've licensed from David Fisher the concept of 'The Stones of Blood.' So I can use the Ogri, I can use Hyperspace, I can use the Stones. The thing that sold me most is the Stones, because I think we could do something not particularly expensive with a bit of CGI, like somebody being trapped between two Stones and now we could envelop them in the Stones very easily, and that could look quite horrific."[15] While there is currently no writer attached, Barnfather sees this as an opportunity to broaden his appeal. "I want to make a horror short for the international film market, but I want to shoot at least double the amount of material, packaging it as a *Doctor Who* video as well. So it will probably be an 18. I'm actually going to go for something a little bit more hard hitting and therein will be a *Doctor Who* story. But there will also be an edited down short to go on the international short film market and I've never done that before and I'm looking forward to it." [16]

2015 also saw the launch of Reeltime Pictures' new website, Time Travel TV, which features remastered DVD, streaming and download versions of Reeltime's back catalogue, including their drama releases and the *Myth Makers* range. The website also features a range of new *Myth Maker* releases.

Another abandoned BBV release may also yet see the light of day. Jon Blum's *The I Job*, a sequel to Lance Parkin's *I Scream,* originally due to be part of the fourth series of *Audio Adventures in Time and Space* and then offered to Magic Bullet but rejected due to its length, has now been re-worked from its initial 75 minute script, as Blum explains.

"It's 90% of the way through post, and only waiting for me to stop working 60–70-hour weeks at my day job!"[17]

Produced by Australian company Mezzacotta Productions, in 2013 the official website called it "A crime caper in space ... 'like *Blake's Seven* meets *Ocean's Eleven*', [which] aims to offer a *Doctor Who*ish combination of thrills, cleverness and scariness, coupled with the humour which Mezzacotta producers David Morgan-Mar and the Comic Irregulars are known for."[18]

The audio's Facebook group stated the first episodes would be premiered at Chicago TARDIS in December 2013, but as of January 2016 the website has been down for some time, and the Facebook group was last updated in November 2013.

The success or otherwise of these new dramas is yet to be seen. The advancement in digital technology over the last decade means filmmaking can now be relatively inexpensive and while there are numerous *Doctor Who* fan films on YouTube it seems odd that nobody has attempted to mount anything of larger scale, something which bewilders Barnfather.

"It's been rather disappointing that we came along when it was really difficult and did what we did, but now there's no-one doing what we did. I don't get it, I don't understand why. I mean I appreciate from the licensing and the professional side of it, you do need to get your licence sorted out. But you don't have to make a *Doctor Who* spin-off by getting licences, there are ways of using *Doctor Who* characters and alluding to *Doctor Who* characters and conceptualise, but no one is bothering and that really surprises me."

Baggs is also surprised, although he feels it may be due to Big Finish's hold on the small market place. "I'm surprised Big Finish have never embarked onto video, although video is expensive, maybe they've saturated the market for everything."[19]

In a 2010 interview with Christian Cawley, Nick Briggs expressed his amazement at recent advances in technology. Commenting on a recent fan film that he had seen, he admitted that "it wasn't half bad. The guy who was playing the Doctor was actually pretty good! I think he was American. And the girl was absolutely, proper, film star drop-dead gorgeous. The CGI wasn't bad either. I seem to remember the script was a bit off. But, of course, the incredible technology that's available to amateur film makers can give such a polished look now. God, I would've loved some of that technology to be available when we were doing *Auton* and *Auton II*, the straight-to-video dramas I directed."[20]

In fact, one fan film was produced on a professional level that, although not part of this book's remit, nonetheless demonstrates what can be achieved by a fan production should someone wish to embark on a low budget spin-off venture.

'Power of The Daleks: Reimagined' was the brain child of Rob Thrush and TNT Films, a group of fans and media professionals who had previously produced stage adaptations of 'The Web of Fear', 'The Dalek Masterplan' and 'The Evil of the Daleks'.

After the success of these three plays they hoped to do a further dramatised production of 'The Power of the Daleks', as Thrush recalls. "The BBC made it clear that we weren't going to be allowed to do 'Power' on stage, so we decided to do it as a film. I therefore decided that if I was going to co-direct and film it, then we might as well pull out all the stops, so we threw the resources of TNT Films behind it and my business partner, Dave Tozer, did a great job behind the scenes on the technical side. Nick [Scovell, who played the Doctor and co-produced] brought in

Nick Briggs, Barnaby Edwards and Lisa Bowerman through his Big Finish work and so it came to pass. The end result was very pleasing, and went down well at conventions round the world."[21]

With the technology available why does Thrush think there aren't more professionally produced *Doctor Who* spin-offs?

"'Power' ate up almost two years of my free time and I was exhausted by the end of it. You have to have that sort of commitment to produce something of quality, allied to a good set of skills, especially if you're doing almost everything yourself. Martin Johnson provided a great original score which added real gloss, but when you're asking people to do something for nothing you can't be surprised when people who initially want to help can't find time and you're back to doing it all yourself. Proud as I am of 'Power', I wouldn't do something on that scale myself again.

"The other thing is that so many of the films are written, directed and starring just one person, and I'm sorry, but you have to be truly exceptional to pull that off and 99% of film makers aren't that good. I valued having the mix of creative people around me. Nick scripted, I edited the script. Nick oversaw the actors and I directed in front of the camera. Dave suggested the basic 'looks' for the lighting, I had a really good First Assistant who ran the floor and made sure we had everything in the can. My other half was Script Supervisor. I had a good Art Department, so the load was spread around and everyone had a say and an input. Not forgetting those who built the seven amazing Daleks we had on set!" [22]

Despite being well received, 'Power of The Daleks: Reimagined' was removed from YouTube at the request of the BBC, much to the bemusement of Thrush.

"I've not been able to get a definite answer on [the reason for its removal]. There was speculation that the originals had been found, but that's unlikely. Another whisper from within the BBC is that it's TOO polished and some confusion between the real series and our efforts might exist, but somehow that doesn't ring true either. There were a lot of column inches and web comment written about us and perhaps it was felt that we were deflecting attention from the series. Who knows? I DO know that Character Options are producing an NSD Dalek in the 'Power' colour scheme as an homage to us, so we're edging towards being canon! Looks like we're destined to become a 'lost classic' ourselves. But maybe one day..."[23]

The removal of 'Power of the Daleks: Reimagined' perhaps demonstrates one major hurdle that any potential film makers looking to cash in on the *Doctor Who* brand would face.

With the BBC now more protective of the show and its brand. Mark Ayres is of the opinion that any fan spin-off would not be tolerated by the BBC.

"I think the BBC would quite rightly stomp all over it. They are using all the characters, I don't know what their deal with people like the Robert Holmes estate on things like the Sontarans is, they may have done an exclusive deal. That's what I would do, I would make sure only we could use them, but I don't know whether that's the case or not."[24]

Daniel O'Mahony thinks that for newcomers it's more about being seen and carving out an identity. "The big problem for anyone coming into the *Doctor Who* audio world today would be standing out among this proliferation of very niche spin-off series. A range as strong as *Kaldor City* could easily prosper now if it was given the chance to establish itself — but getting started and getting noticed is the problem!"[25]

Gary Russell however, does see an outlet for new ventures, if they can acquired or get around a licence. "These days a lot of similar stuff would probably start on YouTube (itself an interesting creative outlet and, I believe, probably the future of the industry finding new talent) or via Kickstarter/pledge-style financing."[26]

Kaldor City's Jim Smith agrees, in the main, with Russell. "If somebody is going to do that kind of stuff in *Doctor Who* now, it's not going to be 30 year old men making things in studios in London to appeal to an audience of a few thousand 30 year old men. It's going to be something like a 19 year old girl in a basement in Alabama, who creates animated gifs, or something, which redefine the way we think about these characters. If my generation of fans could work how it was going to happen we'd do it. We can't. We're too old."

Though Big Finish continues to expand its catalogue with new spin-off ranges including *The Diary of River Song* and *The Churchill Years*, the future of further fan made spins-offs remains unknown. Perhaps Reeltime's web series will open up new possibilities for the genre, or *The I Job* will finally appear and encourage a new group of film-makers.

Whatever happens, *Doctor Who* continues to inspire fans to create, with the internet teeming with cartoons, animations, fan films and spoofs. So it is perhaps just a question of an entrepreneurial youngster taking advantage of new technologies and new distribution methods, in order to create spin-offs for the next generation of fans.

After all, that's how it all started.

Chapter 40 — Cut Here

Despite the minor revival that is currently taking place, the uninitiated fan might be forgiven for thinking that many of the productions discussed in this book are rooted firmly in the past. They might seem to have receded into fan lore as relics of a forgotten time, when *Doctor Who* as a brand was unloved and an all-American reboot was the best return that fans could hope for.

Video productions in particular have been seen as not having stood the test of time. For example, the once bustling online community of the Outpost Gallifrey forum had an entire section dedicated to these productions. But when that site shut down in 2007, its successor, Gallifrey Base, had no place to properly discuss them.

Instead, they were grouped in with fan films, which does a great injustice to the level of professionalism involved in their creation. When they are mentioned on Twitter or the various web fora, it tends to be with a certain amount of cynicism, with some viewers mocking the production values of these "amateur" productions. But as we have seen over the course of this book, some of the reviews they received at the time lauded the production values as being of broadcast standard.

Audio spin-offs have fared better, with Big Finish now the cornerstone of the spin-off market. However, it is easy to forget that from the winter of 1989 to the summer of 1999 there was no Big Finish-produced *Doctor Who*, as Barnfather points out. "Well, Big Finish wasn't around for a large chunk of that period. I think posterity makes its own decisions you know, there's no point worrying about what other people think about what you do, because you'll never do anything else. The fact that what we made is still being bought by people today, means that it had some intrinsic value, otherwise it would just be consigned to a dustbin and they're not. People still buy what we do."[1]

Indeed, Mark Ayres is of the opinion that they share much in common with Big Finish's early years. "Big Finish started out exactly the same as these pro-am things. They had a licence, but it was very rudimentary and they just built and built and built to where they are now, as a very important part of the ongoing commercial part of *Doctor Who* and they are now fully professional. But for a while they were very pro-am and they took over in audio, and no one would dare do now, an actual *Doctor Who* tie in spin-off, as we did with *Shakedown* and *Wartime* and *Downtime*. No-one would dare do that."[2]

Cyberon writer Lance Parkin feels it is very hard to convey the feeling in fandom at the time. "There was a point when BBV started up where the fix of *Doctor Who* stuff was *DWM* every month and either a VHS tape or

New Adventures novel. The market's now so flooded with official merchandise, let alone spin-offs, that it's much harder to keep track. It's difficult now to get across how... special — not quite the right word — 'Summoned by Shadows' and 'More than a Messiah' were. They weren't perfect, but they were part of a movement by fans to reclaim and reinvent *Doctor Who*, to, well, avenge the injustice of it being taken off the air. A lot of the fan videos you see now are incredibly beautifully made, but... empty. I just saw a Batman v Darth Vader thing with great special effects, 'cool moments' and all that, but... there's no spikiness, no challenge. It's slick, but doesn't move anything along, doesn't get to the heart. At their best, BBV's stories were good, imaginative takes on the *Doctor Who* universe that worked as science fiction stories. Bill has always had the spirit that you just get things done, you try stretching the resources and tell the best, most ambitious stories you can."[3]

Kaldor City writer Jim Smith is also quick to point out, that times were changing even before the TV show returned. "This is what people forget, *Doctor Who* spin-offs, apart from Big Finish, were all petering out when the TV show returned. The books had dropped, they'd halved their schedule, BBV were petering out. There was less and less of all of it as time went on. It wasn't the TV series coming back that stopped all that stuff, it was drying up anyway."[4] Nevertheless, he feels the TV show's return had an impact on the creative sector of fandom. "There was a hierarchy. There was a ladder. When the TV series came back, I said that everyone had to move one rung down, because the TV series had come in and become top rung of the ladder, knocking Big Finish down, and they became the second rung, having previously been the top rung. And what was odd to me, a few months after that, *Faction Paradox* which was really like the stand out series from BBV, became kind of merged with *Kaldor City*. It became produced by Magic Bullet, and BBV stopped making new things. So that did sort of happen. It really was like there was a finite number of rungs that the audience could accommodate, and the two bottom rungs became one because somebody had stuck a massive new rung on the top."[5]

Kaldor City creator Alan Stevens has a slightly different perspective. "The majority of audio and video *Doctor Who* spin-offs came from Bill Baggs, and when, for a multitude of reasons, he decided to give it all up , the slack in the spin-off audio market was taken up by Big Finish.

"When I did *Kaldor City* I didn't see myself as being in competition with anyone, I did it because it was an itch to scratch, in fact both Bill Baggs and Jason Haigh-Ellery wished me luck with the project. As for *Faction Paradox*, I took it on because it sounded like a great project, and the fact I'm still selling both *Faction* and *Kaldor* today shows that if you're willing to properly invest in something then people will respect that.

"As for the *Doctor Who* spin-off video market, the biggest drawback is the sheer amount of money and effort involved, which means that to make a profit you either have to skimp, or otherwise prepare yourself for a substantial loss. I personally wouldn't go anywhere near video drama, not just because of the cost, but also because it dates very quickly. Audio drama has a much longer life expectancy, as every couple of years your brain upgrades the visuals."[6]

How then should the video dramas be remembered and how accurate is the term "amateur"?

Former *DWM* editor Gary Russell, feels there was very little amateur about the films. "Let's not forget that many of the people involved with the Reeltime and BBV stables *were* professionals — with many years' experience behind and in front of the camera, so it was more a case of them taking that pre-existing professionalism and transferring it to a medium they loved, i.e. *Doctor Who*. There was very little 'amateur' in any of those company's products. Low-budget, yes, but rarely anything less than professional."[7] Also pointing out that "these things were funded by Keith or Bill or whoever funding out of their own pocket rather than other peoples' — I think they should be applauded for that."[8]

Parkin feels the reputation of these films are perhaps damaged by the digital revolution that took place in broadcasting during the latter part of the 2000s. "It's not that long ago, but in the meantime we've had a revolution in digital cameras, editing, affordable CG effects and so on. Then the whole birth of YouTube and these fan productions that look like the real thing, at times."[9]

Smith feels the production values were of a low standard. "This wasn't anyone's fault, but they were always kiboshed by budget. You say that and everyone sort of goes 'Well, you're *Doctor Who* fans why do you care about budget?' But it's not really true that 20th century *Doctor Who* was a bad, cheap looking cheap series. That's sort of meta myth. It's not really the case." Despite this, he remains a fan. "The earliest BBV ones, they were really exciting at the time. I'm probably alone in this, I like 'Summoned by Shadows', the first one, best of the BBV videos. Because it's not trying to do anything that isn't achievable on its budget. The extras aren't in costume, and the locations are entirely found, but it's not trying to be anything that it can't afford to do. It's got this interesting atmosphere, one that's kind of reminiscent of 'The Greatest Show in the Galaxy' and it's got Michael Wisher in, and Colin Baker is doing things, it seemed to me anyway, that he was doing things as an actor he might have liked to have done as *Doctor Who*, and that he didn't get to do, and he's since followed up in Big Finish. I think the other are all tripped up by budget. Or trying to be *The Bill*." [10]

It is also worth pointing out, that the often mocked production values of these films, may be due to the fact that many of them exist as VHS copies uploaded to You Tube.

How do those that worked on them feel about the spin-offs' place in the Doctor Who *story?*

Nigel Fairs considers them an integral part of the mythos. "I think they're very important. I think they kind of bridge the gap somehow, even if not story wise. It kept the whole thing pushing forward."[11] He also feels they represent the very best of what fandom has to offer. "It was a time of blistering creativity on a shoestring budget, which actually is a pretty good summation of *Doctor Who* its self. [12]"

John Ainsworth is in agreement. "It kept things alive in that gap of years between TV series of *Doctor Who*. It was things like BBV that kept people interested, with new things, and kept it going. It gets forgotten about, but at the time it was actually hugely creative because fans were filling the void."[13]

Simon Gerard agrees that it is a reflection of the BBC's attitude. "The spin-off market helped keep the spirit of *Doctor Who* alive when the show itself had fallen foul of the people who owned it."[14] And as Mark Ayres reminds us, the BBC's approach towards what had once been a flagship show, was less than exemplary. "The BBC's attitude to *Doctor Who* during that time was incredibly woolly. They wouldn't say if it was coming back, they wouldn't say it was cancelled, it was this, it was that. So nobody at the BBC was making any kind of decision and nobody was saying 'no you can't do this'!"[15]

Mark Ayres can see their place within *Doctor Who* history objectively. "Do they get overlooked? No, they don't get overlooked, they were what they were at the time. It's nice that they get recognition, it's nice that people realise that's where it all began. You know it all began with 'The Image Makers' and 'Ocean in the Sky' and on through *Wartime* through *The Stranger* and through *Downtime* and *Shakedown* through the *P.R.O.B.E.* series, and then they kind of petered out. I mean, I know Bill did more things, I know Keith has done a couple of things after that, but they are not as important to my mind, I have to say, because at that time you get this kind of curve coming up to the *P.R.O.B.E*s, then Big Finish come in and take over and take it to a whole new level, whereas the curve of the pro-am things disappears down."[16]

Jim Smith remains proud of his — and others' — efforts in the period. "Lots of people did lots of really good work in those years, and there were lots of exciting things going on. The bits and bobs I did I am proud of. I think they were worth doing, and if people enjoy them I think that's great. If people don't want to engage with them I don't really see that as being their fault." Although he considers it difficult to pin point exactly where these productions sit within the history of *Doctor Who* "There's a complex Venn diagram of these kind of spin-offs, where you have fan fiction at one end, and you have the television series or the film series at the other, and the overlapping circles are all quite complex. Just because there's money involved doesn't make it professional. Just because there isn't money involved, doesn't means it's amateur. Just because it's licensed it doesn't mean it's not fans, just because it's fans doesn't mean it isn't licensed. It's like the pre-Crisis multiverse in DC comics. An extrapolation of extreme of infinite overlapping circles!"[17]

As to their role in keeping the programme alive Barnfather is modest. "I think there can be, if you are not careful, rather deluded with your own self importance and think that what you did was pivotal in keeping *Doctor Who* alive or bringing the programme back. I never believed that, I always knew *Doctor Who* was coming back, from the moment it was cancelled, I knew it would come back one day, there was never a doubt in my mind. So I don't think we did anything to bring it back. I think the only thing I can say, is maybe the independent dramas that were being made when *Doctor Who* was off the air, provided some outlet for those fans who weren't getting any new drama. And if it made people sit down of an evening, in front of the TV set with a cup of tea or a bottle of wine and have a fun evening and something to talk about after, then I'm grateful."[18]

On a personal level, how do those who slaved away tirelessly on these productions look back on their time?

It seems despite the occasional run-in with Bill Baggs, generally a lot of the people involved look back at this time with great affection. David J Howe found it a chance to work in an industry with which he had always been fascinated.

"There's just so many happy memories working on these things. It was just nice to be involved in something creative and I love television and film production, and I love being on set and I love being involved and I've always been so grateful to Keith for involving me so much. Because it's just lovely to have that as part of the stuff that I've done."[19]

Gareth Preston felt it brought him closer to a programme he had loved his entire life. "It had great opportunities to tell good stories and have fun in other people's universes that we enjoy." [20]

Beverley Cressman looks back at the period with warmth. "I am really grateful for the opportunity in playing Kate those many years ago. I loved the *Doctor Who* crowd and I learnt a lot. Still now, somebody finds out that I did these films and of course with the resurgence of popularity of *Doctor Who* they are always quizzing me about them. Brings a big smile to my face."[21]

Cressman's former husband, Miles Richardson, has similar feelings. "On the whole, working for Reeltime Pictures was a lot of fun and seemed like being part of a large, if somewhat quirky, family. Above all there was enthusiasm, a quality which can often be lacking in our modern world, not least from Keith himself, who always assumed that the impossible was achievable, even if it was with cardboard and sellotape. Though it didn't improve my bank balance by much, I certainly gained experience and learnt a lot about film craft, which for an actor like myself — grounded in stage work — is a valuable thing."[22]

Patricia Merrick too viewed the experience as a learning curve and a chance to master her craft, as she later told Kyle Bastaina. "I've learned so much, having worked behind the camera and acting. Working with *Doctor Who* actors has taught me so much about technical things and everything you could possibly want to know about working on a tight budget. And time being tight as well. And when you get into a proper, BBC production, where you've got far more money and resources, you can actually pull it off. It leaves you quite impressed I have to say. "[23]

Nick Briggs still remains on good terms with Barnfather and still works with him on occasion. "These were the jobs I did before I really started to make headway in my career, I suppose. They gave me invaluable experience and taught me so much. And, of course, the Reeltime Pictures *Myth Makers* interviews introduced me to a lot of the old *Doctor Who* actors with whom I still work now in Big Finish.[24]

Conversely, despite a soured relationship with Baggs, Briggs still cites the BBV work as an important stage in his professional life. "I look back on it as vital, rather rough-and-ready, experience. I would love to have got all my experience on big TV or film sets on prestigious productions, but that's not the way things went for me, sadly. So I cut my teeth, as it were, on all this nonsense. I learnt so much and had loads of fun. There was much pain and gnashing of teeth along the way, but I do look back on it with a certain fondness."[25]

And what of Bill Baggs himself? As someone who put so much into the industry, but who left amidst controversy, personal turmoil and business problems, does he have any affection left for this period in his life?

"You can't escape the fact it was born out of Audio Visuals and it's kind of awesome, really. It shaped who I am, it's kind of made a man of me, it has decided who I am. So not only did it shape me as a writer, director, producer but also as a business man, so it invaded all areas of my life largely in a positive way."[26]

And with new projects on the horizon, did he need that time away?

"Yes, to be reborn in a way. I needed to find some motivation. I was very locked into trying to get a job with somebody else, now I'm not locked into that, I'm cued into making my own thing."

And the people he met along the way, what does he have to say to them?

"Just my gratitude to all the people I've worked with, for all the ups as well as the downs — and I have huge amounts jealousy and resentment for all the successes, the Gatisses and Briggses have had," he says jokingly, "but also, for whatever small part I had in their development and just gratitude really." [27]

Perhaps these films do get unfairly mocked in some corners of fandom, but to those who worked on them, and the many fans who enjoyed them, they played an important part in guiding fans though the interim between Classic *Who* and New *Who*.

To judge them by today's standards is as appropriate as judging classic *Doctor Who* by those standards. Yes, they were made on shoestring budgets but so was *Doctor Who*. True, some of the effects don't stand up, but just look at the effects in 'Rose', broadcast over a decade ago and see how badly the effects have aged. And yes, there may be the odd ropey performance, but you can find those in most television dramas, and not only from days gone by.

What these productions were, was a place to nurture creativity and enterprise, and a place for people to learn their trade or put into action skills they had developed in other parts of the industry. Many of these people went on to have successful careers within the industry and while these productions can't claim full credit for their careers, you can guarantee many of them took a wealth of experience away from it, even if in some cases it was just how not to do something. It's just a shame that not all those involved have reaped the success they were after.

Since 1987 the spin-off scene has produced 25 video dramas and 54 audio plays. Although the quality may vary, the level of ambition can never be doubted.

Each release was funded from the producers' own pockets, with no major broadcasters' backing. People like Keith Barnfather and Bill Baggs managed not only to get their films funded, but created a working business model to make further films. Most importantly, they gave fandom a much needed fix of *Doctor Who* related adventures.

As Keith Barnfather, the man who kick started it all, sums the period up that really is "not bad at all!"

Afterword

September 1989, I watch my first ever episode of *Doctor Who*, 'Battlefield' episode one. It stars Sylvester McCoy who manages to be mischievous, scary and instantly likeable all in one go. I'm mesmerised by him and his adventures, and so starts a life-long obsession with the show.

September 1991, I attend my first *Doctor Who* convention and meet my hero, the seventh Doctor, Sylvester McCoy.

Mid 90s, I am fully immersed in *Doctor Who*, despite there being no new TV series. I hoover up books, magazines and spin-offs videos. These spin-off videos often have features which show how these films are put together. The fact people can make these things for a living astounds me.

August 2009, I have my first full time job in TV at QVC, the shopping channel. One of the many guest presenters on my schedule is Beverley Cressman. I'm sure I know that name. When I see her I recognise her instantly as Kate Stewart from *Downtime*. I wonder if there is a book on those spin-offs? I must try and track it down.

January 2013, I'm working on a film with Brian Blessed, Tony Curran and my Doctor, Sylvester McCoy. As I cast my eye down the list of supporting actors, I notice the name Jo Castleton, I'm sure I know that name. When I see her I recognise her instantly as Natasha Alexander from *Auton II* & *Auton 3*. Someone must have written that book by now.

February 2013, nobody has written that bloody book yet. Maybe I'll have a go...

Appendix A – In The Future When All's Well

Keith Barnfather and his partner Anastasia continue to run Reeltime Pictures as a successful business. As well as their corporate work, the company have moved into broadcast television, producing a number of documentary series for an international market.

Nigel Fairs has had a long and varied career in the theatre, as both a writer and an actor. He contributes regularly to Big Finish as writer, actor and composer.

Mark Gatiss went on to garner great critical acclaim as part of the hit comedy troupe, *The League of Gentlemen*. He has written a trilogy of novels for his Lucifer Box character and has written assorted episodes of *Doctor Who* for BBC Wales. He has also had a hugely successful acting career appearing in *Game of Thrones, Being Human* and *London Spy* to name but a few of his roles.

David J. Howe has written numerous reference books, articles, short stories and novellas based on *Doctor Who*. He is co-director of Telos Publishing and has written short stories for numerous anthology works.

John Ainsworth went on to produce several ranges at Big Finish and has directed countless releases. He is currently editing the partwork magazine '*Doctor Who* — The Complete History'

Andy Grant is now Chief Executive of his own specialised broadcasting and events company, Galaxy Light & Power LLC.

Nicholas Briggs went on to have a successful career as a stage, screen and audio actor. He is executive producer at Big Finish Productions, where he oversees the *Doctor Who* range and many others. He is perhaps most famous for providing the voice of the Daleks, Cybermen and various other monsters for the revived series of *Doctor Who*.

James Cooray Smith wrote a lot of books about film and television, almost none of which are still in print, and then spent the best part of two decades working at PlayStation. More recently he has written for *That Mitchell and Webb Sound* and *Private Eye*, and regularly writes on pop culture for *The New Statesman*.

Dan Freeman is currently trying to secure funding for a *Minister of Chance* film and promoting his new audio series *The Light of September*.

Alan Stevens and **Fiona Moore** went on to make the audio series *Radio Bastard.* They have also written reference books on *Blakes 7, The Prisoner* and *Battlestar Galactica* and contribute a regular column to the D.W.A.S. magazine *Celestial Toyroom*

Tim Saward went on to work at the Millennium Dome and The British Library. He now manages a small obscure theatre on the outskirts of London and writes poetry.

Kevin Davies directed two episodes of *Space Island One* for Sky and went on to be Edit Producer on *Cash in the Attic.* He has produced countless DVD extras for shows including *Doctor Who, Dad's Army, Adam Adamant Lives* and *Budgie.* He also has a long association with *Hitchhikers Guide to the Galaxy* and is currently trying to get funding for a documentary about the series in its many guises.

Paul Ebbs went on to write for *Casualty, The Bill,* and *Doctors,* and worked as a mental health nurse.

Mark Ayres continues his career as a successful sound editor, dubbing mixer and composer in both film and television. He was a core member of the *Doctor Who* Restoration Team and he is currently touring with a reformed Radiophonic Workshop.

John Wadmore gave up acting and became a drama teacher. He is now head of department at a secondary school in North London.

Lance Parkin went on to write a number of highly regarded Big Finish releases and a novel for the Tenth Doctor for BBC Books. He has also written reference books based on *Star Trek, His Dark Materials* and *Emmerdale.* He has recently authored *Magic Words,* a biography of Alan Moore.

Alistair Lock is still a sound editor and composer and amongst other things continues to work with Big Finish.

Lawrence Miles co-authored the critically acclaimed *Doctor Who* reference books *About Time.* He also wrote the *Faction Paradox* novel 'This Town Will Never Let Us Go' and edited a number of other volumes. He went onto become a vocal detractor of the revived series of *Doctor Who,* publicly criticising many of the show's writers. He has since retired from fandom and writing to become a "recluse" as he feels his work is unappreciated.

Jeremy Leadbetter aka **Rob Shearman**, went on to write several well received plays, a number of much loved Big Finish audios and one episode of the 2005 series of *Doctor Who*. He has written five critically acclaimed collections of short stories.

After a spiritual awakening **Bill Baggs** quit the broadcasting industry to concentrate on Energy Healing. He has since began retraining as an actor and writer. When it was put to him that Mark Gatiss was the most successful person from the BBV stable, with a grin on his face he quickly retorted "at this point."[1] He remains hopeful of great success with his new projects.

Iain McLaughlin has written for a number of British comics, and set up Thebes Publishing in collaboration with his writing partner Claire Bartlett to print further adventures of their creation, Erimem.

Andy Lane became a teacher and continued to write spin-off novels for TV shows including *Doctor Who*. On television he wrote for Sky One's *Space Island One* TV series and has also contributed to the Big Finish range. He later found success as the writer behind the *Young Sherlock Holmes* range and was able to leave his job as a teacher to write full time. He is still married to his *Wartime* co-writer Helen Stirling.

Appendix B – Mute Witness

What follows are two outlines for unproduced BBV audio adventures. Reproduced for the first time as originally written.

KILL OR CURE
Synopsis by Iain McLaughlin

Katya Dylan (Kat to her pals and fans) is a presenter on a *Blue Peter* type telly programme. When the story kicks off, she's on her final assignment. She's spending the night in a hotel in an unnamed and small South American country before heading out to interview a scientist involved in conservation, which is the subject of the whole assignment. Frankly, she's not enjoying the experience. It's hot, room service is rotten and the air conditioning's on the blink. She thinks things can't get any worse. But then there's a knock at the door. It's not a bloke here to fix the air conditioning, it's her cameraman, Dave McCormick, who also happens to be her ex-boyfriend. The split is recent and still hurts both of them, though they both hide it. She uses sarcasm, he feigns indifference. The inference is that Dave was carrying on with the programme's producer, Maria. (who takes a terrible slagging all through, incidentally).

At the research complex Katya and Dave will be visiting (along with the sound-man and director if they ever get through customs — which they don't), things are not all sweetness and light. Dr Imogen Petersen is talking with a Captain Sanchez of the local army. She's worried about security in the compound — 4 of her colleagues were killed by guerrillas recently and there was a huge explosion in the jungle nearby a few days before. Sanchez is more worried that Petersen will blab to the TV people about guerrillas and terrorists, which would not be good for tourism or the country's international image. It's also clear that Petersen has absolutely nothing to do with conservation. That is certainly part of what goes on here in the compound, but she is working on something totally different. Something extraordinary. A medical discovery so profound it will make penicillin look like the stone age. She's eyeing a Nobel Prize, a place in history and a whopping great stack of cash at the end of this. Eventually she agrees to act like a nice little scientist when the TV people are here. There's a degree of disdain going both ways between Petersen and Sanchez. They may have a certain respect for each other professionally, but personally they're not bosom buddies. Sanchez heads off out into the compound to check on security — and to get away from the scientist. He sees a soldier he doesn't recognise and chases the soldier. He thinks he sees the man run into Doctor Muller's research tent — except Muller's the only one there and he didn't see anybody else. (Muller, incidentally, is the scientist in charge of the conservation work). Sanchez is worried. If a guerrilla has sneaked into the compound, they could be in big trouble.

Dave and Kat are being driven to the compound on the bumpiest, rockiest road ever built. Dave has tried to get a conversation going with Kat but she's giving him the silent treatment. After considerable goading he finally manages to push Kat into telling him to shut up. It's not great conversation but it's a start. And then he spots something out of the window. Kat thinks he's just trying to keep the conversation going. He's not. This is serious. A few seconds later bullets slam into the 4by4 they're riding in. They flatten themselves and their driver drives as fast as he can. Dave seems more worried about his camera than his health. Kat pulls him back down out of sight of the guerrillas until they've rounded a bend and are out of sight. Kat suffers the indignity of getting a bit of glass in the bum. Which Dave tries hard not to find funny. But fails.

At the compound, Sanchez is not a happy captain. No sign of the mystery soldier. He orders that the perimeter fence be examined again, and that the dogs be prepared for patrol duty in the compound at night. Petersen's a bit worried by this, especially with the TV people arriving. On cue, the bullet-ridden 4by4 chunters into the compound. Sanchez greets them. He's appalled by them having been attacked but blames it on a battle from a neighbouring country spilling over the border. Petersen tends to Kat's wounded pride (and bum) while Sanchez gets what info about the guerrillas he can from Dave. Here we get an inkling that Dave knows a sight more about military ops than a cameraman on a Blue Peter type show should. He knows makes of guns, calibre of weapon... that sort of thing. Sanchez clocks this as well, in an understated way. Sanchez heads outside and collars a soldier. There's still no sign of the mystery soldier, and the patrols have turned up a blank on the guerrillas — "Hardly surprising," grumbles Sanchez. "They were too busy shooting at the British TV people to wait around for you to find them. Where are they? Where are they and what kind of artillery do they have that could cause the explosion from a few nights before? He's worried.

Out on the jungle, Marina Silvestra, leader of the guerrillas isn't going to win any smiley-face contests either. She's raging that her troops attacked the 4by4. Don't they understand that if their organisation is ever to be seen as more than a terrorist outfit, they have to win the hearts and minds of the people, not only of their own country but of the world as well. Shooting a kids' TV personality, however understandable (at least in Andi Peters' case if you ask me, not that you did) is not going to make them seem like a credible political force. She's also a bit worried that one of her soldiers and someone from the compund have been found dead. Not just dead, either. Horrible markings on them shwing that they died in pain. A warning to Marina and her troops that they will be horribly executed if they don't clear off. Marina's not for clearing off. And she's more than capable of matching whatever brutality is thrown at her. She's been fighting all her life. She's fought her way out of the gutter, off the streets, away from the perverts and pimps who tried to use and abuse her, she's fought to be more than a nothing. She's fought hard to educate herself. Now she's fighting so that other people won't have to go through the childhood she had. Crossing this woman would be dangerous. She is intelligent, articulate and deadly. She doesn't consider herself a terrorist or a guerrilla — she is a soldier. She knows something's more important than conservation is going on in the compound. And she wants an enemy soldier captured to find out what's going on. She wants to know why her men were brutalised.

In the compound, Kat and Dave can see the high level of security. They are still not on the best of terms. The majority of their conversations consist of sniping and bitching but they both have the idea that there's more going on here than just conservation. They decide to have a shufti at the sort of tent/hut thing Petersen works in. They've been seeing slightly odd shenanigans at this tent. It's got heavier security than any of the others — a more complex number pad "43046721" says Dave. "Eight number combination." He's been paying attention. And it's another hint that there's more than meets the eye to Dave. For the most part, he's relaxed, indifferent. Sometimes, though, there are flashes of him being altogether more tuned in. Kat is quite unsettled by this side of him. They were together for almost two years and she never saw this aspect of his personality. He is at ease creeping about the compound, avoiding sentries and timing their movements against the sweeps of the surveillance cameras. They have almost made it to the tent/hut they are heading for when they see a soldier moving towards it. And he's acting suspiciously as well. Dave starts filming the soldier. The soldier doesn't know the combination — so he shouldn't be going in there obviously. He produces a weird, torch-like device and points it at the lock, which fritzes and crackles and then clocks open. The soldier is about to go in when there's an explosion nearby. He is thrown off his feet by the blast. The compound is immediately full of troops and scientists. Sneaking into the hut is a non-starter. The shady soldier is still down on the ground and Kat goes to help him, but he pushes her aside and runs. Sanchez arrives. He sees the camera, the open hut and the compound under attack. Kat and Dave are, in all but name, arrested and taken to his office for questioning.

In the jungles surrounding the compound, Marina is slightly happier now that she has struck back. Word comes to her that a soldier was seen hurrying out of the compound into the jungle. A deserter? A coward?

Easier to interrogate than a brave soldier. She wants the runaway soldier found and brought to her. He doesn't have to be in perfect health either.

Dave and Kat are being interrogated by Sanchez. He has had them checked out. Kat is a reporter who stumbled into presenting kids' TV by being fun, photogenic and looking for a job. Her real name is Kathy Delaney but she changed it for telly. He's not overly worried by her. Dave, on the other hand, is an altogether different kettle of fish. Dave has a history as a war cameraman. He was behind the lines with the SAS during the Gulf War, worked in Northern Ireland, went undercover in Tennessee with the KKK, and more recently (1998/99-ish — a few years earlier) was in Afghanistan covering human rights violations by the government of the time. And now he's... a children's TV cameraman? Sanchez seems to be jumping to the obvious conclusion that Dave's here to look for a bigger story than a bit of fluffy time-filling for kids at tea-time. Dave protests that he is what he seems to be. He used to be a war cameraman, now he does kids TV. Why the change? She's sitting next to him. Kat had asked him to stop taking the dangerous assignments and he had agreed. Sanchez isn't buying the story, but Kat backs it up. But it's the first time she's heard about some of the stories Dave had covered. He never mentioned some of them — particularly the one with the SAS. Sanchez picks up on that and drops in an interesting tit-bit — the rumour that Dave had been given special privileges by the SAS after killing an enemy soldier to save a member of the SAS. Dave won't confirm or deny that he killed anybody, saying only that it was a long time ago. Kat is now sure that she knows even less about him than she thought.

The soldier who ran from the camp has been caught and knocked unconscious. He is delivered to Marina, who is less than gentle in her interrogation. The soldier seems to fall unconscious again after a few minor thumps. He's been unresponsive, refusing to answer any questions. Marina wonders if he's a good soldier or just plain stupid. She leaves him to stew. She tells her soldiers not to be overly gentle with their guest.

In the scientific compound, Dave and Kat are, in all but name, prisoners. For their own good, naturally, according to Sanchez. They're locked up together and Kat is wary of Dave. She's wondering if he really is a killer. Could she have lived for the best part of two years with someone who had deliberately killed another human being? Dave, on the other hand, is wondering about how to get out. It's clear that there's a damn sight more happening here than conservation. What's in the hut everybody wants to get inside? Who are the guerrillas? What's their objective? He's sure they won't find any answers as long as they're stuck inside. They're going to have to escape.

Sanchez is getting worried. Two of his patrols haven't come back and another reported in as being under attack before being cut off. He asks how far along Imogen's research is. Is it far enough along for them to be able to move it back to a city, where they'll be safe? Imogen's not sure. Some of the experiments could be transplanted but the Wo Jifo flower is very delicate. It doesn't travel well. It would have to be airlifted out. That suits Sanchez. Things are starting to go very wrong here and he doesn't want more dead scientists on his record. He's eyeing a place in the government eventually — an ambitious sort. He decides to call for an airlift.

Marina listens in to the request for an airlift, eavesdropping on a radio. This suits her. A helicopter is a much bigger target to shoot at than a person. When she goes back to the interrogation, both the soldier and his guard are gone. There are signs of a struggle. This has made her mind up for her. If the soldier gets back to the compound, her camp will be under immediate attack. The best option left to her is to attack. Attack the compound and attack the helicopter.

Imogen is discussing the implications of moving back to the city with Muller. He really is a conservationist. He knows that his research here was never the prime concern but it matters to him and he doesn't want to go back, his job half done. Imogen couldn't give a toss if Muller goes back to the city or not but Sanchez has his career to think about so everybody's going to be safe, whether they like it or not.

Kat and Dave have escaped from their makeshift cell. Now they see Sanchez entering the mystery tent/hut. They follow him in — and find Sanchez searching the place. Very suspicious. Why is he looking for something? And what's the something in question? And an equally pertinent question arrives when the hut door opens and who arrives? Sanchez. There are two Captain Sanchezes. Which causes some confusion. (And will have to be carefully handled otherwise the listeners will become just as confused). Imogen enters and she hasn't a clue which Sanchez is which either. The Sanchezes are wary of each other. And then they attack each other. The other people in the room have no idea what to do — how can they begin to explain two Sanchezes? One pulls a gun and tries to shoot the other one — he only manages to wing him. He barges past the other Sanchez and runs off into the night, leaving the other Sanchez with a slightly bloodied head and three shocked people who don't know if he's the real deal or not. And Sanchez is interested to know what Dave and Kat were doing snooping around an off-limits area when they should have been safely locked up like good little prisoners.

And then the attack comes. The guerrillas hit the base hard. Dave and Kat try to get some answers but there's chaos all around them. And then Kat spots something about the blood from the wound (Dave thinks it's a hell of a time for her to get gory) but he and then Imogen agree that something's not right with the blood. The colour is just a bit off, it's thinner than usual blood and it's not congealing properly. She looks at it under the microscope — it's not blood as she knows it. If she didn't know better she'd say that it wasn't human blood.

The battle isn't going well. The guerrillas are over-running the compound — the helicopter is shot down as it gets closer. In the middle of the battle, Marina corners Sanchez. She has a good old gloat and is about to kill him when she sees that he's already nursing an injury. From his own people, no doubt. Sanchez replies that his own people have injured themselves for too long. He gets a bit odd on the subject and then just gets very odd indeed. He changes shape in front of Marina — to a Zygon. She's freaked out and then sees the other Sanchez — just in time to be captured, as is the Zygon, which is pretty much turfed into a cage.

The guerrillas' attack is repelled and Marina is captured. Sanchez is seeing something spectacular in front of himself. If he brings in this alien and the terrorist leader he'll be El Presedente quicker than a hiccup. He thinks the alien is working with Marina. She accuses the government of being involved. Dave and Kat are being kept out of it until Sanchez decides that he needs a record of his great triumph. This would put him right up there with all the great leaders of the world. He quite fancies that idea. Kat is told that she'll be doing the spiel to camera — and that she'd better make Sanchez sound good.

Dave and Kat reluctantly agree to go through with this, given that the alternative would seem to be an accidental but quick death. They are tense and on edge and bicker about their failed relationship. She accuses him regarding his affair with their boss. Which, he finally denies. The first time he's ever just come straight out and said there was no fling. She doesn't believe him. Why didn't he just say so earlier? And what has he been spending so much time with the afore-insulted Maria? You should get the feeling that this is the first time they've actually talked about any of this. They're both stubborn and strong-willed — and very proud. Neither will entertain the possibility that they could have been wrong. As for the story... well, Dave is a cameraman and Kat has always dreamed of reporting as Katherine Dylan, BBC Ten O'Clock news. Maybe this is her chance.

Imogen is fascinated by the captive alien, although Sanchez refuses to let her tend to the Zygon's wound. Muller is also fascinated by the alien. He's been staying out of the way, doing the most sensible thing possible during the battle — keeping his head down and trying to avoid getting shot.

Sanchez has been interrogating both Marina and the Zygon — both of whom show utter disdain for him, and for each other, despite the Zygon's protests that it didn't kill Marina's men in the jungle. It doesn't give a toss that the men are dead, but does want it known that he didn't kill them.

Imogen looks in to check on the two prisoners. Whether Sanchez likes it or not, she's going to make sure they're okay (mainly the Zygon — Gabrielle can pretty much go to hell as far as Imogen's concerned). Gabrielle is asleep or more likely unconscious. The Zygon may well be playing possum but it's an incredible scientific opportunity she's not prepared to miss out on. Muller arrives and warns Imogen to steer clear of the alien. Sanchez won't like her ignoring his orders — and the alien has already shown itself to be dangerous. They are disagreeing when Sanchez arrives. He's not happy that they're with his captives but he's more interested in making his play for power. He's preparing to speak to camera when Marina is wakened. She refuses to speak and then sees Muller — and freaks out (technical medical term). She goes mental. She's seen this guy — and he was dead at the time. Sanchez wallops her and tells her to shut up. But she's insistent. She saw the other one change shape — and it's Dave who goes to the top of the class by piecing together that if the alien is a shape-changer, then maybe this isn't Muller at all. It's another shape-changer. Sanchez pretty much thinks this is nuts, but the already-captured Zygon starts going loopy, trying to get away from Muller. Kat pitches in. How about an easy test. Imogen said that Zygon blood was nothing like human blood. A sample from Muller would do the trick. Sanchez still thinks this is a load of old cobblers — until Muller refuses. He attacks Sanchez and escapes, also attacking Marina as he goes.

It's clear that the Muller Zygon isn't working with Marina. A truce is called — albeit an uneasy one. The Zygon has to be caught. Marina's few guerrillas are sent out with troops (to use the guerrillas' knowledge of the jungle) in a search for the Zygon.

In the compound, Kat is troubled by something. If Muller's also a Zygon, why was the captive Zygon so afraid of it? She tries talking to the beast. It's not overly responsive but she and Imogen eventually get it talking. The creature in the shape of Muller is indeed another Zygon — but one with a different view of life. A different perspective on the plight of the Zygon race, with regards to their lack of a home planet. Most Zygons favour nicking a planet and slowly altering it suit their race's needs. But this is a long-term plan and the Zygons don't have the forces to actively conquer a world. The captive Zygon has a different plan — to alter the Zygons themselves to suit the planet they're on. To do that, it would need a particular drug — which just happens to be the Wo Jifo flower that Imogen's been working with. The drug she's been working on will allow the Zygons to deal more easily with other atmospheres — it'll allow them a degree of enforced evolution. One thing is clear, though. Both factions of the Zygon schism (which is serious inside the Zygon social system) want to take Earth for themselves. Neither is overly keen on sharing Earth with the hairy monkeys who wander about ruining the planet, thinking they own the place and think they are unable to function unless they have a mobile phone. (Nothing to do with the plot but I hate mobile phones, especially when you're on the train.) Both factions of Zygons would look to take humans out of the equation, which rules out helping one side against the other.

Out in the jungle, Marina and Sanchez aren't getting along either. Even though they're supposed to be working together, it's clear that they'd rather tear each other apart. In the jungle, they find a spaceship. They enter and look around. It's a weird kind of ship. They don't see any kind of technology they can snaffle — but on the bright side, there don't seem to be any other Zygons either. Until one slips out, leaving the ship alarmingly active. It's going to blow up.

At the compound, a huge explosion is heard. Sanchez returns, much the worse for wear. The ship exploded and Marina was killed. They have to get the Zygon creature away from the compound. They are getting ready to move the Zygon when Marina arrives. She's in a bad way as well. But she claims that Sanchez is dead and that this must be a Zygon copy. Sanchez claims that Marina is the fake.

The compound shakes — something is overhead. The captive Zygon tries to escape. It has to be the other Zygon's spaceship. Coming to rescue the captive Zygon says Sanchez. Or coming to destroy the compound, suggests Kat. Dave's trying to weigh it all out. He suggests waiting — if they run, the ship may well attack them. If they wait, there's the chance that they won't be attacked because they have at least one alien with them and the Zygons probably wouldn't want to kill their own kind. Marina's against this. Sanchez thinks it would give them time to work out a plan. They argue again. Dave and Kat quietly discuss the fact that either Sanchez or Marina is a Zygon and they don't know which. On the other hand, somebody in the room might be able to tell who it is. They release the captive Zygon, who attacks Sanchez. Sanchez reverts to Zygon form and the two battle their way out into the compound. The humans now can't tell which Zygon is which — not that it matter since they're both intent on taking Earth one way or the other. The Zygon ship is hovering overhead, observing the battle below.

Imogen wants to go to the lab to save her work on the Wo Jifo, which sets minds working. What else does she have in the lab? Marina is convinced that the Zygon technology is organic — and if the Wo Jifo can help the Zygons, Imogen must have something in the lab that's lethal to organic life — or at least harmful to it, if only for experimentation purposes. She does. That would look to be their best bet of getting rid of the ship.

Before setting off, Dave owns up to Kat why he spent so much time with bitch-boss Maria — he was arranging a move for himself from kids TV back to the news. Partly because he wanted to get into the production side, but mainly because (although she hasn't heard yet) when she gets back, Kat is going to be offered a slot with the news — albeit very junior and lowly. At best she'll be 3rd reserve for Jenny Bond and will spend her first year doing the cheery segments that turn up at the end of broadcasts. Budgies that know the words to Rule Britannia, skateboarding grannies, grocers shops that sell vegetables which look remarkably like celebrities — the "and finally" slot. But it's a start. That's what he's been up to. He has not been playing away with Maria. Why didn't he just say that? Because he's stubborn and pig-headed and he was angry that Kat had jumped to conclusions. And he wasn't particularly in the mood to defend himself against stupid accusations she should have known better than make. But as she rightly points out, if he had been more open there wouldn't have been any need for accusations. They agree to talk this out later.

Dave and Imogen make the run to the lab. They get the toxic material, which is stored in flasks, at below zero temperatures. All they have to do now is get it up to the spaceship. How? How should Dave know? He's making it up on the hoof.

One of the Zygons kills the other and goes into the lab. It demands the Wo Jifo extract, which Dave hands over only when Imogen is threatened. The Zygon enters the ship, which takes off again. Marina has been injured again by the Zygon and Kat has a clean shot at it, but Dave stops her from shooting. His then the suggestion is that the survivors run like hell. The Zygon ship is looking unsteady. It wobbles (so we're told in non-clunky expository dialogue) and then starts to fallf rom the sky. It lands in the compound, just giving the humans time to get clear. There's an explosion and fire from the crash. The fire will destroy the dangerous chemicals — but it has ruined the work Imogen did on the Wo Jifo as well. She decides to stay in the jungle and try again, even though there'll be no backing. She's not doing it for humanity — she still wants the glory and eventually, the cash. Marina will help — because it'll show her guerrillas in a good light.

Kat and Dave head back to the city on horseback — the only transport available. They're still bickering, but are on better terms now. His camera's been destroyed — by Marina to stop more people coming into the jungle. Kat mutters that nobody would believe them anyway. Dave lobs something to her — a tape. He took it from the camera before it was destroyed. He's spent too much time behind enemy lines to get caught out that easily. It's her first scoop. As for their relationship? Well, they'll see, although they'll probably be bickering over whether or not they'll see.

PRECIS

Synopsis by Iain McLaughlin

A Zygon infiltrates a medical research facility in the South American jungle. The facility has a conservation operation as its public front, but the the truth is they've found a drug which might just be a universal cure-all. It can hold leukaemia at bay, fight off viruses — it can even cure the common cold. But it's not a stable chemical and it's not easy to make. It can only be produced using a rare flower from the deepest part of the jungle. The Zygon infiltrates at the same time as Kat (a presenter from a Blue Peter type programme) arrives to do her farewell report about the conservation work. She's accompanied by her cameraman ex-boyfriend, Dave. During their visit, people start to act a little odd and appear to be in two places at once. The Zygon wants the drug for its own reasons. And then people appear in three places at once — there's a second Zygon, also trying to get the drug. The Zygons now have factions within their civilisation — hardly surprising given how spread out they are. Most want to change worlds to suit their needs. But a few want to change themselves to suit the worlds they'll be colonising. This drug will help them deal with any infections and ailments the planets have to offer. The other lot of Zygons aren't up for this at all. That's not the way they work. So, in short, it's a telly presenter, her ex-boyfriend cameraman and a couple of scientists in a South American compound with two Zygons who want to kill each other while outside the compound there's the threat of guerrillas. So, do our heroes have to save themselves, save the cure, avoid being killed by the Zygons (neither of whom is a particularly pleasant individual), avoid the guerrillas outside, get themselves off to safety and sort out their relationship. Piece of cake, really.

Appendix C – Reader Meet Author

Wartime
Company: Reeltime
Writer: Andy Lane & Helen Stirling
Release Date: August 1987

While transporting a dangerous cargo across country for UNIT, Benton's mission takes him to an area of the country that he is familiar with, where he is haunted by ghosts from his past.

The Stranger: Summoned By Shadows
Company: BBV
Writer: Christian Darkin
Release Date: September 1991

The Man Who Appeared (as he is called in the film) is at odds with his friends and the universe, cutting himself off and becoming a hermit. His solitude is interrupted when he becomes aware that the Controller is taking advantage of the locals in order to find the pieces of his missing transmat.

The Stranger: More than a Messiah
Company: BBV
Writer: Nigel Fairs
Release Date: February 1992

The Stranger and Miss Brown arrive an idyllic holiday planet, where they encounter Bernard and Charlotte Darton who came to get away from the stresses of life back home. They also come across two students Marc and Nic, who are just there to party and let off steam. When Mark is killed, it appears the planet is fighting back, creating it's own antibody in the form of a young woman, who has a more than passing interest in the Stranger.

The Stranger: In Memory Alone
Company: BBV
Writer: Nick Briggs
Release Date: March 1993

Both suffering from amnesia, the Stranger and Miss Brown arrive at a train station whose only inhabitants are the unresponsive Minor and the robot ticket inspector, Drudger. As a mysterious fog creeps in and engulfs everything, the Stranger must discover what lies a heart of the station.

The AirZone Solution
Company: BBV
Writer: Nick Briggs
Release Date: September 1993

Set in an over-polluted future, weatherman Arnie Davies and activist Anthony Stanwick, attempt to expose a conspiracy by the powerful AirZone Corporation, who have been contracted by the government to clean up the air in Britain. They are helped by Oliver Threthewey and haunted by the ghost of Al Dunbar, a reporter who was mysteriously killed while writing an expose on AirZone.

The Stranger: The Terror Game
Company: BBV
Writer: Nick Briggs
Release Date: July 1994

The Stranger arrives in present day England after returning everything to its proper place in the previous film. As it transpires, his proper place is a night club that he passes out beside and into which he is taken in by Tamora, the duty manger. The club turns out to be the scene of the Stranger's last mission as a Preceptor assassin. Here he meets his former cohorts Egan and Saul who reveal that he is called Soloman and explain the details of his past — he is a terrorist fighting the Protectorate and he is a creature from the dimensional web who merely inhabits this body.

The Stranger: Breach of the Peace
Company: BBV
Writer: Nick Briggs
Release Date: August 1994

Egan and Saul infiltrate the local police purporting to be special investigators from Scotland Yard. However, they are really using police facilities to track down Soloman who has taken refuge with Rose, a local newspaper editor. Meanwhile DCI Sellars is investigating a porn ring run from a night club (last seen in *The Terror Game*) and the disappearance of its owner. While doing so, she uncovers the rather more deadly events of the previous film.

Shakedown: Return of the Sontarans
Company: Dreamwatch Media
Writer: Terrance Dicks
Release Date: October 1994

A group of rich thrill seekers entering a solar race aboard the good ship *Tiger Moth*, captained by Lisa Deranne. Unbeknownst to them a Rutan spy has hidden itself on board. The ship is intercepted and boarded by a group of Sontarans, and the crew find themselves caught in the middle of an age old feud.

P.R.O.B.E.: The Zero Imperative
Company: BBV
Writer: Mark Gatiss
Release Date: December 1994

Liz Shaw and P.R.O.B.E. are investigating a series of mysterious and strange deaths around the Hawthawn Clinic. The investigation unearth not only age old secrets of the hospitals staff and benefactors, but also a supernatural force that has been causing horrific murders for centuries on the hospital site.

The Stranger Chronicles: The Last Mission
Company: BBV
Writer: Nick Briggs
Release Date: January 1995

Soloman carries out his last mission before the events of *Summoned by Shadows*, where he is captured by the Protectorate and put into the estrangement programme in return for the freedom of Egan and Saul.

The Stranger Chronicles: Eye of The Storm
Company: BBV
Writer: Arthur Wallis aka Nick Briggs
Release Date: January 1995

Picking up where *Breach of the Peace* left off, the trio of Soloman, Egan and Saul are travelling through the dimensional web when they see the face of a young woman and are forced out. They become embroiled in the lives of Hunter and Sheila who are conducting a military research operation on a young woman named Meta.

The Stranger: Eye of The Beholder
Company: BBV
Writer: Nick Briggs
Release Date: July 1995

Also following on directly from the last film, Egan, Saul and Soloman are forced out of the dimensional web by a mysterious presence. They soon discover that that presence is Meta, a human with metaphysical powers who is being studied at a local cottage by the military. However, her presence in the web does not go unnoticed, as the web turns the corpses of dead soldiers into antibodies to combat her threat. The only way to save themselves is for Soloman to kill her, but it appears that Egan has fallen in love with her.

P.R.O.B.E. — The Devil of Winterborne
Company: BBV
Writer: Mark Gatiss
Release Date: September 1995

Liz Shaw and her P.R.O.B.E. team investigate the murder of the former headmaster of Winterborne School. Their investigation lead Liz to suspect the current headmaster Gavin Purcell; however she uncovers evidence of a satanic cult led not by Purcell, but by his nephew Christian.

Downtime
Company: Reeltime
Writer: Marc Platt
Release Date: September 1995

With The Great Intelligence now inhabiting Professors Travers' body, it is attempting to manifest itself fully on Earth. It does so via the internet, infecting the computer systems of New World University which is run by Vice Chancellor Victoria Waterfield. The Brigadier must attempt to stop the menace, with a little help from Sarah Jane Smith. But things get even more serious when his daughter and grandson get embroiled in the situation.

P.R.O.B.E. — Unnatural Selection
Company: BBV
Writer: Mark Gatiss
Release Date: October 1996

A series of murders, in which the victims have been horrifically mutilated, attracts the attention of P.R.O.B.E. This leads them to uncover a secret government operation called BEAGLE that took place in the seventies - a project that altered humans to create a superhuman, a super human who is now absorbing people to survive. The team uncover a conspiracy that involves not only the government but P.R.O.B.E. itself.

P.R.O.B.E. — Ghosts of Winterborne
Company: BBV
Writer: Mark Gatiss
Release Date: November 1996

Liz Shaw returns to Winterborne school where the former headmistress' sister has taken over the school. Meanwhile, a body has disappeared and so has a book of black magic and Andrew Powell is seeing visions of his former tormentor Christian. Liz forms an alliance with an imprisoned Gavin Purcell in order to solve the mystery and save lives.

Auton
Company: BBV
Writer: Nick Briggs
Release Date: October 1997

U.N.I.T. employee Doctor Sally Arnold reactivates a Nestene energy sphere left over from one of their previous invasion attempts. With one of her team dead and another duplicated by the Nestene, she calls upon a containment team lead by Lockwood. Trapped inside a U.N.I.T. warehouse with Autons on the rampage, Lockwood reveals his less than human origins as Sally attempts to defeat the Auton menace.

The Time Travellers: Republica
Company: BBV
Writer: Mark Gatiss
Release Date: Early 1998

The Professor and Ace arrive in modern day London only to find fashion, culture and technologically not as it should be. England is ruled over by the old and frail Lord Protector who is being led astray by his astrologer, know only as the Other. The travellers become embroiled in a plot of rebellion and intrigue concerning ousted King Charles XIV.

The Time Travellers: Island of Lost Souls
Company: BBV
Writer: Mark Gatiss
Release Date: Early 1998

Set on a remote research base in Greenland during World War Two, manned by allied forces who are trying to develop sound-based camouflage to help win the war. Soon a German force arrives at the base but there is something more deadly on the island picking off people one by one.

The Time Travellers: Prosperity Island
Company: BBV
Writer: Tim Saward
Release Date: May 1998

Crash landing on Prosperity Island, the Professor and Ace come across former company director Projoy (exiled to the island for past indiscretions) and his son, the psychokinetic Milo. Projoy's wife, and now company leader, Antoinette comes to the island intent on killing him — which she failed to do many years before. Meanwhile Projoy plots to regain the power he once had over the planet.

The Time Travellers: The Left Hand of Darkness
Company: BBV
Writer: Mark Duncan
Release Date: September 1998

Ace is marooned on Yentob Minor, where, suffering from burns and blinded, she is cared for by the synthetic Dorsai. Although initially there is a lack of trust on Ace's part the two learn to get along and develop strong feelings for each other

Mindgame
Company: Reeltime
Writer: Terrance Dicks
Release Date: September 1998

A human, Draconian and Sontaran are kidnapped and placed in a cell located on an asteroid. There they are forced to fight to the death in an experiment by an unseen adversary. The only way for them to escape is for the unlikely trio to form an alliance

Auton 2: Sentinel
Company: BBV
Writer: Nick Briggs
Release Date: October 1998

With the inactive Autons from the previous films missing and Lockwood's signature on their transfer papers, UNIT assigns a new team to investigate led by Colonel Wilson and his scientific advisor, the psychic Natasha Alexander. Lockwood joins them but is forced to leave Doctor Sal behind. Their mission leads them to Sentinel Island where the Autons have been welcomed by the inhabitants and the local vicar has been replaced by Winslet.

The Time Travellers: The Otherside
Company: BBV
Writer: Mark Duncan
Release Date: November 1998

Ace finally returns home to present day London. But before long, she is hit by a passing car. Waking up, she is shocked to find her dead Nan before her. Her Nan informs her that she is there to help Ace pass over to the other side. However it is revealed that she is actually a mind parasite trying to take Ace's consciousness in order to cross over itself.

The Time Travellers: Guests for the Night
Company: BBV
Writer: Nigel Fairs
Release Date: November 1998

On their way to find the legendary Point of Stillness the Professor and Ace encounter Daniel, a young man looking for his missing sister. Their journey takes them to Vespertine Lodge, a house that seems to be shifting in time and is inhabited by a family of vampires.

The Wanderer: Cyber-Hunt
Company: BBV
Writer: Martin Peterson aka Nick Briggs
Release Date: November 1998

On Carson's Planet a team of Marines, accompanied by a Galactic Net News reporter, are on a Cyber Hunt after a successful battle. There they encounter a badly hurt and amnesiac traveller, who adopts the name Fred. Cut off from their ship, they discover a Cyberon Lab and come face to face with a Cyberon that appears to have feelings.

The Time Travellers: Ghosts
Company: BBV
Writer: Nigel Fairs
Release Date: March 1999

The Professor and Ace take a flight to the Hedistic Islands when the Professor unexpectedly passes away. Determined to uncover the truth, Ace discovers that the Professor and a number of other people have not died but been stored in digital format in a plot that leads straight to the planet's leader.

The Wanderer: Vital Signs
Company: BBV
Writer: Tim Saward
Release Date: March 1999

Fred arrives at the Museum of Universal History and Cosmographies where he finds it beset by freak weather conditions and the wolf-like Sandermines. Inside the museum he discovers the museum owners, known only as 'the company' were responsible for the destruction of an entire culture on the planet Ganex and the key to all the problems may be the Vitelica, a holy relic taken from Ganex.

The Time Travellers: Only Human
Company: BBV
Writer: Mark J. Thompson
Release Date: April 1999

The time travellers pick up a passenger, in the form of Omicron, a shape shifter who draws her form from people's memories. Initially she appears as Alice's step-father and in an emotionally fraught scene, reveals a dark history between the two. Omicron eventuality takes the form of the Dominie's friend Samantha. From here the trio visit the far future where a psychopathic droid has killed the last of the human race and is now attempting to make amends for its actions.

Adventures in a Pocket Universe: The Choice
Company: BBV
Writer: Nigel Fairs
Release Date: April 1999

Trapped in Ecto Space, The Mistress is a guest of the Emperor Lukor, whose people honour her for saving them. The Emperor proposes to her which she politely declines and flees in a make shift time space craft she has been constructing. When the machine malfunctions the Mistress & K9 end up in the planet's past where blind cave dwellers are beset by a plague. However it turns out the past and future may not be as far part as The Mistress initially first thought.

Mindgame: Trilogy
Company: Reeltime
Writer: Terrance Dicks, Miles Richardson and Roger Stevens
Release Date: May 1999

'Battlefield'
Field Major Sarg returns to the battlefield he was taken from. Injured and alone, he ponders on his experiences with the Draconian and Human and wonders if collaboration with other races is an option Sontarans should explore.

'Prisoner 451'
The Draconian is now a prisoner of his own people, incarcerated for suggesting that females should be allowed a more prominent place in society, while awaiting his trial he contemplates his experiences and fate..

'Scout Ship'
Space Pilot 692 7896 is now back at the controls of her ship. Drifting through space, with systems running out of power she confronts a few of her demons in the face of death.

The Time Travellers: Blood Sports
Company: BBV
Writer: Nigel Fairs
Release Date: June 1999

The Dominie and Alice are aboard a luxury train to Vienzz, where they find themselves embroiled in a plot concerning racial conflict, age old politics and cultural differences, while a series of suicides turn out to be the work of something altogether more sinister.

Zygons: Homeland
Company: BBV
Writer: Tim Saward
Release Date: June 1999

When the military carries out a raid on the home of Andrew Molton, a business man and philanthropist turned drugs cartel murderer, they discover Molton is actually a Zygon in disguise. Their scientific advisor, Guy Dean, follows a lead which take the team to Columbia, where the real Molton is collaborating with the Zygons, although it turns out their desired outcomes are very different.

Adventures in a Pocket Universe: The Search
Company: BBV
Writer: Mark Duncan
Release Date: September 1999

K9 and the Mistress land on a galaxy sized planet within a poly-alloy dwarf star. There they meet the crew of the Catharis who are on a mission to uncover the secrets of the ancients and the universe. They discover a world in disrepair, full of identical passage ways, earthquakes and chambers that may just contain the secrets of the universe.

Zygons: Absolution
Company: BBV
Writer: Paul Ebbs
Release Date: September 1999

On the world of Ganta 4 or New Eden, a religious order led by Christopher Shaw is shocked by the second coming of one of their group who was killed by a Skarasen some days earlier. This second coming is only the first of many strange happenings as Justine Hallon of Interplanetary Mining discovers. With the colonists out of control it is soon revealed that the Zygons are behind the troubles and that they intend to take over the home world using body prints of the colonists and miners.

Krynoids: The Root of All Evil
Company: BBV
Writer: Lance Parkin
Release Date: September 1999

Eve and Martin of the Ministry of Ecology investigate a new type of weed that has been preventing the growth of any other plants on the farm owned by Jeff and Sally. After some research, Sally identifies it as a Krynoid pod from the Chase Foundation website, although the website says nothing about the plant's dangers, simply noting that it is rare. Jeff attempts to remove the Krynoid from his field but is stung. He immediately begins to transform into a Krynoid and unleashes havoc on the farm.

Sontarans: Silent Warrior
Company: BBV
Writer: Peter Grehan
Release Date: September 1999

When the ship's computer Sentinel brings what appears to be an escape pod on board the cargo ship *Genesis*, the ship's geneticist Sylvia meets the pod's occupant, Alex. The only other crew member is found dead and they quickly uncover a batch of Sontaran clones where the ship should be transporting livestock. Sylvia reveals that she is undercover investigating a smuggling ring but inadvertently got involved in the wrong smuggling operation and ended up dealing with a Sontaran. Now they have further Sontaran craft hiding in the ship's warp signature and Field Major Starn on board hunting them.

Auton 3: Awakening
Company: BBV
Writer: Arthur Wallis (aka Nick Briggs) with additional material by Paul Ebbs
Release Date: September 1999

After his experience on Sentinel Island, Lockwood is physically and mentally weakened. Hunted by UNIT and the Nestene alike, he holds the key to the planet's safety or destruction in his head. He and Natasha head to Millhampton, where the real Winslet was taken to recuperate. As it turns out, Natasha's psychic abilities have been interfered with and she is leading Lockwood straight to the Nestene, who have taken over the town. Dr Sal and Ramsey head to Millhampton under the instructions of Palmer to track down Lockwood and defeat the Autons.

Cyberons: Cybergeddon
Company: BBV
Writer: Paul Ebbs
Release Date: February 2000

After an attack on luxury space liner *Titainia*, Corrigan and his clockwork companion Christian go in search of his daughter Emily, who was a passenger on the ship. The investigation leads them to an asteroid that is inhabited by the Cyberons, a race of cyborgs who disappeared after a war with humanity some 900 years ago. The asteroid also contains the bodies of three million different species, ready to be converted and form an army. Corrigan must first confront his daughter and tell her the truth about her existence, before dealing with the Cyberon threat.

The Dominie: Punchline
Company: BBV
Writer: Jeremy Leadbetter aka Rob Shearman
Release Date: February 2000

The Dominie, going under the name of Dominic Purkins, is trapped in the mundane life of a family sitcom, living through various episodes with seemingly the same story. Slowly, over the course of several episodes, Dominic begins to suspect something strange is going on. He can remember another life where he travelled in time and space.

Sontarans: Old Soldiers
Company: BBV
Writer: Simon Gerard and Colin Hill
Release Date: February 2000

Captain Wells visits the captive Commander Brak as she is investigating a number of military deaths spread over a forty year period, mainly in peace time. These deaths seem to be linked to Cobalt Blue, a multi-purpose substance being found in a variety of weapons. Although Brak initially refuses to help, the two soon start to interrogate each other and learn much about each other and Cobalt Blue.

Infidel's Comet
Company: BBV
Writer: Simon Gerard and Colin Hill
Release Date: April 2000

When a huge comet comes into Earth's orbit and abducts all the non-human life forms hiding on the planet, news reporter Kate Spencer and thieves Jimmy and Henry are amongst them. When they escape their cell they discover they are being taken home by a Pure Crusader who doesn't believe in interspecies breeding. With Henry revealing his darker side, it is up to them to put a stop this and return all the alien life to its rightful place.

The Pattern
Company: BBV
Writer: Marc Duncan
Release Date: April 2000

Mount Chimborazo Radio Observatory is being re-evaluated for its usefulness due to government cuts. But as it is, an anomaly opens up in the area, a mysterious woman called Logan appears, along with an invisible creature. Something called the Pattern is living in their computer systems and if they don't remove it, it will consume all the planet's resources.

I Scream
Company: BBV
Writer: Lance Parkin
Release Date: August 2000

The planet Galspar is the galaxy's largest supplier of Ice Cream - the entire planet is controlled by the company and everybody works for the company. The Narrator is a level F manager in a high end ice cream restaurant. All she wants is to work hard and become a level H, the highest level that can be attained. Then she meets John, an 8 Ball. The 8 Balls are the drop outs who live off the grid. When she starts dating John things get complicated as they hack into the orbital habitat and see things they shouldn't. There are many secrets on Galspar, including a more sinister Force, Level I.

Sontarans: Conduct Unbecoming
Company: BBV
Writer: Gareth Preston
Release Date: September 2000

When Forrest and Maria escape Sontaran custody, they hide away on a Sontaran spaceship. The spaceship in questions contains General Bestock who is on a special mission for the Sontaran council under the orders of Field Major Drell. The two escapees are recaptured once on board and are found to be two high priority prisoners who carry the secrets of the Akara protocols. Bestock begins his interrogation of the two prisoners over a number of days, during this time Maria form a bond, which has ramifications when Bestock is summoned by the Sontaran Strategic Council.

The Rani: The Rani Reaps the Whirlwind
Company: BBV
Writer: Pip and Jane Baker
Release Date: November 2000

The Rani is put on trial by the Tetraps for leaving Urak to die. She is then forced to carry out a experiment on behalf of the Tetraps. The Tetraps kidnap three people from planet Earth — Dean, Sam and Lucy. They kill Dean and impregnate Lucy with Sam's semen. Then they accelerate the gestation process, meaning she is due to give birth soon, despite only having been there ten days. Meeting an alien called Arbitus, they attempt to escape the planet.

Cyberon
Company: BBV
Writer: Lance Parkin
Release Date: January 2001

A hospital run by brain specialist Lauren Anderson is visited by Tom Mordley, who is there to trial a new drug, Cyberon — a drug, he claims, that can reverse the processes of brain damage and dementia. The drug is tested on a number of patients who show signs of recovery straight away; however, they are also seeing sinister robot-like figures in their sleep. Anderson and Mordley begin dating and Anderson learns more about him and Cyberon — which can learn, grow and adapt.

Wirrn: Race Memory
Company: BBV
Writer: Paul Ebbs
Release Date: May 2001

One hundred years after leaving Nerva Beacon the human race are trying to recolonise the Earth. At an isolated station in Africa four people — Sarah, Parker, Charles and Joshua — are using a gene spooler to reintroduce insects back into the environment. When several bits of their tech are sabotaged and a mysterious figure is seen fleeing from the base, Charles and Joshua give chase. Meanwhile Parker starts behaving strangely after being attacked by the intruder and it is soon revealed the intruder was a Wirrn and Parker is slowly becoming one. A race for survival ensues.

The Barnacled Baby
Company: BBV
Writer: Anthony Keetch
Release Date: June 2001

An injured Zygon crashed on earth is put on display in a Victorian freak show owned by the money hungry Jethro. Jethro's daughter, Doris, cares for and nurses the Zygon back to health and the two form an attachment. Having heard of the remarkable creature, scientist Sir Frederick Maltravers wishes to buy the Barnacled Baby to examine. When his offer is rebuffed he enlists the help of Tobias, Doris's former boyfriend, to help him. Tobias realises that Doris is having a breakdown, insisting on referring to the Zygon as Bobby, the name of their dead son. With the Zygon returning to its full strength it agrees to go with Fredrick to find its ship mates. But it also has much bigger plans.

Faction Paradox: The Eleven Day Empire
Company: BBV
Writer: Lawrence Miles
Release Date: October 2001

The Eleven Day Empire is attacked by Sontaran battleships. It is quickly thwarted. Godfather Morlock believes this is no accident as he uncovered that the Sontarans have stolen biodata, and also planted a fusion bomb. Morlock convinces Justine to drop her shadow weapon and pick up the bomb, which destroys her shadow. A further fleet of ships that belong to the other Great Houses then appear in the sky. Faction Paradox have had nothing to do with these Houses for thousands of years. The Houses wish to make peace with the Faction and send delegates, but Morlock suspects the Houses have ulterior motives.

Faction Paradox: The Shadow Play
Company: BBV
Writer: Lawrence Miles
Release Date: October 2001

Justine is successfully bonded to the Grandfather's weapon. This means she is now a siege weapon, with an unlimited arsenal — and that she also carries the Grandfather's shadow.

Meanwhile, the Houses have proposed a treaty that will mean Faction Paradox is recognised as a House again. The Faction will still be subject to their own law but will have to surrender any members who committed crimes against the other Houses.

The treaty is signed and Lolita demands Justine be given into custody, as she now has the Grandfather's shadow attached to her, and must be held accountable for his crimes. Morlock tries to help Eliza and Justine escape, as a further Sontaran fleet arrives and declares martial law.

Do You Have a Licence to Save This Planet?
Company: BBV
Writer: Paul Ebbs & Gareth Preston
Release Date: August 2001

The Foot Doctor arrives in an ordinary suburban neighbourhood. There he meets the Salesman and they are menaced by Cyberons, Autons and Sontarans before being captured by the Licenser, who was also behind the other creatures' attacks. He wants to put a stop to the Foot Doctor's unlicensed adventures.

Kaldor City: Occam's Razor
Company: Magic Bullet
Writer: Alan Stevens & Jim Smith
Release Date: 1st September 2001

Uvanov asks for help from psychostrategist Carnell when several Firstmasters are killed. All the clues point to a new arrival in town, Kaston Iago, but when a squad is sent to arrest him he escapes, only to head straight to Uvanov's house in order to prove that he isn't responsible for the murders. Uvanov in turn employs Iago as his bodyguard, and tasks him with unravelling the mystery.

The Green Man
Company: BBV
Writer: Zoltán Déry
Release Date: March 2002

When two men gathering herbs in the forest are attacked by a wolf/plant like creature, Earl Godfrey sends out Henri D'Arree and some soldiers to investigate. The troops are attacked by one of the men, who has mutated into a Krynoid. The creature gives chase and attacks the local village, while Godfrey's men try various methods to defeat it, all of which fail. Eventually, D'Aree's Knights Templar chop the creature to bits with axes and then burn the pieces. Meanwhile the wolf creature has consumed the local livestock and grown even bigger. With everyone taking refuge in the castle, the Kyrnoid begins an assault on the building.

Kaldor City: Death's Head
Company: Magic Bullet
Writer: Chris Boucher
Release Date: 20th April 2002

When Uvanov is almost killed by a poisoned skull, he asks Cotton to undertake an investigation into the plot to kill him. Cotton delegates duties to Blayes who realises that everything leads to a dead end.

The Killing Stone
Company: BBV
Writer: Richard Franklin
Release Date: May 2002

Mike Yates is taking a holiday in Gibraltar on the advice of the Brigadier, after being discharged from UNIT. While he's there he seeks out an Amphora vase to add to his extensive collection.

Upon finding the vase, the Master — disguised as a snake charmer — makes a snake rise from the vase and spit venom in Mike's eye which knocks him out. He wakes up some time later and returns to his hotel, where he is taken ill with gallstones.

He heads to Scotland to get the stones removed, but upon their removal he realises it is a miniature replica of the Vase. It turns out this is a vital component to the Master's CVE, planted by the snake and grown inside his gall bladder. After the Master tricks Benton into handing the vase over, he lures the Doctor and Brigadier into a trap and only Yates can rescue them.

In 2 Minds
Company: BBV
Writer: Iain Hepburn
Release Date: September 2002

When reporter Nicola McLaren of the *Caledonian* newspaper investigates the strange circumstances of a soldier's death, apparently at the hands of

Al Jazeeran rebels, she finds her self on the run with a former soldier called Wight who was the only survivor of the alleged attack.

Wight reveals the squadron was actually killed by an alien life form from a crashed ship; he has severe burns on his body from the attack and was experimented on by the army afterwards. He finds himself inexplicably drawn south towards a warehouse where the Rutan, which has taken the form of an army officer, is based and has re-appropriated the crashed space craft.

The Quality of Mercy
Company: BBV
Writer: David A Mcintee
Release Date: September 2002

When a man falls from a ship in the sky, the local priest calls in the Church. Also arriving in town is Guy De Carnac, a dishonoured member of the Knights Templar who now lives his life by his own rules and morals. With Father Baldwin set on trying the stranger as a demon to further propagate the church's hold on the region, Brother Reynard sides with De Carnac and the two go on the run with the stranger.

Kaldor City: Hidden Persuaders
Company: Magic Bullet
Writer: Jim Smith & Fiona Moore
Release Date: 30th November 2002

Blayes has joined the Church of Taren Capel and after being provided with some information passed on by a Voc, she meets with church leader Paullus and his followers to plan an act of terrorism.

With Iago away, Uvanov temporarily puts Cotton in charge of his security while Rull investigates the reason why 0.5% of his wages have been docked for something called the Larson Project.

Blayes and her cohorts infiltrate an oxygen cracking centre, with the aim of blowing it up, but their mission coincides with a security practice drill and they are forced to take hostages.

Faction Paradox: Sabbath Dei
Company: BBV
Writer: Lawrence Miles
Release Date: February 2003

Cousins Justine and Eliza find themselves in 18th Century England. They are taken in by Lord Sandwich and the cult, the Order of St Francis. The order is being investigated by Sabbath, a member of the secret service who knows all about Faction Paradox and has a particular interest in the disappearance of a prostitute called Mary Culver.

When the secret service raid a party hosted by the Order, Justine attacks them using her ship. It turns out the raid was ordered by the Earl of Bute, Sabbath's superior and aide to the King.

With an army of Homunculi ready to be unleashed by the King, House Lolita gaining more power and Sabbath tampering with forces and cult relics he doesn't understand. It appears the final battleground of the Houses will be 18th Century Earth.

Kaldor City: Taren Capel
Company: Magic Bullet
Writer: Alan Stevens
Release Date: 15th March 2003

Suspecting there are greater powers at play than even he can control, Carnell inputs all the information he has about Taren Capel into the Voc V31 and the two play a game of chess. Having found evidence that points to Landerchild as the man behind the Larson Project, Rull has him arrested and his property searched. However, the trail then goes cold when Rull's chief witness is found dead.

Meanwhile, Iago and Blayes secretly work together to devise a plan for a Tarenist attack on Company Central. Iago convinces Uvanov that Landerchild and Carnell are behind the attack, but there is something far more deadly about to happen in Kaldor City.

Faction Paradox: In the Year of the Cat
Company: BBV
Writer: Lawrence Miles
Release Date: April 2003

Justine is put on trial as Grandfather Paradox while Eliza, Sandwich and the Sieur d'Eon attempt to stop the King parading his army through the streets and forever throwing history off course. The last survivors of Faction Paradox must find out exactly what Lolita is up to.

Kaldor City: Checkmate
Company: Magic Bullet
Writer: Alan Stevens
Release Date: 20th September 2003

The robots are on the rampage, Landerchild is garnering support to remove Uvanov from power and the Tarenists, lead by Pallus, are about to perform the ritual of 12 to bring Tarren Capel's spirit back, while some greater force is manipulating events.

Faction Paradox: Movers
Company: BBV
Writer: Lawrence Miles
Release Date: December 2003

Justine is trapped in a dream world with her friend Emma. She has no recollection of her previous life and seems quite at home there, but knows something isn't right.

On the Great Houses' prison world, where Justine's physical form is in suspended animation, one of the prison warders, Ordinary Selvynkesh, has gone rogue and let out Demetra Kein, who in turn has set free a number of other prisoners, whom she is able to control through tattoos she has placed on them. Also in the prison is Second Ordinary Keeble who has woken another prisoner, Shuncuker of Faction Paradox, to help him escape the over-run prison world.

Daemos Rising
Company: Reeltime
Writer: David J. Howe
Release Date: December 2003

When Kate Lethbridge-Stewart is summoned to an isolated cottage by Douglas Cavendish, she finds the former UNIT operative sleeping rough and suffering from a mental breakdown. Discharged from UNIT after the Yeti affair, Cavendish took a number of keepsakes. One of these was an ancient book which summons the power of the Daemons. Cavendish was hoping to use the power for good and to help himself but inadvertently brought something else through. With a stone statue that keeps following them and a ghost from the future on the loose, Kate and Cavendish must prepare for the return of the Daemons.

Faction: Paradox: A Labyrinth of Histories
Company: BBV
Writer: Lawrence Miles
Release Date: February 2004

Back in Justine's dream world, Sabbath has found what he looking for, which is Emma's Auntie (who is also, it transpires, Sabbath's grandmother) and so his people attack her house.

Kine meanwhile has asked Selvynkesh to release four prisoners, hunting dogs that were bred to track down members of Faction Paradox. They sniff out Justine, Shuncucker and Keeble in a library where it transpires Justine and Shuncucker's shadow weapons won't work on the hunting dogs; consequently they set fire to the library and build a firewall. We learn that Kine always planned to get imprisoned in order to be woken up so as to be able to track down whoever was carrying the Grandfather's shadow.

Kaldor City: The Prisoner
Company: Magic Bullet and MJTV
Writer: Alan Stevens Fiona Moore
Release Date: 24th April 2004

With Iago captured on the grounds of Landerchild's family estate, a straightforward interrogation soon becomes a debate concerning the nature of belief vs truth and how one perceives reality.

Kaldor City: Storm Mine
Company: Magic Bullet
Writer: Daniel O'Mahony
Release Date: 18th December 2004

Blayes wakes up on a Storm Mine in the middle of the Blind Heart Desert. The Storm Mine is occupied by the Chief Mover, the Commander, and the unseen Chief Fixer, as well as numerous robots. Unfortunately for Blayes, Iago is also there, albeit as a voice inside her head. The rest of the crew were killed by robots who received Taren Capel's message some 18 months ago, and the survivors have been unable to return to the quarantined Kaldor City.

The True History of Faction Paradox — Volume I: Coming to Dust
Company: Magic Bullet
Writer: Lawrence Miles
Release Date: July 23rd 2005

Pennerton and Finton, two members of the Society of Sigismondo di Rimini, discover the imprisoned Great Ape of Posto di Forragio. The locals keep it as a tourist attraction but the society members see it as some kind of dangerous monster. Unsure they can deal with the menace by themselves, Finton suggests they should contact Faction Paradox, whose existence he's aware of through his association with the Earl of Sandwich. The call is answered by Justine, who agrees to help them in return for information, held by society member Corwyn Marne, as to the whereabouts of the Faction Paradox race banks and biodata codices.

The True History of Faction Paradox — Volume II: The Ship of a Billion Years
Company: Magic Bullet
Writer: Lawrence Miles
Release Date: 15th April 2006

On The Ship of a Billion Years, Justine is in the service of Upuat, an Osirian god who finds her presence amusing. The Divine Congress are expecting a visitor; this turns out to be Sutekh, who requests absolute authority over the Osirian Court, following the unexplained absence of his brother, Osiris.

With things heating up in the Osirian Court, it is up to the last survivors of Faction Paradox to stop Sutekh's bid for power.

Zygon: When Being You Just Isn't Enough
Company: BBV
Writer: Lance Parkin, Jon Blum and Bill Baggs (no writer is credited)
Release Date: Spring 2008

After an accident, Mike Kirkwood seeks help from Doctor Anderson. Since the accident he keeps having dreams he is a monster. The two become close and Anderson is told to take some time off work for getting too involved. She is being stalked by Bob Calhoun who encourages her to make Mike remember his past. Anderson and Mike start seeing each other, and they discover the true nature of his alien origin and the history he has with the sinister Bob.

The True History of Faction Paradox — Volume III: Body Politic
Company: Magic Bullet
Writer: Lawrence Miles
Release Date: 3rd May 2008

The War King sends Lord Mortega as Ambassador to the Osirian Court in order to broker an alliance which is crucial to their success in certain areas of battle.

Meanwhile, Justine is determined to bring Osiris back from the dead, to stop Sutekh from taking his brother's place as leader of the Osirian Court, and has sent Eliza to collect Osiris's dispersed biodata from Earth.

The True History of Faction Paradox — Volume IV: Words From Nine Divinities
Company: Magic Bullet
Writer: 24th November 2008
Release Date: Lawrence Miles

Justine's presence on the Homeworld causes discord among the Council, with Lolita trying to block the War King's motion to have Faction Paradox reinstated as part of the assembly. Sutekh, meanwhile, has sent his Mal'akh to kill all those of the Osirian Court who dispute his rule and oppose him. Lolita manoeuvres herself into a position of absolute power on the Homeworld, and Sutekh is preparing for his final assault on the Great Houses.

The True History of Faction Paradox — Volume V: Ozymandias
Company: Magic Bullet
Writer: Lawrence Miles
Release Date: 8th June 2009

Finton and Marne are transported to another planet via a time tunnel. Lord Geb, the father of Sutekh and Osiris/Horus, is overseeing a tribunal to determine which of his sons should be granted accession to the Osirian throne. Sutekh challenges Horus to another battle, which Horus accepts, on the condition that the battlefield is time itself

The True History of Faction Paradox — Volume VI: The Judgment of Sutekh
Company: Magic Bullet
Writer: Lawrence Miles
Release Date: 23rd November 2009

Lolita and Marne arrive in ancient Egypt where the final battle between the forces of Sutekh and Horus has taken place and Sutekh appears to have won, in spite of established history. An epic plot unfolds, a war is fought on many battlegrounds across time and space and the destinies of humans, Osirans and Faction Paradox are revealed.

The Minister of Chance: The Pointed Hand
Company: Radio Static
Writer: Dan Freeman
Release Date: March 2011

Durian, the ambassador from Sezuan, visits the island of Tanto to discuss a peace treaty. The king is automatically aggressive towards him but he remains calm. Sezuan is under threat from the nation Dura, and Durian is worried that Tanto, which lies between the two nations, will be invaded and used as a supply and refuelling station thus giving Dura the upper hand. The king will not hear Durian's pleas and will not be drawn into war, but Durian has some very persuasive methods to make him collaborate.

The Minister of Chance: The Broken World
Company: Radio Static
Writer: Dan Freeman
Release Date: March 2011

Durian, the ambassador from Sezuan, visits the island of Tanto to discuss a peace treaty. The king is automatically aggressive towards him but he remains calm. Sezuan is under threat from the nation Dura, and Durian is worried that Tanto, which lies between the two nations, will be invaded and used as a supply and refuelling station thus giving Dura the upper hand. The king will not hear Durian's pleas and will not be drawn into war, but Durian has some very persuasive methods to make him collaborate.

The Minister of Chance: The Forest Shakes
Company: Radio Static
Writer: Dan Freeman
Release Date: January 13 2012

The Minister and Kitty are imprisoned after they discover the Horseman has left the planet. Their cellmate is a farmer called Sutu, who ended up on this planet after he found the Horseman's door, which should have been shut behind him. Back on Tanto, Cantha is being forced to work on the rocket while debating the ethics of war with her guards. Meanwhile the Horseman is on a rampage murdering soldiers, which naturally angers Lord Rathan. The Minister manages to outwit their captors but stays behind as Kitty and Sutu escape back to Tanto, where she develops a plan to rescue Cantha.

Kaldor City: Metafiction
Company: Magic Bullet
Writer: Alan Stevens and Fiona Moore
Release Date: 7th July 2012

Justina — under instruction from Uvanov — questions Iago over his past. But his story is one all too familiar to the audience.

The Minister of Chance: Plaudin Fields
Company: Radio Static
Writer: Dan Freeman
Release Date: 20th July 2012

The Minister and Kitty go in search of the Sage of the Waves. When they arrive in her vicinity, they find that the locals make regular sacrifices to her by drowning young women. Kitty tries to stop one of these sacrifices and the two of them get into trouble with the local police. Back on Sezuan, Durian is gaining increasing public support, and with the Witch Prime aware of his desire for power, he and the Madam Seer hatch a plan to get Polichar to kill him.

Meanwhile on Tanto Professor Cantha meets Sunflower, who wants her to spearhead the revolution in the name of science. The Minister and Kitty make it into the castle that Sage lives in and while Kitty recovers from an arrow injury she sustained, the Minister prepares for his final battle with the Horseman.

The Minister of Chance. The Tiger
Company: Radio Static
Writer: Dan Freeman
Release Date: March 1st 2013

Lord Rathan orchestrates the invasion of Sezuan air space by Duran craft in order to further propagate Durians need for war. Meanwhile the Horseman and the Minister fight it out before Kitty brokers a peace between them.

The Minister heads back to Tanto leaving the injured Kitty with the Horseman. On Tanto Sunflower and Cantha continue to rally people together in the name of science, while the Witch Prime, admitting defeat, resigns.

The Minister of Chance: In a Bark on the River Hex
Company: Radio Static
Writer: Dan Freeman
Release Date: 17th May 2013

Aware of Rathan's true nature, Kitty and the Minister go about inciting rebellion by contacting Cantha and Sunflower and hypnotizing the former Witch Prime into leading his people against Rathan. They then go to the River Hex, where the Minister must visit the Summer King to find out about Rathan's past.

P.R.O.B.E. — When to Die
Company: BBV
Writer: Bill Baggs
Release Date: 21st April 2015

Liz Shaw is assigned by Patricia Haggard to handle the decommissioning of a secret government project, a super soldier that can live forever. The soldier in question is being kept alive by medication extracted from a Martian meteor, at a cost of millions to the tax payer. With the program discontinued, Paul will die but he is helped to escape by his brother. He goes on the run but starts to experience attacks and surging pain without his medication. If he cannot be recaptured and contained his death will lead to many more.

Acknowledgements

This book would not have been possible without so many people.

A thousand thanks go to Aimee Jayne Kahl for reading and re-reading everything!

Also to Jackson for listening to me rabbit on about this book for about 3 years.

Thanks to Stuart Douglas for publishing the book in the first place and going through the countless rewrites. Blair Bidmead for the cover and an extra special thanks to Alan Stevens for putting me in touch with so many people, fact checking and doing an extra bit of proofing.

My gratitude also goes to Stuart from Misty Moon, Scott Frankton and Sam Clemens.

And thanks to all my interviewees, who took time out of their lives to talk to me about jobs from 20 years ago. Andy Grant, Andy Lane, Anthony Keetch, Alistair Lock, Bill Baggs, Bryonie Pritchard, Bev Cressman, Christian Darkin, David A Mcintee, David J. Howe, Daniel O'Mahony, Fiona Moore, George Telfer, Gareth Preston, Gary Russell, Harvey Summers, Iain Hepburn, Iain McLaughlin, Jan Vincent-Rudzki, John Wadmore, Jon Blum, John Ainsworth, Jo Castleton, Jim Smith, John Guilor, Keith Barnfather, Kevin Davies, Lance Parkin, Mark J Thompson, Miles Richardson, Mark Ayres, Nick Briggs, Nicola Bryant, Nigel Fairs, Patricia Merrick, Peter Grehan, Peter Miles, Paul Cornell, Rob Thrush, Simon Gerard, Sophie Aldred, Steve Cole, Terrance Dicks, Tim Saward, Zoltan Dery and whoever I've forgotten.

And thanks to everyone who made these productions, for helping keep *Doctor Who* alive and making something truly unique.

Notes

Introduction

1 https://www.bigfinish.com/releases/v/the-second-doctor-box-set-430
2 'Living with Levene', BBC/2 Entertain documentary, on 'Claws of Axos' SE DVD
3 'Series and Cereals', Mark Wright, *DWM* 301,p.8

Chapter 1

1 Author interview with Keith Barnfather, London, November 2014
2 Author interview with David J Howe, March 2015, Phone
3 Author interview with Kevin Davies, London January 2015
4 Davies, ibid
5 Author interview with Mark Ayres, London, May 2015

Chapter 2

1 'Benton is Back', Malcolm Hester, *DWM* 129, October 1987
2 Barnfather Interview
3 Author interview with Andy Grant, London, November 2014
4 Ayres Interview May 2015
5 Barnfather Interview
6 *Making of War Time*, Reeltime Productions, 1997
7 ibid
8 Author interview with Jan Vincent-Rudzki - November 14, email
9 Barnfather Interview
10 Author interview with Andy Lane, London, April 2013
11 ibid
12 ibid
13 Skype Interview with John Ainsworth, January 2015
14 Barnfather Interview
15 ibid
16 ibid
17 ibid
18 ibid
19 'A Man with a Vision...', *Dreamwatch* 4, Winter Special 94, pp 13-16
20 Barnfather Interview
21 Nick Briggs Interview, Email. January 2015
22 Barnfather Interview
23 Briggs Email Interview 2015
24 Barnfather Interview
25 Briggs Email Interview 2015
26 *Making of War Time*
27 Briggs Email Interview 2015
28 Ainsworth Skype Interview
29 ibid
30 Lane Interview 2013
31 Briggs Email Interview 2015
32 Barnfather Interview

33 Ayres Interview 2015
34 A Man with a Vision...
35 Ayres Interview 2015
36 Briggs Email Interview 2015
37 Ainsworth Skype Interview
38 ibid
39 Ayres Interview 2015
40 Briggs Email Interview 2015
41 Barnfather Interview
42 Briggs Email Interview 2015
43 Ayres Interview 2015
44 ibid
45 Barnfather Interview
46 Ainsworth Skype Interview
47 Lane Interview, April 2013
48 ibid
49 'Wartime', Paul Travers, *DWM* 140 August 1988, p. 18
50 Lane Interview, April 2013
51 Barnfather Interview
52 A Man with a Vision...

Chapter 3

1 'BBV', Marcus Hearn, *DWM* 216, August 1994, pp. 44-45
2 Author interview with Bill Baggs, Southampton, March 2015,
3 Author interview with Christian Darkin, December 2013
4 ibid
5 'BBV', *DWM* 216
6 *Celestial Toymaker* 201, November 1993
7 Author interview with Nicola Bryant, London, April 2014
8 'BBV', *DWM* 216
9 Heberfelner, Mike, 'An Interview with Bill Baggs of BBV', July 2006 http://searchmytrash.com/cgi-bin/articlecreditsb.pl?billbaggs%287-06%29
10 Author interview with John Wadmore, London, November 2014
11 ibid
12 Lane Interview
13 Baggs Interview
14 'Bill Baggs of BBV'
15 Darkin, email exchange with author, December 2013
16 ibid
17 ibid
18 'Gallifrey Guardian', *DWM* 176, September 1991 p. 8
19 *Celestial Toyroom*, 194, April 1993
20 Darkin 2013
21 'Off the Shelf', *DWM* 181, October 1991, p. 50
22 "Extraordinary Gentlemen', Anthony K McCail, *DWM* 332, July 2003, pp 20 - 25
23 'BBV', *DWM* 216

Chapter 4

1 Author conversation with Peter Miles, Jan 2015, London
2 'Interview: Sophie Aldred', Gary Russell, *DWM* 196, February 1993, pp 10 -13
3 Author Interview with Sophie Aldred, telephone, November 2014
4 Author Interview with Nigel Fairs Interview, Brighton, July 2014

5 Bryant Interview
6 Aldred Interview
7 Fairs Interview
8 ibid
9 Baggs Interview
10 Aldred Interview, *DWM* 196
11 ibid
12 ibid
13 Miles Interview
14 Baggs Interview
15 Fairs Interview
16 ibid
17 ibid
18 Baggs Interview
19 ibid
20 Author interview with Alistair Lock, Telephone, February 2015
21 Lock Interview
22 'Off The Shelf', *DWM* 188, July 1992, p. 49
23 Fairs Interview
24 bid

Chapter 5

1 Fairs Interview
2 Briggs Email Interview
3 ibid
4 ibid
5 ibid
6 *CT* 194
7 ibid
8 'The Auton Diaries', Nick Briggs, *DWM* 270 10/96, p. 26- 30
9 Baggs Interview
10 Briggs Email Interview
11 *CT* 194
12 *Celestial Toymaker* 191, 01/93
13 http://www.searchmytrash.com
14 ibid
15 Author Interview with Harvey Summer, Email, November 2013
16 'BBV', *DWM* 216
17 *CT* 194
18 *DWM* 199
19 Author interview with Gary Russell, Email, November 2014
20 *Stranger than Fiction*
21 'BBV', *DWM* 216
22 *CT* 194
23 'A Stranger in Custody', *DWB* 128 07/94, pp. 13 - 15
24 Nick Briggs podcast 001
25 Briggs Email Interview

Chapter 6

1 'BBV', *DWM* 216
2 Briggs Email Interview
3 ibid

4 'A Stranger in Custody'
5 Author Interview with Tim Saward, London, April 2014
6 Briggs Email Interview
7 Peter Davison Interview, *AirZone Solution* DVD
8 www.searchmytrash.com
9 'Still in Character', *DWM* Summer Special 94, pp 15B – 18B
10 http://www.alancumming.com/1992/2015/5/26/the-airzone-solution
11 http://www.searchmytrash.com
12 'Still in Character'
13 'Doctor #3 – Jon Powetwee', *TV Zone* Dr Who at 30 Special, 12/93, pp 8 - 10
14 http://www.searchmytrash.com
15 'A Stranger in Custody'
16 Nick Briggs Interview January 2016, Email Interview
17 'Still in Character'
18 *Stranger Than Fiction*
19 'Still in Character'
20 http://www.starburstmagazine.com/features/interviews/7587-interview-gary-russell-doctor-who-part-1
21 Baggs Interview
22 Briggs Email Interview
23 'Artistic License', Benjamin Cook, *DWM* 303, 04/01 Pg, 12 - 13
24 *Stranger than Fiction*
25 *CT* 201 11/93, p. 22
26 'Shelf Life', *DWM* 206, p. 48
27 'Still in Character'
28 Starburst Interview with Gary Russell
29 *Dreamwatch* 42 02/99
30 'BBV', *DWM* 216
31 'A Stranger in Custody'
32 'Stranger Tales', Gary Russell, *DWM* 202, pp. 40 - 45
33 Saward interview
34 *TV Zone*, Who at 30 pp. 20 -13
35 *CT* 202 11/93
36 ibid
37 Briggs Email Interview 2016
38 Baggs Interview
39 Bryant Interview
40 Baggs Interview

Chapter 7

1 ibid
2 Author Interview with Iain McLaughlin, Email, March 2015
3 'BBV', *DWM* 216
4 Author interview with John Guilor, Email, March 2015
5 Briggs Email Interview 2016
6 ibid
7 'BBV', *DWM* 216
8 Briggs Email Interview 2016
9 'The Auton Diaries'
10 ibid
11 *Stranger Than Fiction* 2
12 'Stranger Things Have Happened', *Matrix* 51, Summer 1995, pp 6 - 11
13 Briggs Email Interview 2016
14 Wadmore Interview

15 ibid
16 'BBV', *DWM* 216
17 ibid
18 Briggs Email Interview 2016
19 'A Stranger in Custody'
20 Briggs Email Interview 2016
21 Nick Briggs Interview March 2016, Skype
22 Wadmore Interview
23 *The Making of The Terror Game*
24 Briggs Email Interview
25 *Stranger Than Fiction* 2
26 Briggs Email Interview 2016
27 'BBV', *DWM* 216
28 'A Stranger in Custody'
29 Briggs Email Interview 2016
30 Russell Interview
31 http://www.searchmytrash.com/cgi-bin/articlecreditsb.pl?billbaggs%287-06%29

Chapter 8

1 'A Stranger in Custody'
2 'Stranger Things Have Happened'
3 ibid
4 'BBV', *DWM* 216
5 ibid
6 Briggs Email Interview 2016
7 ibid
8 *Stranger than Fiction* 2
9 Wadmore Interiview
10 'A Stranger in Custody'
11 https://www.youtube.com/watch?v=HgGEwrmiSAM
12 'Shelf Life', *DWM* 09/94 217, p 34
13 Review, *Dreamwatch* 01 10/94, p. 29
14 'Stranger Things Have Happened'
218 'The Auton Diaries'
16 ibid
17 Briggs Email Interview 2016
18 ibid
19 Baggs Interview
20 http://www.kasterborous.com/2010/04/interview-with-nick-briggs/
21 Briggs Email Interview 2016

Chapter 9

1 Davies Interview
2 ibid
3 ibid
4 Ayres Interview
5 Davies Interview
6 ibid
7 ibid
8 Terrance Dicks Interview January 2015, Phone
9 Davies Interview

10 Dicks Interview
11 Davies Interview
12 Ayres Interview
13 Davies Interview
14 ibid
15 ibid
16 ibid
17 ibid
18 ibid
19 Aldred Interview
20 Davies Interview
21 ibid
22 ibid
23 Ibid. In fact, Sam West played the role.
24 ibid
25 ibid
26 ibid
27 Ayres Interview
28 Davies Interview
29 ibid
30 ibid
31 ibid
32 Mark Ayres Interview May 2016, London
33 Davies Interview
34 'A Day on the Set', *Dreamwatch* 2 11/94 pp. 17 - 18
35 Davies Interview
36 Aldred Interview
37 ibid
38 ibid
39 Davies Interview
40 ibid
41 ibid
42 ibid
43 Ayres Interview 2016
44 Davies Interview
45 Dicks Interview
46 'Shelf Life', *DWM* 221, p.34
47 ibid
48 Terrance Dicks Interview 2014
49 ibid
50 Davies Interview
51 Ayres Interview 2016
52 Davies Interview
53 ibid
54 Davies directed two episodes of this 1998 series, 'The Barrier of Second Attention' and 'Nemesis', both from season 1
55 Davies Interview
56 ibid
57 Author interview with Paul Cornell
58 Davies Interview
59 ibid
60 Cornell Interview

Chapter 10

1 Briggs Email Interview
2 'Extraordinary Gentlemen'
3 'The Zero Imperative', *DWM* 219, 11/94, pp 12 - 13
4 'Extraordinary Gentlemen'
5 Grant Interview
6 ibid
7 ibid
8 ibid
9 Baggs Interview
10 http://www.searchmytrash.com/cgi-bin/articlecreditsb.pl?billbaggs%287-06%29
11 *Stranger Than Fiction* 2
12 'Extraordinary Gentlemen'
13 *The Zero Imperative*
14 'Extraordinary Gentlemen'
15 Author Interview with Patricia Merrick, Email, December 2014
16 *The Zero Imperative*
17 ibid
18 ibid
19 ibid
20 ibid
21 Ayres Interview
22 ibid
23 *The Zero Imperative*
24 Merrick Interview
25 http://www.searchmytrash.com/cgi-bin/articlecreditsb.pl?billbaggs%287-06%29
26 'Extraordinary Gentlemen'
27 Baggs Interview
28 'Extraordinary Gentlemen'
29 ibid
30 Baggs Interview
31 Ayres Interview
32 *Stranger than Fiction* 2
33 ibid
34 *The Zero Imperative*
35 'Extraordinary Gentlemen'
36 Merrick Interview
37 *The Zero Imperative*
38 *Stranger than Fiction* 2
39 ibid
40 'Starwatch', Graham Kibble-White, *DWM* 450
41 *The Irish Times*. 21 May 1996
42 'Extraordinary Gentlemen'
43 Baggs Interview
44 Ayres Interview
45 'Shelf Life', *DWM* 220 12/94 p. 36
46 ibid
47 ibid
48 *Celestial Toyshop*, *CT* 250, pp. 13 -14
49 ibid
50 *Stranger than Fiction* 2
51 ibid

52 Ayres Interview
53 'Extraordinary Gentlemen'

Chapter 11

1 'Stranger Things Have Happened'
2 http://www.bbvonline.co.uk/fea_nbriggs_int.html
3 ibid
4 ibid
5 Baggs Interview
6 ibid
7 http://www.bbvonline.co.uk/fea_nbriggs_int.html
8 Briggs Email Interview
9 http://www.bbvonline.co.uk/fea_nbriggs_int.html
10 ibid
11 ibid
12 ibid
13 ibid
14 'Shelf Life', *DWM* 223 3/95, p 34
15 'Stranger Things Have Happened'
16 Baggs Interview

Chapter 12

1 'Stranger Still' Graham Fowler, *DWM* 225, pp. 13 - 14
2 Baggs Interview
3 Briggs Email Interview
4 'Stranger Still'
5 http://www.bbvonline.co.uk/fea_nbriggs_int.html
6 *Stranger than fiction 3*
7 'Stranger Still'
8 http://www.bbvonline.co.uk/fea_nbriggs_int.html
9 Matrix 51 Summer 95
10 Stranger Still
11 Stranger Still
12 *Stranger Than Fiction 3*
13 http://www.searchmytrash.com/
14 Stranger Still
15 'Stranger Things Have Happened'
16 *Stranger Than Fiction 3*
17 'Stranger Still'
18 'Stranger Things Have Happened'
19 'Shelf Life', *DWM* 228 8/95 p.43
20 Baggs Interview
21 'Stranger Things Have Happened'
22 ibid
23 'Stranger Still'
24 Baggs Interview
25 Briggs Email Interview
26 Grant Interview

Chapter 13

1 'Shelf Life', *DWM* 215, 08/95 p.34
2 Baggs Interview
3 Briggs Email Interview
4 ibid
5 Briggs Skype Interview
6 ibid
7 ibid
8 ibid
9 ibid
10 Baggs Interview
11 Briggs Skype Interview
12 'Stranger Still'
13 Baggs Interview
14 Briggs Skype Interview
15 ibid
16 ibid
17 http://news.bbc.co.uk/1/hi/england/cambridgeshire/3839733.stm
18 Briggs Skype Interview
19 ibid
20 ibid
21 ibid
22 'Who it yourself', *SFX* 01 06/95 p.36
23 Grant Interview
24 Baggs Interview
25 ibid
26 'Time Gentlemen'
27 ibid
28 ibid
29 *Stranger than fiction 3*
30 'Time Gentlemen'
31 https://www.youtube.com/watch?v=PrusjhgrVQo
32 *Stranger Than Fiction 3*
33 'Time Gentlemen'
34 https://www.youtube.com/watch?v=PrusjhgrVQo
35 Andy Grant Interview
36 ibid
37 ibid
38 *Celestial Toyshop* 235
39 ibid
40 ibid
41 'Shelf Life, *DWM* 245, 11/96 p.42
42 *Stranger than fiction 3*

Chapter 14

1 'War Time', *DWM* 140 pp. 15 - 17
2 Barnfather Interview
3 Andy Lane Interview April 2013, London
4 ibid
5 ibid
6 Barnfather Interview
7 'Gallifrey Guardian', *DWM* 187, 6/92, p.6
8 'Please Release Me', Ben Cook, *DWM* 316, pp. 19 - 23

9 Barnfather Interview
10 'Gallifrey Guardian', *DWM* 202, p 04
11 Barnfather Interview
12 'Origin of Species', Ben Cook, *DWM* 306, pp. 19-23
13 'Origin of Species'
14 'Miss Zygon', Ben Cook, *DWM* 308, pp. 13 - 14
15 'Origin of species'
16 *Dreamwatch* 94 Advert ,DWB 127 06/94, p 02
17 Barnfather Interview
18 http://news.drwho-online.co.uk/DWO-WhoCast-256-Ian-Levine-Interview.aspx
19 'Please Release Me'
20 ibid
21 'Downtime', Graham Fowler, *DWM* 229, pp. 4 - 7
22 'Origin of Species'
23 Richardson Interview March 2015, Email
24 Barnfather Interview
25 ibid
26 Richardson Interview
27 Barnfather Interview
28 'Downtime'
29 Barnfather Interview
30 'Please Release Me'
31 ibid
32 https://www.youtube.com/watch?v=PrusjhgrVQo
33 'Please Release Me'
34 *Still Getting Away with It*, Nicholas Courtney, pp.115-116
35 Beverley Cressman Interview February 2015, Email
36 'Still Getting Away with it'
37 Richardson Interview
38 David J Howe Interview March 2015, Phone
39 'Please Release Me'
40 'Origin of Species'
41 Cressman Interview
42 'Miss Zygon'
43 ibid
44 post production feature DVD, Reeltime
45 'Christopher Barry – Director', *TV Zone* Winter Special 97, pp. 54 – 62
46 http://gallifreybase.com/forum/showthread.php?t=139115
47 'Please Release Me'
48 *TV Zone* Winter Special 97
49 Barnfather Interview
50 'Shelf Life', *DWM* 232 11/95, p.38
51 Barnfather Interview
52 Lane Interview
53 Barnfather Interview
54 ibid
55 http://www.starburstmagazine.com/features/interviews/7587-interview-gary-russell-doctor-who-part-1
56 http://www.doctorwhonews.net/2015/10/dispute-over-downtime-dvd-release.html
57 ibid
58 Barnfather Interview
59 *TARDIS* Vol. 15, No 1, 04/97

Chapter 15

1 Baggs Interview
2 ibid
3 ibid
4 ibid
5 ibid
6 'Time Gentlemen'
7 ibid
8 ibid
9 Baggs Interview
10 'Time Gentlemen'
11 Baggs Interview
12 Patricia Merrick Interview December 2014, Email
13 https://www.youtube.com/watch?v=PrusjhgrVQo
14 https://www.youtube.com/watch?v=HgGEwrmiSAM
15 Baggs Interview
16 'Time Gentlemen'
17 *Stranger Than Fiction 3*
18 ibid
19 'How Zat!', *Dreamwatch* 42, 02/98, pp. 45 - 51
20 ibid
21 'Shelf Life', *DWM* 245, 101/95, p.42
22 ibid
23 *Celestial Toyshop* 237, 12/96, p.15
24 ibid
25 'Shelf Life', *DWM* 245
26 *Celestial Toyshop* 237
27 ibid
28 Baggs Interview
29 'Time Gentlemen'

Chapter 16

1 Alistair Lock Interview February 2015, Phone
2 Barnfather Interview
3 *The Making of Auton*
4 *The Auton Diaries*
5 ibid
6 ibid
7 Barnfather Interview
8 ibid
9 *The Making of Auton*
10 *The Auton Diaries*
11 Briggs Skype Interview
12 ibid
13 ibid
14 ibid
15 ibid
16 'The Auton Diaries'
17 Baggs Interview
18 Barnfather Interview
19 Briggs Skype Interview
20 ibid

21 *The Making of Auton* BBV
22 'The Auton Diaries'
23 ibid
24 Briggs Skype Interview
25 http://www.bbvonline.co.uk/fea_mwade_int.html
26 ibid
27 Briggs Skype Interview
28 Pritchard Interview
29 Briggs Skype Interview
30 'The Auton Diaries'
31 Baggs Interview
32 'The Auton Diaries'
33 Baggs Interview
34 Pritchard Interview
35 'The Auton Diaries'
36 Briggs Skype Interview
37 Lock Interview
38 'The Auton Diaries'
39 http://www.bbvonline.co.uk/fea_mwade_int.html
40 George Telfer Interview November 2015, Phone
41 'The Auton Diaries'
42 Telfer Interview
43 ibid
44 ibid
45 Briggs Skype Interview
46 ibid
47 ibid
48 ibid
49 'The Auton Diaries'
50 'Behind the Scenes of...', *Celestial Toynamker* 251, 1998, pp. 6 - 7
51 Briggs Skype Interview
52 ibid
53 The Making of Auton
54 *Celestial Toyshop* 246, 1997 p.16
55 'The Auton Diaries'
56 *SFX* 32 12/97
57 http://www.searchmytrash.com
58 Baggs Interview
59 Barnfather Interview
60 Briggs Skype Interview

Chapter 17

1 Briggs Skype Interview
2 Baggs Interview
3 https://www.youtube.com/watch?v=34YiRvlE39c
4 Aldred Interview
5 Saward Interview
6 'Time Gentlemen'
7 ibid
8 Aldred Interview
9 Briggs Skype Interview
10 http://www.bbvonline.co.uk/fea_nbriggs_int.html
11 Aldred Interview
12 https://www.youtube.com/watch?v=34YiRvlE39c

13 'Shelf Life', *DWM* 268, 8/98, p.45
14 https://www.youtube.com/watch?v=R3bnHyd9HgE
15 http://www.bbvonline.co.uk/fea_nbriggs_int.html
16 *Celestial Toyshop* 252, 98, pp. 15 -16
17 http://www.bbvonline.co.uk/fea_nbriggs_int.html
18 Saward Interview
19 ibid
20 ibid
21 Miles Interview January 2015, London
22 Saward Interview
23 Miles Interview
24 https://megabytemodem.wordpress.com/2011/09/10/tim-saward-interview-%E2%80%93-an-audio-writer-speaks/
25 'Shelf Life', *DWM* 272, 12/98, p. 57
26 *Dreamwatch* 48, 08/98
27 Saward Interview
28 ibid
29 Ainsworth Interview
30 http://www.bbvonline.co.uk/who_mduncan.html
31 Saward Interview
32 ibid
33 Ainsworth Interview
34 ibid
35 Aldred Interview
36 Richardson Interview
37 'On Tape' Interview, BBV, 'The Other Side' CD
38 ibid
39 Ainsworth Interview
40 Aldred Interview
41 Baggs Interview
42 Summers Interview
43 http://justyce.org
44 Fairs Interview
45 http://justyce.org/
46 Summers Interview
47 Fairs Interview
48 ibid
49 ibid
50 *Dreamwatch* 54, 02/99
51 Ainsworth Interview
52 http://justyce.org/
53 Briggs Email Interview
54 ibid
55 http://justyce.org
56 *Dreamwatch* 54
57 ibid
58 Time Gentlemen
59 'Mark Lawson talks to...' BBC 4, 3 April 2012
60 'The Shelf Life Award', *DWM* 278, 06/99 p.34

Chapter 18

1 Barnfather Interview
2 ibid
3 Dicks Interview

4 Barnfather Interview
5 'Shelf Life', *DWM* 268 8/98 p.44
6 Barnfather Interview
7 ibid
8 ibid
9 ibid
10 Howe Interview
11 Dicks Interview
12 *Making of Mindgame*
13 Richardson Interview
14 Aldred Interview
15 *Making of Mindgame*
16 Sophie Aldred Interview
17 ibid
18 Barnfather Interview
19 Howe Interview
20 Barnfather Interview
21 ibid
22 *'Mindgame', Celestial Toymaker* 253, 1998 pp. 10 -11
23 'Shelf Life', *DWM* 272, 12/98, p.57
24 ibid
25 Barnfather Interview
26 Richardson Interview
27 Barnfather Interview
28 ibid
29 ibid

Chapter 19

1 'Behind the Scenes of...' CT 251, pp. 6-7
2 Saward Interview
3 ibid
4 'The Auton Diaries'
5 'The Auton Diaries'
6 Briggs Skype Interview
7 Ainsworth Interview
8 Bryonie Pritchard 2014, Email
9 'The Auton Diaries'
10 ibid
11 Jo Castleton Interview June 2016, Email
12 'Behind the Scenes of...', *CT* 251
13 George Telfer Interview November 2015, Phone
14 'Behind the Scenes of...', *CT 251*
15 Baggs Interview
16 Briggs Skype Interview
17 ibid
18 ibid
19 ibid
20 Merrick Interview
21 Castleton Interview
22 Telfer Interview
23 'The Auton Diaries'
24 'Behind the Scenes of...', *CT* 251
25 John Wadmore Interview November 2014, London
26 'The Auton Diaries'

27 http://www.bbvonline.co.uk/fea_nbriggs_int.html
28 Briggs Skype Interview
29 'Behind the Scenes of...', *CT* 251
30 ibid
31 Briggs Skype Interview
32 ibid
33 Baggs Interview
34 'Sphere of Influence', *DWM* 284, 10/99, pp. 26 - 28
35 ibid
36 *The Auton Diaries*
37 'Review', *TARDIS* Vol. 16, Issue 2 10/98 pp. 28 - 29
38 http://www.bbvonline.co.uk/fea_nbriggs_int.html
39 Baggs Interview
40 'Sphere of Influence'

Chapter 20

1 Saward Interview
2 Baggs Interview
3 Saward Interview
4 Briggs Skype Interview
5 Ainsworth Interview
6 Baggs Interview
7 Briggs Skype Interview
8 ibid
9 Baggs Interview
10 Steve Cole Interview January 2015, Email
11 Fairs Interview
12 ibid
13 ibid
14 Justyce.org
15 ibid
16 *Dreamwatch* 56 04/99
17 Ainsworth Interview
18 Saward Interview
19 Ainsworth Interview
20 ibid
21 http://www.megabytemodem.wordpress.com/page/2/
22 Ainsworth Interview
23 http://justyce.org/
24 Saward Interview
25 *Dreamwatch* 56 04/99
26 Saward Interview
27 http://justyce.org
28 Baggs Interview
29 Ainsworth Interview
30 https://www.youtube.com/watch?v=34YiRvlE39c
31 Saward Interview
32 Baggs Interview
33 justyce.org
34 Mark J Thompson Interview, April 2014, Email
35 ibid
36 ibid
37 ibid
38 'Shelf Life', *DWM* 280, 07/99, p.42

39 Thompson interview
40 ibid
41 Saward Interview
42 Ainsworth Interview
43 ibid
44 ibid
45 ibid
46 ibid
47 Fairs Interview
48 Ainsworth Interview
49 Fairs Interview
50 Ainsworth Interview ibid
51 ibid
52 Summers Interview
53 ibid
54 'Shelf Life', *DWM* 280, p.43

Chapter 21

1 Barnfather Interview
2 Dicks Interview
3 Briggs Skype Interview
4 ibid
5 ibid
6 Richardson Interview
7 Briggs Skype Interview
8 ibid
9 ibid
10 Barnfather Interview
11 Howe Interview
12 Richardson Interview
13 Barnfather Interview
14 ibid
15 Aldred Interview
16 ibid
17 Barnfather Interview
18 ibid
19 Briggs Skype Interview
20 Wadmore Interview
21 ibid
22 *The Making of Mindgame*
23 Barnfather Interview
24 'Shelf Life', *DWM* 280, p.51
25 ibid
26 ibid
27 Richardson Interview
28 Barnfather Interview
29 Dicks Interview
30 Barnfather Interview

Chapter 22

1 Fairs Interview
2 ibid

3 http://justyce.org/
4 'Shelf Life', *DWM* 281 10/99 p.15
5 http://www.bbvonline.co.uk/news_arch.html
6 Baggs Interview
7 Saward Interview
8 ibid
9 ibid
10 ibid
11 'Shelf Life' , *DWM* 282 8/99 p.24
12 Briggs Skype Interview
13 ibid
14 ibid
15 Ainsworth Interview
16 Pritchard Interview
17 Ainsworth Interview
18 ibid
19 Baggs Interview
20 'Shelf Life', *DWM* 282 8/99 p.23
21 Baggs Interview
22 Ainsworth Interview
23 Baggs Interview
24 http://www.bbvonline.co.uk/news_arch.html
25 Saward Interview
26 http://www.bbvonline.co.uk/fea_pmiles_int.html
27 Saward Interview
28 ibid
29 *Dreamwatch* 65 12/99
30 Saward Interview
31 Lance Parkin Interview August 2014, Emails
32 ibid
33 *Emmerdale* (originally *Emmerdale Farm*) is a rural soap opera which starred Fraser Hines for many years
34 Parkin Interview
35 *CT* 267
36 Peter Grehan Interview April 2014, Email
37 Grehan Interview
38 Saward Interview
39 'Shelf Life' , *DWM* 287 01/00 p.35
40 Grehan Interview
41 Saward Interview
42 ibid
43 Baggs Interview
44 http://www.northernstars.ca/actorsvz/wade_michael.html
45 Baggs Interview
46 Telfer Interview
47 Briggs Skype Interview
48 ibid

Chapter 23

1 Saward Interview
2 Baggs Interview
3 ibid
4 ibid
5 Briggs Skype Interview

6 ibid
7 ibid
8 ibid
9 ibid
10 Baggs Interview
11 https://groups.google.com/d/msg/rec.arts.drwho/CKtOX7DX2Oc/Muu3Or_9bXAJ
12 Baggs Interview
13 Briggs Skype Interview
14 Patricia Merrick Interview December 2014, Email
15 Baggs Interview
16 ibid
17 http://www.bbvonline.co.uk/fea_g_b_int.htm
18 ibid
19 ibid
20 ibid
21 Telfer Interview
22 ibid
23 http://www.bbvonline.co.uk/fea_g_b_int.htm
24 Telfer Interview
25 http://www.bbvonline.co.uk/fea_mwade_int.html
26 Pritchard Interview
27 'Sphere of Influence'
28 ibid
29 Baggs Interview
30 'Sphere of Influence'
31 ibid
32 ibid
33 *Dreamwatch* 56 12/99
34 'Shelf Life' , *DWM* 286 01/00p.39
35 ibid
36 https://groups.google.com/d/msg/rec.arts.drwho/LwrsEHY-Av0/BJIhJaWh4RYJ
37 Baggs Interview
38 Briggs Skype Interview
39 ibid
40 Telfer Interview
41 Castleton interview June 2015, Email
42 http://www.bbvonline.co.uk/fea_mwade_int.html
43 Baggs Interview
44 ibid
45 Saward Interview
46 ibid
47 Saward Interview
48 *DWM* 276, 04/99, p.52
49 Baggs Interview
50 https://groups.google.com/d/msg/rec.arts.drwho/XXJdAFFYLHY/UJkqefgHCCYJ

Chapter 24

1 Baggs Interview
2 ibid
3 https://groups.google.com/d/msg/rec.arts.drwho/XXJdAFFYLHY/dI5XK6IyGgoJ
4 Baggs Interview
5 *CT* 271, 05/00
6 *Getting the Joke*, BBV
7 ibid

8	ibid
9	ibid
10	*DWM* 288 03/00 p.33
11	Baggs Interview
12	*Dreamwatch* 69 05/00
13	Simon Gerard Interview April 2014, Email
14	ibid
15	ibid
16	ibid
17	'Shelf Life', *DWM* 291 05/00 p.43
18	Gerard Interview
19	Baggs Interview
20	Gerard Interview
21	ibid
22	Castleton Interview
23	ibid
24	ibid
25	ibid
26	*CT* 271 05/00
27	Baggs Interview
28	Castleton Interview
29	Gerard Interview
30	ibid
31	Gareth Preston Interview April 2014, Email
32	ibid
33	ibid
34	Baggs Interview
35	ibid
36	*Friends of Doctor Who*, Vol. 12, No.1, Summer 2000
37	Parkin Interview
38	On Web - BBV
39	Parkin Interview
40	On Web - BBV
41	Parkin Interview
42	*CT* 273 07/00

Chapter 25

1	Lock Interview, February 2015, Phone
2	ibid
3	Jim Smith Interview January 2015, London
4	ibid
5	ibid
6	Stevens Interview
7	Smith Interview
8	Stevens Interview
9	ibid
10	Smith Interview
11	Stevens Interview
12	Smith Interview
13	Stevens Interview
14	ibid
15	ibid
16	ibid
17	ibid

18	'J'adore Kaldor!', Alan Stevens. *DWM* 324 12/02 pp. 22 - 23
19	Stevens Interview
20	ibid
21	'Stael Counsel', Alan Stevens, *DWM* 307 07/01 pp. 37 - 37
22	ibid
23	Stevens Interview
24	Smith Interview
25	Stevens Interview
26	ibid
27	Smith Interview
28	Miles interview
29	ibid
30	ibid
31	'J'adore Kaldor!'
32	'The *DWM* Review', *DWM* 310 11/01 p.49
33	'The *DWM* Review', *DWM* 321 09/02 p.52
34	ibid

Chapter 26

1	Preston Interview
2	ibid
3	ibid
4	ibid
5	Anthony Keetch Interview November 2014, Email
6	Preston Interview
7	'Shelf Life', *DWM* 298, 12/00 p.44
8	Baggs Interview
9	Merrick Interview
10	Keetch Interview
11	ibid
12	*CT* 278, 11/00
13	Keetch Interview
14	'The *DWM* Review', *DWM* 300, 02/01, p.47
15	http://www.bbvonline.co.uk/news_arch.html
16	'Sexual Chemistry', Ben Cook, *DWM* 298, 11/00, pp. 8 - 13
17	Keetch Interview
18	On The Web - BBV
19	http://www.bbvonline.co.uk/fea_beetles.htm
20	http://timelord.yuku.com/topic/1585/The-Author-Speaks-Paul-Ebbs#.WBy1uHecZBw
21	The *DWM* Review *DWM* 05/01304 p.49
22	Baggs Interview
23	ibid
24	ibid
25	Parkin Interview
26	Baggs Interview
27	ibid
28	ibid

Chapter 27

1	Saward Interview
2	ibid

3 Baggs Interview
4 *CT* 278 11/00
5 Parkin Interview
6 *CT* 278 11/00
7 Parkin Interview
8 ibid
9 Baggs Interview
10 Keetch Interview November 2014
11 *Cyberon* panel, Gallifrey Convention 2001
12 justyce.org
13 *Cyberon* panel, Gallifrey Convention 2001
14 http://www.bbvonline.co.uk/fea_disco.htm
15 Castleton Interview
16 http://www.bbvonline.co.uk/rev_sb_cyb.htm
17 Baggs Interview
18 Parkin Interview

Chapter 28

1 http://www.searchmytrash.com
2 ibid
3 Preston Interview
4 Baggs Interview
5 Preston Interview
6 ibid
7 ibid
8 ibid
9 Baggs Interview
10 'Artistic License', *DWM* 303, 04/01, pp. 12 - 13
11 Preston Interview
12 ibid
13 Gallifrey 2001 convention interview
14 Jo Castleton Interview June 2015, Email
15 http://www.bbvonline.co.uk/fea_dy_nf.htm
16 Preston Interview
17 Fairs Interview
18 Gallifrey convention 2001 interview
19 Preston Interview
20 'Artistic License', *DWM* 303, 04/01, pp.12 - 13
21 Preston Interview
22 Fairs Interview
23 Preston Interview
24 'The *DWM* Review', *DWM* 308, 09/01, p.43
25 ibid
26 Preston interview
27 ibid
28 ibid
29 ibid
30 ibid
31 Baggs Interview
32 Preston interview

Chapter 29

1 Keetch Interview November 2014
2 ibid
3 ibid
4 http://www.sci-fi-online.com/reviews/audio/Sept_barnacled.htm
5 Keetch Interview
6 https://www.facebook.com/note.php?note_id=10151088227093447
7 Baggs Interview
8 ibid
9 http://www.ninthart.co.uk/display.php?article=739
10 http://www.bbvonline.co.uk/news_arch.html
11 http://www.radiodramarevival.com/malleus-interview-nigel-fairs-speaks-on-the-faction-paradox-protocols/
12 ibid
13 http://www.bbvonline.co.uk/feat.html
14 'The *DWM* Review', *DWM* 314, 03/02, p. 45
15 'The *DWM* Review', *DWM* 314, p. 46
16 http://www.radiodramarevival.com/malleus-interview-nigel-fairs-speaks-on-the-faction-paradox-protocols/
17 Zoltan Déry Interview January 2015, Email
18 ibid
19 Nigel Fairs Interview
20 'The *DWM* Review', *DWM* 317, 05/02, p.40
21 Déry Interview
22 ibid
23 Richard Franklin, *Myth Makers*, Reeltime Pictures, 1989
24 'Gallifrey Guardian', *DWM* 296, 10/00, p.05
25 Baggs Interview
26 ibid
27 ibid
28 *The Killing Stone* CD, BBV
29 'Reviews', *DWM* 324, 12/02, p.47
30 http://www.radiofreeskaro.com/2012/02/19/radio-free-skaro-297-no-more-janus-thorns/
31 Iain Hepburn Interview November 2014, Email
32 ibid
33 ibid
34 Fairs Interview
35 'Reviews', *DWM* 327, 03/03, p.41
36 Fairs Interview
37 Hepburn Interview
38 David A Mcintee Interview April 2014, Email
39 ibid
40 Mcintee Interview

Chapter 30

1 Stevens Interview
2 Moore Interview
3 Stevens Interview
4 Jim Smith Interview
5 Moore Interview
6 Stevens Interview

7 *CT* Issue 299
8 Stevens Interview
9 ibid
10 ibid
11 'Silver Jubilee', Alan Stevens, *DWM* 329, 04/03, pp. 37 - 38
12 http://www.kaldorcity.com/people/bailie.html
13 Details of the game can be found on the Magic Bullet website.
14 Lock Interview
15 Stevens Interview
16 ibid
17 'Reviews', *DWM* 329, 04/03, p.42
18 'Reviews', *DWM* 332, 07/03, p.46
19 ibid
20 ibid
21 http://www.radiodramarevival.com/the-true-history-of-magic-bullet-an-interview-with-alan-stevens-producer-of-kaldor-city-and-faction-paradox-part-1-of-2/#more-913
22 http://www.dalesmithonline.com/rejection/kaldor-city
23 http://www.kaldorcity.com/people/rhtribute.html
24 *Shockeye's Snack Bite* 14, 04-05/03

Chapter 31

1 Baggs Interview
2 ibid
3 Keetch Interview
4 Iain McLaughlin Interview March 2015, Email
5 Jon Blum Interview November 2014, Email
6 http://www.doctorwhonews.net/2001/03/bbv-productions.html
7 Mcintee Interview
8 Preston Interview
9 'Gallifrey Guardian', *DWM* 323 11/02 06
10 Fairs Interview
11 ibid
12 Lawrence Miles interview, 29.12.2013
13 Fairs Interview
14 ibid
15 Castleton Interview
16 http://www.radiodramarevival.com/malleus-interview-nigel-fairs-speaks-on-the-faction-paradox-protocols/
17 ibid
18 *DWM* Review *DWM* 332 07/03 p.47
19 *DWM* Review *DWM* 333 08/08 p. 48
20 ibid
21 http://www.bbvonline.co.uk/news.html
22 Baggs Interview
23 http://www.bbvonline.co.uk/news.html
24 http://www.radiodramarevival.com/malleus-interview-nigel-fairs-speaks-on-the-faction-paradox-protocols/
25 ibid
26 *DWM* Review *DWM* 341 03/04 p. 36
27 ibid
28 http://www.radiodramarevival.com/malleus-interview-nigel-fairs-speaks-on-the-faction-paradox-protocols/
29 Stevens Interview

30 Baggs Interview
31 Gallifrey Guardian *DWM* 339 02/04 p. 04
32 Briggs Skype Interview
33 ibid
34 ibid
35 Ainsworth Interview
36 Briggs Skype Interview
37 Grehan Interview
38 Hepburn Interview
39 ibid
40 Castleton Interview
41 Gary Russell Interview November 2014, Email
42 Mcintee Interview
43 Saward Interview
44 http://timelord.yuku.com/topic/1585/The-Author-Speaks-Paul-Ebbs#.VZ_6Rjnaa_E
45 http://www.bbvonline.co.uk/news/script.cgi
46 http://www.bbvonline.co.uk/news/script.cgi
47 Baggs Interview

Chapter 32

1 *Daemos Rising* DVD
2 ibid
3 Howe Interview
4 Barnfather Interview
5 ibid
6 Howe Interview
7 ibid
8 ibid
9 Barnfather Interview
10 Howe Interview
11 ibid
12 ibid
13 ibid
14 Beverley Cressman Interview February 2015, Email
15 Barnfather Interview
16 Richardson Interview
17 *Daemos Rising* DVD
18 Cressman Interview
19 Howe Interview
20 ibid
21 Richardson Interview
22 Cressman Interview
23 'Reviews', *DWM* 344, 06/04, p. 48
24 Barnfather Interview
25 Richardson Interview
26 ibid
27 Howe Interview
28 ibid
29 Cressman Interview
30 Howe Interview
31 ibid
32 Richardson Interview
33 Howe Interview

Chapter 33

1 Stevens Interview
2 ibid
3 Ibid
4 Smith Interview
5 Daniel O'Mahony Interview January 2015, Email
6 O'Mahony Interview
7 Stevens Interview
8 O'Mahony Interview
9 ibid
10 Stevens Interview
11 O'Mahony Interview
12 ibid
13 ibid
14 *CT* 323
15 *CT* 321
16 O'Mahony Interview
17 *CT* 321
18 *CT* 324
19 'Off The Shelf', *DWM* 355, 09/05, p. 60
20 *CT* 332
21 http://pagefillers.com/dwrg/kcstorm.htm
22 http://www.radiodramarevival.com/the-true-history-of-magic-bullet-an-interview-with-alan-stevens-producer-of-kaldor-city-and-faction-paradox-part-1-of-2/
56 Conversation with Alan Stevens, 09.01.17
24 http://www.dalesmithonline.com/rejection/kaldor-city
25 ibid
26 ibid
27 Smith Interview
28 Fiona Moore Interview February 2015, Email

Chapter 34

1 Stevens Interview
2 ibid
3 ibid
4 ibid
5 ibid
6 ibid
7 http://www.radiodramarevival.com/the-true-history-of-magic-bullet-an-interview-with-alan-stevens-producer-of-kaldor-city-and-faction-paradox-part-1-of-2/
8 Stevens Interview
9 ibid
10 ibid
11 Alistair Lock Interview
12 *CT* 386
13 Stevens Interview
14 http://www.kaldorcity.com/people/ibinterview.html
15 *CT* 340
16 'Off The Shelf', *DWM* 362, 11/05, p. 63

17 'Off The Shelf', *DWM* 375, 11/06, p. 63

Chapter 35

1 Preston Interview
2 ibid
3 ibid
4 'Back Page', *DWM* 383, 06/07
5 Parkin Interview
6 ibid
7 Blum Interview
8 ibid
9 ibid
10 Baggs Interview
11 Parkin Interview
12 Blum Interview
13 ibid
14 Castleton Interview
15 ibid
16 ibid
17 ibid
18 Baggs Interview
19 'Back Page', *DWM* 392, 03/08
20 ibid
21 Lock Interview
22 Blum Interview
23 Baggs Interview
24 Fairs Interview
25 Briggs Skype Interview
26 Mcintee Interview
27 Andy Grant Interview
28 Saward Interview
29 Telfer Interview
30 Baggs Interview
31 ibid
32 ibid
33 Saward Interview
34 Mcintee Interview
35 ibid
36 ibid
37 ibid
38 ibid
39 ibid
40 Baggs Interview
41 Castleton Interview
42 Lock Interview
43 ibid
44 Blum Interview
45 ibid
46 ibid
47 ibid
48 ibid
49 ibid
50 'Back Page', *DWM* 292 03/08
51 ibid

52 Baggs Interview
53 ibid
54 Castleton Interview

Chapter 36

1 http://www.radiodramarevival.com/the-true-history-of-magic-bullet-an-interview-with-alan-stevens-producer-of-kaldor-city-and-faction-paradox-part-1-of-2/#more-913
2 http://www.radiodramarevival.com/the-true-history-of-magic-bullet-an-interview-with-alan-stevens-producer-of-kaldor-city-and-faction-paradox-part-2-of-2/#more-980
3 http://podcasts.resonancefm.com/archives/11713
4 Stevens Interview
5 ibid
6 *CT* 335
7 http://podcasts.resonancefm.com/archives/11713
8 Stevens Interview
9 Fiona Moore, *CT* 384
10 Stevens Interview
11 Conversation with Alan Stevens, 06/12/2016
12 Lock Interview
13 Stevens Interview
14 http://podcasts.resonancefm.com/archives/11713
15 http://www.radiodramarevival.com/the-true-history-of-magic-bullet-an-interview-with-alan-stevens-producer-of-kaldor-city-and-faction-paradox-part-2-of-2/
16 ibid

Chapter 37

1 Grant Interview
2 Saward Interview
3 Briggs Skype Interview
4 George Telfer Interview November 2015, phone
5 Keetch Interview November 2014
6 Saward Interview
7 Mcintee Interview
8 ibid
9 Blum Interview
10 Bryant Interview
11 Saward Interview
12 Briggs Skype Interview
13 ibid
14 Ayres Interview
15 Fairs Interview
16 ibid
17 ibid
18 ibid
19 Baggs Interview
20 ibid
21 Briggs Skype Interview
22 Nick Briggs podcast 001
23 ibid

24 Baggs Interview
25 ibid
26 ibid
27 http://justyce.org/
28 Briggs Skype Interview
29 ibid
30 https://www.leagueofgentlemen.co.uk/newopen.shtml
31 Baggs Interview
32 ibid
33 Preston Interview
34 Parkin Interview
35 Ayres Interview
36 Gerard Interview
37 Summers Interview
38 Aldred Interview
39 Ainsworth Interview
40 ibid
41 Saward Interview
42 Briggs Skype Interview
43 ibid
44 ibid

Chapter 38

1 http://geekcrashcourse.com/2012/04/01/interview-dan-freeman-the-minister-of-chance/
2 http://www.geekplanetonline.com/index.php/features/interviews/item/3206-the-minister-of-chance-dan-freeman-interview
3 ibid
4 http://nerdbastards.com/2012/10/24/interview-minister-of-chance-producer-clare-eden-on-the-adventure-of-the-audio-drama/#klP3yVW4lljJOUco.99
5 http://www.geekplanetonline.com/index.php/features/interviews/item/3206-the-minister-of-chance-dan-freeman-interview
6 http://geekcrashcourse.com/2012/04/01/interview-dan-freeman-the-minister-of-chance/
7 http://www.shadowlocked.com/201103111600/interviews/interview-sylvester-mccoy-on-the-hobbit-minister-of-chance-doctor-who.html
8 http://www.starburstmagazine.com/features/interviews/4796-interview-dan-freeman-the-minister-of-chance
9 http://www.geekplanetonline.com/index.php/features/interviews/item/3206-the-minister-of-chance-dan-freeman-interview
10 http://geekcrashcourse.com/2012/04/01/interview-dan-freeman-the-minister-of-chance/
11 http://www.shadowlocked.com/201103161619/reviews/review-the-minister-of-chance-episode-1.html
12 http://www.sliceofscifi.com/2011/04/01/dan-freeman-writer-diretor-and-producer-of-the-minister-of-chance-a-slice-of-scifi-interview/
13 https://www.wired.com/2011/07/review-the-minister-of-chance-is-simply-superb-and-quite-the-adventure/
14 http://nerdbastards.com/2012/10/24/interview-minister-of-chance-producer-clare-eden-on-the-adventure-of-the-audio-drama/#klP3yVW4lljJOUco.99
15 http://www.denofgeek.com/tv/doctor-who/20808/sylvester-mccoy-interview-doctor-who-tiswas-fire-the-minister-of-chance-the-hobbit#ixzz3jHFgsMms)
16 http://geekcrashcourse.com/2012/04/01/interview-dan-freeman-the-minister-of-chance/

17 http://www.entertainment-focus.com/book-section/book-interviews/dan-freeman-interview/#sthash.i5kw53py.dpuf
18 http://www.radiodramareviews.com/id1213.html
19 http://www.entertainment-focus.com/book-section/book-interviews/dan-freeman-interview/#sthash.IZ0vsdCX.dpuf
20 http://tinyurl.com/hxwx7gv
21 http://www.starburstmagazine.com/reviews/audio-reviews/4714-audio-review-the-minister-of-chance-episode-4-tiger
22 http://nerdbastards.com/2012/10/24/interview-minister-of-chance-producer-clare-eden-on-the-adventure-of-the-audio-drama/#klP3yVW4lljJOUco.99
23 http://redrocketrising.com/2013/05/minister-of-chance-5-in-a-bark-on-the-river-hex-reviewed//
24 http://tinyurl.com/hxwx7gv
25 http://who-natic.blogspot.co.uk/2014/02/review-minister-of-chance-prologue-film.html0

Chapter 39

1 Moore Interview
2 Stevens Interview
3 ibid
4 Barnfather Interview
5 Howe Interview
6 http://www.doctorwhonews.net/2013/05/daemons-white-witch-returns-dvd-230513062117.html
7 Barnfather Interview
8 ibid
9 ibid
10 ibid
11 Baggs Interview
12 ibid
13 ibid
14 ibid
15 Barnfather Interview
16 ibid
17 Jon Blum, Facebook conversation, 5 Dec 2016
18 www.theijob.net
19 Baggs Interview
20 http://www.kasterborous.com/2010/04/interview-with-nick-briggs/
21 Rob Thrush Interview January 2015, email
22 ibid
23 ibid
24 Ayres Interview
25 O'Mahony Interview
26 Russell Interview

Chapter 40

1 Barnfather Interview
2 Ayres Interview 2015
3 Parkin Interview
4 Smith Interview
5 ibid
6 Stevens Interview

7 Russell Interview
8 ibid
9 Parkin Interview
10 Smith Interview
11 Fairs Interview
12 ibid
13 Ainsworth Interview
14 Gerard Interview
15 Ayres Interview
16 ibid
17 Smith Interview
18 Barnfather Interview
19 Howe Interview
20 Preston Interview
21 Cressman Interview
22 Richardson Interview
23 *Whotopia* 11 Issue One
24 http://www.kasterborous.com/2010/04/interview-with-nick-briggs
25 Briggs Skype Interview
26 Baggs Interview
27 ibid

Appendices

1 Baggs Interview